Sigmund Freud
AND
His Impact
ON THE
Modern World

To submit new manuscripts, send the original manuscript (double-spaced, including references, footnotes, quoted passages, and dialogue) and three copies to:

Jerome A. Winer, M.D., Editor
THE ANNUAL OF PSYCHOANALYSIS
122 South Michigan Avenue
Chicago, IL 60603

THE
ANNUAL
OF
PSYCHOANALYSIS
VOLUME XXIX

Sigmund Freud
AND
His Impact
ON THE
Modern World

Edited by

Jerome A. Winer and James William Anderson

for the Chicago Institute for Psychoanalysis

and the Chicago Psychoanalytic Society

THE ANALYTIC PRESS
2001   Hillsdale, NJ   London

Chapters in this volume are abstracted and indexed in
Psychoanalytic Abstracts.

© 2001 by the Institute for Psychoanalysis, Chicago.

Published by The Analytic Press
Editorial offices:
101 West Street
Hillsdale, NJ 07642

www.analyticpress.com

ISSN: 0092-5055
ISBN: 0-88163-342-9

Printed in the United States of America
10 9 8 7 6 5 4 3 2 1

Acknowledgment

We would like to thank Ms. Christine Susman, who provided secretarial and editorial assistance.

Contents

III

FREUD'S IMPACT IN SPECIFIC AREAS

IV

FREUD'S IMPACT ON HUMANISTIC STUDIES

Contents

Contributors

James William Anderson, Ph.D. (ed.) is Faculty, Institute for Psychoanalysis, Chicago, and Associate Professor of Clinical Psychology, Northwestern University Medical School.

Virginia C. Barry, M.D. is Faculty, Institute for Psychoanalysis, Chicago, and in private practice.

Marcia Cavell, Ph.D. has taught at several universities, including the University of California at Berkeley and the State University of New York at Purchase, and has authored *The Psychoanalytic Mind: From Freud to Philosophy* (1993).

Alan C. Elms, Ph.D. is Professor of Psychology, University of California, Davis, and author of *Uncovering Lives: The Uneasy Alliance of Biography and Psychology* (1994).

Paul J. Emmett, Ph.D. is Associate Professor of English, University of Wisconsin, Manitowoc.

Glen Gabbard, M.D. is Professor of Psychiatry at Baylor College of Medicine and Training and Supervising Analyst at the Houston/Galveston Psychoanalytic Institute. He is the author or editor of 14 books, including *Psychiatry and the Cinema*, with K. E. Gabbard (1999), and *Love and Hate in the Analytic Setting* (1996).

Benjamin Garber, M.D. is on the faculty of the Institute for Psychoanalysis, Chicago, and is the Director of the Barr-Harris Children's Grief Center, Chicago.

John E. Gedo, M.D. has retired as a member of the faculty of the Institute for Psychoanalysis, and has been Visiting Professor of Psychoanalytic Thought, University of Chicago. He has written or edited 18 books including *The Evolution of Psychoanalysis* (1999) and *Conceptual Issues in Psychoanalysis* (The Analytic Press, 1986).

Jack L. Graller, M.D. is Faculty, Institute for Psychoanalysis, Chicago, was one of the founders in 1968, and is now Emeritus Faculty of the Family Institute of Chicago at Northwestern University.

Roy R. Grinker Jr., M.D. is Faculty, Institute for Psychoanalysis, Chicago, and is Senior Attending Physician, Emeritus, Michael Reese Hospital and Medical Center, Chicago.

Peter Loewenberg, Ph.D. is Dean, Southern California Psychoanalytic Institute and Professor of History and Political Psychology, University of California at Los Angeles. He authored *Decoding the Past* (1996) and *Fantasy and Reality in History* (1995).

Paul Meyer, B.A. His paper in this volume, "Freud and the Human Sciences," won the Thomas James Pappadis Award, sponsored by the University of Chicago and the Institute for Psychoanalysis. (pauldavidmeyer@hotmail.com)

Mary Ellen Ross, Ph.D. is Associate Professor of Religion, Trinity University, San Antonio.

Fred M. Sander, M.D. is Faculty, New York Psychoanalytic Institute Psychotherapy Training Program and the Association for Psychoanalytic Medicine; Associate Clinical Professor of Psychiatry, Cornell-Weill Medical School. He serves as chairman of the Psychoanalysis and Theater Series of the New York Psychoanalytic Society. He has authored *Individual and Family Therapy* (1979).

Nellie L. Thompson, Ph.D. is Curator, Archives and Special Collections, A. A. Brill Library, the New York Psychoanalytic Institute.

Joseph Tobin, Ph.D. is the Nadine Mathis Basha Professor of Education at Arizona State University and author of *Good Guys Don't Wear Hats: Children's Talk about the Media* (2000) and *Preschool in Three Cultures: Japan, China, and the United States*, with David Wu and Dana Davidson (1989).

Harry Trosman, M.D. is Faculty, Institute for Psychoanalysis and Professor of Psychiatry, University of Chicago. He wrote *Freud and the Imaginative World* (The Analytic Press, 1985) and *Contemporary Psychoanalysis and the Masterworks in Art and Film* (1996).

William Veeder, Ph.D. is Professor of English, University of Chicago. He wrote *Henry James: The Lessons of the Master* (1975) and *Mary Shelley and Frankenstein: The Fate of Androgyny* (1988).

Jerome A. Winer, M.D. (ed.) is Director, Institute for Psychoanalysis, and Professor of Psychiatry, University of Illinois, Chicago.

I

SIGMUND FREUD THE MAN

Introduction

JAMES WILLIAM ANDERSON
JEROME A. WINER

Freud's Impact

As the year 2000 approached, there was much speculation about who were the most influential figures in the twentieth century. Several political leaders, such as Wilson, Gandhi, Lenin, Roosevelt, Hitler, Churchill, and Mao, dominated the world stage, but it is questionable whether the effect of any of them had much staying power. Lenin's Soviet Union has disappeared. Hitler's Third Reich, which was supposed to last a thousand years, is now a ghastly memory. Roosevelt's "New Deal" is no longer "new," and much of it has been abandoned.

Commentators turned their attention from politicians to thinkers, and the name of Sigmund Freud came up regularly. *Time* magazine (March 29, 1999), in an issue on "The Century's Greatest Minds," featured Freud and Albert Einstein on the cover, with John Maynard Keynes, Jonas Salk, and Rachel Carson in the background.

There is wide agreement that few if any people had more of an effect during the past 100 years; our goal in this volume is to explore just what Freud's impact has been.

He had one area of influence that is unarguable. He was the founder of psychodynamic psychology. The practitioners of psychotherapy, who include psychiatrists, psychologists, social workers, and counselors, are all descended from Freud. Although psychiatric medications have become widespread, thousands of people who need help still are able to find it in the "talking cure," a method of treatment that was unheard of a century ago. The self-help movement, to the extent that it is based on the assumption that people's psychological problems are rooted in their childhood experiences—in the "inner child," as one variation would have it—is also a legacy from Freud.

But Freud had another kind of influence that is more pervasive. It is what W. H. Auden (1974, p. 4) had in mind when he wrote:

3

to us he is no more a person
now but a whole climate of opinion
under which we conduct our different lives.

We see ourselves and everything around us from a perspective that did not exist in the pre-Freudian era. We know that all people have motivations of which they are unaware. A person's inner life (dreams, fantasies, private thoughts) is as important as the external life.

One psychologist, Henry A. Murray (1940) suggested that, before he was exposed to psychoanalysis, he viewed people as being almost like robots. Now, he went on,

> I visualize . . . a flow of powerful subjective life, conscious and unconscious; a whispering gallery in which voices echo from the distant past; a gulf stream of fantasies with floating memories of past events, currents of contending complexes, plots and counterplots, hopeful intimations and ideals [p. 160].

Today there may be as many people as ever who find sexuality disquieting, but there is no longer a pretense that it is an incidental part of life. In law attention is paid to a defendant's state of mind. In the cinema even action films are expected to give some consideration to psychological motivation. Schools recognize that when children have trouble at home there will be repercussions in the classroom. The media scrutinize the private lives of politicians. There is controversy about Freud, but he has so permeated our culture that combatants on both sides are psychologically minded. The critics of Freud pay homage to him even as they point out his errors and shortcomings.

This Volume

We began planning this volume when we learned that the exhibit, "Sigmund Freud: Conflict and Culture," mounted by the Library of Congress, would be coming to the Field Museum in Chicago. We set out to create what we thought of as an unofficial companion volume to the exhibit.

The two papers in the opening section are tied in most closely to the exhibit. The volume opens with "Sigmund Freud's Life and Work: An Unofficial Guide to the Freud Exhibit." James William Anderson looks at Freud's biography with the intention of providing a larger context for understanding the meaning of the objects in the exhibit. Roy R. Grinker Jr. gives a more personal view of Freud by describing his father's trip to Vienna to have an analysis with the founder of psychoanalysis.

In the second section, several thoughtful commentators were given free rein to take a broad perspective on Freud's impact. John E. Gedo, an influential psychoanalytic theoretician in his own right, evaluates "The Enduring Scientific

Contributions of Sigmund Freud." Peter Loewenberg, a historian who has had psychoanalytic training, describes "Freud as a Cultural Subversive." Marcia Cavell, who specializes in philosophy, considers Freud's continuing importance as a thinker. Alan C. Elms, a psychobiographer, came up with an original way of viewing Freud's influence. He looks at the three supposed comments from Freud that are most often quoted, examines whether he actually said these things, and asks why these particular statements are so often cited. Virginia C. Barry, a psychoanalyst with an interest in neuroscience, looks at a central area of Freud's thinking—symbolization—and considers how his approach to this process has stood up in the light of recent neurological knowledge.

The third section, rather than assessing Freud's overall impact, looks at his influence in specific areas. Joseph Tobin, a researcher with an interest in early childhood education, uses an experimental method to investigate how Freud's idea of childhood sexuality has fared. Freud welcomed women into the profession he created. Nellie L. Thompson examines the result of this by looking at the women who became psychoanalysts in the United States from 1911 to 1941. Jack Graller assesses "Freud's Impact on Marriage and the Family." Benjamin Garber, aware that Freud is usually associated with therapeutic work with adults, assesses "Freud's Impact on Therapeutic Work with Children."

In the final section, the authors assess Freud's influence in several of the major areas of humanistic studies. The authors and the areas they examine are Paul J. Emmett and William Veeder, literature; Fred M. Sander, drama; Mary Ellen Ross, religious studies; Paul Meyer, human sciences; Harry Trosman, visual arts; and Glen Gabbard, cinema.

The Institute for Psychoanalysis in Chicago

Apart from his writings, the greatest instrument of Freud's influence has been the psychoanalytic institutes, of which the Institute for Psychoanalysis in Chicago is a prime example. Because psychoanalysis has never had a strong presence in universities, the institutes have been the main locus of training and research.

At first psychoanalytic training was haphazard. Some of Freud's early followers read a few of his papers, attended some meetings, and became analysts without even going through analysis themselves. Freud realized what a large step forward was being taken with the formation of the first psychoanalytic institute in Berlin in 1919. When Helene Deutsch established an institute in Vienna in 1925, Freud gave his approval; Deutsch became the director and Freud's daughter, Anna Freud, her assistant.

The early American psychoanalysts generally had to go to Europe for their training. In the early 1930s, institutes were formed in New York, Chicago, Boston, and Washington-Baltimore, the first institutes in the United States (Hale, 1995, pp. 25–37).

When Hitler gained control of Germany and later Austria, the psychoanalytic institutes in those countries were disbanded, and the center of the psychoanalytic world shifted from the German-speaking countries to the United States. Hence it can be said that in the period since Freud's death in 1939, the institutes such as the Institute for Psychoanalysis in Chicago have played a pivotal role in carrying on Freud's influence and also in the reassessment and expansion that have taken place in psychoanalysis.

Franz Alexander founded the Institute for Psychoanalysis in 1932. Alexander was a special favorite of Freud's. Freud once said he counted Alexander "as one of our strongest hopes for the future" (Pollock, 1964, p. 24), and he sent his own son, Oliver, to Alexander for analysis (Young-Bruehl, 1988, p. 115). The first graduate of the Berlin Psychoanalytic Institute, Alexander set out to develop an institute that was modeled on the one where he had received his training.

He brought in Karen Horney, a leading teacher at the Berlin Institute, as his original associate director. Although Horney soon moved to New York, the Chicago Institute has a reputation for consistently having women in major roles. Helen Ross served as administrative director; Joan Fleming was the dean. Therese Benedek was a leading researcher and a legendary supervisor. Marian Tolpin today is one of the most sought-after teachers and supervisors at the Institute.

As with other institutes, the primary function of the Chicago Institute is to provide psychoanalytic training; each candidate goes through analysis, attends courses for five or more years, and analyzes several patients while receiving supervision. Graduates of the Chicago Institute include five people who would be on the short list of the most influential psychoanalysts of the past 60 years: Karl Menninger (the first graduate), Heinz Kohut, George Pollock, John Gedo, and Arnold Goldberg. A sixth person, Merton Gill, had his first analysis as a research subject in one of the Institute's studies, and, after receiving his training at the institute which Menninger founded in Topeka, became a faculty member at the Chicago Institute.

Research and the development of theory have been a central concern of the Institute since Alexander established several large-scale projects in the 1930s. Faculty members publish dozens of articles and books each year.

Psychoanalysis is a field that has often been riven by bitter arguments and controversies. The Chicago Institute has managed to remain whole all these years, but twice a split almost occurred. The first time the issue was Alexander's attempt to shorten the length of psychoanalytic treatment; he believed a psychoanalysis could take place less frequently than the usual four or five times per week and could last less than the usual three or more years. The second time the controversy was over Kohut's theoretical innovations, which in essence amounted to extending psychoanalysis to a group of patients, so-called "narcissistic patients," who were seen as being different from the patients usually treated by this method.

The outcome both times was to find room within the Institute, and within psychoanalysis in general, for both traditional psychoanalysis and the newer initiatives. Now most psychoanalysts treat some patients in the usual way and offer shorter-term, less intense treatment for other patients. If the latter kind of treatment is not literally called "psychoanalysis," it hardly matters to the patients. And psychoanalysts now treat both the traditional, so-called "neurotic" patient, as well as other patients who do not fit that diagnosis.

The Chicago Institute has expanded the training it offers beyond the original program for those becoming psychoanalysts. It also has programs for learning child psychotherapy and adult psychotherapy. Each year it sponsors a variety of continuing education classes and conferences. There is also an attempt to reach into the community and to provide activities that are of interest to people outside the helping professions.

In addition to the private treatment offered by faculty and graduates, the Institute has a clinic that makes psychoanalysis and psychoanalytically oriented psychotherapy available to the public. The Institute also sponsors the Barr-Harris Grief Center, a clinic treating children who have lost a parent through death or divorce.

Two of the Institute's activities come together in this volume. Each year the Chicago Institute for Psychoanalysis produces *The Annual of Psychoanalysis*, a volume of peer-reviewed papers. And the Institute attempts to bring recent thinking about psychoanalysis to the public. With the coming of the Freud exhibit to the Field Museum in Chicago, we saw the opportunity of devoting the current volume of the *Annual* to a theme, "Sigmund Freud and his Impact on the Modern World." Our hope is that this volume will enhance the experience of those attending the exhibit and that it also will be of interest to anyone else who wants to know more about the reverberations and consequences set off by the work of Sigmund Freud.

References

Auden, W. H. (1974), In memory of Sigmund Freud. *Internat. Rev. Psycho-Anal.*, 1:3–4.

Hale, N. G., Jr. (1995), *The Rise and Crisis of Psychoanalysis in the United States*. New York: Oxford University Press.

Murray, H. A. (1940), What should psychologists do about psychoanalysis? *J. Abnormal and Social Psychol.*, 35:150–175.

Pollock, G. H. (1964), *Franz Alexander, M.D.* (pamphlet). Chicago: Institute for Psychoanalysis.

Young-Bruehl, E. (1988), *Anna Freud*. New York: Summit Books.

Sigmund Freud's Life and Work:
An Unofficial Guide to the Freud Exhibit

JAMES WILLIAM ANDERSON

"Sigmund Freud: Conflict and Culture" is an exhibit created by the Library of Congress, scheduled to travel to several cities, and sure to be seen by hundreds of thousands of people. It consists of approximately 116 objects—most of them manuscripts and books written by Freud and photographs related to his life— along with written comments, videotapes, and selections from his collection of antiquities.

One time, before reading a story to my son, who was then nine years old, I warned him that it might be frightening. "There's nothing to be scared about, Dad," he said. "It's only ink on a page." Before going on I must observe that my son's comment cannot be understood without Freud's concept of defense mechanisms. My son had learned a way of protecting himself against threatening feelings; he practiced a variation of the defense of "isolation of affect," in which the content (in this case, what happens in the story) remains in the conscious mind while the associated emotion (in this case, fear) is stripped away.

No one can deny that the story was ink on a page. But that is not all it was. The ink was arranged into letters, and the letters were organized into words that told a story. The context of the ink gave it its meaning.

Similarly one can say that the most valuable and attractive of the objects in the Freud exhibit, the manuscripts that he himself wrote, are no more than ink on a page. They derive their meaning from the role they played within the context of Freud's life and work. My goal in this essay is to explain that context, to provide an overview of Freud's experience and the development of his thinking. People who plan to attend, or have attended, the Freud exhibit are my primary

---

The author would like to thank Alan C. Elms and Dan P. McAdams for their help in the preparation of this essay.

audience, but I hope that this essay will also appeal to anyone who would like to read a concise summary of Freud's life.

Although this essay represents my own point of view and is not sanctioned by the Library of Congress, it might be thought of as an unofficial guide to the Freud exhibit. I organize my narrative of Freud's life around a number of the objects in the exhibit. (These objects are listed in headings; three of them will be reproduced in this essay as illustrations.)

Manuscript: "Rat Man Process Notes"

An example is Freud's account of his sessions with an obsessional patient whom he called, in his published case history, "the Rat Man." Freud generally did not take notes while talking with a patient, but, using his unusually sharp memory, he sometimes wrote down in detail what had gone on in a session. Freud almost always destroyed these notes; only those from the case of the Rat Man have survived (Freud, 1909, p. 259).

The notes tell us much about the difference between what he heard from the patient and what he chose to talk about in his case study. The patient, for example, mentions his mother much more frequently than Freud does. Freud put his emphasis on the patient's hostility toward his father and his discomfort with this hostility. The name Rat Man derives from a fantasy the patient had which was horrifying to him. The patient pictured his father being subjected to a cruel torture: a rat is attached to the man's buttocks in such as way that it would inevitably bore into his anus.

This case played a part in Freud's making a connection between obsessiveness and an interest in anal phenomena. As with many other areas of his thought, Freud's ideas have permeated our culture. It is not unusual to hear an obsessive person referred to as being "anal."

Document: Sigismund Schlomo Freud's Birth Certificate, May 6, 1856

Freud started life in 1856 with the more Jewish and eastern-European name of Sigismund Schlomo Freud and did not permanently become Sigmund Freud, a name that reflected his identity as a secularized, Viennese Jew, until he was a student at the university (Gay, 1988, pp. 4–5). He spent his first three years in Freiberg, a small town in Moravia (now part of the Czech Republic, then a province in the Austro-Hungarian Empire). After a brief period in Leipzig, his family moved in 1860 to Vienna, where he lived for 78 years (Jones, 1953–1957, I, pp. 1–13).

One characteristic of Freud's that must have started to develop in early childhood was his inner conviction of being destined for greatness. "A man who has been the indisputable favorite of his mother," Freud once wrote, no doubt with himself in mind, "keeps for life the feeling of a conqueror, that confidence of success that often induces real success" (Jones, 1953–1957, I, p. 5). His mother, hoping that her firstborn child would be special, fastened on several superstitious indications of his golden future, and Freud too was well aware of these indications. The first dates precisely from the time of his birth; he was born in a caul, a circumstance seen as promising future fame. Later a peasant woman informed his mother that he would become a great man. When he was 11 or 12, a fortune-teller prophesied Freud would become a cabinet minister. That this prediction settled into his mind is likely, because as an adult he had a dream in which he held such a position (Jones, 1953–1957, I, pp. 4–5).

His father, though, did not view Freud in quite the same way, and so there must have been some tension between the two parents in their ambitions for their son. When Freud was seven or eight, he urinated one time in his parents' bedroom. Whether he used a chamber pot or urinated on the floor is not known for certain. But his disapproving father commented, "The boy will come to nothing" (Freud, 1900, p. 216). Freud's lust for achievement not only was grounded in his mother's faith in him but also in his determination to prove his father's doubts to be wrong.

Photograph: The Jacob Freud Family, Circa 1878 (Figure 1)

In this picture, taken when Freud was about 22, Freud's father looks as if he could be the father of Freud's mother, and he was old enough to be. Freud's mother was 21 years older than Freud, and his father was 20 years older than his mother. Freud experienced an intense form of what he called the Oedipus complex: the little boy craves closeness and sexual intimacy with his mother while having rivalrous and murderous feelings for his father. It is easy to see how his family constellation was conducive to his developing these feelings. Because he was as close to his mother in age as his father was, I can imagine him saying to himself, "Why should my father—rather than I—be the one who gets to sleep with my mother?"

Freud's particular experience helped him detect oedipal conflicts in others, and he gave us a useful concept. But, in the view of many modern commentators, he erred in declaring the Oedipus complex to be universal. It was so immediate and overwhelming in his own experience that he thought it must be a defining event in everyone's childhood.

At the Gymnasium (the Austrian high school), from 1864–1873, and at the University of Vienna, from 1873–1881, he was an outstanding student. He continued to imagine that he would achieve greatness one day. After just two years at the university, he had a fantasy of being an "explorer" who is able "to strike out on new therapeutic paths" (Ferris, 1997, p. 33). Ten years later—well before

Figure 1. The Freud Family, along with some relatives, circa 1878. Sigmund Freud, in his early twenties, is in the back row, third from the left. His mother is seated in front of him, and his father is seated to the right. Freud Museum, London.

he had had any significant accomplishments—he announced in a letter that he had destroyed most of his letters and notes. "[A] number of yet unborn and unfortunate people will one day resent" it, he announced; "they are my biographers" (E. Freud, 1960, p. 140).

His interests at the university turned to research in the hard sciences. It cannot be wholly coincidental that the first major research project of this man— who became known for finding hidden sexuality—involved searching for the elusive testes of male eels. Scientists had been unable to locate this sexual organ until one scientist reported a finding; Freud, after cutting open 400 specimens, offered a partial confirmation of this other scientist's claim (Gay, 1988, pp. 31–32).

Soon he gravitated to the university's professor of physiology, Ernst Brücke, and worked in his laboratory for six years. Although studying for a medical degree, Freud did not aspire to become a practicing physician but rather a research scientist.

Freud later described Brücke as "the greatest authority who affected me more than any other in my whole life" (Jones, 1953–1957, I, p. 28). Physiology was an inspiring discipline in the late nineteenth century, and the leading scientists set out to blaze new paths. Brücke and three other professors saw themselves as having a sacred mission which had to it something of an antireligious theme. The accepted belief at the time was that a life force, an *élan vital*, animated living beings. As a young scientist , Brücke signed a pledge declaring, "No other forces than the common physical chemical ones are active within the organism." He and his fellow rebels wanted to demonstrate the body works according to systematic forces that can be traced physiologically. They made progress in this quest. Brücke's colleague, Helmholtz, for example, was the first to measure the speed of the impulse that operates in the nervous system (Fancher, 1973, pp. 15–17).

Freud's later work can be summarized as an attempt to study the mind in the same way. Psychoanalysis, as he developed it, argues that the mind does not work in a mysterious or haphazard way. Rather all thoughts—along with psychiatric symptoms and irrational behavior—operate according to systematic forces that are grounded in the body (Fancher, 1973, p. 20). Brücke probably would not have recognized Freud's work as being like his own if he had lived long enough to become acquainted with it, but Freud saw himself as extending his teacher's approach into the realm of psychology.

Photograph: Wedding Album Photograph of Sigmund Freud and Martha Bernays, 1886 (Figure 2)

Freud's hopes of becoming a physiological researcher came to an abrupt end when, in 1882, he met and instantly fell in love with an acquaintance of his

Figure 2. Wedding photograph of Sigmund Freud and Martha Bernays, 1886. Freud Museum, London.

sisters, a young woman named Martha Bernays. Within two months, and after just a few meetings, they were engaged. Brücke took Freud aside and gave him some fatherly advice. Freud, Brücke pointed out, could never hope to get married and support a family on his earnings as a physiological researcher (Freud, 1925, p. 10). The only way would be to become professor of physiology. Anyone would have trouble attaining one of those few positions, and for a Jew it would be virtually impossible. If Freud had not met his fiancée, he never would have gone down the path that led to the creation of psychoanalysis.

Freud quickly left behind his low-level position at the Physiological Institute and set out to become a physician. "I became a doctor," he later noted, "through being compelled to deviate from my original purpose." His greatest aspiration, beginning in his childhood, was "to understand something of the riddles of the world in which we live and perhaps even to contribute something to their solution" (Jones, 1953–1957, I, p. 28). Initially, becoming a doctor represented a defeat for Freud; he felt he had to give up his deep desire to be an explorer.

Manuscript: Freud's Sketch of His Room at the General Hospital in Vienna

Having received his medical degree the previous year, he began working at the General Hospital in Vienna in order to develop his clinical skills. It took him four years to be in a position to get married, and it was possible in 1886 only because some friends lent him money.

Freud's growing preoccupation with sexuality probably owed much to his long and almost certainly chaste engagement. He had to wait four years for his wedding night, and during most of that period, Martha was living hundreds of miles away in Hamburg. He wrote her frequently, and from the few letters that have been published, it is clear that sexual desire, despite his efforts to suppress it, was much on his mind. Before a visit he wrote, "Woe to you, my princess, when I come. I will kiss you quite red." And he added that she would see who is stronger, "a gentle little girl" or "a big wild man who has cocaine in his body" (Jones, 1953–1957, I, p. 84). Freud's severe sexual frustration made him sensitive to the claims of sexual desire.

Publication: "Contribution to the Knowledge of Cocaine," 1885

The reference Freud made to cocaine in his letter to Martha points to his attempts to do research on cocaine during this period. He hoped to hasten his marriage by making a major discovery about this little-known drug, the effects of which seemed so remarkable before its addictive potential became known. Freud used it himself, recommended it to friends, including Martha, and wrote about its effectiveness as, for example, a treatment for morphine addiction. As more and more evidence accumulated regarding the dangers of cocaine, he reluctantly accepted that it was not a magical solution—either for medical ills or for his bachelorhood—and turned his attention back to neurology.

His experiences with three older physicians (Charcot, Bernheim, and Breuer) introduced him to ideas that readied him to create psychoanalysis, although, ironically, all three of them later became hostile or indifferent toward psychoanalysis.

Manuscript: Freud's Translation of Charcot's Lectures into German

Freud received a grant to travel to Paris in 1885–1886 to study at the Salpêtrière, a hospital in Paris, with Jean Martin Charcot, who was the most celebrated neurologist of the day. Charcot specialized in explaining the disease of hysteria. Hysterical patients were those with symptoms that appeared physical—such as a paralyzed arm or a pain in the leg—but which had no physical basis.

Photographs: Images of Hysterics Under Hypnosis at Salpêtrière

Without a number of coincidental factors, Freud never would have followed the path that led to his career as the founder of psychoanalysis. He specialized in neurology, not because he had a particular interest in patients with brain-related illnesses and injuries, but because he had studied the nervous system in his years as a physiological researcher. As a young neurologist, he probably would have preferred working with patients with obvious brain disorders, such as those who had suffered injuries to their heads. But he had to settle for the hysterical patients that many senior physicians shunned. They saw these patients as being malingerers and complainers; moreover they felt unable to help them.

In a typical demonstration, of the kind Freud would have observed, Charcot would hypnotize a patient with hysteria. If the patient had a paralyzed arm, Charcot could take away the paralysis or even move it from one arm to the other. Any cure, unfortunately, was only temporary (Gay, 1988, p. 49). But the demonstration showed Freud that forces in the mind, which could be manipulated by hypnosis, were in control of the hysterical symptoms.

Even though these public demonstrations fascinated Freud, a private comment from Charcot impressed him even more. At an evening reception, Freud overheard Charcot talking to another professor, P. C. H. Brouardel. Brouardel mentioned a patient, a woman who was an invalid. Her husband had difficulties in the bedroom. "But in such cases," Charcot replied with animation, "it's always the genital thing, always—always—always." Freud wondered why, if Charcot knew this, he never talked about it in public (Freud, 1914, pp. 13–14). The answer is that Charcot had observed how central sexuality was to hysteria, but he did not consider this insight something that could be discussed openly.

Picture Postcard: Hippolyte Bernheim

Freud was interested in the work of another French physician, Hippolyte Bernheim, and traveled to Nancy to study with him in 1889. As with Charcot, Freud translated some of his work from French to German. Bernheim was a specialist in hypnotism, and Freud observed him giving the following demonstration. After putting his umbrella in the corner of the ward, Bernheim hypnotized a patient and gave him a rather absurd posthypnotic suggestion. Bernheim told the patient that later he, Bernheim, would return to the ward and then, "You will come to meet me with my umbrella open and hold it over my head." When Bernheim entered, with Freud accompanying him, the patient picked up the umbrella, unfurled it, and held it over Bernheim's head. Bernheim asked him what he was doing. The patient, searching for an explanation, said something like, "I only thought, doctor, as it's raining outside you'd open your umbrella in the room before you went out." Freud knew the explanation was obviously wrong because he had observed the posthypnotic suggestion (Freud, 1940, p. 285).

In a demonstration like this, or a similar one, Bernheim went on to insist to the patient that he knew the real reason for his action. With Bernheim pressuring him, the patient eventually was able to realize that he had opened the umbrella because Bernheim had told him, while he was in a hypnotic trance, that he would do so. Freud (1915–1917) noted that the patient had to know the reason all along; "it was merely inaccessible to him" (p. 103).

From such demonstrations Freud received an unshakable conviction that behavior can be unconsciously motivated. And there also was the kernel of the idea that, when people tried, and especially when someone else urged them on, they often could get access to ideas that had been unconscious.

Painting: Portrait of Josef Breuer

Of the three physicians, the third, Josef Breuer, had by far the greatest influence on Freud. A respected, successful doctor 14 years older than Freud, Breuer was Freud's mentor when Freud opened his private practice as a neurologist a few months before his marriage in 1886.

Photograph: Bertha Pappenheim (Anna O.)

Breuer told Freud about his treatment of a hysterical patient in the early 1880s. The patient's name was Bertha Pappenheim; when featured in *Studies on Hysteria* (Breuer and Freud, 1893–1895), she was given the pseudonym "Anna O."

Pappenheim had numerous hysterical symptoms. As her physician Breuer visited her frequently and fell into talking with her at length. He found that when she traced back a symptom to the memories that were associated with it, and vented her feelings as she talked of the memories, she found relief for the symptom. For example she was unable to drink liquids. (She kept alive by eating fruit and other foods that had liquid in them.) During one of her meetings with Breuer, she recalled seeing the governess let a dog drink out of a glass and expressed her disgust as she talked about it. Afterward she was able to drink liquids again. Pappenheim called this "the talking cure." At the time it was an astounding idea that simply talking could help a patient with neurotic symptoms.

Hearing about this case brought Freud another step closer to the discovery of psychoanalysis. Gaining access to thoughts that were unconscious seemed to be the key to obtaining relief from neurotic illness.

But there was a fundamental difference in the approaches that Freud and Breuer took. Freud was convinced that sexual conflicts lay at the root of neurotic problems; Breuer was much more cautious and omitted any mention of sexual themes when he wrote the case of Anna O.

Freud, though, knew that sexuality had been deeply implicated in the case. Pappenheim, a vivacious woman in her early twenties, had fallen in love with her physician and even fantasied becoming pregnant by him. Today no one would be shocked that a patient develops a "sexual transference" to her therapist. But Breuer, probably feeling attracted to her and guilty about it, terminated his treatment of her because of the sexual feelings that had been aroused (Jones, 1953–1957, I, pp. 224–225).

Book: *Studies on Hysteria,* 1895

Studies on Hysteria included the case of Anna O., as well as four of Freud's cases. When Freud wrote about his patients, he invariably argued that sexual issues played a central role in their hysterical symptoms. The best example is the patient called Fraulein Elisabeth von R. One of her symptoms, pain in her legs, increased shortly after her sister died. During her treatment she recovered a memory that she found mortifying; after her sister's death, the thought popped into her mind that her sister's husband would now be free to marry her. Freud concluded she had had to repress that thought because it threatened to make her feel so guilty. He concluded that an illicit sexual desire—for her brother-in-law—was at the heart of her neurotic problems (Breuer and Freud, 1893–1895, pp. 135–181).

If Freud, always ambitious, hoped to make a name for himself with *Studies on Hysteria*, he was disappointed. Over the next 13 years, only 626 copies were sold. A single bookstore can easily sell that many copies of a Harry Potter book. The reviews by the medical establishment also disappointed Freud. But a professor of literature at the University of Vienna seems to have grasped the potential power of the vision that the book presented. "We dimly conceive the idea that it may one day become possible to approach the innermost secret of personality," wrote Alfred von Berger, and he compared the underlying approach of the book with "the kind of psychology used by poets," such as Shakespeare. He gave Lady Macbeth as an example of a character in literature who could be understood according to the ideas in the book (Jones, 1953–1957, I, p. 253).

Manuscript: Freud's Letter
to Wilhelm Fliess, November 2, 1896

The last years of the nineteenth century were the most creative of Freud's career, and, to our great good fortune, they are the best documented of his life. As his friendship with Breuer dissolved, Freud felt isolated in Vienna, but he had one close confidante, a physician in Berlin named Wilhelm Fliess. Freud shared his intellectual struggles, his emotional turmoil, and his fears and dreams—including literal dreams—with Fliess.

In 1936 Fliess's widow sold the nearly 300 letters to a dealer who in turn sold them to Marie Bonaparte, a wealthy friend of Freud's. Freud tried to persuade her to burn them but she had, as she told him, "an immense aversion to the destruction of your letters and manuscripts," and she carefully preserved them (Masson, 1985, pp. 6–11).

During the period of the correspondence, Freud not only was experimenting with ways of treating the neuroses of his patients but was delving into, as he put it to Fliess, "the deepest depths of my own neuroses" (Masson, 1985, p. 255).

Photograph: Freud, His Three Sisters,
and Mother at His Father Jacob's Grave, 1897

His father's death in 1896 seemed to precipitate a period of intense emotional suffering that was marked by anxiety, depression, and superstitious fears of his own death.

Manuscript: Letter to Wilhelm Fliess, November 2, 1896

In a letter to Fliess shortly after Freud's father's death, Freud wrote about how much he valued his father and how deeply the loss had affected him. He also told Fliess about a dream he had had the night after the funeral in which he read a sign that said, "You are requested to close the eyes," that is, to shut the eyes of the deceased person. The statement, Freud concluded, referred in part to his not having done his duty to his father; the family had been angry at him for arranging for a simple funeral and for arriving late (Masson, 1985, p. 202).

Through the attention he paid to his own dreams, Freud was getting close to discovering his own oedipal hostility toward his father. Despite his professed love for his father, he had a deep-seated wish for his father's death, going back to when he saw his father as his rival for his mother's love. According to this line of reasoning, his hidden negative feelings toward his father had motivated his undutiful behavior at the time of the funeral.

He also got in touch with the other side of his oedipal complex, his sexual desire for his mother. Contemplating a vague memory from his third year of life, he speculated in another letter to Fliess that "my libido toward *matrem* was awakened, namely, on the occasion of a journey with her from Leipzig to Vienna, during which we must have spent the night together and there must have been an opportunity of seeing her *nudam*" (Masson, 1985, p. 268). His discomfort even so many decades later with these thoughts led him to use the Latin words for "mother" and "naked."

Soon he was ready to tell Fliess of a revelation. "I have found, in my own case too," he wrote, "being in love with my mother and jealous of my father, and I now consider it a universal event in early childhood" He immediately connected this phenomenon to the "gripping power of *Oedipus Rex*" (Masson, 1985, p. 272).

Manuscript: Letter to Wilhelm Fliess, September 21, 1897

Meanwhile he took an unfortunate detour in his thinking about psychopathology. He developed what he called his "neurotica," a theory of the development of neurosis. The theory held that in every case the individual had been sexually abused early in childhood. He gave talks and published papers espousing this point of view.

In a letter on September 21, 1897, he wrote Fliess, "I no longer believe in my *neurotica*." Among the reasons he gave for abandoning his theory was the improbability that "in all cases, the *father*, not excluding my own, had to be accused of being perverse." He had the kernel of another idea: "that the sexual fantasy invariably seizes upon the theme of the parents" (Masson, 1985, pp. 264–265). In other words, the child has sexual fantasies—as Freud no doubt had regarding his mother—and, because of the guilt that is aroused, the child ends up in conflict.

There has been much controversy over this crucial moment in the development of Freud's thinking. Some have charged him with cowardice for recognizing the devastating effect of sexual abuse and then discounting its importance (Masson, 1984). Freud, though, never suggested that sexual abuse does not occur or that it is not harmful. The whole thrust of his thinking was that such experiences profoundly influence a child; merely seeing his mother naked had a lasting effect on him, he believed. But the crux of the matter, he argued, is how each person, in his or her own individual way, reacts to, uses, and elaborates on those experiences. What the external world does to a person is important, but what the individual does with those experiences is decisive.

Book: *Die Traumdeutung* (*The Interpretation of Dreams*), 1900

Freud emerged from this period of self-analysis with the book that he always considered his fundamental contribution, *The Interpretation of Dreams* (Freud, 1900). This work marks the birth of psychoanalysis, because it contains all the basic elements of Freud's theory of personality.

Freud saw a dream as being a compromise formation. His formula was that a wish—often an illicit sexual wish—comes into conflict with the part of the person that disapproves and feels guilty about having such a wish. The result of this clash is the dream. It is a production—a sort of hallucination or fantasy—that reflects both sides of the conflict.

An example of Freud's dream interpretations, taken from a later publication (Freud, 1915–1917, p. 186), provides a typical illustration. A Jewish man whose uncle was observant reported a dream consisting of two pictures: "His uncle was smoking a cigarette although it was Saturday. A woman was caressing and fondling him [the dreamer] as though he were her child." The man said the woman reminded him of his mother, and he noted that his religious uncle would never smoke on the sabbath. Freud gave the following interpretation of what the dream meant for the man: "If my uncle, that pious man, were to smoke a cigarette on a Saturday, then I might let myself, too, be cuddled by my mother." In other words the man had found an outlet in the dream for his desire for sensuous contact with his mother. The dream also reflected his disapproval of this desire; not only is it disguised (the woman is a mother substitute, not his mother), but also he has made his behavior acceptable ("if my uncle can do that, it's no worse for me to do this").

Soon after the book was published, Freud wrote Fliess that he did not think of himself as a "man of science" or an "experimenter." "I am by temperament nothing but a conquistador—an adventurer, if you want it translated—with all the curiosity, daring, and tenacity characteristic of a man of this sort" (Masson, 1985, p. 398).

His next adventure was to try to conquer three more areas—hysterical symptomatology, Freudian slips, and jokes—by applying the very same model. Because illicit sexuality was so central to his model, he also turned his attention to the development of sexuality.

Manuscript: Letter to Wilhelm Fliess,
October 14, 1900

His opportunity to analyze a characteristic hysterical patient came when Ida Bauer—called Dora in his first full-length case study—began treatment with him. He wrote Fliess that this was "a case that has smoothly opened to the existing collection of picklocks" (Masson, 1985, p. 427).

But before he published the case, his relationship with Fliess came to a bitter end. Freud had anticipated the change in his feelings about Fliess in a passage in *The Interpretation of Dreams*. He recalled the closest friend of his early childhood, his relative Johann Freud, who was about a year older than he was. "All my friends have in a certain sense been reincarnations of this first figure," he noted. "My emotional life has always insisted that I should have an intimate friend and a hated enemy . . . and it has not infrequently happened that the ideal situation of childhood has been so completely reproduced that friend and enemy have come together in a single individual" (Freud, 1900, p. 483). Just as Freud's previous most intimate male friend, Josef Breuer, became an enemy, so did Fliess.

Photograph: Carl Jung, circa 1910

The same thing happened successively with three more men; each of these men was Freud's most trusted follower and then had a bitter break with Freud: Carl G. Jung, Sándor Ferenczi, and Otto Rank.

Photograph: Ida Bauer (Dora) with Her Brother Otto, 1890
and
Book: *Fragment of an Analysis of a Case of Hysteria,* 1905

When I teach Freud's theories, I like to tell my students, "Sexuality is of great importance. No one can doubt that today. It is hard to imagine that someone can overestimate its importance, but that is just what Freud did." Freud certainly went too far in placing sexuality at the center of virtually all psychopathology.

But we have to imagine what it must have been like for him. According to the establishment view, sexuality hardly mattered at all. William James (1890) attempted to cover psychology comprehensively in his widely read textbook, *The Principles of Psychology*, and yet, in 1378 pages, he devoted only three pages to sex.

When Ida Bauer's father brought her to Freud for treatment, 18-year-old girls like her were expected to be virtually innocent of sexual knowledge. As her story came tumbling out, no observer—least of all Freud—would have overlooked the centrality of sexuality to it (Freud, 1905a). By using his method of free association—encouraging the patient to speak as freely as possible about whatever came to mind—Freud repeatedly received evidence of the major role that sexuality plays in each person's experience.

Ida, plagued with various symptoms such as depression, a nervous cough, and periods of losing her voice, told Freud of the intrigue that had gone on between her family and another couple, the Zellenkas (Ferris, 1997, p. 192), who were close friends of her parents. Ida was aware that her father and Mrs. Zellenka were having an affair. When Ida was only 13 or 14, Mr. Zellenka had lured her to his office, grabbed her, and given her a passionate kiss. Two years later he propositioned her; Ida angrily declined and told her parents, but they did not believe her. She believed that her father had unofficially sold her out to Mr. Zellenka in exchange for Mr. Zellenka tolerating his affair with his friend's wife. Ida's father, who had brought her to treatment, wanted Freud to convince Ida that these ideas of hers were fantasies, but Freud believed Ida and let her know he did.

From today's perspective Freud's method of treatment seems tactless, awkward, and overbearing, although, of course, today's perspective would not exist if he had not invented the whole enterprise of dynamic psychotherapy in the first place. He applied his theory and confronted Ida with his conclusions. He told she had illicit sexual desires for Mr. Zellenka, an older man and a family friend, and yet she felt guilty about her desire, and the clash had produced her hysterical symptoms. Ida, not surprisingly, quit treatment.

I remember thinking, when I first read his interpretation to her, how far-fetched it seemed. Freud told her that she was so upset by Mr. Zellenka's proposition because she was in love with him and wanted him to propose to her—not to treat her like a house servant with whom he would have a sexual fling. To my surprise Ida confirmed that Freud was right.

There can be no dispute that Freud's handling of the case drove her out of treatment. And it also may be that sexuality was not as central to her problems as the infidelity and exploitation that she saw all around her (Erikson, 1968, pp. 250–252). But we have to admit that Freud's intuitive understanding of people enabled him to tune into conflictual experiences that would elude most others.

Book: *The Psychopathology of Everyday Life,* 1901.
and
Book: *Wit and Its Relation to the Unconscious*
(first english translation), 1916

Freud (1901) wrote one book explaining common mistakes—such as forgetting something, dropping something, or using the wrong word; from this work the phrase "Freudian slip" has entered the English language. He wrote another book (1905c) analyzing humor.

Manuscript: "War Jokes," 1915

Freud loved jokes, often told them to patients to illustrate a point, and kept collections, one of Yiddish humor, another of war jokes. Before giving an example of his analysis of a joke, I wish to warn the reader that what may have been funny 100 years ago is not likely to make anyone laugh today.

Freud analyzed the following joke: "A wife is like an umbrella—sooner or later one takes a cab" (Freud, 1905c, pp. 110–111). According to Freud, a joke, like a dream or a symptom, is a compromise formation. In this case, Freud reasoned, the joke stemmed from the joke-teller's illicit wish for sex with a prostitute, but the joke-teller realizes this wish is considered immoral. So he justifies his wish indirectly, as is typical with a joke. The joke says, in essence: a man marries to have his sexual needs satisfied, but a wife does this inadequately (just as an umbrella at times offers inadequate protection against the rain), and hence it is only natural that at times a man will turn to prostitutes to get his erotic desires quenched.

Book: *Three Essays on the Theory of Sexuality,* 1905

Freud's study of sexuality included his theory of the psychosexual stages: oral, anal, and phallic (Freud, 1905b). No one can deny that he was on to something. For example what parent has not noticed how much of the world an infant experiences through her mouth and what parent has not faced the challenge of toilet training? Freud's focus on these phenomena is certainly far too narrow; so much more is involved during the first five or six years of life than that which his theory encompasses. Yet he was the first to propose developmental stages and also the first to offer a theory that recognized how important childhood experiences are to the formation of personality.

Letter to the Mother of a Homosexual, April 9, 1935

In the "Three Essays," Freud also looked at homosexuality and proposed a view that was far ahead of the common view of his day although not in accord with the dominant view in psychology today. He also described his approach in a letter to an American woman who wrote him with concern about her gay son:

> Homosexuality is assuredly no advantage, but it is nothing to be ashamed of, no vice, no degradation; it cannot be classified as an illness; we consider it to be a variation of the sexual function, produced by a certain arrest of sexual development. Many highly respectable individuals of ancient and modern times have been homosexuals, several of the greatest men among them. . . . It is a great injustice to persecute homosexuality as a crime—and a cruelty too. . . .
>
> By asking me if I can help, you mean, I suppose, if I can abolish homosexuality and make normal heterosexuality take its place. The answer is, in a general way we cannot promise to achieve it. . . .
>
> What analysis can do for your son runs in a different line. If he is unhappy, neurotic, torn by conflicts, inhibited in his social life, analysis may bring him harmony, peace of mind, full efficiency, whether he remains homosexual or gets changed [cited in E. Freud, 1960, pp. 423–424].

While Freud saw homosexuality as being an arrest in development, he was not judgmental about it. He believed that all people are bisexual: they start out with sexual desire for both sexes and retain at least some of the capacity to feel sexual attraction to members of their own sex. Some follow the complicated path to heterosexual maturity, but many of them may suffer from neurotic symptoms that stem from their discomfort with their illicit sexual desires, a common type of which is homosexual desire. Freud believed that homosexuals tended to do better than neurotics. A homosexual lives out his or her desires for a person of the same sex; a neurotic represses them and suffers the consequences.

Photograph: Group at Clark University, September 10, 1909 (Figure 3)

Freud was invited to Clark University in Worcester, Massachusetts, to receive an honorary degree in 1909. He felt "despised" in Europe. He was saddened and disappointed, but not surprised, throughout his career that there was so much hostility to his work. When he came to America, he was pleased to be received by the leading figures "as an equal." He was especially delighted that William James, for whom he had a special respect (Rosenzweig, 1992), was among those who came to Worcester to meet him.

Manuscript: "Five Lectures on Psycho-Analysis," 1910

When he came forward to give the talks later published as "Five Lectures on Psycho-Analysis," he recalled, "it seemed like some incredible day-dream: psychoanalysis was no longer a product of delusion, it had become a valuable point of reality" (Freud, 1925, pp. 51–52). In these lectures he presented his first organized introduction to psychoanalysis (Freud, 1910a).

Manuscript: "Introductory Lectures on Psycho-analysis—Transference"

Five years later Freud began presenting another series of lectures. Published as "Introductory Lectures on Psycho-analysis," they provided his first comprehensive account of psychoanalysis. He included a description of the process of treatment (Freud, 1915–1917, pp. 286–302 and pp. 431–463). The patient lies on the couch (but as the old joke[1] goes, is encouraged to tell the truth) and attempts to practice free association, that is, to speak as openly as possible. The analyst listens, preferably with his unconscious as well as his conscious mind, and concentrates

---

[1] Here is one version of this joke. Analyst-in-training: "I did what you said. I told the patient to lie on the couch." Supervisor: "So, what's wrong then?" Analyst-in-training: "He did what I told him and he lies on the couch—the whole session—one lie after another."

Figure 3. Participants in the conference at Clark University in 1909. The front row includes William James (third from left), Sigmund Freud (seventh from the left), and Carl G. Jung (eighth from the left). By permission of Clark University, Massachusetts.

Key to Figure 3:

1. Franz Boas
2. E. B. Titchener
3. William James
4. William Stern
5. Leo Burgerstein
6. G. Stanley Hall
7. Sigmund Freud
8. Carl G. Jung
9. Adolf Meyer
10. H. S. Jennings
11. C. E. Seashore
12. Joseph Jastrow
13. J. McK. Cattell
14. E. F. Buchner

15. E. Katzenellenbogen
16. Ernest Jones
17. A. A. Brill
18. Wm. H. Burnham
19. A. F. Chamberlain
20. Albert Schinz
21. J. A. Magni
22. B. T. Baldwin
23. F. Lyman Wells
24. G. M. Forbes
25. E. A. Kirkpatrick
26. Sándor Ferenczi
27. E. C. Sanford
28. J. P. Porter

29. Sakyo Kanda
30. Hikoso Kakise
31. G. E. Dawson
32. S. P. Hayes
33. E. B. Holt
34. C. S. Berry
35. G. M. Whipple
36. Frank Drew
37. J. W. A. Young
38. L. N. Wilson
39. K. J. Karlson
40. H. H. Goddard
41. H. I. Klopp
42. S. C. Fuller

on making interpretations. Transference is seen as providing fertile ground for interpretation; the same conflicts, patterns, and feelings that the patient had early in life for important figures, such as parents, the patient now has for the analyst. The underlying goal is to make the unconscious conscious. In Freud's view what is repressed is at the root of the patient's symptoms. If the patient is able to discover these inner feelings, to own up to them, to ease off on condemning them, and to make a place for them in the patient's approach to the world, then relief will follow.

Does this process work? The short answer is that sometimes it does and sometimes it does not. For certain patients, to whom Freud's formulations apply especially well, traditional psychoanalytic treatment can seem like a miracle. For the other patients? The entire history of post-Freudian psychoanalysis can be seen as an attempt to broaden its understanding so that it can make sense of other kinds of patients and to expand its treatment methods so these other patients can be helped (see Summers, 1994).

Freud's basic theory was in place by the time of the "Introductory Lectures on Psychoanalysis." In the following two decades, he made refinements but few major changes.

Manuscript: "The Ego and the Id," 1910

He did not introduce his famous concepts of the id, ego, and superego until 1923 (Freud, 1923). These concepts merely provided a more structured way of talking about compromise formation. The id is the part of the mind that is the repository of the desires and wishes, some of which are unruly and illicit. The superego comprises the conscience and the ego ideal; on the basis of the superego, one judges certain desires to be immoral or unworthy. The ego is the part of the mind that finds the best compromises possible given the demands of the id and the superego and the constraints of reality.

The most significant revision Freud made to his theory in the later years was his addition of the "death instinct" to go along with the "sex instinct" (Freud, 1920). His introduction of the death instinct led to his positing an inborn aggressive tendency. The death instinct, he argued, caused people to be self-destructive, but they could get some relief from this tendency to harm themselves by diverting it outward and by expressing aggression toward others.

Photograph: Freud with Sons Ernst and Martin, 1916

It seems likely that Freud's experiences with death and aggression influenced his opinion about these matters. He was a close observer of the slaughter and brutality of World War I. All three of his sons—Ernst, Martin, and Oliver—served in the Austro-Hungarian army, and Freud was terrified that they would be killed. One of them, Martin, was especially a cause for concern because he was a prisoner-of-war. Altogether about 800,000 Austro-Hungarian soldiers died during the war, but all three of Freud's sons survived. One of his nephews, though, died in action (Gay, 1988, p. 352 and pp. 380–381).

The early 1920s was an especially painful time for Freud. His daughter Sophie Halberstadt died of influenza in 1920, shortly before he introduced the concept of the death instinct. In 1923 he was diagnosed with cancer. He had numerous operations in his remaining years as malignancies kept reappearing inside his oral cavity on his jaw and palate. Later in 1923 his four-year-old grandchild, Heinz Halberstadt, lay dying from tuberculosis. "I myself know," he wrote to some friends, "that I have hardly ever loved a human being, certainly never a child, so much as him." After the boy died, Freud felt that life had lost its value (Gay, 1988, p. 421).

Manuscript: "Future of an Illusion," 1927

He turned more and more to writings about larger social forces, and these writings reflected his deepening pessimism.

"The Future of an Illusion" (Freud, 1927) is his most detailed examination of religion. He argued that life is cruel and almost unbearable; therefore people had invented gods as an illusory solution. Life seems less terrible when people feel they can turn to a supernatural being for protection, and the promise of an afterlife quells the fear of death.

Manuscript: "Civilization and Its Discontents," 1930

In one of his earliest works on the nature of society, "'Civilized' Sexual Morality and Modern Nervous Illness," Freud (1908) argued that civilization is based on the suppression of the sexual instinct. Life would be in chaos if all people pursued their sexual desires; so civilization was born in order to suppress these desires. But, he concluded, people lose out either way. If there is too much expression of unbridled desires, then there is increased conflict among people, and if there is too much suppression of these desires, then, in line with his theory of compromise formation, the neuroses reach epidemic proportions.

Freud (1930) expanded on this point of view in one of his most widely read works, "Civilization and Its Discontents." By this time Freud saw aggressive desires as being on a par with sexual desires. Civilization, he noted, was formed to suppress aggression as well as sexuality. Once more, however, there was no workable answer. If there is too much suppression of aggression, he claimed, then people do not have an outlet for their death instinct and they become self-destructive.

He argued that groups of people try to protect themselves from their aggression and to bind themselves together by directing their aggression toward alien nationalities or ethnic groups. The Jews, scattered as they were throughout much of the world, provided a ready-made target for this form of scapegoating. He added, with bitterness, that the wide-scale massacres of Jews during the Middle Ages did not seem to enable their fellow citizens to avoid numerous wars.

Freud's deeply skeptical view of civilization did much to increase the prestige of his work in later years, because it seemed to foretell what was to come in European history with the rise of nazism, the Holocaust, and the ruthlessness of Stalin's Soviet Union.

In these and other works, Freud turned to the largest questions. As noted earlier his most cherished goal from an early age was "to understand something of the riddles of the world in which we live and perhaps even to contribute something to their solution." Late in his life, he concluded that "the triumph of my life lies in my having, after a long and roundabout journey, found my way back to my earliest path" (Jones, 1953–1957, I, p. 28).

Another large question that fascinated Freud throughout his career was the mystery of artistic creation.

Manuscript: "Leonardo da Vinci and a Memory of His Childhood," 1910
and
Manuscript and Pen and Ink Sketch: "The Moses of Michelangelo," 1914

Among the figures whom he examined, some in more detail than others, were Leonardo da Vinci, Michelangelo, Dostoevsky, and Shakespeare. For his basic formula, Freud returned again to the concept of compromise formation. He argued that art is an expression of the conflicted desires of its creator. He also drew heavily on his pet concept, the Oedipus complex. As an example of his psychobiographical interpretations, he looked at the mystery of the famous smile on the face of Leonardo's *Mona Lisa*. Freud argues that Leonardo's mother, who was unwed, lavished attentions and caresses on him when he was a little boy. This intensified his sexual feelings toward his mother to the point where they were overwhelming, and hence he was left with an image of a woman's smile that promised "unbounded tenderness" but had a "sinister" undertone to it (Freud, 1910b, pp. 107–118).

Photograph: The Committee

Convinced that his ideas were invaluable for mankind, Freud was concerned throughout his career with forming an international movement that would help his vision to spread. He formed a small "committee" of loyal followers who were entrusted with safeguarding the purity of his creation.

Photograph: International Psychoanalytic Congress, 1920

He also founded the International Psycho-Analytical Association to oversee psychoanalysis throughout the world.

Selections from Freud's Collection of Antiquities
and
Photograph: Freud in His Study in Vienna in 1938

Freud had a passionate interest outside his work: collecting ancient objects, such as statuettes and pottery. His study was crammed with his antiquities. In a sense his hobby was inseparable from his involvement with psychoanalysis: it appealed to him because he saw the archaeological artifacts as being tied into his psychological vision.

Images of Sergei Pankejeff

Sergei Pankejeff, the patient whom Freud called, in a case study, the "Wolf-Man," remembered Freud referring to his collection to illustrate the process of psychoanalysis. "The psychoanalyst, like the archaeologist in his excavations," Freud reportedly said, "must uncover layer after layer of the patient's psyche, before coming to the deepest, most valuable treasures" (Gardiner, 1971, p. 139). In "The Interpretation of Dreams," Freud made a similar comment. "The deepest and eternal nature of man . . . lies in those impulses of the mind which have their roots in a childhood that has since become prehistoric" (Freud, 1900, p. 247). Freud seems to have felt that his artifacts put him in connection with the early, determinative stratum of mankind just as his psychoanalytic probings enabled him to gain access to a similar stratum in the individual.

Photograph: Freud at Work in His Study in London, 1938

After Hitler took over Austria in 1938, Freud's life was endangered. Because of his worldwide fame and his powerful friends, he was able to get permission to leave Vienna, and he and his immediate family moved to London. Before departing Freud was required to sign a document attesting that the authorities had treated him with "respect and consideration." There is a story, probably apocryphal, that he asked if he might add a few words of his own, and he wrote, "I can heartily recommend the Gestapo to anyone" (Ferris, 1997, p. 393). Whether this happened it is a perfect illustration of Freud's theory of humor. In his view a joke expresses the inner feelings of the person which cannot be stated directly, in this case, his disdain and anger toward the Nazi officials. In keeping with Freud's change in emphasis during the later years, the feelings expressed here are aggressive rather than sexual.

Photograph: Adolfine, Marie, Rosa, and Pauline
—Freud's Sisters

Four of Freud's sisters were not as fortunate as Freud's immediate family. They remained behind in Vienna and later perished in Nazi death camps.

Manuscript: "Moses and Monotheism," 1939

The rise of anti-Semitism no doubt turned Freud's attention to his Jewishness, and his last major work, *Moses and Monotheism* (1939), is a fanciful examination of Moses and the early origins of the concept of a single God. Throughout his life Freud's sense of being Jewish was central to his identity, but because of his atheism, he characterized himself as "an infidel Jew" (Gay, 1988, p. 599).

Manuscript: For the BBC Recording, 1938
and
Sound File: The BBC Recording, 1938

If Freud had an opportunity near the end of his life to say just a few words to posterity about what mattered to him, what would he say? We have the answer to this question. While Freud was living in London, representatives of the British Broadcasting Corporation persuaded him to let them record him speaking. Freud had time to plan his statement ahead of time, and he said the following words:

At the age of 82, following the German invasion, I left my home in Vienna and came to England where I hope to end my life in freedom. I started my professional activity as a neurologist trying to bring relief to my neurotic patients. Under the influence of an older friend and by my own efforts I discovered some new facts about the unconscious in psychic life, the role of instinctual urges, and so on. Out of these findings there grew a new science, psychoanalysis, a part of psychology, and a new method of the treatment of the neuroses. I had to pay heavily for this bit of good luck. People did not believe in my facts and thought my theories unsavory. Resistance was strong and unrelenting. In the end I succeeded in acquiring pupils and building up an international psychoanalytic association. But the struggle is not yet over [National Psychological Association for Psychoanalysis, n.d.].

Several comments can be made about this statement. As Freud thinks back to the beginning of his career, he notes that his purpose was to "bring relief" to his patients. Seeing that his patients did not benefit from the inadequate methods of treatment that were available, he set out to find something else. Nearing the end of his life, he still remembers the part that ("an older friend") Breuer played in the early discoveries. He does not think of himself as having developed merely a provisional theory; Freud's view is that he came upon "new facts" and developed "a new science." In speaking of what he discovered, he highlights two points: first, his learning about the "unconscious," and, second, his uncovering "the role of instinctual urges." His emphasis was on the desires and wishes of compromise formations, the underlying sexual and aggressive drives which he believed motivate much of thought and behavior. He was distressed that his findings met with so much resistance but pleased that he had followers and had built up an international association. He ends by urging posterity to continue his work and declaring "the struggle is not yet over." He called himself a conquistador years earlier; now he seems to see himself as a crusader fighting a sacred war.

A few months after Freud made this statement, his cancer became inoperable. He died on September 23, 1939.

References

Breuer, J. & Freud, S. (1893–1895), Studies on hysteria. *Standard Edition*, 2. London: Hogarth Press, 1955.

Erikson, E. H. (1968), *Identity: Youth and Crisis*. New York: W. W. Norton.

Fancher, R. (1973), *Psychoanalytic Psychology: The Development of Freud's Thought*. New York: W. W. Norton.

Ferris, P. (1997), *Dr. Freud: A Life*. Washington, DC: Counterpoint.

Freud, E., ed. (1960), *The Letters of Sigmund Freud*. New York: Basic Books.

Freud, S. (1900), The interpretation of dreams. *Standard Edition*, 4 & 5. London: Hogarth Press, 1953.

———— (1901), The psychopathology of everyday life. *Standard Edition*, 6:1–290. London: Hogarth Press, 1960.

———— (1905a), Fragment of an analysis of a case of hysteria. *Standard Edition*, 7:3–124. London: Hogarth Press, 1953.

———— (1905b), Three essays on the theory of sexuality. *Standard Edition*, 7:125–248. London: Hogarth Press, 1953.

———— (1905c), Jokes and their relation to the unconscious. *Standard Edition*, 8:9–236. London: Hogarth Press, 1955.

———— (1908), "Civilized" sexual morality and modern nervous illness. *Standard Edition*, 9:177–204. London: Hogarth Press, 1959.

———— (1909), Notes upon a case of obsessional neurosis. *Standard Edition*, 10:153–318. London: Hogarth Press, 1955.

———— (1910a), Five lectures on psycho-analysis. *Standard Edition*, 11:3–58. London: Hogarth Press, 1957.

———— (1910b), Leonardo da Vinci and a memory of his childhood. *Standard Edition*, 11:59–138. London: Hogarth Press, 1957.

———— (1914), On the history of the psycho-analytic movement. *Standard Edition*, 14:3–66. London: Hogarth Press, 1957.

———— (1916–1917), Introductory lectures on psycho-analysis. *Standard Edition*, 15 & 16. London: Hogarth Press, 1963.

———— (1920), Beyond the pleasure principle. *Standard Edition*, 18:3–66. London: Hogarth Press, 1955.

———— (1923), The ego and the id. *Standard Edition*, 19:3–68. London: Hogarth Press, 1961.

———— (1925), An autobiographical study [1924]. *Standard Edition*, 20:3–76. London: Hogarth Press, 1959.

———— (1927), The future of an illusion. *Standard Edition*, 21:3–58. London: Hogarth Press, 1961.

———— (1930), Civilization and its discontents [1929]. *Standard Edition*, 21:59–148. London: Hogarth Press, 1961.

———— (1939), Moses and monotheism: Three essays [1934–1938]. *Standard Edition*, 23:3–140. London: Hogarth Press, 1964.

———— (1940), Some elementary lessons in psycho-analysis [1938]. *Standard Edition*, 23:281–286. London: Hogarth Press, 1964.

Gardiner, M., ed. (1971), *The Wolf-Man by the Wolf-Man*. New York: Basic Books.

Gay, P. (1988), *Freud: A Life for Our Time*. New York: W. W. Norton.

James, W. (1890), *The Principles of Psychology* (2 volumes). New York: Henry Holt.

Jones, E. (1953–1957), *The Life and Work of Sigmund Freud* (3 volumes). New York: Basic Books.

Masson, J. M. (1984), *The Assault on Truth*. New York: Farrar, Straus & Giroux.

————, ed. (1985), *The Complete Letters of Sigmund Freud to Wilhelm Fliess*. Cambridge, MA: Harvard University Press.

National Psychological Association for Psychoanalysis (n.d.), "The Voice of Sigmund Freud" (audio recording).

Rosenzweig, S. (1992), *Freud, Jung, and Hall, the King-Maker*. St. Louis, MO: Rana House Press.

Summers, F. (1994), *Object Relations Theories and Psychopathology*, Hillsdale, NJ: The Analytic Press.

My Father's Analysis with Sigmund Freud

ROY R. GRINKER JR.

I like to joke that I am the "last living man who met Sigmund Freud." It is an exaggeration, but, if I live long enough, it may become true. My interaction with him was brief, but my father's was far more extensive, because he had an analysis with Freud. He was often urged to write a book about his experiences with Freud, as did several others (Aldington, 1926; Wortis, 1954; Dorsey 1976; Kardiner, 1977). He refused, claiming that Freud had wanted him to preserve his, that is, Freud's, confidentiality.

Grinker (as I will sometimes refer to my father in the portions of the essay describing his analysis) explained this point by bringing up the following anecdote. During the analysis, Grinker had difficulty understanding the concept of transference, which holds that a person in analysis has strong feelings about the analyst, feelings that are fueled by the unconscious. Once Grinker was at a party at the residence in Vienna of a Dr. Sippy (inventor of the famous "Sippy diet" for peptic ulcer) and his wife. He repeated a joke Freud had told him. Apparently Mrs. Sippy passed the story on to her analyst, Freud's daughter, Anna Freud, who in turn repeated the story to Freud. In Grinker's next session, Freud said, "I thought that we decided that this analysis was confidential." "To my surprise," Grinker recalled, "I burst into tears at this criticism. And [Freud] said, 'Well, now you know what transference is'" (Grinker, 1979, p. 10).

Another aspect of this anecdote is that Grinker was surprised at being accused of a breach of confidentiality. He thought that confidentiality was supposed to protect the patient's privacy, not the analyst's. Current codes of ethics describe confidentiality in just that way; there is no such thing as confidentiality for the analyst or psychotherapist. Grinker, moreover, noted that no mention was made of Anna Freud's egregious transgression of her patient's confidentiality.

I wish to thank Jennifer Grinker Miller, Roy R. Grinker III, and James William Anderson for their helpful suggestions.

35

Despite his often repeating this anecdote, Grinker discussed some of his memories of his analysis in two of his writings (Grinker, 1940, 1979). He also told additional stories to me and other members of his family, and, because I was in Vienna with him at the time, I have some memories of my own from that period. By putting together these sources of information, I will reconstruct his experiences with Freud.

The story begins with his father, my grandfather. Julius Grinker was a prominent neurologist in Chicago early in the twentieth century. He was best known for introducing phenobarbital into this country in 1903 for the treatment of epilepsy.

In January 1911, Ernest Jones, who later headed the British Psycho-Analytical Society for many years and wrote the authorized biography of Freud, addressed a joint meeting of the Chicago Medical Society and the Chicago Neurological Society. Jones provided a rebuttal to the most common criticisms of psychoanalysis. Several of the physicians, including Julius Grinker, discussed the presentation. Julius Grinker also directed those in attendance to give Jones a standing ovation (Grinker, 1963).

Julius Grinker showed considerable interest in psychoanalysis. He attempted to use the method himself and wrote an essay (1911) in support of psychoanalysis. He argued that it "has as its basis a plausible psychology, splendid reasoning, and a profound acquaintance with the innermost depths of human nature." He added that "it has certainly opened our eyes to facts hitherto completely ignored or not at all recognized" (p. 53).

His style of treatment as a neurologist was to present himself as the ultimate expert: authoritarian, autocratic, rigid, and tough. His patients were expected to worship him, and they generally did so. When he tried practicing psychoanalysis, his patients—freed to voice their feelings openly—began to express ambivalence and even outright hostility toward him. He became scared and indignant and abruptly stopped using psychoanalytic techniques.

Julius Grinker (1912) wrote an essay just a year after the first, declaring that psychoanalysis was "of no use" (p. 185).

When I had my training analysis, I imagined that he had been scared away because one of his patients had professed sexual feelings for him, but I do not have any solid evidence for this fantasy.

In the same essay in which he dismissed psychoanalysis, Julius Grinker noted, "The vehemence of an attack on a scientific problem is often in inverse proportion to the degree of ignorance of the attacking party" (p. 194). He had no idea this point applied to himself, but, given the paucity of experience with psychoanalysis, it did.

In 1924 my father, Roy R. Grinker Sr., who had also become a neurologist, married and went with his wife on a European honeymoon. He already had a beginning interest in psychoanalysis and wired his father that he wished for some money to be able to have an analysis there. His father wired back, "If you have nothing better to do with my money, return home at once. Your loving father, Julius" (Grinker, 1979).

When a psychoanalyst, Franz Alexander, who had been a favorite of Freud's, was recruited to come to the University of Chicago Medical School, Grinker, who was an associate professor of neurology there, was delighted. Alexander accepted but, according to Grinker (1979, p. 6), insisted on being appointed a visiting professor in the Department of Medicine. He received the appointment, and it carried with it the requirement that he give a series of lectures.

Soon after becoming established at the Medical School in 1930, he presented his first lecture. In it he discussed a female patient who had suffered from constipation. He explained that he arranged for the patient's husband to give her a bouquet of roses, and she was cured. Most of the physicians other than Grinker were outraged by this story and quickly turned against Alexander (Grinker, 1979, pp. 6–7).

Another incident caused even more trouble for Alexander. It came out that a medical student, who was in analysis with Alexander, was charged for his treatment. Alexander was seen to be violating the American tradition that doctors do not pay doctors for their medical care (Grinker, 1979, p. 7). This custom, of course, makes no sense in relation to psychoanalysis, which in those days consisted of four to six sessions per week for a year or more. By this point most of the faculty of the Medical School were outraged with Alexander.

Alexander, knowing his unpopularity at the University of Chicago, seized an opportunity to work in Boston, and moved there in 1931, but he returned to Chicago in 1932 as the founding director of the Institute for Psychoanalysis.

In the same year, 1932, Franklin McLean, the head of the Medical School of the University of Chicago, invited Grinker to set up the Department of Psychiatry and to become a full professor. Grinker accepted, but, having seen Alexander's experience there, he knew of the animosity toward psychoanalysis. McLean himself did not share in this antagonism; in fact, his wife, Helen McLean, became one of the first four candidates to undergo training at the Institute for Psychoanalysis.

Grinker's original problems at the medical school did not have to do with psychoanalysis but rather with a general hostility toward psychiatry. Psychiatry was a fledgling discipline; in all of Illinois there were only about 35 psychiatrists, and he was given few beds at the hospital (Grinker, 1979, p. 6).

Meanwhile, Grinker's interest in Freud grew. He had trouble finding Freud's books because none of them were in the medical library. He learned that the psychology library had some of his books. The librarian restricted who was allowed to read the books, and the books could not be taken out of the library, so he had to read them without leaving the building. They were kept secure in a locked case.

Grinker later claimed that his own background in neurology is what attracted him to Freud's work. Grinker was impressed with Freud's early writing on neurological research, and he felt his psychoanalytic theories were similar to the neurological theories of Hughlings Jackson (Grinker, 1940, p. 180, 1979, pp. 7–8).

Grinker decided he wanted to have a psychoanalysis. He contacted Sándor Ferenczi, in Budapest, whom Freud, at least at one time, had considered to be his foremost living follower, but, before final arrangements could be made, Ferenczi died.

Ferenczi's secretary suggested that Grinker go to Freud. Alexander considered that an excellent idea and wrote to Freud in Grinker's behalf, but Freud said no.

My father wrote Freud and tried to persuade him to change his mind. Apparently my father also tried to argue for a low fee, because Freud wrote back, "[T]here are material needs to be considered. I am still forced to make a living. I cannot do more than five hours of analysis daily; and I do not know how much longer I shall work at it" (Grinker, 1979, p. 8).

Alan Gregg, the head of the Rockefeller Foundation, had an interest in psychoanalysis and approved Grinker's request for a grant to go to Europe for an analysis. Grinker was able to pay Freud the hefty fee of $25 per session, and Freud agreed to treat him.

So off we went, four Grinkers—my parents, my sister, age eight, and I, only six years old. When we arrived in Vienna late in the summer of 1933, we found a huge apartment with many rooms, a fraulein, and a cook-maid named Liesl.

Grinker (1940) first met Freud at the villa outside Vienna where he spent the summer. He described Freud in this way:

> He impressed me as extremely energetic, with long fingers and hands, constantly moving about. He appeared much younger than his actual age. His hair was white and sparse, beard short and well trimmed. Behind rather thick spectacles were eyes that were magnetic and gave a reassuring feeling of great kindliness. Freud's manners were charming and immediately gave one a feeling of ease and security, yet his questions were direct and searching [p. 181].

Grinker arranged to meet Freud six days per week for an analysis. For some years Freud had conducted analyses with American and British patients in English.

My father recalled coming to Freud's office for a typical session. He would ring the bell and wait "while dogs barked and growled." The maid, Paula Fichtl, would usher him into a hallway and then into the waiting room. It was small and had furniture that seemed ancient. "Suddenly the door of the sanctum would open and Freud appeared," Grinker (1940) noted.

> He invariably grasped the oustretched hand only by the fingers and swept or pulled his analysand into the analytic chamber. This room always smelled

musty, was well lighted by a modern indirect lamp and heated with a coal oven. On the wall were many Egyptian figures of priests. Directly through a wide opening without doors was the Professor's own study. The central attraction was the desk covered with ivory figures and relics. The walls were lined with shelves filled with reference books and sets of the Professor's works translated into numerous languages. The Professor sat in a comfortable armchair, with a footstool for his slippered feet [pp. 181–182].

After Grinker had had just two discussions with Freud and one analytic session, Freud became ill with heart failure and pneumonia and was unable to work for about three weeks. "I thought—in the magical way that analysands think— that perhaps it was I who had made him sick" (Grinker, 1979, p. 9). After Freud's return, he seemed sick, feeble, and fatalistic. His boundless energy had disappeared, and he walked slowly. Grinker (1940) felt Freud "was tired of living and would gladly have given up" (p. 181).

With Freud in such a diminished state, Grinker was reluctant to criticize him, and he also thought it was hard to express "hostility to a genius. I couldn't tell Freud certain things I thought about him: I had to use certain indirections" (Grinker, 1979, p. 9).

Grinker, along with another American named Jake Finesinger, was reading Freud in German. Finesinger was unrestrained in his criticisms. "In my analysis," Grinker recalled, "I found I could quote Finesinger's negative remarks: I did not say those things; Jake did" (1979, p. 9). He found he could also scold the dog.

Dogs played a prominent part in the analysis. Both Freud and Anna Freud, who shared a waiting room with him, had dogs—Freud, a chow; Anna, a giant wolfhound. Both would bark at the doorbell, and the wolfhound would immediately poke his snout into Grinker's genitals. "I entered Freud's office," Grinker remarked, "with a high level of castration anxiety" (Grinker, 1979, p. 9). Once at the seminar the dog lay next to him and barked. Anna Freud said, "Dr. Grinker, he's perfectly safe. Of course, when he was younger, he used to eviscerate sheep, and I couldn't take him out. But now he's perfectly safe; just pull his tail and he'll stop barking." Grinkers's response was that there was not the remotest possibility that he was going to touch that ferocious dog (p. 10).

Sometimes during a session Freud's dog, named Jofi, would scratch at the door, and Freud would let him out. Upon returning, Freud would say, "Jofi doesn't approve of what you're saying." Later, after Jofi scratched at the door to get back in, Freud would comment, "Jofi wanted to give you another chance" (Grinker, 1979, p. 10).

Once, when Grinker was emoting a great deal, Jofi jumped right on top of him, feet-to-genitals, nose-to-nose. Freud said, "You see, Jofi is so excited that you've been able to discover the source of your anxiety" (Grinker, 1979, p. 10). Grinker, well trained in wild-animal behavior, closed his eyes and did not move a muscle, as one is taught to do with big brown bears, wild boars, and ferocious, charging rhinosceroses.

Grinker found another way to express his hostility toward Freud. "I told him repeatedly that I had made a mistake and should have gone to Helene Deutsch [for analysis]" (Grinker, 1979, p. 13). Deutsch, who had been analyzed by Freud, was the director of the Vienna Psychoanalytic Institute. Grinker and his wife had become friendly with five Viennese couples who were all closely associated with psychoanalysis: the Deutsches, Bibrings, Waelders, Krises, and Hartmanns. Grinker suspected that these couples—who all eventually emigrated to the United States—wanted to improve their English, but, nonetheless, he and his wife enjoyed socializing with them. Grinker was especially fond of Deutsch and told Freud that "[s]he would not have said such things as he was saying to me" (Grinker, 1979, p. 13).

Deutsch may have been implicated in one of Grinker's choicest anecdotes from his analysis, although I am not sure. Freud often used stories, jokes, or metaphors to make a point. He knew that Grinker was taken with a woman in Vienna who was extremely intelligent; this may have been Helene Deutsch. Freud had also learned about his wife, who was generally seen as being beautiful and charming. But Grinker pointed out that this other woman was an intelligent professional and told Freud that he liked to talk to her as he did to an intelligent man. Freud related a story about "a man who loved to hear a particular wind instrument":

> One day, when an artist on this particular instrument came to town, he took his son to hear the man play. He turned to his son and said, "Doesn't this sound just like a violin?" And the son answered, "Why don't we go listen to the violin, then?" [Grinker, 1979, p. 12].

The meaning of the story is that Freud disbelieved Grinker's claim that he liked this woman because she was as enjoyable to talk to as an intelligent man. Freud was implying that Grinker liked her because of her attractiveness as a woman. Deutsch, by the way, is known to have been a lovely woman with sex appeal.

Despite his criticisms of Freud, Grinker was impressed with him. Writing to another psychiatrist at the time, he commented, "Perhaps you may credit my feelings toward him as transference during analysis, but from the very first day I felt his personality as being the most inspiring and confidence giving one I have ever met" (Hale, 1995, p. 108).

About three months into our stay in Vienna, my mother was dissatisfied with her husband's progress in analysis. She told me later one of her complaints: Her husband was not telling Freud that he failed to treat his mother-in-law "nicely enough." Grinker suggested she write Freud a letter. He mentioned the idea to Freud, who replied, "Yes, let her write me, providing she doesn't expect me to answer the letter." She wrote "three pages of accusations," and this became something my father discussed in the analysis (Grinker, 1979, p. 12). My mother believed that Grinker's treatment of his mother-in-law never improved.

My mother decided that she wanted an analysis too. Grinker went to Helene Deutsch for a recommendation, and she suggested Siegfried Bernfeld, who had been the analyst of her husband, Felix Deutsch. Bernfeld, later an analyst in San Franciso, became well known for his writings on education.

After she was in analysis, there was a coincidental meeting in the lobby of a spa. My parents, Bernfeld, and an unknown woman approached the registration desk at the same time. My mother, seeing Bernfeld with this much younger red-head whom she assumed was "obviously his mistress," went up to him, scolded him, and quit her analysis on the spot. Bernfeld stopped her short by saying, "Mrs. Grinker, let me introduce you to my wife." There was more than enough embarrassment and discomfort in that lobby for everyone.

At the beginning of her analysis, Bernfeld made a pact with my mother; there would be six months of a trial analysis. After five months, my mother said she felt it was coming time to terminate. Bernfeld said, "I think you had better stay on," and she did. In later years she had few clear memories of her analysis except for commenting on Bernfeld's tallness.

My father, in contrast to my mother, had detailed memories of his analysis, and, despite his avowed intention to respect Freud's so-called "confidentiality," he ended up sharing a great many of them.

Grinker remembered that Freud's voice was "very low," as a result of losing part of his tongue during his many surgeries for cancer of the jaw and palate. Many patients, according to Grinker, wonder whether the analyst ever goes to sleep during their analyses. Grinker would break the unwritten rule and look back at Freud to see whether he was awake; he never found him to be asleep (Grinker, 1940, p. 182).

"When [Freud] was ready to make an interpretation that he thought was quite fitting and related to uncovering some important material," Grinker noted, "he would become excited and would pound the edge of the couch. As he talked, the prosthesis in his mouth would make him spew saliva, and the saliva would cover my face." Grinker concluded that "every time my face was covered with saliva, I knew that I was making progress in my analysis" (Grinker, 1979, pp. 10–11).

Grinker was impressed with Freud's "great zest for details in associations and dreams." When a town was mentioned, Freud would get a map and ask to be shown its location. He also wanted to know just how a house, such as Grinker's childhood house, was configured and often asked that Grinker draw him diagrams (Grinker, 1940, p. 182).

Freud had a light next to his chair, but there was no electrical outlet nearby, so there was a long cord reaching over to an outlet across the room. One time when Freud jumped up to consult a map, he tripped over the cord, fell, and bumped his face on the floor. "And there I was," Grinker remembered, "lying on the couch with Professor Freud lying on the floor with a bloody nose. It took me a while to recover from that!" (Grinker, 1979, p. 9).

In his papers on technique Freud laid down a number of ironclad rules which have been taken as holy dogma by many analysts. Freud, however, broke a great many of them. The emphasis in the papers is on the analyst acting like a blank screen on which the patient can project whatever comes from inside him; the analyst is supposed to have little human interaction with the patient and certainly never to give anything to the patient.

Once Grinker told Freud of a story he had heard about him. It was said that Freud could not smoke cigars any more because of his struggle with cancer, and so he would light up a cigar and draw the smoke up through his nostrils in order to enjoy the smell. Instead of treating this story as something to be interpreted, Freud denied it flatly. Grinker then noted that he could not find a good cigar in Vienna. Freud got up, went to his desk, took out a fine cigar, and gave it to Grinker. Never smoking it, Grinker saved it as a momento until it finally crumbled into pieces (Grinker, 1979, p. 14). There is an apocryphal story, almost certainly incorrect, that Freud once said "sometimes a cigar is only a cigar." In this instance, the cigar, for Grinker, was much more than a cigar; it was a reminder of Freud's way of relating to him.

Another story relates to the question of whether everything is interpretable. Freud told Grinker about how he had suffered from intractable headaches for months, and he noticed that they were milder on Sundays than on other days. Freud worked in his study every evening except for Saturday night, when he had a standing card game with three of his old friends. Freud had the realization that his study might be the source of his headaches. A small gas leak was found there; if it had not been discovered, he might have died of carbon monoxide poisoning (Grinker, 1940, 184). In this case, a headache was a headache, not a neurotic symptom.

Far from sticking to interpretations, Freud often talked with Grinker about his followers and former followers. Freud believed not only that every analyst should go through analysis but also he or she should return every five years for a "refresher." A rare exception was Karl Abraham, who had been president of the International Psycho-Analytical Association at the time of his death in 1925. Freud believed Abraham had been a "normal" individual who had not needed analysis (Grinker, 1940, p. 182).

Freud did not hesitate to make critical comments to Grinker about the early followers with whom he had had breaks. He had "no use" for Alfred Adler, one of his first colleagues, and explained "that he had to make the best of those co-workers available at the time." He spoke positively of Otto Rank but said he was "a naughty boy." He was bitter toward Carl G. Jung. According to Grinker, "Freud remember[ed] Jung telling him of a personal dream six months before his overt antagonism came to the surface. The Professor stated that he should have known from this dream what was to happen" (Grinker, 1940, p. 183).

Grinker received permission to attend the meetings of the analytic society. He was shocked at the rages and the irrationality of these experienced analysts who supposedly had been "thoroughly analyzed." When he told Freud about this, Freud replied, "Why be surprised? Analysts are still human and possess emotions" (Grinker, 1940, p. 185).

Grinker was much more impressed with Freud than with the other Viennese analysts. During his analysis, he wrote to an American psychiatrist that he considered Freud to be the "one and only genius." He said that Freud's followers tried to come up with new theories but Freud "studies his material and waits until he has the evidence." Grinker added that the 11 volumes of the [*Collected Works*] are my Bible right now" (cited in Hale, 1995, p. 108).

Freud talked with Grinker about "lay analysis," which refers to the question of whether people other than medical doctors should be allowed to learn and to practice psychoanalysis. Freud was a strong proponent of lay analysis and was contemptuous of the opposition of the American psychoanalytic establishment toward it. He may have made a special point of bringing up this issue with Grinker because Grinker was the chairman of his department at a prominent medical school. "I was forced to admit," Grinker noted, "that nothing I had known medically or neurologically had helped me in understanding [psychoanalysis as it was taught in Vienna]" (Grinker, 1940, p. 184).

My father detected in Freud not only a critical attitude to the American position on this issue but also a general negativity toward the United States. Freud told Grinker about one incident from his only visit to the United States, in 1909. After receiving an honorary degree at Clark University, Freud spent some time with one of his first American followers, James Jackson Putnam, at a camp in the Adirondacks. He remembered suffering from intestinal cramps while he was there. "'That's too bad' still rang in his ears twenty-five years later," Grinker noted, "for this expression and nothing more was all he received" when he told people of his illness. Freud was still bitter about the American response to his suffering (Grinker, 1940, p. 183).

Despite his unambiguous support of lay analysis, Freud had kept up his interest in his original field of neurology. Although Grinker had just completed a textbook of neurology before he left for Vienna, he was impressed with Freud's knowledge in this area.

A secretary at the psychoanalytic publishing house died of Landry's ascending paralysis, a neurological disease that was little known in Vienna at the time. Freud wanted to discuss it at length with Grinker during an analytic session. Grinker was irritated. "I tried to get off the subject," he recalled, "but I had to spend the whole hour talking about Landry's paralysis rather than about myself, who should have been the center of attention" (Grinker, 1979, p. 11).

When Freud read Grinker's textbook, Grinker recalled, "he pointed out the omission of several references to important classical research in neurology" (Grinker, 1940, p. 180).

Freud struck Grinker as having a "warm, gentle and kindly manner in personal contact," but at the same time he had "extreme intolerance for intellectual mediocrity" (Grinker, 1940, p. 185). Freud could be rigid in the rules he set for the patient. For example, he did not tolerate absences. There were some bitterly cold days, and the office was poorly heated, but Grinker was expected to come for his session. During one period, after a political uprising, the streets were barricaded with barbed wire and patrolled by soldiers, but Grinker felt obligated to find a way to Freud's office (Grinker, 1940, p. 182).

Grinker had a concern during analysis; he was afraid he would change too much. Freud said to him, "Don't worry, Dr. Grinker. Your friends in Chicago will still recognize you."

I remember my father often and fondly quoting Freud as saying, at the end of the analysis, "Dr. Grinker, your analysis has been one of the last great pleasures of my life."

Although I was so young while we were in Vienna, I have some of my own memories. We were there during turbulent times. I remember that our apartment building had an illegal printing press in the basement. I spent hours squatting on the pavement, peeking at it down through the open windows. Later it was closed down.

My mother took me to first grade, and the principal said he would give me two weeks to learn to keep up with the class, which was conducted, of course, in German. My mother told him that was impossible and that he was being totally unreasonable. He stood firm. Principals in Vienna at that time were the authorities; they did not listen to parents. Amazingly, I was soon able to understand the lessons in the classroom. During the latter part of our trip, I poked fun at my parents for their poor pronunciation. In college, when I had trouble with German, my teacher asked me why I was so bad in the language but had a perfect Viennese accent.

School was very different in Vienna from what it is now like in the United States. There was no allowance for play. We sat at desks like little soldiers, wrote with pen and ink, and had our mid-morning roll and jam. We carried the food to school in little wicker baskets hung around our necks, and we had briefcases strapped to our backs with our books and our homework papers.

One of the most traumatic moments of my life occurred when the fraulein tiptoed at night into the room to show my sister and me off to a friend. I woke up with a startle and started crying. She was so angry—and, no doubt, humiliated— that she squeezed my thick, rubber, blow-up Popeye doll and ruptured it permanently with her long red fingernails. I was left with a lifelong aversion to red nail polish, but at least it was Popeye's neck and not mine.

I was free to go to the nearby Ringstrasse, the grand avenue circling the inner city, to play. One day I excitedly ran home to tell my mother of a parade she should come to see with me. She accompanied me and recognized that the marchers were brown-shirted Nazis. Within hours we fled the city. We moved to Baden-am-Wien, about 15 miles away, for about three weeks, and my father commuted to his analysis at Freud's office.

After we returned a friend showed me the shell holes in the walls of his government-housing high-rise and and took me into the basement to point out the barrel in which he had hidden during the shelling.

As a 7-year-old, it seemed to me that life returned to normal. My favorite food was *Kipfel*, which Liesl made every day and hid from me. The aroma was and still is divine to me. My first task of the day was to discover the hiding place of this pastry. She was inventive in finding new and obscure places for it.

Once Liesl and my sister put a box of tea on top of a slightly ajar door. When I opened it, the box fell on my head. Everyone laughed but me. I shrieked in terror and made them repeat the same trick over and over until I was able to laugh too. This is the earliest experience I can remember of using repetition in the service of mastery.

In July 1934 the Austrian Nazis staged an abortive coup and assassinated Engelbert Dollfuss, the chancellor of Austria. We returned to Baden-am-Wien, and my father again travelled to Vienna for his analysis.

One day as we were driving into Vienna from Baden-am-Wien, my father asked me what kind of work I hoped to do for a living. I replied, "Papa, why should I work? I'll just write out American Express checks like you do."

I have a clear memory of the time my father took me along to one of his appointments. Freud patted me on the head and said, "Nice boy." When I asked my father what he was talking about with Freud, he said, "I am telling the Professor what a bad boy you are." I replied, "Oh no. You are telling him what a bad boy *you* are."

After my father completed his analysis, we went to London, where he worked in neurology and brain dissection at Guy's Hospital. In 1935 we returned to the United States, and our memorable trip abroad was over.

Back in the United States, my father became increasingly impatient with the attitude at the Medical School, which was as antagonistic to psychoanalysis and psychiatry as it had ever been.

In 1937 a major hospital in Chicago, Michael Reese Hospital, offered him the position of chief of psychiatry and promised he would have authority to run the department as he saw fit. He consulted with Alan Gregg of the Rockefeller Foundation, who had financed our trip to Vienna for the benefit of the University of Chicago. Gregg was totally sympathetic to the change and told my father that he should see himself as a "Johnny Appleseed" who was spreading the seeds of psychoanalysis wherever they might take hold.

During this period my father also underwent formal psychoanalytic training at the Chicago Institute for Psychoanalysis. Each graduation certificate is numbered beginning with certificate No. 1, which went to Karl Menninger. My father received certificate No. 27.

He had three analyses during his career. The first was with Freud, whom he liked but felt was more interested in proving his theories than in helping his patient benefit from treatment. The second was his training analysis, with Franz Alexander. My father thought Alexander's priority was in proving himself right. He felt his third analysis, with Therese Benedek, did the most for him. She was only interested in him, his character, and his neuroses. He liked all three analysts and was able to develop transferences with all of them, but he believed that of the three Freud was the least effective. He saw Freud as a genius who had invented psychoanalysis but not as the best of clinicians.

In 1951 my father established a freestanding institution at Michael Reese Hospital called the Psychosomatic and Psychiatric Institute. The inpatient units had 80 beds, and there was a large outpatient clinic. One hundred twenty people were on the professional staff, 115 of whom were either analysts or psychiatrists in training to become analysts. He was especially proud of the psychoanalytically oriented training that was provided for psychiatric residents.

As a graduate of that program, I can testify that P&PI, as it was called, was a ferment of excitement, learning, and scientific activities. Residents came early and stayed late. My father was pleased that he had helped foster the development of many distinguished psychiatrists, including 19 who became chairs of psychiatry departments across the country.

My father published many books and papers, conducted extensive research projects, and gave hundreds of talks. He liked to think of himself as an "intellectual gadfly," and his favorite targets were the psychoanalytic and psychiatric "establishments." He generated great animosity, and no one had neutral feelings toward him.

It is an open question how much credit his analysis with Freud should receive either for his substantial contributions to the field or for the unresolved aspects of his personality that made him seem, in the eyes of many, to be a difficult person.

References

Aldington, H. D. (1926), *Tribute to Freud*. New York: Pantheon Books.

Dorsey, J. M. (1976), *An American Psychiatrist in Vienna, 1935–1937, and His Sigmund Freud*. Detroit, MI: Center for Health Education.

Grinker, J. (1911), Freud's psychotherapy. *Bull. Northwestern Med. School*, 13:53–56.

———— (1912), Freud's psychotherapy. *Illinois Med. J.*, 32:185–195.

Grinker, R. R., Sr. (1940), Reminiscences of a personal contact with Freud. *Amer. J. Orthopsychiat.*, 10:850–855; reprinted in *Freud as We Knew Him*, ed. H. M. Ruitenbeek. Detroit, MI: Wayne State University Press, 1973, pp. 180–185.

———— (1963), A psychoanalytic historical island, 1911–1912. *Arch. Gen. Psychiat.*, 8:392–404.

———— (1979), *Fifty Years in Psychiatry*. Springfield, IL: C. C. Thomas.

Hale, N. G., Jr. (1995), *The Rise and Crisis of Psychoanalysis in the United States*. New York: Oxford.

Kardiner, A. (1977), *My Analysis with Freud: Reminiscences.* New York: W. W. Norton.

Wortis, J. (1954), *Fragments of an Analysis with Freud.* New York: Simon & Schuster.

II

FREUD'S IMPACT:
LARGER PERSPECTIVES

Freud and Symbolism: Or How a Cigar Became More Than Just a Cigar

VIRGINIA C. BARRY

Freud profoundly altered the ways in which we understand ourselves when he demonstrated how things are not always what they seem. Through his treatises on dreams, on everyday slips of the tongue, on jokes, on art, on history and more, Freud taught us that though consciously we believe we are in control of how we act and what we think, unconscious motivations are continuously driving our actions and our thoughts. Others before Freud had spoken of what was nonconscious, but it was Freud's genius to describe what came to be known as the *dynamic unconscious*. Consciousness gives the illusion of control over one's thoughts and actions, but unconscious mentation is what actually drives the machinations of the mind. Man's instincts are only barely reined in by the pressures of civilization.

Freud believed that seething inner urges—instincts and drives—were constantly pressing to find expression and satisfaction in the world. The conflict between these inner urges and the forces of civilization is what Freud thought lead to the development of the human mind. But the conflict could never be finally resolved, and the unconscious acts that Freud so carefully enumerated provided evidence of the conflicts universal to all mankind. Thus the life instincts (Eros) continuously battle death instincts (Thanatos); sex wars with aggression. And all these inner drives fight the sanctions imposed by civilization in order to gain expression.

The question of how these inner psychobiological strivings come to be transformed into the stuff of human psychology—otherwise known as the mind/body problem—fascinated Freud. How does *mind* emerge out of *body*? Philosophers have traditionally wrestled with the matter of the duality of the mind and body, and Freud threw his hat into this ring as well as he investigated and theorized about the formation of the *psychic apparatus*.

51

Understanding symbol formation and symbolization was a cornerstone of Freud's theorizing. Although Freud may not have wished for it, he has become known in the popular mind for his writings about the sexual symbols he viewed as inherent in practically everything we think and do. Freud hypothesized that the psychic apparatus was energized by the sexual instincts (called *libido*). When he looked for evidence of the influence of the (unconscious) sexual drives in conscious behavior and thinking, he believed he found evidence in the everyday symbols that occur in dreams, fantasies, and waking thought. In the 21st century, we are quite comfortable with the idea that phallic-shaped objects might be symbolic references to actual phalluses. However, in the 21st century, we also believe that phallic objects might equally denote a broader range of symbolic references that include much more than just phallic symbols; phallic symbols represent just one of a multitude of possibilities for what a cigar might signify. Whereas a cigar might represent a penis or masculine, sexually aggressive behavior to one person, to another person the image of a cigar might indicate warm memories of childhood walks with a father who smoked cigars. In this second denotation, cigars would conjure up images of safety and warmth, not sex or aggression. And to another person, a cigar—via its torpedo-like shape and foul odor—might reference turds.

In this essay, I demonstrate how Freud used his late-19th-century work with patients suffering from language disorders (*aphasias*) and/or hysteria to develop a theory of how the mind operated. This theory of mind anticipated neuroscientific findings of the late 20th and early 21st centuries. Freud's theory was limited in that he believed only sexual and aggressive drives fueled the development of the mind. It was also limited by 19th-century knowledge of the brain. In recent decades knowledge about brain function has grown astronomically, and, I believe, this new knowledge can incorporate Freud's theories of symbol formation into a broader theory which can account for the use of symbols that reflects all the multiple ways in which the body can interact with the environment, *including* sexual and aggressive ways. It can also account for symbols that have more universal meanings, as well as symbols with highly personal, idiosyncratic meanings.

Everyday parlance nods at Freud when we play upon the phallic symbolism of cigars, snakes, guns, knives, steam engines, hoses, monuments, skyscrapers, volcanoes, and so forth *ad infinitum*. Becoming bald, losing one's teeth, being decapitated or dismembered all could represent castration. And boxes, ovens, rooms, shells, undulating landscapes, and so forth are easily understood representations of female sexual organs. The actions of sexual intercourse are symbolized in scenes of being run over, climbing stairs, flying, and so forth. Oceans, rivers, and bodies of water can represent the watery uterine environment out of which all of us are born. Once Freud (1900) laid this out so meticulously, it seemed commonsensical, but as we know today, these symbols can also have many different kinds of referents.

In the early 1900s, Freud observed that the abundant symbolism for representing sexual material in dreams is also found in folklore, popular myths, legends, linguistic idioms, proverbial wisdom, and jokes. According to Freud sexual symbolism emerged from man's unconscious and impregnated his conscious thinking. To state this even more starkly, thinking itself was motivated by the need to gratify biological instincts; thinking, by way of *symbolization*, was the way in which these instincts came to be given a presentable facade by which they could gain expression. The manner in which the physical body interfaces with the external environment is what shapes the mind. Freud's statement—"the ego[1] is first and foremost a body ego"—captures the idea that who we are and even the way we think is shaped by our bodies' physical interactions with the world.

Although Freud may have been limited by his science that viewed biological development as driven only by life (sexuality) and death instincts, and limited by the deficiencies of late-19th-century neurology, his hypothesis that symbols and thinking emerge out of the body's interface with the environment has stood the test of time and can be seen to be quite consistent with contemporary theories of how many symbols are indeed derived from the complex interaction of the body and the world. Freud's (1891) early work on *aphasias*[2] helped him grasp that language functions are distributed throughout the brain. This meant that in speaking or listening, areas of the brain involved in vision, audition, tactile senses, emotions, timing, coordination, and so forth, are all functioning in an integrated way in order to produce a symbol, understand a sentence, or develop a concept. The postulate that language functions recruited widely distributed areas of the brain contrasted with many of Freud's teachers who had theorized the presence of "centers" in the brain. The centers were purported to support discrete functions of language. That prevailing theory held that damage to a center for expressive language (Broca's area) caused difficulty finding words to say things or damage to a center for receptive language (Wernicke's area) caused difficulty in understanding what was said. Freud contested these hypotheses and asserted that language production and reception is not localized within particular brain regions, and that word images are not contained within cells. Instead he contended that language dysfunction occurs because of a disruption of the network of communications between brain cells.[3] The idea that different

---

[1] "Ego" was a term variously defined by Freud, but generally came to mean a psychic structure that experiences and interfaces between the unconscious drives and the outside world.

[2] Aphasias are problems in verbal communication. They include the inability to understand words and/or the inability to produce cogent speech. Aphasias are most often studied in patients who have suffered strokes, but they are also seen in hysterical patients where the speech abnormality has no organic basis.

[3] Freud was greatly indebted to John Hughlings Jackson who conceptualized the hierarchical organization of the nervous system. Jackson's observations of how manifestations of earlier formed, more primitive neural organizations reappear when higher-level neural organizations have been damaged informed Freud's use of the concept of regression in describing neurotic illnesses.

areas of the brain are associated with one another through networks of communication was an integral part of a working hypothesis that led Freud to the therapeutic technique of *association* by which the meaning of symptoms came to be elucidated.

Contemporary science supports Freud's hypothesis of the distribution of language functions over the entire brain. And just as contemporary science has demonstrated the distributed nature of language functions, current scientific research also helps us understand how the body is used to form the basis of how we think, including the basis for symbolization. The ability to use symbols could be considered a highly developed mode of thinking. Some people consider the use of symbols to be that which distinguishes man from lower animals. How man has achieved the ability to use symbols can be examined and debated from many angles—philosophical, linguistic, neuroanatomical, evolutionary, and others. But it is important to understand that conjectures about how a symbol is constructed and how it operates have changed dramatically over the centuries. Traditionally it was thought that the brain operated in a way to somehow produce interior replicas of the external world, and that representations in the brain duplicated external reality. For example, if one saw a dog, an image of this specific dog was created in the brain. Therefore, when one saw a medium-size white dog with black spots and a narrow tail, a corresponding image (or symbol or representation) of a medium-size white dog with black spots and a narrow tail was thought to be created in the brain. Likewise a big long-coated black dog with a bushy tail was believed to stimulate the rendering of a different image in the brain. (The creation of images of objects includes entities as diverse as material objects like dalmatians, or auditory images like the melody of "I'm Dreaming of a White Christmas," or the image of your mother's stern look when you sampled dinner with your fingers.) Rather than static images being created in the brain, however, it is more accurate to think in terms of potential patterns of activation of neurons that are stimulated by objects in the universe. Stimulation from the environment, for example the sight of the dalmatian, will activate a particular pattern of neuronal firings. Although sight of the dalmatian will stimulate firings uniquely specific to our medium-size white dog with black spots and a narrow tail, many of the neurons firing to represent the dalmatian could be called into action with the sight of the Bernese mountain dog. Indeed, there is a generalized pattern of firing that correlates with the category of dog. (More about this later.) The point to remember now is that specific images are not stored in the brain as such. What is stored is a *potential* for activating the firing of a particular set of interconnected neurons.

Over time philosophers and scientists have come to agree that the images (more accurately conceptualized as patterns of firings of neurons) formed in the brain are profoundly influenced by the individual forming the images. To say this another way, because inner representations of reality are associated networks of information from *all* our senses, including sight, sound, taste, olfaction, touch, inner senses, and so forth, the representation of reality is necessarily influenced by our particular body's capacities for sensing sensations. The representation of reality must be a highly subjective, individual experience constrained by the mechanisms that our brains and bodies have to sense the world. And yet there are universals in the ways we experience, represent, and ultimately come to symbolize reality.

For a moment let us retreat from the concept of symbolization and consider instead how we use our bodies to understand the world. From birth the infant is provided with certain tools and preferences (values) that he or she can use to interact with the world. The area of vision processing has been one of the more extensively studied areas of sensory processing systems, and thus lends itself for example. The neurons in the retina pass through various relay stations *en route* to specialized areas of the brain. Take, for example, seeing the dalmatian of the earlier example as he fetches a kong[4] thrown by his master. Aspects of this visual experience are parceled out to specific areas distributed throughout the brain for processing. In these distributed areas, the stimulus response is refined, and then relayed to other areas in the brain (some people speak of these discrete functional units as *modules*) in the service of ultimately creating a unified visual experience. Thus specific areas of the brain process the blackness and whiteness of this dog with spots (the differing wavelengths of light are what we experience as color). Other areas stimulated by motion process the forward loping trajectory of the dog as he sprints to retrieve the thrown object, and the discontinuity of movement as he suddenly brakes to grab the kong in his mouth and turns to race back to his owner. The dalmatian's attributes, specified by the angles of how his longer legs meet his thinner doggy body, or how the narrow tail expressively attaches to his rear end, are distributed to brain areas capable of encoding these distinctions. And these are only a few of the myriad of ways in which aspects of vision are processed in the brain. A unified experience of vision is created through the (degenerate[5]) interconnections of all these various modes of the (deconstructed) visual stimuli. In other words, although experienced as a unitary phenomenon, the operations that underlie vision are distributed throughout the brain. For our purposes it is not necessary to know precisely where each facet of vision is processed, but it is essential to note that it is a distributed process.

---

[4] For the uninitiated, a kong is a rubber cylinder (about 6 inches long and 2 inches in diameter) attached to a sturdy rope of about 12 inches. Dogs proudly carry their kongs to the park for use during exercise outings. Somehow (a physicist would know) a kong's construction makes it a magnificent object for throwing and retrieval, and the rubber substance makes it practically indestructible.

[5] "Degenerate" refers to the idea that a particular output—such as a motor act or a memory—can occur through the activation of different subsets of neuronal connections. There is not just one road to Rome, but many separate paths.

As you can surmise, our vision is limited by the equipment we have to process the visual stimuli. It can be assumed, therefore, that we may not see everything there is to be seen. Certain preferences (capabilities) are hardwired into the brain, and one must presume that other capabilities are absent. We all know that dogs can hear higher pitches than humans, so that what is silence for us, is the call to dinner for them. In the human dimension, preferences might include some of the following: If an infant is exposed to two objects that move in synchrony, the infant makes an assumption that the objects are one. The infant's surprise when the objects are made to move out of synchrony is evidence of this assumption that the two objects were conceived of as one. The underlying preference, then, is that a gestalt (whole) image is preferred to part images. The ability to differentiate horizontal from vertical lines is another inborn preference. The capacity to detect noxious stimuli and to withdraw from them exists even in utero. Infants prefer to look at structured patterns rather than unstructured; they prefer images of faces with the features organized in human fashion rather than images in which facial features have been dislocated (as in a Picasso painting). Infants also prefer novelty in stimulation, and get bored with repetition. Infants demonstrate an innate ability to be able to understand what something should feel like from looking at it. (This is called cross-modal or amodal perception.) In other words certain basic behavioral tendencies are inherited and govern later adaptation. We have all heard the adage "use it or lose it," and this applies to many of these early preferences or possibilities. If they are not invoked and exercised during certain critical periods of development, certain possibilities will be nullified. (This is the basis of why a native Korean speaker is unable to hear the difference between the sounds of "R" and "L"; the ability to distinguish those phonemes is lost early in life because the language does not require its use.)

Now let's take these ideas a little further as we try to understand how thinking is embodied, and how symbolization, in the Freudian sense, is also embodied. We use our nature-given bodies to investigate the world. We use our eyes to see. Our eyes move up to follow a ball as it bounces high into the air and then down as the ball falls to the ground. (If you prefer to stay with our dalmatian example, imagine viewing again the dog's loping gait.) Our eyes follow the ball's trajectory into the street. We reach our arms out and down to grasp the ball, and then bring our arms up and in to lift the ball; we bring it closer to our body, stabilizing it and ourselves as we counterbalance our bodies against the ball's weight. All our senses are co-opted into this process and, miraculously, integrated perceptions and actions ensue. It is with actions, or more precisely interactions, that we come to categorize (sort out) our experiences in the world. This idea is brought home most dramatically in the instance of individuals who have been blind since birth. In those cases where vision has been restored, the now-sighted individual cannot make heads or tails of what he is "seeing." The retina is now capable of transmitting signals, but the brain has no way of ordering what is being signaled. Only active interaction with the envisioned world will provide an opportunity to translate the stimuli exciting the retina into meaningful information. A particularly dramatic example of this kind of restored sight was documented by Oliver Sacks (1995). His patient, Virgil, had undergone a surgical procedure that restored the capacity to see; Virgil, however, became able to "see" only when he was able to begin to correlate the stimuli to his retina (and brain) with tactile stimuli that had previously been categorized. (Cross-modal perception must be activated.) This was dramatically demonstrated when Virgil visited the apehouse in the zoo; he began to "see" when he understood that shape of the bronzed primate statue that he stroked with his hands correlated with the visual stimuli now exciting his retina and his brain as he looked at the apes.[6]

Repeated interactions of the body with the world allow input from all the body's sensors to be organized and "understood." For example, repeated actions of following a ball's movements with a goal of grasping, catching, kicking, picking it up, and so on become encoded in the brain in categories or *image-schemas* (Lakoff, 1987) relevant to what one does with balls. It should be understood that one does not have to have a word "ball" in order to conceptualize ball and the possibilities for actions of balls and interactions with balls. All this categorizing can be accomplished by an infant before he or she has the brain capacity to use language.

As the infant interacts with his environment, he or she uses these interactions to form concepts about how things work. Keep in mind that the brain constantly strives toward greater levels of organization and higher complexity. Concept formation infuses every aspect of life, from maximizing the soothing effect of sucking on one's own thumb, to understanding that nipples are also delightful to suck on, to learning that a hearty scream will bring help (or not). A concept informs expectations of what will happen next. Concept formation, deeply reliant on categorizations, begins with the body. (As I noted earlier, Freud wisely observed that "the ego is first and foremost a body ego" [1923].) The first concepts are in the form of image-schemas and comprise a kind of universal language. Eventually acts of the imagination extend these more concrete concepts to structure abstract concepts and reasoning. How we think and reason has its origins in the early interactions of the body with itself and with the world.

---

[6] An experiment illustrates how interaction or action is a necessary part of learning to categorize experience. In this experiment individuals wear lenses that invert what they are seeing. Thus the world appears upside-down to them, in a manner inconsistent with other sensory, vestibular, and proprioceptive inputs. As they walk about, they are gradually able to adjust and once again report that they see the world as right side up. Individuals who cannot walk around (yet are sitting on a chair with wheels) are unable to make the adjustment, indicating the importance of the direct interaction. This experiment also underscores brain plasticity in that people who have had practice using these lenses come to be able to put them on or take them off and instantly perceive the world as right side up.

What does it mean to say that thinking and reasoning have their origins in the early interactions of the body with the world? Perhaps an example will help elucidate this idea. The following example demonstrates how conceptual metaphors appear in everyday language and thought. You will note that how we reason about things is an extension of our original interactions with objects and events. Imagine being in love. Then think of telling a friend, as you attempt to express the ecstasy you feel because you are in love, "I'm flying on the wings of desire!" (You had forgotten how Victorian you could sound.) What do you mean? And what does it mean that you speak this way? When you describe yourself as flying, you are speaking (and thinking) in terms that use travel or journey as its point of reference. You are talking about a love relationship as if it were a journey. In this instance, your journey is on board a vehicle of flight—wings of desire. And your destination will be some kind of consummation of your love relationship. General principles and correlations that govern our thinking about journeys are applied when thinking about relationships. In a journey a traveler (often the self) uses a vehicle to reach some destination. (In infancy, a hand reaches out to grasp an attractive toy or mothers cross the room to bring a bottle.) Along the way there can be obstacles to travel or facilitators of travel. Applying these principles to a love relationship in which love is conceptualized as a journey, one understands that the lovers are the travelers who are riding on the wings of love to their destination of a shared life. Along the way they encounter turbulent weather that threatens to unseat them or trade winds that speed them on. You can see all the possibilities for the metaphorical mappings of the concepts that underlie thinking about love as a relationship, and also get a sense of how the way we think is grounded in how our body works. (Let me repeat for emphasis that this use of metaphor in reasoning *is* how we think and is not simply a linguistic device.) Some primary metaphors (that take origin from the body) that form part of a universal grammar (image-schemas) include concepts like up/down, left/ right, balance/symmetry, hot/cold, higher/lower, inside/ outside, in/out, front/back, light/dark, warm/cold, male/female, near/far, and so forth Thus to be off-balance, referring to some difficulty in negotiating a situation be it physical or emotional, is a concept that evolves from the body's ability to navigate and maintain its center of gravity, implicitly referencing factors that interfere with the ability to maintain balance. In another example consider the bodily expressions of grief or sadness—head drooping, shoulders slumped, features slack, mouth turned down. Then consider the linguistic expression of feeling down, down in the dumps, under the weather, in the pits. All these expressions and, more important, the way we conceptualize about emotions arise from the bodily experiences (when one feels happy, the body is carried with erect posture, thus happy is up) and are ultimately conveyed through the language we use.

Let's return to Freud. Freud thought that his hysterical patients were "symbolizing" their neurotic conflicts. The gestures of everyday life fascinated Freud, who routinely documented their occurrences (see Freud, 1901, 1905) as he went about his daily life, and incorporated them into his theories of the functioning of the mind and his theories of psychological pathology. Gestures such as covering one's eyes in order to not "see" the significance of some "insight," or loudly sniffing as an involuntary expression of moral disgust commanded a significant part of Freud's focus as he tried to understand the baffling presentations of his patients in the late 19th-century. He came to call the bodily expression of emotional conflict "conversion phenomena" (Breuer and Freud, 1893–1895, p. 206).

The case of Frau Cäcilie (Breuer and Freud, 1893–1895) was paradigmatic, in Freud's mind, of hysterical conversion phenomena. Frau Cäcilie had suffered from facial pain which first occurred when she was unable to give voice to the injury of emotional assault and then remained as the presenting symptom. Neurological evaluation had demonstrated that the pain did not conform to any nerve distribution (i.e., it did not conform to the distribution of the trigeminal nerve that innervates the region of the face and jaws). As Freud attempted to determine whether the patient's pain could be traced to a psychical cause, he discovered that as he

> began to call up the traumatic scene, the patient saw herself back in a period of great mental irritability towards her husband. She described a conversation which she had had with him and a remark of his which she had felt as a bitter insult. Suddenly she put her hand to her cheek, gave a loud cry of pain and said: 'It was like a slap in the face.' With this her pain and her attack were both at an end [Breuer and Freud, 1893–1895, p. 178].

Freud argued that the process underlying the symptom was one of symbolization; extensive theorizing about how the mind operated rested on this notion of "symbolization." Briefly stated, however, for Freud, symbolization meant that the verbal registration of the experience was converted into a nonverbal form, such that the action/gesture came to stand for the words that could not be said. Frau Cäcilie *felt* as if she had actually been slapped in the face. Symbolization seemed to reflect a process of substituting a gesture for the words. Freud argued that the words were present first, and symbolization was a secondary and defensive process. However, as you will see, Freud equivocated on this point and also wondered if in fact the verbal expression was not constructed from the physical source. In the second hypothesis, symbolization would reflect a kind of regression back to an earlier mode of representing experience.

Other examples of symbolization included the patient who, as a child, had experienced the piercing looks of her strict grandmother as a literal pain in her forehead. She had felt that her grandmother was viewing her with suspicion and could look right into her brain. Or consider Freud's patient in whom certain experiences were accompanied by a stabbing sensation in the region of the heart; Freud interpreted the symptom to mean that the split-off affect was experienced as if "it stabbed me to the heart." The complaint of a headache, as if "nails were being driven into the head," was confidently explained as pain related to thinking. ("Something's come into my head.") A hysterical difficulty swallowing, which appeared after receiving an insult, symbolized the idea that "I shall have to swallow this." Freud ventured to guess that sometimes the sensations could call up an explanation of the thinking process, but that often the idea "would create the sensation by means of symbolization" (Breuer and Freud, 1893–1895, p. 180). (Here is the equivocation.) In either case Freud noted that pains of this kind were always cleared up as soon as the problems involved were cleared up. Therapeutically it didn't seem to matter whether symbolization was a primary or secondary process.

Freud, as you will recall, was developing a theory to account for thinking. Arguing for the idea that unconscious mentation is powerful and operates according to identifiable laws, Freud asserted that when ideas become associated with speech the ideas acquire consciousness. (Edelman, 1992, and Edelman and Tononi, 2000 also assert that language is necessary for higher-order consciousness.) Unconscious ideas, on the other hand, retain their power, but operate according to the laws of a lower functional level. This concept became especially important as Freud was arguing that the symptoms of hysterical patients had an unconscious meaning. In other words hysterical symptoms are a function of ideas. Freud believed that affect associated with upsetting and ultimately identifiable events functioned traumatically, leading to a dissociation between the memory of the event and the affect. Normal psychic processes, Freud hypothesized, allow emotional events to be processed and disposed of *through language*, and hence "forgotten." The "talking cure" brought these powerful unconscious ideas under the control of a higher functional organization through language. This hypothesis developed at the same time as he was witnessing the disappearance of patients' symptoms after the patients were able to give feeling-laden utterance to the events under which the symptoms had first developed. Symbolic expression of painful thoughts formed the core of the patients' incapacitating symptomatology. (In maintaining that hysterical symptoms are a function of ideas, Freud had to distinguish hysterical lesions from organically-based lesions:

[I]n its paralyses and other manifestations hysteria behaves as though anatomy did not exist or as though it had no knowledge of it. . . .
It has no knowledge of the optic chiasma, and consequently it does not produce hemianopsia. It takes the organs in the ordinary, popular sense of the names they bear: the leg is the leg as far up as its insertion into the hip, the arm is the upper limb as it is visible under the clothing. There is no reason for adding paralysis of the face to paralysis of the arm. A hysteric who cannot talk has no motive for forgetting his understanding of speech [Freud, 1893, p. 169].

The creation of symptoms is based on *linguistic* knowledge.

Freud used common linguistic usages as support for his thesis that language structures human experience in ways that are outside of human conscious awareness. Idioms like "blowing off steam" or "crying oneself out" illustrated this concept of the need to affectively work through a memory in order to be rid of it and get on with life as normal. His hypothesis maintained that everyday "wearing-away" processes allowed emotional events to be dealt with through a process of "association." Association referred to the ways in which the brain operates to place experience within categories of previous experience in order to bring order and understanding to events. Freud thought that if the associative process is suppressed (and the idea sequestered in the unconscious mind), the affect remains attached to the memory and continues to exert its ongoing effect via the production of symptoms. The theory that the unprocessed memory of traumatic events continues to act and cause illness is contained in the statement that "hysterics suffer mainly from reminiscences" (Breuer and Freud, 1893–1895, p. 7). Working backward from the observation that *affective* recollection of the events that brought on the illness (in other words, reexperiencing the original psychic event in the consultation room) brought relief from symptoms, Freud came to view these patients as locked in the grip of the "unrememberable" and the "unforgettable." The physical/bodily symptoms expressed what had not been remembered in words, and it was up to the psychoanalyst to decode the meaning of the symptoms through the analytical process.

The following paragraph, quoted in totality because of its import, lays out Freud's theory of symbolization.

I have not found such an extensive use of symbolization in any other patient [besides Frau Cäcilie M.]. It is true that Frau Cäcilie M. was a woman who possessed quite unusual gifts, particularly artistic ones, and whose highly developed sense of form was revealed in some poems of great perfection. It is my opinion, however, that when a hysteric creates a somatic expression for an emotionally-coloured idea by symbolization, this depends less than one would imagine on personal or voluntary factors. In taking a verbal expression literally and in feeling the "stab in the heart" or the "slap in the face" after some slighting remark as a real event, the hysteric is not taking liberties with words, but is *simply reviving once more the sensations to which the verbal expression owes its justification.* How has it come about that we speak of someone who has been slighted as being "stabbed to the heart" unless the slight had in fact been accompanied by a precordial sensation which could suitably be described in that phrase and unless it was identifiable by that sensation? What could be more probable than that the figure of speech "swallowing something," which we use in talking of an insult to which no rejoinder has been made, did in fact originate from the innervatory sensations which arise in the pharynx when we refrain from speaking and prevent ourselves from reacting to the insult? All these sensations and innervations belong to the field of "The Expression of the Emotions," which, as Darwin [1872] has taught us, consists of actions which originally had a meaning and served a purpose. These may now for the most part have become so much weakened that the expression of them in words seems to us only to be a figurative picture of them, whereas in all probability the description was once meant literally; and hysteria is right in restoring the original meaning of the words in depicting its unusually strong innervations. *Indeed, it is perhaps wrong to say that hysteria creates these sensations by symbolization.* It may be that it does not take linguistic usage as its model at all, but that *both hysteria and linguistic usage alike draw their material from a common source* [Breuer and Freud, 1893–1895, pp. 180–181; emphasis added].

It is in this last paragraph that Freud equivocated about whether the hysteric's symptoms represented a concrete representation of what could not be spoken, or whether the words, and by extension one can assume symbols, actually draw on the lessons of the body in their creation. One might suggest (as has Valerie Greenberg, 1997) that Freud had two theories, one dealing with speech acquisition and the other with language acquisition. The theory of language acquisition is a more encompassing theory, and the one more consistent with certain current hypotheses of the way mind arises out of the body. In his speech acquisition theory, he attempted to understand how specific words came to represent objects in the world. In this attempt he failed in large measure because he did not have an adequate developmental schema for understanding word acquisition. His broader theory of language acquisition, however, holds up. This theory addressed how features common to one event or an object, via the mechanisms of displacement and condensation, mediated by the networks within the brain, could come to represent a different event or object. This returns us to the territory of how a cigar can stand for a penis or an umbrella can serve as a symbol of security. Neurologically a connectionist theory can help us hypothesize how this process might occur in the brain. Features of events and objects are encoded in the brain by the patterns of activity that they invoke. Thus the pattern of activity engendered by the rigid physical shape of a cigar can also be activated by the image of an erect penis. (And, of course, a cigar also lends itself to represent anal matters via its color and shape.) Or the literal protection provided by an open umbrella can be activated by the protection offered by an insurance policy. (Clearly a closed umbrella can also elicit those same connections stimulated by the erect penis and the cigar.) One hypothesizes that similar neuronal mappings occur to underlie many of the expressions that serve our thinking processes. Thus expressions like "blowing off steam" are elaborations of the body's physiological changes as anger is induced. The feelings of fullness in the chest as one's heart pounds, the rushing noise of blood pulsing by one's eardrums as blood pressure rises, the explosive readiness of the muscles as one is ready to spring into action are physiological states that are all referenced in the expression "blowing off steam," and, indeed, linguistic usage arises from the projection of these bodily responses as mediated by language.

I hope it is clear that, in contrast to Freudian theory that rested on only two libidinal drives, contemporary theory hypothesizes more than just a libidinal motivator to drive the mind machine. All the symbols that Freud made reference to drew their power from the sexual drives that could not find direct expression. And certainly sexuality does inform and embody many of our symbols. But so do other bodily functions. Thus the ability to see underlies how we think about understanding, as if seeing is knowing. We say we are blind to a partner's pain when we ignore that person's distress. Or our symbol of justice is depicted as wearing a blindfold to represent her impartiality. Freud's patient who presented with ataxia (problems with balance on walking), was expressing her sense of being off-balance in a social situation. She didn't have a leg to stand on. The image-schema having to do with balance was imaginatively extended to meta-phorically express the patient's emotional state. These ways of thinking and sym-bolizing are so viscerally understandable to us that we hardly even think about them, yet it is with precisely these transformed bodily understandings that we do actually think and reason.

Naturally not all verbal expressions continue to rest on the concrete physical experience. We can speak of feeling off balance even though we are not literally off balance. In symbolic systems, the words and metaphors are detached from the direct indexical meanings, allowing greater flexibility of thought. It remains true, however, that the origin of these ways of thinking was in the body. And patients like those treated by Freud presented symptoms reflecting a regression of mind, such that their symptoms did in fact literally refer to the origins of the expressions. What Freud called unconscious ideation of a symbolic nature re-ferred to these conceptual systems and conceptual metaphors upon which every-day language is based.

Let's consider some symbols and see how these ideas hold up. In the tradition of Freud, I have turned to popular culture in order to explore this topic further. I have consulted a book (Miller, 1984) that claims to interpret dream symbols. My browsing took me to "eagles." The book confidently states that "to see one soar-ing above you, denotes lofty ambitions which you will struggle fiercely to real-ize, nevertheless you will gain your desires" (p. 211). The interpretation takes off from the attributes of birds. (I am aware that my use of the term "takes off" is using the image-schema of a journey to think about these ideas, and is coinci-dentally synchronous with the subject of the flight of birds.) The image-schema that refers to orientation in space first comes to mind. In the up/down orienta-tion, getting "up" and "above" something connotes mastery and dominance. Physical prowess is also connoted by being up as in the expression that says someone is at the peak of his powers. Foreseeable events are also up in the way that when one looks at an object moving toward one, that object seems to be moving upward in one's line of vision. Ambition is an emotional, ideological, abstract concept as opposed to a concrete object; it is symbolized through the linking of concrete imagery to these abstract concepts through the use of conventional metaphor and metonymy. As I read down in my dream book to examine the other meanings of how eagles might appear in a dream, almost every reference includes the concept of ambition—eating the flesh of an eagle denotes the possession of a powerful will that would not turn aside in ambitious struggle, to kill an eagle portends that no obstacle will stand before your reaching your ambition. The eagle's symbolic denotations arise from more sophisticated observations of his character than are attributable only to the bodily image–schemas projected into the world. Hence arises the notion of single-mindedness of purpose, intensity and ferocity that derive from how the eagle "goes in for the kill" with no apparent sense of empathy for his victim. Still the original bodily attributions (the image-schemas of up and over) are a significant foundation for this symbol of power, intelligence, and ability.

In considering how a cigar becomes more than a cigar, it is essential to remember that symbols also take meaning from the context in which they are employed. Therefore a cigar lying pristinely in the display counter of a tobacco shop doesn't primarily conjure up virile males locked in aggressive combat, whereas an image of a woman—seated at a conference table in what appears to be a board room—holding a chewed and smoking cigar, emphatically conveys that this woman has the balls to stand up to any competitor. The letter A printed as part of the word "shame" is an arbitrary symbol insofar as it has become associated with a particular phoneme, but colored scarlet and attached to a woman's dress, the letter takes its reference to shame from the deep red color of the cheeks when they are involuntarily suffused with blood as a physiologic manifestation of shame and humiliation, and to the flush of passion or the blush of guilt. In Hawthorne's (1850) novel, *The Scarlet Letter,* the "A's" cardinal reference is to words beginning with the letter "a," namely "adultery," "adulteress," and "angel." But the "scarlet" of the letter lends the overtones associated with the blush and flush of affective responses related to the passionate acts of the heroine and the punishment meted out to censure her behavior. A sparkling gem comes to represent intelligence the way a person's eyes are widened, alert, and reflective of light when they are interested and engaged in an activity.

In conclusion allow me to review where our investigations have taken us. Emerging out of his examinations of patients with disorders of language and observations of hysterical patients whose symptoms seemed to reflect a concretization of a verbal idea, Freud hypothesized the process called "symbolization." His studies on aphasia led him to consider how the organization of brain processes could be used to understand the organization of psychological processes. Similar to the brain's hierarchical organization in which networks of associations of brain cells—sensory and motor—were interconnected to produce speech and language, Freud hypothesized similar associational networks within the psychological domain. Just as a literal interruption of these intercommunicating networks would cause a regression of function as observed in patients with an organic brain disease, Freud thought that a loss of the ability to articulate an idea (and thus hold it in consciousness) could be explained by an interruption of the network of associations. The speculations about how the mind is structured as a network of associations developed into the cornerstone of his psychoanalytic theory. "Symbolization" in this context referred to a regressive phenomenon through which an idea became represented by a concrete manifestation, yet Freud also understood that it was out of the concrete physical components that symbols and language were (progressively) created. He identified the way in which all the senses and attributes of the body contributed to language, and it has been up to contemporary linguists and neuroscientists to flesh out Freud's original ideas and demonstrate how the body's interactions with the world are represented in the brain and becomes the basis for how we think, how we represent reality, and how we form symbols. Now we understand that the body's interaction with the world is central to the structure of thought and that many symbols derive their meanings from the projection of the body onto objects in the world. This is how a cigar comes to be more than just a cigar.

References

Breuer, J. & Freud, S. (1893–1895), Studies on hysteria. *Standard Edition,* 2:1–309. London: Hogarth Press, 1955.

Edelman, G. (1992), *Bright Air, Brilliant Fire: On the Matter of the Mind.* New York: Basic Books.

Edelman, G. & Tononi, G. (2000), *A Universe of Consciousness: How Matter Becomes Imagination.* New York: Basic Books.

Freud, S. (1891), *On Aphasia,* trans. E. Stengel. New York: International Universities Press, 1953.

———— (1893) Some points for a comparative study of organic and hysterical motor paralyses. 1888–1893. *Standard Edition,* 1:160–172. London: Hogarth Press, 1955.

———— (1900), The interpretation of dreams. *Standard Edition,* 4 & 5. London: Hogarth Press, 1953.

———— (1901), The psychopathology of everyday life. *Standard Edition,* 6. London: Hogarth Press, 1960.

———— (1905), Jokes and their relation to the unconscious. *Standard Edition,* 8. London: Hogarth Press, 1960.

————(1923), The ego and the id. *Standard Edition,* 19:12–66. London: Hogarth Press, 1961.

Greenberg, V. (1997), *Freud and His Aphasia Book:Language and the Sources of Psychoanalysis.* Ithaca: Cornell University Press.

Hawthorne, N. (1850), *The Scarlet Letter.* New York: Knopf.

Lakoff, G. (1987), *Women, Fire, and Dangerous Things: What Categories Reveal about the Mind.* Chicago: University of Chicago Press.

Miller, G. (1984), *The Dictionary of Dreams.* New York: Prentice-Hall.

Sacks, O. (1995), *An Anthropologist on Mars: Seven Paradoxical Tales.* New York: Knopf.

Seeing Through Freud

MARCIA CAVELL

When I first discovered Freud many years ago, my excitement needed no apology. Many of America's best artists and writers were on the couch, still a centerpiece in many of our favorite movies. Psychoanalysts were sought after by the most prestigious medical schools for the most prestigious positions. Freud was not merely an important figure but, as W. H. Auden said, a whole climate of opinion, riding high on a wave of honor that carried him well into the 1980s.

But for many reasons the crest has broken. There are moments now in which I have to defend Freud even to myself. What puts me on the spot are not the attacks by people unfamiliar with what goes on in the consulting room. Some of Freud's critics claim that the "data" are contaminated by suggestion and so can be dismissed. The first part of this claim is undoubtedly sometimes true. The second part is false. The problems people bring us and the way they think about them, or fail to think about them, call for explanation: regardless of his or her particular theoretical bent, every psychoanalyst has to grapple with the sorts of speech, thought, and behavior that puzzled Freud and got him going.

What puts me on the spot are arguments by a number of different psychoanalysts to the effect that whole chunks of Freudian theory are deeply mistaken. These analysts would reject, or fundamentally revise, Freud's drive theory, his libido theory, his various forms of the dual instinct theory—sex versus self-preservation, Life versus Death—his psychosexual development stages, his idea that the oedipal complex is at the root of every neurosis, even, as I say later, the view of the Unconscious as a special mental system with laws of its own.[1] In most cases the arguments are persuasive. Yet I continue to believe that the peculiar discipline Freud invented—part theory, part therapy, part method of investigation—is one of the big achievements of the 20th century. Freud is so much a

---

[1] See Macmillan (1997) for a summary of many of these arguments.

part of how I, personally, see the human condition that I cannot imagine its look without him.

The particular tack I take here is to defend Freud as I would a great philosopher. Sometimes we think of philosophy as pure conceptual analysis, or as imaginative speculation. This is the view of philosophers as absentminded denizens of an ivory tower. But, like Freud's work, philosophy straddles a line between the conceptual and the imaginative on the one hand, empirical research on the other. Indeed philosophers have long been interested in many of the things Freud was and others that analysts have been discovering only recently: the explanation of irrationality, the relationship between thought and language, what a concept is and how concepts are formed, how words manage to convey roughly the same meaning within a given language community, how indeed we are able to understand each other at all, the extent to which another person's mind is knowable, the authority and the limits of self-knowledge. All these philosophical investigations continue to draw on and fertilize empirical studies; all continue to prompt questions that open our eyes, that engage us in arguments that sharpen our wits about what to make of what we see. For most philosophers, Socrates set the model for our practice: He does not argue his interlocutor out of a possibly wrong-headed view. Rather he attempts, first, to get inside the thinking of the other; then to make him feel the tensions in that thinking, perhaps begin to ask questions he hasn't asked, note where his thoughts are oddly gappy, and then to discover illuminating connections among them.

The good philosopher takes us on a process of discovery in which he first calls our attention to certain ordinary, ubiquitous facts of human experience that we may have taken for granted, for example, that we are able to group the vast multiplicity of things and qualities in the world, no two of which are identical, into kinds; or that though we often blame ourselves for our mistakes and congratulate ourselves for our honors, as if the things we do were all up to us, we also think that some of the causes of our actions are outside of us. The philosopher next shows us that the ordinary facts to which he called our attention contain within them certain rather extraordinary problems. What happens then is as much a process of self-discovery as of the world, or rather it is both; for the very idea of experience looks in two directions, toward us as experiencers and toward the objects of our experience. When we see that we have been making certain unfounded assumptions, or that our thinking is somehow self-contradictory, our reflections may finally bring about a change in the way we look at things, and so a change in the way things look.

To give an example: Plato is the philosopher who discovered the first problem I alluded to about our ability to group things into kinds, the so-called problem of the One and the Many. He showed us that while my Aunt Milly's favorite brown chair, and my circular, blasted front tire, and this sunny day are particular items or events, the words that name and describe them refer to a possible infinity of objects. This is obvious. What may not be obvious before we read Plato is, first, that no experience, or thought, would be possible unless we were able to group particular things under terms that can refer to a great many; and second, that these many-referring terms seem to name entities which, like brown-ness and circularity, and unlike Aunt Milly's brown chair and my blasted tire, are immutable.

This insight drove Plato to a dualistic ontology according to which there are two orders of reality, our familiar everyday world with its dying creatures and its changing seasons that will surely change and vanish, and another, glimpsed to the thoughtful eye, which is perfect and unchanging. Intrinsic to this ontology was the idea that our groupings of things reflect a structure of reality that is also timeless. Our concepts are not merely local facts about us but, Plato thought, images of reality. Genus and species are forever, and Noah's ark has no new inhabitants. Darwin has made us reject at least this aspect of Plato's ontology. Indeed many of Plato's arguments are no longer persuasive, and were not so even to his student Aristotle. But the fit between mind and world is a problem that, along with many others equally interesting and perplexing, Plato set for all time. Few philosophers today go along with the details of his views, or those of Descartes, or Kant. Yet we continue to read and value them, and not merely as historical curiosities.

In the way it navigates between theory and practice, in particular clinical practice, psychoanalysis is not like philosophy, nor indeed anything else. Freud was developing simultaneously a method of treatment, a peculiar conversational mode that explores the human mind and tries to untie its knots, and a theory that attempts to explain what he found. But like the philosopher, Freud called our attention to certain familiar aspects of ordinary life, showing us how problematic they are. Both as theorist and as clinician, Freud resembles in broad ways the Socrates I invoked earlier. Freud too thought along a line that straddles the empirical and the conceptual, and though many of Freud's claims are largely speculative, many are in principle open to verification. Over the years some have been found false, many true; but even his errors often struck out paths of investigation that have led to important, earlier hidden aspects of the mind.

In what follows I am going to focus on Freud's quasi-philosophical investigations of sex, unconscious processes, intention, and temporality. I address these topics under their separate headings, but as will be quickly apparent, all but the first name threads in the same terrain, which leads into a tangled knot of philosophical problems about freedom of the will and agency. I'll begin, as Freud did, with sex.

Sex

In "Three Essays on the Theory of Sexuality" (Freud, 1905) Freud refers to the "poetic fable" in which our first ancestors were rounded creatures, each with a body that had four arms, four legs, one head with two faces turned in opposite directions, and two sets of sexual organs. When these creatures, who were male, female, or hermaphrodite, attacked the gods, they were punished by being cut into two. Sexual love is the doomed attempt to find one's other half. Freud does not mention that the fable comes from Plato's dialogue on the nature of love, *The Symposium*, where it is told by the character of Aristophanes. Plato agrees with Aristophanes that sexual love is our attempt to achieve a wholeness that was once ours and will never be so again, not in this earthly life. But Plato thinks that Aristophanes has his eye on the wrong sphere of being, on body instead of soul and mind. Plato thinks that Aristophanes, like most of us, is under a certain gripping illusion.

Freud thinks so as well, though he and Plato disagree in turn about how to conceive this illusion. Plato held that before its embodied existence, the mind dwells in a state of union with a timeless, incorruptible, immaterial Being, in which the physical and psychological experience of longing so familiar to us has no parallel. It is that blissful oneness we perpetually seek, and that we will find only after death, or if here on earth, only through philosophical reflection. For Freud, on the other hand, there is no other order of existence, nor any soul without body; the union we dimly remember was at the mother's breast. Freud famously says in "Three Essays" that "The finding of an object is in fact a refinding of it" (p. 88). I happen to think this idea of Freud's is evocative but wrong, rooted in a conservative theory of instincts that has been discredited. Nevertheless the idea is part of an examination of the dialectic between longing for another and the wish for separation that Freud opened in "Three Essays," which grew in richness across his work and marked out areas of research for decades of psychoanalysts to come.[2]

In this work Freud also explicitly took on sexual perversion, a concept that presumes an idea of "normal" sexuality and that provides a screen, Freud (1905) showed, for a number of damaging prejudices and anxieties. He wrote:

> Popular opinion has quite definite ideas about the nature and characteristics of this sexual instinct. It is generally understood to be absent in childhood, to set in at the time of puberty . . . and to be revealed in the manifestations of an irresistible attraction exercised by one sex upon the other; while its aim is presumed to be sexual [p. 1].

This definition, which Freud ascribed to popular opinion some 100 years ago, is not so foreign to it today, though by the end of the essay Freud had managed to subvert every one of its assumptions. The sexual instinct is absent in childhood, popular opinion says.[3] Yet which parent has not observed a child masturbating?

---

[2] Among the most famous studies are those by Mahler, Pine, and Bergman (1975) and McDevitt and Settlage (1971).

[3] This opinion was echoed recently by Colin McGinn (1999).

The instinct is revealed in the attraction of one sex upon the other. Is homosexuality not a sexuality? The aim is sexual union. What about all the so-called sexual perversions: fetishism, sodomy, sadomasochism? Activities such as sucking, shitting, tickling, taking in and extruding, mastering and being mastered, seeing and being seen, hurting and being hurt, even destroying and being destroyed, need none of them be sexual; yet all readily take on a sexual significance. This puzzled Freud and should puzzle us. It leads us to wonder what indeed we mean by "sexuality."

Among the many illuminations in these essays is the extent to which those aspects of sexuality that the popular definition leaves out are disturbing. Freud distinguishes between the sexual object, that is, the person or creature who attracts us, and the sexual aim, or the activity through which one hopes to achieve gratification. According to the popular definition, sexual instinct by nature chooses a heterosexual object, where "nature" means something like, "the way God means things to be," such that any deviation from this essence must be attributed to a fall from Grace, a willful turning away from the Good that so many religious people believe. But curiosity about these matters asks: Why do we bring such heavy artillery to bear on a sexual choice that is different from ours?

The Academy Award–winning film *Boys Don't Cry* is a true story about a girl who masqueraded as a boy and got away with it for a while. When the boys in that story found out the girl's sexual identity, they repeatedly raped and finally killed her. What was going on in their minds to enrage them so? Was it the idea of homosexuality itself? If so, what about it? Perhaps that homosexuality is linked to anxieties about not conforming to the expectations that come with one's having the body of a male or a female sort? Or to conflicts about having to accept— so we are early taught—that one is a girl or a boy, never both, and that one must be excluded from the possibilities that are open to the other? Or to some wish to transgress the limits that one's gendered body seems to lay down? But why would a boy who knows he is a boy and acts like one, experience conflicts and anxieties like these to begin with? Is his grip on own gender more precarious than he thinks? In a sketchy way, Freud made all these suggestions, which later more systematic research has confirmed.[4]

Another illumination in "Three Essays" is the extent to which sexuality is a matter of mind as well as body, so that the simplest, seemingly "innocent" thing can take on sexual meaning, and different meanings for you than for me. How can my friend Mary find that creep exciting? Why am I excited or turned off by things that repulse or seduce you? Why does the way he lifts his hat or sings off key turn her on? We usually don't ask these questions. When we do we chalk it

---

[4] For an account of some of these see Person, 1999.

up to "chemistry" or "taste" or pheromones and genes. It's not that they aren't part of the answer, but they can't chart the ways in which sexual fantasies get going for each of us and hook up to our behavior. Steven Marcus (1962) aptly called "Three Essays" Freud's meditation on the mind/body problem.

Freud's answer to the questions about the diversity of sexual behaviors, and their interconnectedness with aspects of experience that are not in the first instance sexual, is that sexuality begins much earlier than we had thought, and that it is structured by those bodily activities that bring the infant into daily, intimate, pleasurable, highly charged, often conflicted contact with its caretakers. He suggests a number of different continua: from child to adult, from homosexuality to heterosexuality, from so-called "normal" to "perverse" sexual thinking and behavior. Children have erections, they masturbate, and they have orgasms, though of course the child is not yet ready for intercourse or procreation and has only an inkling of the meanings of grown-up sexuality. The child means one thing by his or her flirtatious behavior, the adult takes it in another sense. In this space between them, there is room for the sad misunderstandings that Sándor Ferenczi, one of Freud's brilliant followers, began to explore (Ferenczi, 1955).

Recent studies of the interaction between parents and children have resulted in a decisive rejection of Freud's idea that at first the infant has no interest in the outside world and that its first love object is itself (Emde, 1981; Stern, 1985). Other studies indicate that Freud was wrong in thinking that girls do not value being girls and are not aware for a long time of their sexual organs; that girls want babies only as substitutes for a penis; that children begin to understand themselves as boys or girls only after observing genital difference; that the male superego is stronger than the female's and that it derives primarily from fear of castration (de Marneffe, 1997). Furthermore, for many psychoanalysts, conflicts around dependency have replaced conflicts about sexuality as organizers of the childhood psyche. These are some of the points that many of us think Freud got wrong.

But it was he who first proposed in a serious way that children have a sexual life; that what gender they are matters to them psychologically; that children observe more than we think they do; that just as adults have an inner, subjective, life, so do children, intelligible to us but different from ours; and that because the life situation of a child is very different from that of the adult, the child's inner life will normally reflect these differences. There is a culture of childhood, we have learned in this century, and Freud was its first anthropologist.

Freud also changed the way sexologists and psychoanalysts think about impotence, assigning to it a psychological cause. His interest in the sexual perversions led to an understanding of the central role of erotic fantasy in desire, and of how complex fantasy can be, not only gratifying forbidden wishes, as Freud thought, but also attempting to repair damage to self-esteem, to keep anxieties about gender at bay (Kaplan, 1979; Stoller, 1979). And it was Freud who first said that homosexuality is neither an innate nor a degenerate condition. Interestingly research has recently come around to the view that there may after all be an inborn disposition to homosexuality. But how different that conclusion looks once we have prised it apart from the issue of degeneracy, and begun to entertain the idea that every sexual orientation, heterosexual as well as homosexual, has its reasons. For example, heterosexual love, too, can be defensive in function (Chodorow, 1994). Freud was given to binary oppositions: sexual instincts versus ego instincts in his early theory, life against death in a later revision, narcissistic or object love, male or female. But his way of thinking leads to a tolerance for ambiguities that escapes all his own dualisms.

The Unconscious

Freud said that conscious thought processes are shadowed by others that are unconscious, determining, beyond our knowledge and control, how we perceive the world, how we feel, and how we act. Freed from Freud's own metapsychology, the idea has even more support now than when Freud pronounced it. Gerard Edelman (1992) writes:

> The postulation of an unconscious is a central binding principle of Freud's psychological theories. Since his time, ample evidence has accumulated from the study of neurosis, hypnotism, and parapraxes to show that his basic theses about the action of the unconscious were essentially correct [p. 145].

Fifteen years ago cognitive scientists assumed that the most important cognitive processes are conscious. The idea of long-term memory implied that some mental contents are unconscious, but the implications had not been explored. The consensus now is that human thought and memory involve at least two systems, one conscious, called explicit memory, the other unconscious, called implicit memory. The latter contains rules of skills or procedures, from knowing how to ride a bicycle to how close to stand to the person with whom you are talking. We have reason to think it also contains associations that guide thinking and feeling; that feeling-laden evaluations often precede conscious thought processing; that without knowing it, people censor information they perceive only subliminally; and that they can be particularly vigilant about such information (Westen, 1999).

The philosopher Jean-Paul Sartre said that the idea of repression involves a self-contradiction, for "the censor" must be aware of what is to be repressed (Sartre, 1956). Sartre has since been echoed by other philosophers (Pears, 1982; McGinn, 1999). They are right, if we think of awareness as an all-or-nothing phenomenon. But a number of studies suggest instead that perception is a process with a number of stages, only the last of which is fully explicit (Neisser,

1967). It is this multistage-process of awareness that Freud (1926) suggested long ago in *Inhibitions, Symptoms and Anxiety*.

Of course there cannot be direct, first-person experience of repression, since by definition the process is out of awareness. Nevertheless there is a good deal of evidence of an indirect sort. Certain studies with a tachistoscope, for example, are best explained by positing a motivated failure to register consciously a perception that has been registered unconsciously (Shevrin and Dyckman, 1980; Shevrin et al., 1996). The concept of repressed memories of childhood sexual abuse, which some analysts prefer to describe as dissociated rather than repressed (Davies, 1996), has elicited the harshest response from Freud's critics. Undoubtedly some of these memories have been fabricated, often under the benighted guidance of poorly trained therapists. But however we describe it, there is a body of evidence that here too is convincing (Westen, 1999).

If there is so much observation in support of the idea of unconscious mental functioning, why are many people still skeptical? One reason is ignorance of contemporary research. Another is that the idea has to be rescued from Freud himself. He thought he had discovered the *Unconscious*, a peculiar mental system with its own nonrational laws that is nevertheless the mind's fount. Supposedly his grand discovery, the *Unconscious* carries an enormous body of speculation on its shoulders, much of which I think is misguided or mistaken but that continues to burden psychoanalytic thinking. Some contemporary research suggests that instead of one unconscious system, there are many different kinds of unconscious processes serving many different functions; that some of the features which Freud attributed only to the system Unconscious characterize conscious thinking as well; and that conscious and unconscious thinking may be generally more similar than Freud thought (Westen, 1997; Westen, 1999).

Intention, Mental Mechanisms, and Anxiety

What is a doing that is truly one's *own* doing, an action for which one can be held responsible? The presence of intention might seem to capture this domain, which is why so many philosophers beginning with Aristotle have been interested in articulating what we mean, or should mean, by "intention." A lot of the things we do are clearly unintentional: for instance, sneezing, or bumping into someone on the subway when the train suddenly lurches. I apologize, but it wasn't my fault. Neither is it if on my way to your kitchen with your Ming vase, my knee gives way and so does your Ming vase. My knee didn't break the vase; I did. But I didn't do it intentionally. It was an accident. Unfortunately, however, because we are creatures who are adept at disguising our intentions even from ourselves, the consciously accidental may not be the end of the story. Any of the above might be done intentionally, or carelessly in a way that invites a longer account of what happened.

Calling a deed unintentional is usually the same as calling it involuntary. And if an act is truly unintentional and involuntary, then in an important sense it is not a free act. Aristotle said that those things are involuntary that we do under compulsion or out of ignorance. He added that something is compulsory if its origins are outside the agent, but he noted some important qualifications, one of which is that with regard to things we do from fear of greater evil, it is debatable whether the action is voluntary. For example, in *Sophie's Choice,* Sophie is told by the Gestapo to decide which of her two children is to be killed, and that if she doesn't decide, both will be. She chooses her daughter, but of course it isn't a free choice, not one she would have made except under the severest constraint.

Kierkegaard (1954) reminds us of a similar example from the Bible. Introducing the story with the equivocal words "God did tempt Abraham," *Genesis* says that God commanded Abraham to sacrifice Isaac, his only son, and that Abraham was prepared to do so. We are told little about what was going on in Abraham's mind; but this is precisely the question that a genius of subjectivity and the moral life like Kierkegaard wants to investigate. For what, precisely, is going on in someone's mind, consciously or unconsciously, when he or she drops a vase, or sacrifices a child, has everything to do with just what his or her action is, and for what, if anything, the agent might appropriately feel guilty.

So Kierkegaard uses the equivocal opening words "that God did tempt Abraham" to spark our imaginings. Was it a temptation because Abraham might (wrongfully) have resisted God's command? Or because Abraham should never have been willing to obey the command in the first place? Or because something untoward in Abraham, something of which he was scarcely conscious, wished for Isaac's death? In which case the act that would have looked from the outside like extreme piety would have been, from the inside, closer to murder. The look from inside is a crucial factor when guilt and forgiveness are in question, or when we are trying to decide between accidental death, manslaughter, and murder.

The biblical scholar will be quick to supply other readings of the Abraham story, as the psychoanalyst will urge us to keep in mind that harboring a murderous impulse on which one does not act is categorically different from putting the impulse into action. Both scholar and psychoanalyst are right, but neither blunts Kierkegaard's scary point. Some fifty years before Freud, Kierkegaard was meditating on the possibility that under the best of public reasons, more private motives may lurk which make all the difference to what we should correctly be described as doing.

Here the problems begin to multiply, first, because of course there are many things in anyone's mind at any one moment, not all of which that person can possibly know at the time. Second, because though we hope that our action will have certain consequences, it will inevitably also have others that we not only hadn't wanted but couldn't have anticipated. (This is how I read the multiple ironies in Sophocles' *Oedipus the King*, not as the expression of unconscious desire but of the fact that the world itself so escapes our knowing that even the best intention can have terrible results. These results may point us to unconscious intention, but they also may not.) Third, because of the damnable unconscious. In the absence of our awareness of them, motives can move us in a semimechanical way.

The groundwork for the concept of a mechanism of defense was laid by Janet (1889), who viewed memory as the central organizing apparatus of the mind. His work with hysterics led him to think that memory can function automatically, in a way that is shared both by human beings and other animals, and also in a peculiarly human way, integrating new experience into existing mental schema. If an experience is frightening or very novel, it may not be remembered as an integrating narrative. It becomes dissociated from conscious awareness and from voluntary control. When it does, one is unable to tell what happened. Instead the person "remembers" by repeating the traumatic scene in action.

Psychoanalysts continue to speak of dissociation, which may manifest itself in a quick shift of attention, a change of subject, a failure to note or be bothered by the contradictions between one line of one's own thinking and another, or a way of talking about something "hot" in a strangely cold and disconnected way. Such forms of dissociation overlap with the mechanisms of defense that Freud called isolation—idea from affect—and splitting one group of thoughts from another with which it is connected. But the major point is that the mind has quasi-automatic, subrational ways of defending itself against trouble, in particular, anxiety.

In "Inhibitions, Symptoms and Anxiety," Freud (1926) described anxiety as the affect that signals danger, or what one construes as a danger. All creatures have ways of defending themselves from danger, but because we are the complex sort of thinking creatures we are, things that would not be dangerous for a lion or a rabbit are dangerous for us. Not only are they construed by us as dangerous, but also they may truly endanger mental functioning. So in a defensive move the mind manages not to understand or take note of its own perceptions. There is a signal of impending danger in the form of a moment of anxiety just sufficient to set defensive strategies in motion, strategies that defend both against the danger situation and against the full recognition of the anxiety itself.

Let's talk about the child. A child needs not only to be loved but also to feel that she is loved, not only to have a parent who is able to take care of her and who is admirable, but also to believe that she does. She needs a parent powerful enough to keep her safe, but also respectful enough of her not to intrude himself in ways that would be overwhelming or frightening. So depending on the situation of the child, it may be imperative for her not to see what she sees, not to know what she knows, for the knowledge, for example, that the person she loves and needs has malevolent intents toward her, might be too great to bear. Of course, because no person is entirely malevolent, or entirely good, the child will have perceptions of him that are both. The thoughts about the good parent may then be split off from the thoughts about the bad. Unfortunately one of the ways in which a child can ignore the badness of the behavior which she cannot help but perceive is by demonizing herself as the all-bad child who justly deserves such punishment.

In this little scenario, a sort that is very familiar to psychoanalysts, we have a set of defensive strategies that create dangers of their own in the form of self-hatred and lasting habits of thinking and behaving which hamper one's perceptions. We are creatures who learn from experience; on the basis of past experience, we learn to anticipate danger in certain situations and respond accordingly. The trouble is that we may assimilate the present to the past on the basis of superficial and irrelevant similarities, so that what might have been adaptive for the child is now destructive for the adult, who needs to see his troubles, and his pleasures, with eyes clear of the sand of childhood.

Freud always saw conflict as central in the workings of the mind. Not conflicts like that between becoming a pianist or a physicist, or going to Maine or to Paris for a vacation. In these cases it is clear what one wants, and that one can't have it all. The conflict is visible both to others and to oneself. But the kinds of conflicts that Freud saw are unconscious, typically organized in childhood, where they were affect laden, involving imperative needs that could only be satisfied at the expense of other needs which were equally imperious. Conflict sets in motion defensive thought processes that acquire their own force and that tend to twist knowing and wanting themselves. In his early work, Freud threw us off the track of understanding childhood conflicts by locating them in a nexus of sexual wish and desire versus the constraints of society. This is not to say that sex is unimportant, but that its importance may better be revealed in the context of a conflict between dependency and autonomy. The child wants his parents' love, and he feels he must do what he needs to do to keep that love. But increasingly he also wants to explore the world on his own, to do things not all of which his parents want him to do, and some of which he feels would make them ashamed, perhaps not of him but of themselves, or threatened with their own sense of loss, or critical of him and angry.

Some children navigate these conflicts without great difficulty. Others do not, and what can happen then is a kind of self-blinding about what one sees or wants. Or it can make for a constriction of wanting itself, so that instead of recognizing one's wants as *his*, the child feels that something is being demanded or required of him from outside. He may then vacillate between compliance and resentment, never feeling the pleasure and sense of potency that comes with wanting, knowing what you want, and going after it as best you can. Or he may be chronically unable to make decisions, filled with doubt about his own abilities. These are what psychoanalysts mean by symptoms, ways of structuring one's experience and one's thinking that, in the case I have just imagined, stunt wanting before it grows sturdy enough to put one in the dangerous situations he fears. The formation of symptoms is again the sort of behavior that defies Aristotle's distinction between the voluntary and the involuntary.

The concept of a symptom, in its usual sense as a sign that something is wrong, is misleading. In this sense a symptom merely points the doctor to the underlying illness, and it is this that he hopes to find and treat. But the symptoms the psychoanalyst treats are themselves the illness, the mind's strategies, though out of the person's conscious awareness, for controlling anxiety but which interfere with thinking itself. Anxiety helps to create false beliefs; to prevent acknowledgment of one's own perceptions, reflection on what one knows; to keep separate in the mind pictures, beliefs, fantasies, that are not compatible with each other. It strips feeling from thinking, caricatures the bad and the good, and is in general intolerant of ambiguity. A mind like this is not a mind that is able to exercise reason fully. In the place of the kind of thinking that makes connections, that explores the implications of a thought, relatively free of fantasies which blur one's own perceptions of what is, there are symptoms.

Yet at the same time, psychoanalytic theory extends the domain of explanation in terms of reasons. Freud insisted, rightly, I believe, that the kinds of behavior he saw in his consulting room can be explained to a large extent in terms of beliefs, desires, memories, and so on, namely the sorts of mental attitudes that figure in our everyday understanding of the reasons why people act as they do, reasons that are also causes, though causes of a special sort. When we begin to understand someone's behavior in terms of her wants, what she believes, what frightens her and why, then we understand her reasons for doing what she does.

If the person is a child, this understanding can be particularly difficult; so also when one is dealing with an adult, namely all of us, in whom the child lives on. In their investigation of the five-year-old Little Hans, Hans's father and Freud discovered the child believed his penis might be cut off, a belief that at the time seemed to these grown-ups irrational. Years later in "Inhibitions, Symptoms and Anxiety," Freud (1926) wrote that those of a child's beliefs that strike the adult as absurd may show their sense, once the adult is sensitively attuned to the world as it presents itself to the child.

Was Freud the master of the irrational, or the rational? Both, here again coax us beyond our familiar categories. He deepens the puzzles about who is the agent of our actions, at the same time as he brings to light mental phenomena we had dimly discerned but for which we previously had no vocabulary. Interestingly Freud does for us as philosophers something like what the psychoanalyst may accomplish with his patient.

Aristotle suggested we ask: Inside the agent or outside? Compelled or free? Thing done in ignorance or done knowingly? But some compulsions seem to come from within ourselves. And "ignorance" may have its reasons in an inarticulate awareness that foretells depression or massive anxiety. Aristotle was concerned with overt actions in the world. But the mind also acts: it thinks, chooses, decides, worries, evades, pays attention, tunes out. One of Freud's big contributions to the philosophy of mind was the idea that the mind does some things, like defend itself against psychological threats to its own functioning, that are purposive, yet more automatic and mechanical than intentional. His concept of a mechanism of defense opens a wedge between outside and inside, involuntary and voluntary, compelled and free, a-rational (like the behavior of an inanimate object or an animal) and rational.

What are the implications of psychoanalytic ideas about conflict and unconscious motivation for philosophical issues of free will? Let me first set aside two claims that are often thought to decide the question. The first is that everything we do and think has an organic substrate. The second is that everything we do has a cause. Both claims are true, and both are irrelevant to freedom of the will. Freud seems to have thought otherwise, but this was a confusion. Nor is the idea of the unconscious by itself decisive. What matters is not that body has its place— of course it does because there is no mind without body—nor that the agent's behavior is caused—of course, again—nor that some of the causal factors were unconscious, but the way in which the agent's wantings, conscious or unconscious, figured in the causal story. Did she do what she did because she wanted to do it? And was this wanting itself more or less in harmony with her other desires?

These are the questions of volition that Aristotle took up and about which psychoanalysis has had much to say, though to my knowledge no philosopher writing about free will and determinism has yet put the insights of psychoanalysis to a systematic use. The reasons may be that it's a hard problem at best, and that psychoanalysis reveals it to be even harder than we had thought. Freedom, it tells us, like wanting itself, comes in degrees. Does the person in my earlier example, who allows herself to do what she wants only by thinking of herself as complying with or as being coerced by someone else, do what she wants to do? Only to an extent. And similarly with the addict, the pervert, the sex offender.

Temporality

In a monumental canvassing of Freud's theories and those of his followers, Malcolm Macmillan (1997) argues that the changes Freud made in his theory were prompted not by new observations but by internal contradictions within it, that saving a pet idea was always the guiding motive. The argument is convincing up to a point, but singularly missing is an appreciation of the phenomena Freud was trying to explain. An example: Freud gradually realized he could not accommodate anxiety dreams to his theory that every dream is the fulfillment of a wish. In fact the "repetition" phenomenon, in which a person seems willfully to get himself again and again into a kind of situation that has been painful to him in the past, does not seem to fit the more general idea that people are motivated by the wishes for survival and for pleasure, an idea that had been fundamental to Freud's system. So in 1920 he proposed a radical revision that figured "the death instinct" (Freud, 1920).

Many psychoanalysts were unhappy with the idea from the first. But however we explain it, the phenomenon of something like a willful repetition of a painful past remains. Along with a good many other clinical phenomena, it showed Freud that the mind is vulnerable to problems of a peculiarly temporal character (Cavell, 1999). This is not surprising, given that there is no such thing as a human mind without memory and that memory is notoriously unreliable, both absentminded and creative. What is surprising is that we unconsciously provoke experiences in which earlier passions are lived now as if all the circumstances were the same; we construct fantasies and forego pleasures in the effort to ward off catastrophes that have already occurred.

The mind's temporality is one of the big psychoanalytic ideas that Anglo-American philosophy has yet to absorb. We tend to think of self-knowledge as success or failure in capturing present mental content. But content is guided by acts of attention, which always have a history; present desires, beliefs, and fears necessarily contain ones that are older. This earlier mind is ground of the present mind, not as foundational axiom to inference but as lens to vision. Or to change the metaphor: The mind is made of time; but the mind is anxious and the watch gets stuck.

Rather late in his career, Freud arrived at his structural theory, which invites us to think of the mind in terms of three overlapping structures that he called "the It," "the I," and the "Over-I" (Freud, 1923). Many psychoanalysts have argued that the structural theory does not serve us very well (Klein, 1976; Holt, 1989). Yet whatever its lacks, one can see it as Freud's attempt to think about the mind in a way that does justice to the ambiguities I have noted, exploring that no-man's-land between the clearly intentional and the clearly unintentional, inside and outside oneself, the "I" and the "not-I," free and un-free, past and present.

Psychoanalytic therapy itself increases a tolerance for ambiguity. To revert to one of my earlier examples: the child of a violent, malicious father may unconsciously protect her idea of a strong, benevolent parent by splitting her perceptions into two groups, caricaturing each, and turning fall-guy in the process. As she grows up, her relations to the important persons in her life may continue to be stamped in this pattern. In therapy she may begin to acquire a third-person view from which she now sees what she was and is responding to, and sees also perhaps the ghosts that haunted her own nursery (Fraiberg, 1975). One of the incidental consequences of psychoanalytic therapy can be a kind of objectivity in which radical discontinuities between good and evil disappear, and the moral landscape broadens to include oneself in interaction with others: one is not only doer but done to, or, rather, the distinction between passive and active loses sense, for it denies the extent to which who one is at any moment emerges from an interplay between not only inside and out, but also self and other.

Which of Freud's theses in particular will survive, and in what form, I cannot say. Nor am I willing to predict the fate of psychoanalysis as therapy. But as an intellectual enterprise, psychoanalysis guides our vision of ourselves in a way that is peculiarly modern and that I believe will be enduring. Like Wittgenstein, and, despite his own dogmatisms, Freud unsettles our quest for the unquestionable. Behavior that shows up from one point of view as in the service of a certain set of needs and values proves itself in the service of a conflicting set from another. A thought I had yesterday that struck me as an important piece of insight may strike me today as self-deception, and vice versa. As my self-congratulatory judgments may mask a baser motive, so my feelings of guilt may hide disappointment with someone else. We are less grown-up than we think we are, less important, less self-sufficient, not so strong, and much stronger, more alone, and less. In the Freudian landscape nothing is what it seems, or, rather, nothing is only what it seems to me now, in this light.

The proper conclusion is not that there is no such thing as truth, or that everything is "subjective," as some psychoanalysts have claimed, but that an increase in knowledge comes with widening the place where we stand, so reconciling differences, adjusting our partial perspectives, mine with yours, my own with each other. The psychoanalytic process strikes me as something like this. I put it as a matter of knowing and seeing; but perhaps the major lesson of psychoanalysis is that there is neither without human passions and interests.

References

Cavell, M. (1999), Keeping time: Freud on the temporality of mind. In: *Analytic Freud: Philosophy and Psychoanalysis,* ed. M. P. Levine. London: Routledge.

Chodorow, N. (1994), *Femininities, Masculinities, Sexualities: Freud and Beyond.* Lexington, KY: University Press of Kentucky.

Davies, J. M. (1996), Dissociation, repression and reality testing in the countertransference: The controversy over memory and false memory in the psychoanalytic treatment of adult survivors of childhood sexual abuse. *Psychoanal. Dial.,* 6:189–218.

de Marneffe, D. (1997), Bodies and words: A study of young children's genital and gender knowledge. *Gender and Psychoanalysis,* 2:3–33.

Edelman, G. E. (1992), *Brilliant Air, Bright Fire.* New York: Basic Books.

Emde, R. N. (1981), Changing models of infancy and the nature of early development: Remodeling the foundations. *J. Amer. Psychoanal. Assn,* 29:179–219.

Ferenczi, S. (1955), Confusion of tongues between adults and the child. In: *Final Contributions to the Problems and Methods of Psychoanalysis.* New York: Brunner Mazel, 1980.

Fraiberg, S. (1975), Ghosts in the nursery. *Amer. Acad. Child Psychiat.,* 14:387–421.

Freud, S. (1905), Three essays on the theory of sexuality. *Standard Edition*, 7:130–243. London: Hogarth Press, 1953.
———— (1920), Beyond the pleasure principle. *Standard Edition*, 18:7–64. London: Hogarth Press, 1955.
———— (1923), The ego and the id. *Standard Edition*, 19:12–66. London: Hogarth Press, 1966.
———— (1926), Inhibitions, symptoms and anxiety. *Standard Edition*, 20:87–175. London: Hogarth Press, 1959.
Holt, R. R. (1989), *Freud Reappraised*. New York: Guilford Press.
Janet, P. (1889), *L'Automatisme Psychologique*. Paris: Société Pierre Janet, 1978.
Kaplan, H. S. (1979), *The Sexual Desire Disorders: Dysfunctional Regulation of Sexual Motivation*. New York: Brunner/Mazel.
Kierkegaard, S. (1954), *Fear and Trembling*. Princeton, NJ: Princeton University Press.
Klein, G. S. (1976), *Psychoanalytic Theory*. New York: International Universities Press.
Macmillan, M. (1997), *Freud Evaluated, The Completed Arc*. Cambridge, MA: MIT Press.
Mahler, M. S., Pine, F. & Bergman, A. (1975), *The Psychological Birth of the Human Infant: Symbiosis and Individuation*. New York: Basic Books.
Marcus, S. (1962), *Introduction to Sigmund Freud: Three Essays on Sexuality*. New York: Basic Books.
McDevitt, J. B. & Settlage, C., eds. (1971), *Separation-Individuation: Essays in Honor of Margaret Mahler*. New York: International Universities Press.
McGinn, C. (1999), "Freud under analysis." *New York Review of Books* (November 4).
Neisser, U. (1967), *Cognitive Psychology*. Englewood Cliffs, NJ: Prentice-Hall.
Pears, D. (1982), Motivated irrationality, Freudian theory and cognitive dissonance. In: *Philosophical Essays on Freud*, ed. R. Wollheim & J. Hopkins. Cambridge, England: Cambridge University Press.
Person, E. S. (1999), *The Sexual Century*. New Haven, CT: Yale University Press.
Plato (n.d.), Symposium. In: *Plato, The Collected Dialogues*, ed. E. Hamilton & H. Cairns. Princeton, NJ: Princeton University Press, 1973.
Sartre, J. P. (1956), *Being and Nothingness*. New York: Philosophical Library.
Shevrin, H. & Dyckman, S. (1980), The psychological unconscious: A necessary assumption for all psychological theory. *Amer. Psychologist*, 35:421–434.
———— Bond, J. A., Brakel, L. A. W., Hertel, R. & Williams, W. J. (1996), *Conscious and Unconscious Processes: Psychodynamic, Cognitive, and Neurophysiological Convergences*. New York: Guilford Press.
Stern, D. (1985), *The Interpersonal World of the Infant: A View from Psychoanalysis and Developmental Psychology*. New York: Basic Books.
Stoller, R. (1979), *Sexual Excitement: Dynamics of Erotic Life*. New York: Pantheon.
Westen, D. (1997), Towards a clinically and empirically sound theory of motivation. *J. Amer. Psychoanal. Assn.*, 78:521–549.
———— (1999), The scientific status of unconscious processes: Is Freud really dead? *J. Amer. Psychoanal. Assn.*, 47:1061–1107.

Apocryphal Freud: Sigmund Freud's Most Famous "Quotations" and Their Actual Sources

ALAN C. ELMS

Sigmund Freud wielded a mighty pen. His many books and essays transformed our ways of thinking about ourselves and others. His technical terminology has become a part of our everyday language. Yet his most often quoted sentences were not written down by Freud and may not even have come from his tongue.

Over the past two decades, I have collected Freud quotations from the mass media, from scholarly works outside of strictly Freudian treatises, and more recently from the Internet. By my running count, three quotations have emerged as what we might informally call Freud's Greatest Hits. One of the three could have been spoken aloud by Freud pretty much as we have it; an eager disciple quoted it in her journal soon after a session with him. Another was possibly said by Freud, in some form vaguely resembling the currently cited version. But it did not appear in print until eleven years after Freud's death, and its final form may owe more to the writer who published it than to Freud. A third quotation often attributed to Freud probably did not come from him in any form. It may instead have been invented by an anonymous humorist, perhaps borrowing from Kipling or Turgenev.

These three favorite Freud quotations are:

A number of colleagues have made helpful suggestions during the preparation of this essay, and I thank them all. In addition to the specific indebtednesses identified in the text of the paper, I would like to express special thanks to several individuals who volunteered information on critical points: James W. Anderson, Alyson Burns, Kurt Eissler, Seymour Howard, Pearl King, Ralph Keyes, Phyllis Magnani, Roland Marchand, Michael Molnar, Betsy W. Pitha, and Eva Schepeler. I would also like to thank the Humanities Institute at the University of California, Davis, for support early in the essay's development.

(1) Freud's gift to his later feminist critics: "What do women want?"
(2) Freud's wise-old-man pronouncement on what a psychologically healthy person should be able to do: "To love and to work."
(3) Freud's ultimate anti-Freudian joke: "Sometimes a cigar is just a cigar."

These quotations circulate in America mainly in English, but the "original" German of the first two is also available. All three have entered the oral tradition, passing from one person to another. Versions of one or all can be found in novels, television dramas and comedy shows, popular magazines, newspaper headlines, and advertisements. At least two of the three (1 and 3) have appeared on commercially marketed T-shirts. A few key phrases and sentences from Freud's own writing are quoted less often and less widely, mostly in reference to specific psychoanalytic concepts. But as statements credited to Freud that many people know and repeat, these three quotations enjoy a special status not shared by anything Freud himself wrote. (Several quotations actually written by Freud also competed, in my tabulations, for the status of Freud's Greatest Hits: "Anatomy is destiny," "The goal of all life is death," "Where id was, there shall ego be." But judged by the basic criterion of widespread general usage, they soon fell by the wayside.)

This special status is problematic in at least two ways. First, these apocryphal remarks provide many people with their principal exposure to what they assume are Freud's own words. If the quotations are inauthentic Freud, they convey false impressions of an important cultural figure. Second, even if Freud did say something like the statements now before us, the absence of context for them in Freud's own writing permits unchecked distortion of their original meaning. Such distortion may occur even if the words are used by someone sympathetic to Freud, and is even more likely when Freud is "quoted" by a critic of psychoanalysis. It seems only fair to Freud that efforts be made to track down the most accurate versions of these widely used quotations, and to establish the original contexts within which Freud himself may have said them. If he did not say them, it also seems fair to stop crediting him—or blaming him—for someone else's words.

Freud on Women

The All-Time Number One Hit, as Freud quotations go, is the question, "What does Woman want?" That is the most accurate way to translate what Freud is reported to have said in German: "Was will das Weib?" (A more literal translation would be, "What does the woman want?" as long as the phrase "the woman" is understood to be a collective singular, representing all women.) Frequent variants in English, which also convey the sense of the German, include "What does a woman want?" and "What do women want?"

Where did this quotation originate? In his own writings, Freud often referred to the psychology of women as a riddle, an enigma, "a dark continent" (1926, p. 212), "veiled in impenetrable obscurity" (1905, p. 151). But in his written remarks on women, Freud never asked, "What does Woman want?" The question's uneasy position in the Freudian canon is suggested by the way it is handled in the most authoritative quotation reference, *Bartlett's Familiar Quotations*. In both the fourteenth and the fifteenth editions (Beck, 1968, 1980), *Bartlett's* attributes the quotation to Freud, but the only cited source is a 1963 book edited by Charles Rolo, *Psychiatry in American Life*. If you look at that book, or at the July 1961 special issue of the *Atlantic Monthly* on which it was based, you will find a page of Freud quotations (Freud, 1961) under the rubric "From the Writings of Sigmund Freud." The page includes "What does a woman want?" but gives no information about where in Freud's writings this or the other quotations may be found. Wide dissemination of "What does a woman want?" probably occurred initially through the *Atlantic Monthly's* special issue and then through the 1968 *Bartlett's*, so it is not surprising that subsequent users of the quotation often failed to cite a source beyond Freud's name.

Some users have gone so far as to make up a specific source, as well as to elaborate on the basic quotation. The February 1970 cover of *Harper's Magazine* consisted of a color photo of a miniskirted woman's thighs, plus this quotation attributed to Freud: "What does woman want? Dear God! What does she want?" Inside the magazine, in an article titled "In Pursuit of the American Woman," the quotation was given in slightly different form, along with the attribution: "Freud, age 77, to his diary" (Grossman, 1970, p. 48). *Harper's* failed to acknowledge that the latter half of the cover quotation—"Dear God! What does she want?"—was created from thin air. So was the attribution. Freud was 69 rather than 77 at the time his famous question was apparently asked, and his sparse diaries include nothing resembling this remark during any year of his life.

Many users of the quotation seem primarily interested in making fun of foolish Freud for ever having asked the question; they don't care when or where or why he said it. For instance, a German film's American advertising campaign simply quoted Freud as asking "What does a woman want?" and then answered with the film's title: *Men*. In the October 1989 issue of Columbia University's alumni magazine (*Columbia Magazine,* p. 16), a cartoon shows Freud lying on his psychoanalytic couch, musing "What does woman want?" while his aproned wife sweeps the office with a broom and fantasizes an aproned Sigmund with broom in hand. An ad in the August 26, 1990, *Parade Magazine* shows a very grim Freud with the caption, "And Freud thought he knew what women really wanted." The ad then provides its own answer: "Really comfortable shoes, that's what" (p. 13). The December 1994 *Vanity Fair* (p. 191) displays Hugh Grant outspread on the floor, with the caption, "Memo to Freud: Is this what women really want?" The 2000 Hollywood film *What Women Want* tells us that Freud died without answering the question, and that Mel Gibson can answer it only by becoming telepathic.

The quotation and its connection with Freud have become so widely known that quoters can afford to be coy about who said it. In a full-page *New York Times* advertisement for *Cosmopolitan* (October 17, 1983, p. 48), a young woman dressed only in a long metallic scarf says, "What do women *want*? Remember that funny old question? I think it's been pretty firmly established by now we want what *men* want . . . someone to love and be cherished by and work that fulfills us." The ad thus manages to incorporate two of the three most popular Freud quotations without mentioning Freud at all.

Still other quoters not only fail to mention Freud but also alter the quotation to serve their own purposes. The titles of published social-scientific papers have asked such questions as "What Do Women Want from Men?" and "What Do Women and Men Want from Love and Sex?" A computer column in *Newsweek* (Hackett, 1994) asks, "What do women want? Who knows? What do men want? Something bigger, faster, and cooler than yours" (p. 54). A *New York Times Book Review* headline (Masson, 1993) asks, "What Do Dogs Want?" An essay by analyst Enid Balint (1993) is titled, "The Analysis of Women by a Woman Analyst: What Does a Woman Want?" An announcement by the Washington (DC) Psychoanalytic Foundation lists a weekend conference scheduled for February 22–24, 2002: "The Psychology of the Analyst: What Does the Analyst Want?"

Few usages of the quotation have correctly identified its original published source or have quoted it fully. The quotation was first published in Ernest Jones's (1955) classic biography, *The Life and Work of Sigmund Freud*, volume 2. In a discussion of Freud's character, Jones stated, "There is little doubt that Freud found the psychology of women more enigmatic than that of men. He said once to Marie Bonaparte: 'The great question that has never been answered and which I have not yet been able to answer, despite my thirty years of research into the feminine soul, is 'What does a woman want?'" (p. 421). Jones added the German words *"Was will das Weib?"* in a footnote, but offered no other information about the quotation. (*Bartlett's Familiar Quotations*, in its sixteenth edition [Kaplan, 1992, p. 569], finally got all that right, perhaps in part because its new editor was married to Freud's grandniece.)

Even quoters familiar with the published source have argued about the quotation's meaning. Erich Fromm (1959) was one of the first to use "What does a woman want?" as evidence for Freud's general "lack of understanding of women" (p. 36). Walter Kaufmann (1963, p. 339) then accused Fromm of failing to recognize that Freud had been making a "mildly humorous remark." Other instances can be cited in which Fromm did indeed fail to grasp the subtleties of Freud's language. But in this case, how did Kaufmann know that Freud was being "mildly humorous"? Perhaps Kaufmann was responding to the rather florid language of the rest of the quotation ("The great question . . . my thirty years of research into the feminine soul"). But Freud's mood is hard to establish on the basis of the quotation's wording alone. What we have, at best, is the Frenchwoman Marie Bonaparte's written rendition of her recollection of Freud's German, as later translated into English by the Welshman Ernest Jones. The only context Jones provides is that Freud "once said it to Marie Bonaparte." James Strachey, the official translator of Freud's works into English, was bothered enough by this lack of context to complain, in a summary of Freud's comments on female psychology, "Unfortunately Jones gives no date for this remark" (1961, p. 244).

What was the context? Fortunately Marie Bonaparte's journals of her analysis by Freud have survived, and a psychoanalyst with access to them (Frank R. Hartman) has given me the specific date on which she wrote down the quotation, as well as some of the immediate context in the journals. Knowing the date of the quotation, we may also look at Freud's correspondence and published writings for other evidence of his state of mind at the time.

The date of the quoted remark was December 8, 1925. Princess Marie Bonaparte had entered analysis with Freud only ten weeks earlier. She soon made it a habit to rush home from each session with Freud to record in her personal journal everything she could recall of his statements during the analytic hour. At times she may even have made notes during the sessions themselves (Bertin, 1982, p. 155). Such a practice may not have been helpful to Marie's analysis, but she was already convinced that Freud was a great man, and she wanted to be his student, as well as his patient.

Princess Marie was directly descended from Napoleon's younger brother. She had married Prince George of Greece at a time when being a prince or princess still meant something. Both she and the prince were fabulously wealthy, yet Marie suffered from a variety of personal problems. Among other matters she quickly discovered that her husband's sexual preference was for his uncle rather than for her. Marie herself, during several passionate affairs, had such difficulty attaining orgasm that she eventually obtained a surgical relocation of her clitoris (Bertin, 1982, p. 170). As Freud confronted such contrasts of great wealth, high social position, and powerful private miseries, he might well have exclaimed, in one of his occasional explosions toward a difficult patient, "What *does* a woman want?"

Had Freud been gently reminded of his own concepts of countertransference and overdetermination at this point, he might have acknowledged that other issues also converged upon his resonant question. At the time Marie Bonaparte heard him ask it, Freud was especially worried about a set of issues concerning the most important woman in his life: his daughter Anna.

Five days earlier Anna Freud had celebrated her thirtieth birthday. (Note Sigmund's reference in the full quotation to his "thirty years of research into the feminine soul." Indeed several of his most important psychoanalytic discoveries had emerged during the period surrounding Anna's birth in 1895; see Elms, 1980.) Anna had long since become Sigmund's favorite among his six children, and she had to a considerable extent replaced her mother Martha in his emotional life. In her turn Anna had strongly identified with Sigmund, psychologically and professionally. It was hard for her even to dream of reaching a level of achievement near that of her genius father. But she had already come to play a significant role in the psychoanalytic movement as his secretary, advocate, and occasional surrogate speaker. Though Freud gave her a kind of training analysis, as he did with other promising candidates for the psychoanalytic profession, he was strongly ambivalent about the possibility that she would become a full-time analyst. He also seems to have felt guilty about having diverted her from traditional paths of feminine development. In a letter written in English to his nephew Sam, Freud praised Anna's accomplishments, then lamented, "Yet she has just passed her 30th birthday, does not seem inclined to get married, and who can say if her momentary interests will render her happy in years to come when she has to face life without her father?" (quoted in Clark, 1980, p. 480).

For her part Anna had been experiencing an identity crisis that extended over at least six years. She had been courted by several of her father's male disciples and family friends, without regarding any of them as a good match. She had worried a great deal over her lack of decisiveness, not only about potential mates but also about a serious career choice. She experienced a strong conflict between her altruistic urges, which included taking care of her aging father, and what she saw as her more selfish urges, mostly involving desires for strong approval and affection from those close to her. She described these desires with a hyphenated term, almost as if it were the name of a syndrome: "Etwas-Haben-Wollen," or "wanting-to-have-something [-for-myself]" (Young-Bruehl, 1988, p. 133). As she reached age 30, the various things Anna wanted were coming together in a satisfying way. She had decided definitely to become a full-time psychoanalyst, focusing on child patients. Though she wished to remain close to her father, she also wanted to share her life with a woman, an American named Dorothy Tiffany Burlingham, as well as to become a coparent to Dorothy's children.

Anna Freud's relationship with Dorothy Burlingham may never have involved an overtly sexual component. (Anna's most thorough biographer, Elisabeth Young-Bruehl [1988], says it did not. Dorothy's most thorough biographer, her grandson Michael John Burlingham [1989], thinks it might have but probably did not.) Even if the relationship were physical as well as emotional, it should be noted that Anna's father was, for his time, unusually tolerant of homosexuality. Nonetheless he appears to have been deeply troubled to learn that Anna had finally decided against getting married and having her own children, and furthermore that she was developing an intense emotional relationship with a woman.

Anna had ended her long indecisiveness about issues of love and work, but in ways that Freud found difficult to endorse wholeheartedly. "What does Woman want," indeed!

Following Erich Fromm, Freud's critics typically use the quotation to indicate his general failure to understand female psychology. Freud might well have acknowledged this point as another of the quotation's overdeterminants. His understanding of male psychology was to a considerable extent based on, or validated by, his firsthand perceptions of what it had been like to be a boy and to develop into a man. Lacking such firsthand experience of being a girl or woman, he repeatedly emphasized his inadequacy as a theorist of female psychology.

Yet Freud should not be sold short in this regard, even if he often sold himself short. Many of his patients, from whom he collected massive amounts of psychological data, were women. They seem often (though not always) to have attained psychological relief through the shared working-through of their problems. A variety of intellectually and emotionally sophisticated women, including not only Marie Bonaparte but also Lou Andreas-Salomé, Hilda Doolittle, and Helene Deutsch, responded enthusiastically to his insights into themselves and other women. He encouraged a number of women besides Anna to become practicing psychoanalysts, at a time when such encouragement from a well-established medical patriarch was rare. When a male participant at a Vienna Psychoanalytic Society meeting made crudely sexist remarks about women medical students, Freud chastised him in terms that anticipated gender-related affirmative action: "Woman, whom culture has burdened with the heavier load (especially in propagation) ought to be judged with tolerance and forbearance in areas where she has lagged behind man" (quoted by Nunberg and Federn, 1962, p. 199). Freud wrote several essays and book chapters on female psychology that go well beyond the stereotypically dogmatic discussions of penis envy. These have served as powerful inspiration for later feminist writers, including Juliet Mitchell, Nancy Chodorow, and Carol Gilligan. Freud did not get everything right about women, and on certain issues he proposed extreme formulations that others have pushed to further extremes. But critics who quote his intensely personal question "What does Woman want?" without qualification, implying that Freud was a simple sexist, ignore the remarkable complexity both of his ideas about women and of his attitudes toward them.

Freud on Psychological Health

"What does Woman want?" is a quotation popular among Freud's critics and enemies. Our next quotation is popular among Freud's defenders and friends. As the standard account goes, "Freud was once asked what he thought a normal person should be able to do well." He responded: "Lieben und arbeiten," which translates neatly into English as, "To love and to work."

Perhaps the most frequent users of this quotation have been mental health professionals, as they try to convey in nontechnical shorthand what the goal or outcome of psychotherapy should be. At least a dozen books about the attainment of psychological health have used the phrase in their titles, in such forms as *To Love and to Work: A Demonstration and Discussion of Psychotherapy* (Kapelovitz, 1987), *Work, Love, Play: Self Repair in the Psychoanalytic Dialogue* (Shor, 1992), and *Beyond Love and Work: Why Adults Need to Play* (Terr, 2000). Many book chapters, journal articles, and convention papers have been similarly titled. These books and papers typically cite Freud as the source of the phrase without quoting him directly or trying to identify a specific source in his writings. For example, in *Work and Love: The Crucial Balance*, Jay B. Rohrlich states, "To the best of my knowledge, no one has ever repudiated Freud's contention that the basic requirements of human existence are love and work" (1980, p. 21).

The phrase has become so popular in analytic circles that it is now often employed without citing Freud as its source. In *Psycho-Analysis as History*, Michael S. Roth writes that "there are those who do not sublimate and who have their 'pathologies,' *but who remain socially functional*, which I take to be one of Freud's major criteria for normality" (1987, p. 107). This passage is footnoted, "Functional here simply means the ability to love and work." A president-elect of the American Psychoanalytic Association told a reporter that the unique potential of psychoanalysis compared with other therapies "is that after a long period of time, it can affect personality or characterologic change. It can [improve] a person's ability to love and work" (Sylva, 1988). Elisabeth Young-Bruehl, in her biography of Anna Freud, remarks without explaining the source of her sentence's key phrase, "During her personal psychoanalysis and afterward, in an ongoing, lifelong self-analysis, Anna Freud reflected on herself and on how she came to love and to work as she did" (1988, p. 19).

Uses of the phrase by nonpsychotherapists vary in their degree of attribution to Freud and in their paraphrasing. At least two modern novels, by Reynolds Price (1968) and Gwyneth Cravens (1982), have been titled *Love and Work*; neither directly credits Freud. In Carol Shields's novel *The Republic of Love* (1992), a character refers to love and work as "the two good Freudian anchors." In a comic novel named after its psychoanalyst protagonist, *Fine*, author (and psychiatrist) Samuel Shem (1985) not only cites Freud but also offers the phrase in German and English: "Freud stated the purpose of life to be *lieben und arbeiten* (love and work), and Fine's life work now was *The Fine Theory*, a modern attempt to link biology and psychology" (p. 53). In a later novel, Shem (1997) has another psychotherapist repeat the same phrases in English and then in German (pp. 241–242). Daniel Goleman (1984) began a *New York Times* article on the psychology of love with the statement, "Freud counted the ability to love, along with the capacity for work, as a hallmark of full maturity" (p. C1). An article about a popular New England discount chain deviated in an interesting but not wholly inaccurate way from the usual phrasing: "Sigmund Freud identified work and sex as the two pillars of human endeavor. Building #19 playfully panders to an unacknowledged but equally compelling third: bargain-shopping" (Diamant, 1986, p. 36). Likewise, Woody Allen's character in his 1997 film *Deconstructing Harry* tells his son, "Freud said the two most important things in your life are the work that you choose and sex."

None of these users of the Freud phrase bothers to tell us where it is from. That may be because they don't really know. In his edition of Freud's letters to Wilhelm Fliess, Jeffrey Masson does make a guess as to the source. He quotes a letter from the French neurologist Jean Martin Charcot to Freud, about a patient of Freud's whom Charcot had examined: "She is, in fact, and she acknowledges it herself, to a certain extent prepared for the struggle of life, which she was not formerly." Masson (1985) then asks, "Might this not be the origin of Freud's later famous dictum (for which no source can actually be found) that the goal of analysis is to be able to work and love?" (p. 20). Masson appears to be stretching Charcot's remark a great deal, but he is correct that at least in the body of Freud's own writings, "no source can actually be found."

The dictum's first public appearance, in both German and English, is no mystery at all, though Masson fails to cite it. The phrase was published in 1950, in one of the most popular psychoanalytic books after Freud's own works, Erik Erikson's *Childhood and Society*. Erikson (1963) says there that he is going to quote "what has come to me as Freud's shortest saying":

> Freud was once asked what he thought a normal person should be able to do well. The questioner probably expected a complicated answer. But Freud, in the curt way of his old days, is reported to have said: "Lieben und arbeiten" (to love and to work). It pays to ponder on this simple formula; it gets deeper as you think about it. For when Freud said "love" he meant *genital* love, and genital *love*; when he said love and work, he meant a general work-productiveness which would not preoccupy the individual to the extent that he loses his right or capacity to be a genital and a loving being. Thus we may ponder, but we cannot improve on "the professor's" formula [pp. 264–265].

For all the weight Erikson places on this quotation, he is cautious in attributing it to Freud. Note his qualifying phrases: "what has *come to me* as Freud's shortest saying. . . . Freud was *once asked.* . . . [by an unidentified] *questioner* [who] *probably expected* a complicated answer. But Freud . . . is *reported to have said.*" And in terms of dating the quotation, all we get is Erikson's remark about its style: "Freud, in the curt way of his old days." On the other hand, Erikson gives us the precise formulation, "Lieben und arbeiten," and then tells us not only what Freud *said* but what Freud *meant.* Let us not worry yet about how Erikson knew what Freud meant. The prior question is, how did he know what Freud said?

Erikson does not try to pin the quotation down to a written source, because there is none. The concordance to Freud's published writings in English translation, which indexes every occurrence of every substantive word Freud used (Guttman, Jones, and Parrish, 1980), identifies no passage in all his writings in which "love" and "work" occur together in a sentence or even on the same page. By Erikson's account, Freud *said* "Lieben und arbeiten," rather than writing it; but Erikson does not claim that he himself *heard* Freud say it. Erikson had known Freud personally, but not well. They never engaged in substantive conversations that Erikson later thought worth recounting. Anna Freud could have reported to her patient, Erik, on one of her father's sayings, but there is no evidence that she did.

On several occasions Erikson was asked to be more specific concerning the source of his wonderful Freud quotation. The Adlerian psychologist Heinz Ansbacher (1981) says Erikson told him that "the origin of the story is unknown" (p. 439). When I interviewed Erikson on August 10, 1982, I also asked about the quotation's source. Erikson replied, "Oh, I simply don't know. I heard it in Vienna and it impressed me. I've never seen it in print. And some people now have said I made it up. If I did, I'm proud."

Perhaps Erikson to some degree shaped the specific wording of "Lieben und arbeiten," but the sentiment expressed was not foreign to Freud. Richard Sterba (1982), a Viennese psychoanalyst, has reported:

> When once the discussion in a meeting turned to the question of what means we have at our disposal to motivate a patient to undergo analysis, Freud pointed out that we promise him relief from his symptoms, an increase in his working capacity, and an improvement of his personal and social relationships [p. 119].

That's not nearly as elegant a formulation as "Lieben und arbeiten," but the general idea is there. Of course Sterba's own memories of what Freud had said some 50 years earlier may have been helped by his having read or heard Erikson's anecdote more recently.

We, however, need not depend on such old and uncertain memories. Freud's writings often referred to love, work, and roughly equivalent concepts, though he never quite put "lieben" and "arbeiten" together on one page. The equivalent terms he was most likely to use were (in English translation) "sex" and "ambition." He sometimes even discussed sex and ambition in the same passage. More than once he characterized his own infantile motives in these terms. He (1908) proposed that the "motivating forces" of young men's and women's fantasies

> fall naturally into two main groups. They are either ambitious wishes, which serve to elevate the subject's personality; or they are erotic ones. In young women the erotic wishes predominate almost exclusively, for their ambition is as a rule absorbed by erotic trends. In young men egoistic and ambitious

wishes come to the fore clearly enough alongside of erotic ones. But we will not lay stress on the opposition between the two trends; we would rather emphasize the fact that they are often united [pp. 146–147].

In a slightly later work, Freud repeated that daydreams "have two principal aims, an erotic and an ambitious one—though an erotic aim is usually concealed behind the latter too" (1909, p. 238).

At times Freud specifically discussed love rather than sex or eroticism. When he did his views were usually positive. Even in a book where he compared being in love with a kind of hypnotic devotion, Freud (1921) could also add that "in the development of mankind as a whole, just as in individuals, love alone acts as the civilizing factor in the sense that it brings a change from egoism to altruism" (p. 103).

Freud was even more emphatic about the value of work, to himself and to others. He wrote to a correspondent in 1910, "I cannot imagine life without work as at all comfortable; giving my imagination free play and working coincide for me; nothing else amuses me" (as translated by Kaufmann, 1980, p. 160). In one of his classic footnotes, Freud (1930) later wrote about the general value of work, then added a sentence that appears self-referential:

No other technique for the conduct of life attaches the individual so firmly to reality as laying emphasis on work; for his work at least gives him a secure place in a portion of reality, in the human community. . . . Professional activity is a source of special satisfaction if it is a freely chosen one—if, that is to say, by means of sublimation, it makes possible the use of existing inclinations, of persisting or constitutionally reinforced instinctual impulses [p. 80].

On those occasions when Freud discussed both something like love (or sex) and something like work (or ambition or creative achievement), he usually presented them as inversely related: the less a person is able to satisfy sexual drives directly, the more psychological energy is available for productivity in other areas. That is the basic assumption in Freud's concept of sublimation. His revision of his drive theories to include a destructive or death-seeking drive did not change this assumption of reciprocity; creativity/constructiveness/work generally continued to depend on the leftovers from the more basic drives, whether they were sexual and self-preservative drives or "life instincts" and "death instincts." Nonetheless Freud began at times to conceptualize certain forms of love and work as complementary rather than inversely proportional. For example, throughout most of his psychobiography of Leonardo da Vinci (1910b), Freud strongly emphasized the inverse relationship of Leonardo's sexuality and his creativity: Because Leonardo's direct sexual satisfaction was blocked by the peculiarities of his upbringing, he had vast energies available for creative work. But Freud also speculated about a set of circumstances in Leonardo's middle age when a rearousal of his early sexual feelings, stimulated by his fascination with the woman usually identified as Mona Lisa, revivified his declining creative urges. Though Freud assumed that Leonardo remained unable fully to satisfy his sexual urges with anyone, he suggested that Leonardo's long-dormant erotic impulses needed to be stirred again in order for him to create his last great artistic works.

Freud did not regard Leonardo as a psychologically healthy or "normal" individual, though he saw him as a genius. It is when Freud describes the desired outcome of psychoanalytic therapy that he is most likely to link something like love and something like work in a complementary or equally valued way. For instance, in a now-famous letter to a mother who seemed to be asking Freud to "cure" her son's homosexual tendencies, Freud stated (in his own English):

> Homosexuality is assuredly no advantage, but it is nothing to be ashamed of, no vice, no degradation, it cannot be classified as an illness. . . . By asking me if I can help, you mean, I suppose, if I can abolish homosexuality and make normal sexuality take its place. . . . What analysis can do for your son runs in a different line. If he is unhappy, neurotic, torn by conflicts, inhibited in his social life, analysis may bring him harmony, peace of mind, full efficiency, whether he remains a homosexual or gets changed [April 9, 1935; in E. Freud, 1960, p. 423].

The key words here are *harmony* (as a response to "inhibitions in his social life") and *efficiency* (as a response to being "torn by conflicts"). Freud (1923) elaborated on these ideas in more formal publications, such as this one:

> It may be laid down that the aim of the treatment is to remove the patient's resistances and to pass his repressions in review and thus to bring about the most far-reaching unification and strengthening of his ego, to enable him to save the mental energy which he is expending upon internal conflicts, to make the best of him that his inherited capacities will allow and so to make him as efficient and as capable of enjoyment as is possible [p. 251].

In this and similar passages, the recurring German terms are *Genussfähigkeit* and *Leistungsfähigkeit*. The former term refers not to sexual pleasure as such, but to a general capacity for enjoyment or for experiencing pleasure in whatever form. The latter term, usually translated as "efficiency" in the English editions of Freud's writings, may be reasonably translated instead as "capacity to get work done." However translated, these passages that bring together the individual's capacities for enjoyment of pleasure and for efficient work are distinctly positive statements of the goals of analysis. Indeed these passages indicate that Freud at least sometimes thought we can eat our cake and have it too— that we can satisfy our yearnings for pleasure, erotic and otherwise, and still retain enough psychological energy to achieve genuine realistic accomplishments, through hard work.

Does Erik Erikson's quotation of what he thought Freud once said actually misrepresent "the professor's" views? It is surely a selective quotation, emphasizing social relationships and culturally valued activities in an optimistic tone. In that regard it sounds much like Erikson's own writings. Freud could be much more pessimistic about analysis—as when he wrote, early in his career, that analysis works mainly to transform "hysterical misery into common unhappiness" (1895, p. 305). In other writings Freud appeared to stress genital orgasms as the desired endpoint of adult development or of effective psychotherapy, preferably accompanied by "finding an [erotic] object" (1905, p. 222). Sometimes he referred to love, in the now common Western sense of romantic love, as a delusion. Freud, who was frustrated in his own sexual life and disappointed that his romantic dreams of marriage had not been fully realized, at times even described his own work, mightily creative as it was, as a sort of consolation prize in the risky game of life. So Erikson, who knew Freud's writings as well as anyone, was not totally forthcoming when he offered us "Lieben und arbeiten" as the simple formula for psychological health that Freud had arrived at in "his old days."

On the other hand, the picture that Freud's detractors often present—of Freud as a cynical young man and a bitter old man—is also far from complete. As I have noted, Freud did sometimes come close to writing just what Erikson has told us he said about love and work. If Freud as an old man had been asked, on one of his good days, what he thought of the formula "Lieben und arbeiten," he might well have answered, "Well, some people have said I made it up, and if I did, I'm proud."

Freud on Cigars

Though recent editions of *Bartlett's Familiar Quotations* (Beck, 1980; Kaplan, 1992) list our final quotation merely as "Attributed" to Freud, it too is often quoted as having come directly from the pen or mouth of the master. In this case, however, not only do we lack any written record of Freud as the direct source, but also there are many reasons to conclude that Freud never said it or anything like it.

This quotation comes in several minor variations. The most popular are "Sometimes a cigar is only a cigar" (as a dramatized Freud says, for instance, in a BBC-TV miniseries based on his life) and "Sometimes a cigar is just a cigar" (as quoted, for example, by California artist Darrell Forney when a critic asked him about "the omnipresent phallic forms that pepper his paintings" [Dalkey, 1986].) The quotation's basic form appears to have been established in English. My colleague Eva Schepeler has translated it into German for me as "Manchmal ist eine Zigarre nur eine Zigarre." But despite her wide reading of psychoanalytic and popular literature in her native language, she does not recall ever having seen the quotation printed in a German publication.

It has, however, popped up in all sorts of odd places in English. A *Dictionary of Literary Symbols* (Ferber, 1999, p. 5), in discussing poetic references to nightingales, tells us that "What Freud said about cigars is sometimes true of literary symbols: sometimes a nightingale is just a nightingale, or little more than a way of saying the night has come." A *New York Times* article about a new psychoanalytic bookstore in Manhattan (Boynton, 2000) begins, "Sometimes a bookstore is just a bookstore," then goes ahead to tell how this one is much more. A *New York Times* review of a lesbian film titled *Just Desserts* assures us, "Sometimes a cigar is not just a cigar, and a Venetian fritter is not just a Venetian fritter" (Holden, 1996). In their combination of real recipes and half-imagined Freudiana titled *Freud's Own Cookbook*, James Hillman and Charles Boer (1985) present Freud as telling the reader in an introduction:

> Here, too, I can make corrections that have been needed for years and years; for instance, the irritating interpretation of a casual remark, since become notorious, that I let pass one evening after a very good *Sauerbraten mit Eiernudel*: "Sometimes a cigar is only a cigar." I was simply referring to the oral delight of smoking which was then being subtly undermined by my followers—far too many of whom were nonsmokers—by giving to the cigar a genital significance. This interpretation of cigar betrays an unfortunate, un-recognized, cigar-envy and a desire to castrate the father who smokes for pleasure [p. 7].

In a later passage, Hillman and Boer's Freud discusses the first psychoanalytic case, Josef Breuer's treatment of the patient called "Anna O." In this (totally apocryphal) version, Anna's symptoms are resolved when Breuer feeds her a kind of Viennese banana split. According to the cookbook's Freud, "Anna's banana was neither sublimated into mere talk nor reduced to its symbolic significance, Dr. Breuer's phallus. Sometimes a banana is just a banana" (p. 63).

Hillman and Boer may not have realized that their banana-for-cigar substitution had been anticipated years earlier by the television show *Saturday Night Live*. In a skit starring Dan Aykroyd as Freud and Laraine Newman as his daughter Anna, the teenage Anna sits on her father's lap and tells him about a dream she has just had. In the dream she was surrounded by naked men offering her their bananas—but, she says, she ate only the banana offered her by a man who looked just like her father. Sigmund grows increasingly uncomfortable with this naively transparent dream, and when Anna asks for an interpretation he grumbles, "Sometimes a banana is just a banana."

In recent years the cigar quotation has gone political. When Paula Jones's lawyers filed a petition for summary judgment against President Clinton for sexual harassment, Clinton's lawyer told a press conference that Jones's claim to have developed sexual aversion was a joke. He then hastily explained that it was a joke only because it was filed so late in the case, and he concluded, "I mean no more than that. . . . As Freud said, sometimes a good cigar is just a good cigar" (Clines, 1998). When the details of Bill Clinton's liaisons with Monica Lewinsky emerged a few months later, "Sometimes a cigar is [or is not] just a cigar" jokes swept the Internet like wildfire. None will be repeated here.

The *Saturday Night Live* banana skit dates from the late 1970s. Do we have a significantly earlier source for the quotation—one with cigars rather than bananas? And did Freud really say it? Over the past fifteen years, I have talked or corresponded with a number of Freud scholars about this significant issue: Kurt Eissler, Paul Roazen, Peter Swales, Nathan Hale Jr., and others. They have been generous with their help, but none has had a clue about the quotation's origin. I have examined not only Freud's formal writings but also his published letters and many unpublished letters, in the Library of Congress, the Archives of the British Institute of Psycho-Analysis, and elsewhere. I have looked at every memoir of Freud I could find, by anyone who knew him personally. I too have drawn a blank on the cigar quotation's source.

The earliest version that I have located is a 1961 scholarly paper by Peter Gay, the distinguished intellectual historian who has written a major biography of Freud (1988). Gay concluded his 1961 paper, on interpretations of the rhetoric of the French Revolution, with this statement: "After all, as Sigmund Freud once said, there are times when a man craves a cigar simply because he wants a good smoke." No source is given, and Gay did not surround Freud's comment with quotation marks. When I asked Gay in 1985 about his knowledge of any earlier appearances of the quotation, he responded:

> I first quoted this particular point . . . in a paper I gave in 1960 at a French Historical Society meeting at Rochester, New York, and then published in the *American Historical Review* the following year. At the time I covered myself carefully because I could not find the source of that quotation. Since then, despite all my reading in Freud material, both published and unpublished, I have not found it. This may turn out to be one of those wonderful apocryphal things that people attribute and the first reference to which remains unknown.

When I recently asked Gay whether he had located anything new on the matter, his answer was much the same.

There does, however, seem to be an oral tradition referring to a much earlier source. This tradition is hinted at in the *Little, Brown Book of Anecdotes* (Fadiman, 1985), which presents the quotation this way:

> Cigar smoking is often thought of as a symbolic activity, the cigar itself frequently interpreted as a phallic symbol or emblem of masculinity. Freud

himself was an inveterate cigar-smoker. A curious student once asked him if his cigar smoking carried any particular symbolic weight for him. He puffed reflectively, then replied, "Sometimes a cigar is just a cigar" [p. 223].

That account offers an interesting detail: "a curious student" to whom Freud responds. The anecdote book gives as its source a 1982 article in the *Los Angeles Times*. Upon examination, however, the *Times* article, at least in its microfilm version (July 5, 1982), turns out to have said a lot about cigars but nothing about a curious student. Its reference to Freud, in full and lacking any citation of sources, is:

> John F. Banzhaf III, executive director of Action on Smoking and Health, a non-smokers rights group based in Washington, says men smoke and pass out phallic-shaped cigars on the birth of a child to symbolize a particular fantasy. Taking a thoughtful puff, the father of psychoanalysis replied, "Sometimes a cigar is just a cigar."

But maybe the editors of the *Little, Brown Book of Anecdotes* did not invent the curious student all by themselves. Several people have told me that as they had heard the story, Freud made the cigar statement during his only visit to the United States, in a lecture at Clark University in 1909. Some of these informants have added that Freud was answering a student's question. One woman told me she had heard this information at Clark University, from one of her professors, sometime in the early 1960s. Unfortunately the professor (Heinz Werner) is now deceased, and he did not arrive at Clark University until nearly 40 years after Freud's visit. Nobody else who has told me a similar story could trace it back to a specific source.

An article on "Sexual Jokes," published in the professional journal *Medical Aspects of Human Sexuality*, provides the most elaborate instance of the Clark University version that I have found (though it lacks the inquiring student):

> Early in his psychoanalytic career, Sigmund Freud was invited to the United States to lecture to eager audiences on his new and engaging theories. During one of his first appearances, he decided to discuss penis envy and phallic symbolism. In the midst of his lecture, he lit up his now famous cigar and continued to speak. The audience, making an obvious connection between his topic and the cigar, broke out in laughter. After a few moments, Freud, realizing what the audience was finding so funny, removed the cigar from his mouth, and quipped: . . . "and sometimes a good cigar, is *just* a good cigar" [Gold, 1985, p. 212].

When I asked the article's author, a clinical psychologist named Michael I. Gold, about his source for the Freud anecdote, he said he got it from his fellow clinical psychologist, Harvey Mindess. When I asked Mindess, he said he thought he had heard it from Michael Gold.

After I had heard the Clark University attribution a few times, I checked the published accounts of Freud's visit to the United States, but found no mention of the cigar anecdote. I then wrote to Clark University's official University Historian, William A. Koelsch, who has published several papers about the Freud visit (e.g., 1984). Koelsch responded, "I had not previously heard that Freud is said to have made his celebrated cigar statement while at Clark. I have seen nothing here which would indicate that the statement was made at Clark"—that is, nothing in the University's archives and nothing in "all extant local newspaper accounts" of Freud's visit. "I think I would have caught it," Koelsch added, "because our public relations people would have loved it." I might add that C. G. Jung, who accompanied Freud on his visit to Clark University and who was then beginning to have strong doubts about Freud's "authority," would have loved the story too, but in gossiping about Freud later he never mentioned it. Nor did anyone else who published recollections of the Clark University conference, as far as either I or the University Historian can determine. Saul Rosenzweig, who has written a nearly 500-page history of the conference (1992), tells me he has never come across the anecdote in all his research. All these negative findings strongly suggest, without proving definitively, that the story originated somewhere and sometime else—much as, according to Freud, human beings commonly take later experiences or fantasies and attach them in memory to much earlier events.

So much for the story's external validity: that is, for any factual evidence that Freud did indeed make the cigar statement, at Clark University or elsewhere. What about internal validity—evidence that it's the sort of thing Freud *might* have said, whether at his Clark University lectures or at any other time in his long life? We do know a good deal about what Freud actually said at Clark, because he wrote out his lectures in detail soon after he returned to Vienna. "During one of his first appearances," according to the version of the anecdote published in *Medical Aspects of Human Sexuality*, "he decided to discuss penis envy and phallic symbolism" (Gold, 1985). Freud did indeed, in the third of his five Clark University lectures, refer to how "the analysis of dreams has shown us that the unconscious makes use of a particular symbolism, especially for representing sexual complexes" (1910a, p. 36). Freud (1910a) then moved from dream symbolism to such things as slips of tongue and pen, "to which as a rule no importance is attached," he said. He continued:

> Besides these there are the actions and gestures which people carry out without noticing them at all, to say nothing of attributing any psychological importance to them: playing about and fiddling with things, humming tunes, fingering parts of one's own body or one's clothing, and so on. These small things, faulty actions and symptomatic or haphazard actions alike, are not so insignificant as people, by a sort of conspiracy of silence, are ready to suppose. They always have a meaning, which can usually be interpreted with ease and

certainty from the situation in which they occur. . . . A man's most intimate
secrets are as a rule betrayed by their help [pp. 37–38].

Now, did Freud at this point make an exception to his line of argument, and
insist that his own cigars involved no symbolism, revealed no "intimate secrets"?
That seems hardly likely. According to the evidence of the published lectures,
he (1910a) instead emphasized the exact opposite:

As you already see, psycho-analysts are marked by a particularly strict belief
in the determination of mental life. For them there is nothing trivial, nothing
arbitrary or haphazard. They expect in every case to find sufficient motives
where, as a rule, no such expectation is raised. Indeed, they are prepared to
find *several* motives for one and the same mental occurrence, whereas what
seems to be our innate craving for causality declares itself satisfied with a
single psychical cause [p. 38].

In the Clark University lectures and for the rest of his life, Freud continued to
stress these two essentials of psychoanalytic theory: first, complete psychological determinism (the idea that no human behavior lacks psychological significance, and that all behavior is determined by discoverable motives), and second,
overdetermination (the idea that virtually all behavior is determined by "*several*
motives," not just by "*a single* psychical cause"). The statement, "Sometimes a
cigar is just a cigar," flatly contradicts both these assumptions, especially the
second. Freud enjoyed telling jokes, but such essential components of his core
theory were not matters about which he would have dismissively joked, especially to an audience who knew little about psychoanalysis.

Perhaps he was simply caught off guard by a brash student's question and
gave an unprepared and self-defensive answer? In the first place, Freud's lecture
style was not such as to produce unprepared and self-defensive answers. By
1909 he was a master of the art of public speaking, at the height of his intellectual powers, and thoroughly experienced at responding to a wide variety of challenges that his many patients had thrown at him concerning any and all of his
discernible behavior patterns. In the second place, Freud was quite aware of the
neurotic aspects of his cigar smoking. He hardly needed to pretend, to himself or
to others, that a cigar was "just" a cigar for him. He admitted repeatedly that his
cigar smoking was an addiction. As early as 1897, he acknowledged to a friend
the neurotic basis of such addictions:

The insight has dawned on me that masturbation is the one major habit, the
"primary addiction," and it is only as a substitute and replacement for it that
the other addictions—to alcohol, morphine, tobacco, and the like—come into
existence. The role played by this addiction in hysteria is enormous; and it is
perhaps there that my major, still outstanding obstacle is to be found, wholly
or in part [Masson, 1985, p. 287].

Freud was extremely reluctant to reduce the number of cigars he smoked (usually 20 per day), let alone give them up entirely, even when his physicians demanded that he do so for serious health reasons. His cigars were not just a matter of pleasure. As he told more than one correspondent in approximately the same words, "I owe to the cigar a great intensification of my capacity to work and a facilitation of my self-control" (quoted in Schur, 1972, p. 62; see also E. Freud, 1960, p. 403). Is a cigar *only* a cigar? No: Freud felt certain that cigars were an essential part of his personality and of his life.

But if Freud didn't say it, then where *did* the cigar quotation originate? Perhaps from a professional comedian, pre–*Saturday Night Live*? (Groucho Marx? George Burns?) It is a good comic line, and it has worn well. Perhaps from a hostile biographer of Freud? I have not found the quotation in any Freud biography prior to the 1970s. Perhaps from Peter Gay? The wording used in his 1961 paper, which is not as neat as the subsequent "Sometimes a cigar is just a cigar" variants, suggests the possibility of a still earlier inspiration, not from Freud but from Rudyard Kipling. Again, Gay's version is this: "After all, as Sigmund Freud once said, there are times when a man craves a cigar simply because he wants a good smoke" (1961, p. 676). Rudyard Kipling's similar lines, first published in 1885, are far more sexist than Freud ever was: "And a woman is only a woman, but a good Cigar is a Smoke" (Kipling, 1940, p. 49). Perhaps Gay or a previous writer preconsciously crossed Kipling's line with Freud's "What does a woman want?" to tell us that "a man craves a cigar simply because he wants a good smoke." Perhaps someone else just misremembered Kipling's original, replacing "woman" with "cigar" in the first part of his line: "And a cigar is only a cigar, but . . ." Either or both possibilities seem to me as likely a derivation for the "Sometimes a cigar" quotation as any so far suggested.

A less likely but still possible source is even earlier than Kipling. Turgenev's pre-Freudian but very oedipal novel *Fathers and Sons*, published in 1862, includes a scene in which the liberated Madame Kukshin first meets the young nihilist Bazarov. When she offers Bazarov a cigar, their mutual friend Sitnikov says, "A cigar's a cigar [in Russian, "Sigarku sigarkoi"], but do let's have some lunch" (p. 71). So for all these years we may have been missing part of the apocryphal Freud quotation. Perhaps in full it should read something like, "A cigar is just a cigar, but a couple of pirozhki are a real meal."

As I mentioned earlier, "What do women want?" is usually quoted by Freud's critics, and "To love and to work" is usually quoted by his advocates. "Sometimes a cigar is just a cigar" tends to be quoted by people who are ambivalent about Freud and who would like to find an exception to his strict motivational determinism—a way to deny the psychological implications of their own behavior, or of the behavior of someone important to them. Freud scorned such evasions. He spent much time and psychic energy revealing how his own dreams, as well as those of his patients, developed intricate disguises for the true significance of acts and impulses. It is still remotely possible that Freud tossed off the "cigar" statement in a weak moment. He was not so perfect that he never made what would be, from his usual perspective, such an irrational remark. But if anyone does come across firm evidence that Freud said it, I'll still want to consider what the special circumstances may have been, and I'd suspect that Freud himself soon analyzed the unconscious reasons for his temporary aberration.

Now that we know something about the sources (or nonsources) and the contexts (or noncontexts) of these three very popular quotations, do I assume that people will stop using them inappropriately? By no means. The quotations have developed a life of their own, and for one unanalyzed reason or another, many people will go on believing that Freud said them. Whether a person reveres or resists his ideas, idealizes him or feels eager to bash him, a short and convenient set of quotations such as these offers a way to connect with Freud and simultaneously to communicate with others about him. Anyone who wants to quote him more thoughtfully, however, should turn to Freud's own writings—to his many marvelous letters, more of which are becoming available each year, as well as to his formal essays and books. They contain enough wise, provocative, and truly Freudian quotations to carry us through at least another century.

References

Ansbacher, H. (1981), "To love and to work": Adlerian thoughts on an anecdote about Freud. *Bull. Menn. Clin.,* 45:439–441.

Balint, E. (1993), The analysis of women by a woman analyst: What does a woman want? *Before I Was I: Psychoanalysis and the Imagination.* New York: Guilford.

Beck, E. M., ed. (1968, 1980), *Bartlett's Familiar Quotations,* 14th and 15th editions. Boston: Little, Brown.

Bertin, C. (1982), *Marie Bonaparte.* New York: Harcourt Brace Jovanovich.

Boynton, R. S. (2000), Getting alienated Freudians to associate. *The New York Times,* March 17.

Breuer, J. & Freud, S. (1893–1895), Studies on hysteria. *Standard Edition,* 2:1–309. London: Hogarth Press, 1955.

Burlingham, M. J. (1989), *The Last Tiffany.* New York: Atheneum.

Clark, R. W. (1980), *Freud: The Man and the Cause.* New York: Random House.

Clines, F. X. (1998), President's team demands dismissal of Jones lawsuit. *The New York Times,* March 21, p. A10.

Cravens, G. (1982), *Love and Work.* New York: Knopf.

Dalkey, V. (1986), A world turned inside out. *Sacramento Bee,* December 14, Encore section, p. 23.

Diamant, A. (1986), On your markdown, get set, go. *Boston Globe Magazine,* June 22, p. 16ff.

Elms, A. C. (1980), Freud, Irma, Martha: Sex and marriage in the dream of Irma's injection. *Psychoanal. Rev.,* 67:83–109.

Erikson, E. H. (1963), *Childhood and Society,* 2nd edition. New York: Norton.

Fadiman, C., ed. (1985), *The Little, Brown Book of Anecdotes*. Boston: Little, Brown.

Ferber, M. (1999), *A Dictionary of Literary Symbols*. Cambridge, England: Cambridge University Press.

Freud, E. L., ed. (1960), *Letters of Sigmund Freud*, trans. T. Stern & J. Stern. New York: Basic Books.

Freud, S. (1905), Three essays on the theory of sexuality. *Standard Edition*, 7:130–243. London: Hogarth Press, 1953.

——— (1908), Creative writers and day-dreaming. *Standard Edition*, 9:141–153. London: Hogarth Press, 1959.

——— (1909), Family romances. *Standard Edition*, 9:235–241. London: Hogarth Press, 1959.

——— (1910a), Five lectures on psycho-analysis. *Standard Edition*, 11:9–55. London: Hogarth Press, 1957.

——— (1910b), Leonardo da Vinci and a memory of his childhood. *Standard Edition*, 11:63–137. London: Hogarth Press, 1957.

——— (1921), Group psychology and the analysis of the ego. *Standard Edition*, 18:69–143. London: Hogarth Press, 1955.

——— (1923), Two encyclopaedia articles: (A) Psycho-analysis [1922]. *Standard Edition*, 18:235–254. London: Hogarth Press, 1955.

——— (1926), The question of lay analysis. *Standard Edition*, 20:183–258. London: Hogarth Press, 1959.

——— (1930), Civilization and its discontents [1929]. *Standard Edition*, 21:64–145. London: Hogarth Press, 1961.

——— (1961), From the writings of Sigmund Freud. *Atlantic Monthly*, July, p. 78.

Fromm, E. (1959), *Sigmund Freud's Mission*. New York: Grove Press, 1963.

Gay, P. (1961), Rhetoric and politics in the French revolution. *Amer. Historical Rev.*, 66:664–676.

——— (1988), *Freud: A Life for Our Time*. New York: Norton.

Gold, M. I. (1985), Sexual jokes. *Med. Aspects of Human Sexuality*, 19:210–214.

Goleman, D. (1984), Psychologists start to take the measure of love. *The New York Times*, November 20, p. C1.

Grossman, E. (1970), In pursuit of the American woman. *Harper's Magazine*, 240 (February):47–69.

Guttman, S. A., Jones, R. L. & Parrish, S. M. (1980), *Concordance to the Standard Edition of the Complete Psychological Works of Sigmund Freud, Vol. 1*. Boston: G. K. Hall.

Hackett, G. (1994), Online: alt.men-waste-time. *Newsweek*, May 16, p. 54.

Hillman, J. & Boer, C. (1985), *Freud's Own Cookbook*. New York: Harper & Row.

Holden, S. (1996), A lesbian perspective. *The New York Times*, July 19.

Jones, E. (1955), *The Life and Work of Sigmund Freud, Vol. 2*. New York: Basic Books.

Kapelovitz, L. H. (1987), *To Love and to Work*. New York: Aronson.

Kaplan, J., ed. (1992), *Bartlett's Familiar Quotations*, 16th edition. Boston: Little, Brown.

Kaufmann, W. (1963), *The Faith of a Heretic*. Garden City, NY: Doubleday Anchor.

——— (1980), *Discovering the Mind, Vol. 3*. New York: McGraw-Hill.

Kipling, R. (1940), *Complete Verse*. Garden City, NY: Doubleday, 1989.

Koelsch, W. A. (1984), *"Incredible Day-Dream": Freud and Jung at Clark, 1909*. Worcester, MA: Friends of the Goddard Library.

Masson, J. M., ed. & trans. (1985), *The Complete Letters of Sigmund Freud to Wilhelm Fliess 1887–1904*. Cambridge, MA: Harvard University Press.

———— (1993), What do dogs want? *The New York Times Book Review*, August 1, p. 12.

Nunberg, H. & Federn, E., eds. (1962), *Minutes of the Vienna Psychoanalytic Society, Vol. 1*. New York: International Universities Press.

Price, R. (1968), *Love and Work*. New York: Atheneum.

Rohrlich, J. B. (1980), *Work and Love*. New York: Summit Books.

Rolo, C., ed. (1963), *Psychiatry in American Life*. Boston: Little, Brown.

Rosenzweig, S. (1992), *Freud, Jung and Hall the King-Maker*. Seattle: Hogrefe & Huber.

Roth, M. S. (1987), *Psycho-Analysis as History*. Ithaca, NY: Cornell University Press.

Schur, M. (1972), *Freud: Living and Dying*. New York: International Universities Press.

Shem, S. (1985), *Fine*. New York: St. Martin's/Marek.

———— (1997), *Mount Misery*. New York: Fawcett Columbine.

Shields, C. (1992), *The Republic of Love*. New York: Viking.

Shor, J. (1992), *Work, Love, Play*. New York: Brunner-Mazel.

Sterba, R. F. (1982), *Reminiscences of a Viennese Psychoanalyst*. Detroit, MI: Wayne State University Press.

Strachey, J. (1961), Editor's note to "Some psychical consequences of the anatomical distinction between the sexes." *Standard Edition*, 19:243–247. London: Hogarth Press, 1961.

Sylva, B. (1988), Matters of the mind. *Sacramento Bee*, September 6, pp. B1, B9.

Terr, L. (2000), *Beyond Love and Work*. New York: Touchstone Books.

Turgenev, I. (1862), *Fathers and Sons*, trans. G. Reavy. New York: New American Library, n.d.

Young-Bruehl, E. (1988), *Anna Freud*. New York: Summit Books.

The Enduring Scientific Contributions of Sigmund Freud

JOHN E. GEDO

Psychoanalysis as a Natural Science

The Freud Exhibition organized by the Library of Congress marks the centenary of the birth of psychoanalysis. Its sole parent, Sigmund Freud, has been dead for over sixty years—indeed, he was born before the American Civil War, relatively early in the reign of Queen Victoria—yet his contribution to modern civilization has been so profound that his work has stayed in the center of attention (whether to be praised or denigrated) throughout the twentieth century. The current exhibition therefore provides a suitable opportunity to reappraise Freud's achievements in all their multiplicity.

One way to summarize his life's work is simply to state that he invented a new scientific discipline that has steadily grown for over a hundred years and in every part of the developed world—an intellectual and organizational feat of some magnitude. His scientific writings (in English translation) comprise 24 volumes (Freud, 1886–1957) and continue to be read, not only by professional psychoanalysts. In fact, so great has Freud's prestige been in educated circles that, even today, two to four generations after its original publication, his oeuvre is commonly equated with the conceptual world of psychoanalysis.

In recent years discussions of Freud's work aimed at the general public have tended to focus on those of his hypotheses that have been invalidated by a variety of scientific advances. Because Freud unequivocally adhered to the conception of psychoanalysis as a branch of biological science, he attempted to correlate his observational data with the biology of his own time—specifically with the prevalent theories of contemporary neurophysiology. Brain science was in its infancy a hundred years ago, and the concepts Freud (1895) borrowed from his neurological and physiological mentors—Wilhelm Brücke, Theodor Meynert, Josef Breuer—have not stood the test of time. In the most general sense, the functions of the central nervous system were then conceptualized in power engineering terms (as if the brain were an electrical apparatus), a paradigm that turned out to be incorrect (Toulmin, 1978). Most of Freud's scientific errors followed from these invalid neurophysiological assumptions.[1]

It has taken psychoanalysis half a century (and the availability of valid neurophysiological information)[2] to overcome the conceptual difficulties caused by Freud's mistaken assumptions. It is very odd that commentators who would not dream of dismissing current brain science because of the inadequacies of that discipline at the end of the nineteenth century often try to discredit contemporary psychoanalysis because it relied on the very same hypotheses, applied to mental life. Such critics appear to ignore one of the cardinal methodological principles of science as a whole, that progress in knowledge can best take place through the disproof of existing hypotheses. It is to Freud's credit that he generally stated his speculative propositions in such a manner that they could be invalidated by subsequent scientific findings.

Another way to put this point is to reemphasize that Freud placed his new discipline on *scientific* foundations—meaning that it did not spring from his head fully formed as a doctrine; rather it was a first attempt to explain a broad array of novel observations, subject to continuous modification in the light of further experience. The *Standard Edition* of Freud's psychological works is still deserving of careful study, for it contains important observational data and sophisticated thinking about them, but it is not a currently acceptable exposition of the valid knowledge that constitutes psychoanalysis.

Readers unfamiliar with contemporary psychoanalysis—the current consensus as well as the ongoing controversies within the field—may have difficulty in evaluating Freud's writings in terms of which of his propositions continue to have scientific validity, which have been invalidated although they attempted to answer important questions (and therefore possessed great heuristic value), and which of them turned out to be useless because the problems they were supposed to address were misconceived. In this respect, however, Freud's contributions are no different from those of other authors in the biological sciences who wrote 60 to 100 years ago.

Development of the Analytic Observational Method

In my judgment Freud's most lasting and valuable scientific contribution was not conceptual; hence it tends to be overlooked by nonspecialist historians. This achievement was the development of a novel observational method through which

---

[1] For detailed discussions of these complex issues, see Rosenblatt and Thickstun, 1977; Holt, 1989; Dorpat and Miller, 1992; and Rubinstein, 1997.

[2] The relevant findings are reviewed by Levin, 1991 and Schore, 1994.

it became possible for the first time to gain reliable data about man's inner life. From about 1890, when he began to practice the "talking cure" invented by Breuer, it took Freud roughly twenty years to standardize a "psychoanalytic method" that permitted independent observers to collect such data. It is these unprecedented observations about mental functions and the control of human behavior that have defined the boundaries of psychoanalysis as a scientific domain. In other words Freud accomplished a methodological breakthrough whereby, single-handedly, he founded a new discipline.

It is difficult to discern whether Freud himself fully realized that his method was no mere pragmatic tool to be used therapeutically. His most extensive exposition of the procedure was given in his "Papers on Technique" (Freud, 1911–1915), written shortly after he stopped modifying it. The context there was entirely pragmatic. Nor have subsequent commentators emphasized the *scientific* importance of Freud's observational method. I suspect that the clumsy attempts of some psychoanalysts to rebut critics by claiming that those who have not been in analysis have no way of assessing the truth value of psychoanalytic data were inadequate efforts to point out that the standard psychoanalytic situation permits the collection of information that is simply not observable in other settings.

A psychoanalytic situation requires periods of observation ("analytic hours") almost every day—at any rate, as frequently as possible; in the course of these, the analysand must make good-faith efforts to free associate, while the analyst has to act as an empathic witness of the resulting productions, as well as of the analysand's concomitant (nonverbal) behaviors. Free association differs from ordinary human discourse, which is almost always guided by social rules and the speaker's interest in preserving the privacy of much of his or her inner life. Its precondition of total candor, promoted by the reciprocal guarantee of complete discretion on the part of the analyst, tilts the associative process in the direction of veracity, authenticity, and the emergence of mental contents most people even prefer to keep out of their own awareness. The resultant observations reveal aspects of mental functioning otherwise hidden from the view of the analysand, not to mention others.

Not only does the psychoanalytic situation yield data inaccessible to the nonanalytic observer, but such data also almost never become available through private introspection. This is true partly because we tend to view ourselves through the distorting lens of strong emotional bias and partly because hardly anyone is able to persevere with the introspective effort in the face of intense shame, guilt, or anxiety. The presence of an empathic witness serves to challenge the analysand's prejudices and to push for perseverance despite emotional discomforts.

Because the manifold schools of psychoanalysis have disagreed about the significance of the data of observation they share, it has not been sufficiently recognized that they have few disagreements about the nature of those data. Albeit there seems to be widespread agreement about the fact that the analyst's therapeutic activities are bound to affect the subsequent emergence of fresh material, it has become fairly clear how particular interventions tilt the field of observation in various specific directions. The simplest illustration of this tendency is that analysands generally focus their thoughts on matters that seem to interest the analyst (and to neglect those to which the analyst appears to be unresponsive). In other words intersubjective factors influence the emergence of the observational data in particular settings, but this circumstance does not compromise the relevance of those observations for the analysand's mental life. In summary Freud succeeded in devising a procedure that has led to the reliable collection of previously unobserved data about the human mental condition. Psychoanalysis is the science that has attempted to explain the significance of these novel observations.

The Significance of the Unconscious

Only one of Freud's conclusions on the conceptual level can approach the scientific value of his methodological discovery—that is his realization that human mentation proceeds predominantly outside of subjective awareness (Freud, 1900, chapter 7). Freud was not the first to record that unconscious mentation is possible; his great discovery was that conscious thinking (reflection) is the exception rather than the rule. By placing this insight at the center of his conceptual system, Freud differentiated the discipline he created from the science of conscious mental states; that is why psychoanalysis is also called "depth psychology." By correctly discerning the topography of mental life, Freud went beyond the expansion of our understanding of the control of behavior—he made possible the improvement of that adaptive system by way of psychological intervention.

From this perspective a large array of psychological therapies that have rejected various other Freudian propositions (such as the schools of the early secessionists from psychoanalysis, C. G. Jung and Alfred Adler) owe their genesis to Freud's discovery of the true significance of unconscious mentation.[3] It is important to note that Freud's hypothesis was a biological proposition that awaited validation within neurophysiology. Such proof became available with the development of PET-scan techniques for the visualization of the activities of the brain. These have amply demonstrated the validity of Freud's view on the relative significance of both conscious and unconscious mental life (Lassen, 1994). Thus psychoanalysis was built on the valid assumption that, in order to understand

---

[3] For dispassionate examination of these controversies, consult Homans (1979) and Stepansky (1983).

vital aspects of behavior, we have to discern the effects of what has hitherto been unconscious thought.

From such a "topographic" perspective, Freud (1926) reached another crucial conclusion: certain mental contents that had previously been conscious may arouse sufficient shame, guilt, or anxiety to set in motion a variety of mental processes that either render them entirely unconscious or deprive them of their emotional charge, disavow their significance, or shift responsibility for them to someone else. Arguably, Freud's description of these defensive operations—repression, disavowal, projection, and so on—may have gained wider public acceptance than any of his other scientific contributions.[4] In recent years brain science has made sufficient progress to explain the neurophysiological basis of a number of these defense mechanisms (Levin, 1991).

The scientific importance of the conceptualization of a system of defenses against the experience of painful emotions is that it has illuminated both the adequate and the maladaptive organization of behavior. Both the failure of defense and the need to suppress vital aspects of one's true self through continual defensive operations constitute psychopathology, although of course there are many other types of maladaptation (Gedo, 1988). Freud's insight about the great frequency of conflicts between aspects of personal motivation and the need to avoid painful emotions has made it possible to intervene therapeutically (not only by means of analytic treatment proper but also through a variety of psychotherapies based on psychoanalytic principles) in a manner that may establish effective defenses without stifling the individual.

The Compulsion to Repeat

The third major Freudian achievement was the insight that human behavior is characterized by a variety of automatic repetitions. Freud observed that analysands were never aware of any motive for these behaviors, nor could an observer discover any in every instance; hence Freud (1920) rightly concluded that there has to be a fundamental biological basis, inherent in the organization of the central nervous system, for the tendency to repeat. The first type of repetition he discerned (Freud, 1912) was that of patterns of behavior and attitudes initially experienced in relation to the primary caretakers of childhood. Freud observed that analysands reexperienced these patterns vis-à-vis the analyst—a process he named "transference." He proposed (Freud, 1914a) that transference repetition takes place in lieu of the recollection that might make it possible to transcend persisting childhood mental dispositions that lead to intrapsychic conflict.

---

[4] The most complete review of these mental operations is that of Anna Freud, 1936. See also Gedo and Goldberg, 1973.

From the clinical perspective, the conceptualization of transference made it feasible in most instances to transcend therapeutic difficulties caused by analysands' seemingly irrational emotional reactions to the analyst through interpretation of their significance as repetitions of aspects of the past (Freud, 1915). Transference interpretation is the therapeutic tool that has made it possible to conduct long-term analyses in the course of which the voice of reason may gain a hearing despite any initial distress caused by its message.

Freud (1920) eventually observed the obligatory occurrence of repetitive behaviors that produce neither pleasure nor profit; as he put it, these compulsive repetitions are "beyond the pleasure principle" that governs most unconsciously motivated activities. These were the instances for which Freud was never able to discover any motive, so that he was forced to provide a purely biological explanation for them. His commitment to an energetic model of mental functions led him to the mistaken conclusion that the compulsion to repeat is caused by the operation of entropy (that is, the loss of organization). Because this hypothesis turned out to be unacceptable to most psychoanalysts, the important observations it was meant to explain were for some time neglected. In recent years theoretical biology has emphasized the need to perpetuate the organization of complex living systems; this overriding biological principle provides a rationale for the automatic repetition of existing patterns, even if in current circumstances they violate the pleasure principle (Gedo, 1979, 1988; Modell, 1993). Thus Freud's twin discoveries, of transference and the repetition compulsion, turn out to be crucial components of adaptive behavior.

The Genetic and Structural Viewpoints

The last Freudian scientific discovery of major import (Freud 1900, 1909, 1923, 1926) is the role of early childhood vicissitudes (the traumatic consequences of stressful experiences, of illness and, above all, of unfortunate family relationships) in personality development and pathogenesis. This concept is called the "genetic viewpoint" of psychoanalysis (Rapaport and Gill, 1959). For the most part, Freud was able to reconstruct these traumatic events only if they occurred during the era he labeled "oedipal"—roughly between the ages of three or four and five or six; it remained for some of his successors to postulate the pathogenic consequences of even earlier vicissitudes.[5] The exceptions to this generalization demonstrate that his conception of a genetic point of view was, however, potentially broader than the period to which he applied it. For instance he described the devastating effects of congenital abnormalities on character formation as a result of early injury to self-esteem (Freud, 1916).

---

[5] For an overview of these developments, see Gedo, 1986, 1999.

A close corollary of the conceptualization of a genetic viewpoint was Freud's (1918) realization that the long-term effects of early experience imply that it has left behind affect-laden memories that continue to act as structured mental dispositions, that is, enduring functional propensities. From this functional perspective, insight into the enduring effects of the (childhood) past constitutes the "structural viewpoint" of Freudian theory. It is the concurrent use of the motivational (dynamic), the topographic, the genetic, and the structural frames of reference that qualifies Freudian psychoanalysis as the most comprehensive attempt to characterize the regulation of human behavior (Rapaport and Gill, 1959). Freud conceived all these metatheoretical viewpoints from a biological perspective, but that commitment is clearest in the case of the structural point of view, because it refers not to the *contents* of mind but to the manner in which those contents are processed (Freud, 1923). In other words it was the structural viewpoint that provided Freud's psychological theory with its connection to neuroscience.[6]

Primary and Secondary Processes

Freud has rightly been dubbed a "biologist of the mind" (Sulloway, 1979), for the foregoing list of his important and lasting scientific contributions (including the development of a novel observational method) can properly be characterized as valid biological discoveries. Paradoxically his fame was not to be based on any of the contributions I have thus far discussed. The popular imagination was captured by Freud's reports of the conflictual mental contents he typically encountered in his clinical work. Because he was ever trying to find human universals, Freud's necessarily limited clinical experience was seldom sufficient to yield universally applicable conclusions about intrapsychic conflicts, so that most of his hermeneutic claims have subsequently proved to be of limited applicability. In other words, in the infinitely variable territory of mental contents, Freud's overly ambitious efforts to generalize turned out to be based on sampling errors.

Nonetheless, Freud (Freud, 1900, chapter 7) made one discovery of universal import about the contents of human thought, that of the distinction between the consensual language of adult discourse and the language of dreams, neurotic symptoms, parapraxes, and jokes (Freud, 1900, 1901, 1905a; Breuer and Freud, 1893–1895). He gave these distinct languages the designation of secondary and primary processes, respectively. Much of Freud's magnum opus, *The Interpretation of Dreams*, deals with a detailed description of how the primary process

---

[6] Freud tried to amplify that connection by postulating a complementary "economic viewpoint" that dealt with putative vicissitudes of psychic energy. His ultimate statement on this subject (Freud, 1940) continued to maintain this concept. The hypothesis of psychic energy has become untenable as a result of more recent knowledge about the operations of the central nervous system.

operates and how it may be translated into rational discourse. Freud himself believed that his decipherment of the language of dreams was the greatest of his accomplishments. If there is no general agreement about that judgment today, such an alteration in the appreciation of Freud's masterful clinical discovery has come about because he tried to fit his observations into the metapsychological (psychoeconomic) framework that has been invalidated by subsequent scientific findings, thus obscuring their significance.

The Yield from Invalid First Thoughts

The foregoing list of Freud's lasting scientific contributions is by no means exhaustive, but from a contemporary perspective these are his observations and conclusions that continue to have the greatest value in explicating human behavior and its regulation. By contrast a valid proposition such as Freud's (1905b) assertion that human beings are ever bisexual has not, for the moment, found a prominent role in explaining these matters. In my judgment, however, through the development of a novel observational method, Freud discovered a universe of fresh data that for the first time permitted proper appreciation of the role of childhood experience in structuring mental dispositions of crucial import for adult adaptation, gave rightful emphasis to the dominant role of unconscious mental processes as well as of primary process thinking, and highlighted the essential part played by the automatic repetition of old behavioral patterns in health and disease. These contributions alone would justify Freud's reputation as one of the foremost scientists of the past century.

The assessment of a scientist's stature should not, however, be based on the number and importance of valid hypotheses alone; it should include contributions to scientific progress through raising crucial questions and/or proposing hypotheses that may miss the mark but subsequently promote fruitful inquiry. Freud put forward too many heuristically useful ideas that are no longer regarded as entirely valid to allow me to discuss them all in this essay; rather I hope to convey the importance of such "first thoughts" about scientific puzzles by focusing on a few examples.

When the clinical experience of the early psychoanalytic circle began to broaden, they encountered character types who did not develop the kind of transference Freud had initially observed in his work with patients who only suffered from well-defined neurotic symptoms. This new finding confronted Freud with the inadequacy of the theory of motivation he was then espousing, one based on the concept of instinctual drives. He was not ready to scrap that theory because of a single "anomaly"; instead he amended it (Freud, 1914b) by postulating another form of drive, that of "narcissism." (Later investigators were able to discern specific transferences displayed by "narcissistic" personalities [see Kohut, 1971], thus substantiating that through this concept Freud had come to grips with a real psychological entity.) In contemporary psychoanalysis, narcissism is no longer understood as the product of an instinctual drive (Gedo, 1979)—in other words Freud's initial contribution on the subject was in large measure invalid. Yet the notion of narcissism was of such heuristic value that it has truly suffused modern views of humanity, and all students of human behavior have had to tackle the behavioral correlates of narcissism: selfish ruthlessness, arrogance, vanity, and ingratitude. Thus the conceptualization of narcissism turned out to be one of Freud's most fruitful scientific notions.

The Freudian concept of psychic trauma has had a similar fate. Originally the idea was borrowed from neuropathology (Breuer and Freud, 1893–1895); when Freud gave up on the effort to base his work on the brain science of the 1890s, he retained the notion without specifying the physiological mechanisms it involves. Clinical observation has amply confirmed the reality of traumatic states— psychoanalysts encountered them in pure culture, so to speak, in numerous casualties during both world wars (Abraham et al., 1919). There is no controversy about the observation that psychological traumata suffered in early childhood may lead to maladaptive consequences. Late in his career, however, Freud (1926) offered an explanation of trauma on an untenable psychoeconomic basis that has now been abandoned by most psychoanalysts. Despite this invalid hypothesis, recent views of psychopathology (e.g., Modell, 1993) have frequently been centered on the concept of trauma (now understood as the disorganization of established structure), so that this early Freudian idea has proved to have led to illuminating theoretical progress.

I shall have to content myself with offering only one additional example of a partially misconceived notion that led to fruitful results. Clinical experience led Freud to the realization (Freud, 1914a) that correct interpretation of the analysand's mental contents did not by itself produce behavioral change. He postulated that, beyond interpretation, a process of "working through" is needed in order to master the affects previously warded off by defensive operations. There is universal agreement about the necessity of working through to achieve therapeutic success. It is not widely understood, however, that such a process is not merely a matter of mastering the unpleasure of facing the truth: behavioral change is contingent on the establishment of new neural networks (through novel activity patterns), thus disestablishing automatic reliance on those previously available (Gedo, 1996). Although Freud's understanding of working through was inexact, the concept forever altered the technique of treatment by putting an end to unrealistic expectations that rapid change should follow "insight."

The Freudian Legacy

Within psychoanalysis, Freud's prestige remained enormous well beyond his lifetime. As the founder of the discipline so many of whose ideas proved to be valid and/or fruitful, for many he exerted an aura approaching infallibility. Happily, such unrealistic attitudes of idealization have gradually disappeared; in contemporary psychoanalysis each of Freud's specific contributions can generally be assessed on its particular merits. (Those psychoanalysts who cannot dispense with an idealized *Meister* can choose among a number of more recent contributors to put on a pedestal.) I believe psychoanalysis is now ready to give Freud credit *only* where credit is due.

Whether the general public can forgive Freud for not having been infallible remains to be seen. It is not unusual for great contributions to go into temporary eclipse with a change in intellectual fashions, and the postmodern era has not been conducive to introspection—for that matter, to the *vita contemplativa* as a whole. Yet Dark Ages are generally followed by a Renaissance.

References

Abraham, K., Ferenczi, S., Jones, E. & Simmel, E. (1919), *Psychoanalysis and the War Neuroses*. London: International Psycho-Analytic Press, 1921.

Breuer, J. & Freud, S. (1893–1895), Studies on hysteria. *Standard Edition*, 2. London: Hogarth Press, 1955.

Dorpat, T. & Miller, M. (1992), *Clinical Interaction and the Analysis of Meaning*. Hillsdale, NJ: The Analytic Press.

Freud, A. (1936), *The Ego and the Mechanisms of Defense*. New York: International Universities Press, 1946.

Freud, S. (1895), Project for a scientific psychology. *Standard Edition*, 1:295–391. London: Hogarth Press, 1966.

———— (1900), The interpretation of dreams. *Standard Edition*, 4 & 5. London: Hogarth Press, 1953.

———— (1901), The psychopathology of everyday life. *Standard Edition*, 6. London: Hogarth Press, 1960.

———— (1905a), Jokes and their relation to the unconscious. *Standard Edition*, 8. London: Hogarth Press, 1960.

———— (1905b), Three essays on the theory of sexuality. *Standard Edition*, 7:136–248. London: Hogarth Press, 1953.

———— (1909), Analysis of a phobia in a five year old boy. *Standard Edition*, 10:3–147. London: Hogarth Press, 1955.

———— (1911–1915), Papers on technique. *Standard Edition*, 12:89–174. London: Hogarth Press, 1958.

———— (1912), The dynamics of transference. *Standard Edition*, 12:97–108. London: Hogarth Press, 1958.

———— (1914a), Remembering, repeating, and working-through (Further recommendations on the techniques of psycho-analysis: II). *Standard Edition*, 12:146–156. London: Hogarth Press, 1958.

———— (1914b), On narcissism: An introduction. *Standard Edition*, 14:73–102. London: Hogarth Press, 1957.

——— (1915), Observations on transference love (Further recommendations on the techniques of psycho-analysis: II). *Standard Edition*, 12:158–174. London: Hogarth Press, 1958.

——— (1916), Some character-types met with in psycho-analytic work: II. Those wrecked by success. *Standard Edition*, 14:311–336. London: Hogarth Press, 1957.

——— (1918), From the history of an infantile neurosis. *Standard Edition*, 17:7–124. London: Hogarth Press, 1955.

——— (1920), Beyond the pleasure principle. *Standard Edition*, 18:3–64. London: Hogarth Press, 1955.

——— (1923), The ego and the id. *Standard Edition*, 19:3–66. London: Hogarth Press, 1961.

——— (1926), Inhibitions, symptoms and anxiety. *Standard Edition*, 20:87–172. London: Hogarth Press, 1959.

——— (1940), An outline of psycho-analysis [1938]. *Standard Edition*, 23:141–207. London: Hogarth Press, 1964.

Gedo, J. (1979), *Beyond Interpretation*, rev. ed. Hillsdale, NJ: The Analytic Press, 1993.

——— (1986), *Conceptual Issues in Psychoanalysis*. Hillsdale, NJ: The Analytic Press.

——— (1988), *The Mind in Disorder*. Hillsdale, NJ: The Analytic Press.

——— (1996), *The Languages of Psychoanalysis*. Hillsdale, NJ: The Analytic Press.

——— (1999), *The Evolution of Psychoanalysis*. New York: Other Press.

——— & Goldberg, A. (1973), *Models of the Mind*. Chicago: University of Chicago Press.

Holt, R. (1989), *Freud Reappraised: A Fresh Look at Psychoanalytic Theory*. New York: Guilford.

Homans, P. (1979), *Jung in Context*. Chicago: University of Chicago Press.

Kohut, H. (1971), *The Analysis of the Self*. New York: International Universities Press.

Lassen, N. (1994), Where do people think? Presented at meeting of Psyche '94, October, Osaka, Japan.

Levin, F. (1991), *Mapping the Mind*. Hillsdale, NJ: The Analytic Press.

Modell, A. (1993), *The Private Self*. Cambridge, MA: Harvard University Press.

Rapaport, D. & Gill, M. (1959), The points of view and assumptions of metapsychology. *Internat. J. Psycho-Anal.*, 40:153–162.

Rosenblatt, A. & Thickstun, J. (1977), *Modern Psychoanalytic Concepts in a General Psychology. Psychological Issues*, Monograph 42/43. New York: International Universities Press.

Rubinstein, B. (1997), *Psychoanalysis and the Philosophy of Science. Psychological Issues*, Monograph 62/63. Madison, CT: International Universities Press.

Schore, A. (1994), *Affect Regulation and the Origin of the Self*. Mahwah, NJ: Lawrence Erlbaum Associates.

Stepansky, P. (1983), *In Freud's Shadow: Adler in Context*. Hillsdale, NJ: The Analytic Press.

Sulloway, F. (1979), *Freud: Biologist of the Mind*. New York: Basic Books.

Toulmin, S. (1978), Psychoanalysis, physics, and the mind–body problem. *The Annual of Psychoanalysis*, 6:315–336. Madison, CT: International Universities Press.

Freud as a Cultural Subversive

PETER LOEWENBERG

*The stone which the builders refused is
become the head stone of the corner.*
—Psalms 118:22

This essay argues that Freud was a major initiator of the ambiguity, irony, deconstruction, and perspectivism that define the modern cultural temper of the 21st century. Psychoanalysis is currently under attack on three fronts: (1) from biological psychiatry which claims to have superseded the "talking cures"; (2) from aspects of postmodernism that dismiss Freud as historically time-specific and socially static, paternalistically gendered, and irrelevant; (3) from those within the field of psychoanalysis who say it is now time to leave Freud behind in order to exclusively engage newer theories. Even should, as Freud hoped, neurochemical understandings of brain function and psychopharmacology one day offer accurate, speedy, and lasting symptomatic relief for the neuroses, the relationship that he made between our unconscious and the real ambiguities of our everyday life will remain integral to our 21st-century culture because they are subversive of binary thinking and therefore liberating of personal and cultural repression. Binary thinking is elemental and irreducible: either/or, yes/no, in/out, win/lose, for us/against us; it is primary process thought—the primitive, nonrational, wish fulfilling, and fearful thought of dreams and of the unconscious. Binary thought is defensive; it is destructive of complexity and the emotional richness flowing from struggles and ambivalence. What makes Freud a fascinating thinker and writer is that he deconstructed the seemingly self-evident binary oppositions of our lives and experience: good and bad, crime and guilt, success and failure, love and mourning, kindness and selfishness.

I thank Gerald Aronson, José Brunner, Alain Cohen, David James Fisher, Volney Gay, Samuel Loewenberg, and Herbert Morris for their ideas, discussion, and inspiration.

117

Radical postmodernism ignores claims that presume to be based on factual evidence; it deconstructs all values in the natural and humanistic sciences by postulating that "the systems of knowledge humans create constitute the only source of meaning."[1] Although Freud did not share that radical level of postmodern skepticism, he was the original postmodern, or at least proto-postmodern, in decentering the subject; he dissolved the polarities between self and object, inner and outer, society and psyche, private and public, mental and social. His thought is counterintuitive to the Enlightenment's clear and perfect Kantian categories of mind—time, space, and causality, and to Kant's separation of public from private thought and conduct (Kant, 1784). Psychoanalysis is racially anti-institutional and liberating because it undercuts the universal need to claim knowledge and to institutionalize it with power.[2] The psychoanalytic task of confronting, evaluating, and "corralling" binary thinking, of allowing space for irony, ambiguity, and nuance, is lifelong for the individual and permanent for the culture. Therefore psychoanalysis will inextricably be a part of our lives and culture in the 21st and coming centuries.

The platonic tradition that dominated Western thought for the last twenty-four centuries structured a sharp cleft between the realms of the ideal and the material, reason and passion, consciousness and the unconscious, the intellect and the emotions. In Greco-Christian thought it is absolutely clear that the soul is superior to the body, which is lower and soiled, animal-like and impulse-driven, inferior and preverbal. The platonic view, in line with Socrates' famous imperative to "Know Thyself!" is an injunction to self-purification—to know our true higher human self and to purge or expel our lower animal self. Plato conceived of two kinds of love, *Eros*—sensuous love of the body, and *Agape*—altruistic love for one's fellow humans. For Freud there is only one kind of love—to deny it is self-deception, although it often is aim-inhibited. He affirmed that "we all still show too little respect for Nature which (in the obscure words of Leonardo which recall Hamlet's lines) 'is full of countless causes [*ragioni*] that never enter experience.'" Freud (1910, p. 137, n.1) enjoyed quoting Hamlet's address to Horatio:

> There are more things in heaven and earth, Horatio,
> Than are dreamt of in your philosophy.

---

[1] See, for example, Mary Poovey (1998, p. 327). As a historian I know that interpretations differ, sometimes crucially. I also assume that something not fully knowable, but something real, definable, and, within broad areas of consensus, ascertainable, happened then and there—in 1789, 1914, 1933, and 1945—and in our lives and those of our analysands.

[2] "Once it is fully established, bureaucracy is among those social structures which are the hardest to destroy . . . as an instrument for 'societalizing' relations of power, bureaucracy has been and is a power instrument of the first order—for the one who controls the bureaucratic apparatus . . . where the bureaucratization of administration has been completely carried through, a form of power relation is established that is practically unshatterable" (Weber, 1925, p. 228).

Freud broke the chains that bound us to the Greek idea that we have a "human nature" that, once discovered, will confer values, will tell us how to live the good life. By demonstrating how we are shaped by often distorted memory traces of encounters between our bodies and particular significant people, events, and surrounds, Freud left us able to forthrightly examine the ambiguities of life that Greco-Christian thought tried to foreclose. He moved us from an ethic of ideal purity to one of individuation, contingent chance, and unique self-definition.

Freud's subversion of Judeo-Christian and Victorian sexual morality is most eloquently stated when he postulates a more humane sexual and cultural ideal by relativizing both historically and anthropologically. For example, in the "Dora" case, Freud (1905a) set a culturally subversive and historically relative standard of sexual behavior:

> We must learn to speak without indignation of what we call the sexual perver-
> sions—instances in which the sexual function has extended its limits in re-
> spect either to the part of the body concerned or to the sexual object chosen.
> The uncertainty in regard to the boundaries of what is to be called normal
> sexual life, when we take different races and different epochs into account,
> should in itself be enough to cool the zealot's ardour. We surely ought not to
> forget that the perversion which is the most repellent to us, the sensual love
> of a man for a man, was not only tolerated by a people so far our superiors in
> cultivation as were the Greeks, but was actually entrusted by them with im-
> portant social functions. The sexual life of each one of us extends to a slight
> degree—now in this direction, now in that—beyond the narrow lines imposed
> as the standard of normality. The perversions are neither bestial nor degener-
> ate in the emotional sense of the word [p. 50].

In Freud's parallel text of psychodynamic theory, the "Three Essays on the Theory of Sexuality" (Freud, 1905b), which was published the same year as the "Dora" case, he argues: "Account must be taken of the fact that inversion [Freud's term for homosexuality] was a frequent phenomenon—one might almost say an institution charged with important functions—among the peoples of antiquity at the height of their civilization" (p. 139). In a profoundly radical shift, he advo-cated the turn from ethnocentric marginalization of homosexuals to a historical ethnographic relativism: "The pathological approach to the study of inversion has been displaced by the anthropological" (n. 2). A third of a century later, when writing to an American mother, Freud offered her the comfort of historical and cultural relativism:

> I gather from your letter that your son is a homosexual. I am most impressed
> by the fact that you do not mention this term yourself in your information
> about him. May I question you why you avoid it? Homosexuality is assuredly
> no advantage, but it is nothing to be ashamed of, no vice, no degradation; it
> cannot be classified as an illness; we consider it to be a variation of the sexual

function, produced by a certain arrest of sexual development. Many highly respectable individuals of ancient and modern times have been homosexuals, several of the greatest men among them. (Plato, Michelangelo, Leonardo da Vinci, etc.) It is a great injustice to persecute homosexuality as a crime—and a cruelty, too.[3]

Freud helped us to become more tolerant of ourselves and others, of human situations, and more creative in seeing possibilities, options, and new self-definitions.

Long before it became fashionable to debunk the "spin management" of war coverage, Freud was subversive of the enthusiasm and self-righteous tunnel vision of chauvinistic nationalism. He was not immune to the intense nationalistic passions that swept Europe in the late summer of 1914. As the war began, Freud participated in the patriotic nationalism that inflamed the populace, including the left and the intellectuals, of all the belligerent countries. In the euphoric last days of July 1914, he wrote to Karl Abraham in Berlin: "For the first time in thirty years I feel myself to be an Austrian and feel like giving this not very hopeful Empire another chance. Morale everywhere is excellent. Also the liberating effect of courageous action and the secure prop of Germany contribute a great deal to this."[4] Three days later, ever the skeptic, Freud asked Abraham: "Can you perhaps tell me whether in a fortnight's time we shall be thinking half ashamedly of the excitement of these days?"[5] Unlike most of Central Europe's intellectuals, for example, Thomas Mann or Max Weber, Freud's early enthusiasm did not last through the first month of the war. At the end of August 1914, Freud gave Ferenczi a piece of his self-analysis of this turn of his libido from nationalist chauvinism to disillusionment with the war:

> The inner process has been as follows: The rush of enthusiasm in Austria swept me along with it, at first. . . . I hoped to get a viable fatherland from which the storm of war had wafted away the worst miasmas and in which the children could live with confidence. . . . I suddenly mobilized libido for Austria-Hungary. . . . Gradually a feeling of discomfort set in [with] the strictness of the censorship and the exaggeration of the smallest successes. . . . I am experiencing the ferment of my libido into anger, which I can't begin to deal with.[6]

By December 1914 he was writing to van Eeden in Holland of his bitterness at the atmosphere of pervasive lying propagated by governments: "Just look at

---

[3] Freud to Anonymous, April 9, 1935 (original in English) (cited in E. Freud, 1960, p. 423).
[4] Freud to Abraham, July 26, 1914 (cited in Abraham and Freud, 1965, p. 186).
[5] Freud to Abraham, July 29, 1914 (cited in Abraham and Freud, 1965, p. 186).
[6] Freud to Ferenczi, August 23, 1914 (cited in Falzeder and Brabant, 1996, p. 13).

what is happening in this wartime, at the cruelties and injustices for which the most civilized nations are responsible, at the different way in which they judge of their own lies, their own wrong-doings, and those of their enemies, at the general loss of clear insight."[7] Freud (1915) was appalled that the war revealed "an almost incredible phenomenon: the civilized nations know and understand one another so little that one can turn against the other with hate and loathing" (p. 279). A later generation of psychoanalysts would refer to this primitive mental phenomenon of bifurcation as "splitting"—people being conscious and enacting one side of themselves, in this case their hatred of the enemy, while repressing the side of themselves that is aware of the opponent's good qualities. Freud accurately predicted the deleterious consequences of the denial of losses and the inflated successes claimed by war propaganda. The German and Austro-Hungarian publics were not psychologically prepared for the disastrous defeat and its costs when the collapse came three years later, resulting in the projection of blame for the loss of the war on the left and the Jews. He was disgusted by the hypocrisy practiced by governments and pointed to the suspension, indeed the reversal, of all the acquired moral values of civilization in wartime. In the Central Europe of 1915, this is a highly political statement which, in the guise of science, defied the wartime censorship (Freud, 1915):

> A belligerent state permits itself every such misdeed, every such act of violence, as would disgrace the individual. It makes use against the enemy not only of the accepted *ruses de guerre*, but of deliberate lying and deception as well—and to a degree which seems to exceed the usage of former wars. The state exacts the utmost degree of obedience and sacrifice from its citizens, but at the same time it treats them like children by an excess of secrecy and a censorship upon news and expressions of opinion which leaves the spirits of those whose intellects it thus suppresses defenceless against every unfavorable turn of events and every sinister rumor. It absolves itself from the guarantees and treaties by which it was bound to other states, and confesses shamelessly to its own rapacity and lust for power, which the private individual has then to sanction in the name of patriotism [pp. 279–280].

Freud was the initiator of the great subversive movement of modernity that destroyed the rational illusion that man is master of his mind and soul. In our post-Freudian era, we accept that we are not the center of the universe, nor of our culture and society, and indeed that we are not even masters of our own psyche which is a battleground between unconscious strivings and conscious wishes. We must content ourselves, as Freud (1916–1917) put it, "with scanty information of what is going on unconsciously in [our] mind" (p. 285). Freud uses personal societal necessity and the metaphor of political censorship to explain

---

[7] Freud to van Eeden, December 28, 1914 (cited in Jones, 1955, pp. 368–369).

repression and dream distortions and displacements. He argued that those who would fool the censor must be clever and this also applies to the unconscious (Freud, 1900):

> The politeness which I practice every day is to a large extent dissimulation . . . and when I interpret my dreams for my readers I am obliged to adopt similar distortions. The poet [by which Freud means Goethe] complains of the need for these distortions in the words:
>
> > *Das Beste, was du wissen kannst*
> > *Darfst du den Buben doch nicht sagen.*
>
> > [You cannot tell the boys
> > the best of what you know.][8]

A similar difficulty confronts the political writer who has disagreeable truths to tell to those in authority. If he presents them undisguised, the authorities will suppress his words. . . . A writer must be aware of the censorship, and on its account he must soften and distort the expression of his opinion. According to the strength and sensitiveness of the censorship he finds himself compelled either merely to refrain from certain forms of attack, or to speak in allusions in place of direct references, or he must conceal his objectionable pronouncements beneath some apparently innocent disguise: for instance, he may describe a dispute between two Mandarins in the Middle Kingdom, when the people he really has in mind are officials in his own country. The stricter the censorship, the more far-reaching will be the disguise and the more ingenious too may be the means employed for putting the reader on the scent of the true meaning [p. 142].

This Freudian model of cunning dream censorship and its practice of evasion by coded allusion and deciphering by clever educational interpretation was developed by the political philosopher Leo Strauss (1899–1973) as an influential model of the transmission of ideas. Strauss argued that writing in the Western tradition since Plato has functioned on two levels, a public *exoteric* level and behind that an *esoteric* level of meaning open to those who know how to read it. Science and the world are changed by subversive texts that constitute a disguised critique of prevailing assumptions but are only understood by the *cognoscenti*. The purpose of the *esoteric* texts, said Strauss (1952), was explicitly to exercise a generational, aggressive, sexual and homoerotic subversive appeal, to seduce the young.[9] "Exoteric literature presupposes that there are

---

[8] Mephistopheles to Faust in Goethe, *Faust*, Part I, Scene 4.

[9] "[T]he young men who might become philosophers: the potential philosophers are to be led step by step. . . . All books of that kind owe their existence to the love of the mature philosopher for the puppies of his race, by whom he wants to be loved in turn: all exoteric books are 'written speeches caused by love' " (p. 36).

basic truths which would not be pronounced in public by any decent man. Because they would do harm to many people who, having been hurt, would naturally be inclined to hurt in turn him who pronounces the unpleasant truths" (p. 36). This is one of the reasons psychoanalytic teachings have been banned and psychoanalysts have been persecuted wherever governments are totalitarian and fear private truths.[10] The price of detection would be persecution, which Strauss defined in the most nuanced way to include, not only exile and destruction, but also being ostracized or marginalized within a group.[11] Those trusted benevolent minds who are the initiates to this encoded esoteric knowledge constitute an elite who carry on a disguised discourse whose secret texts are public, but whose revolutionary levels of meaning can only be comprehended by those who know how to read them. Modern readers of the unconscious are no longer philosophers, priests, and oracles, but, as Freud said, poets and writers, and on a less aesthetic and more mundane level, the psychoanalysts. The contemporary philosopher Richard Rorty (1991) expresses his appreciation of comfort with an ambivalent unconscious that Freud provided.[12]

Freud studied deceptions and self-deceptions as means of self-comfort and relief of anxiety. He was a century ahead of his time in forthrightly confronting issues of his personal death; such issues are now on the American political agenda as a major public policy debate. American society, as expressed in our courts and popular referenda, has in the past decade been engaged in a fierce clash on fundamental beliefs about life, death, current informal practices, personal

---

[10] Since Socrates was given the hemlock, it has been too dangerous to tell the truth: "Philosophy and philosophers were 'in grave danger.' . . . The exoteric teaching was needed for protecting philosophy. It was the *armor* in which philosophy had to appear. It was needed for political reasons" (pp. 17–18, italics added). The Reichian connotation of "armor" is evocative.

[11] "Persecution covers a variety of phenomena, ranging from the most cruel type, as exemplified by the Spanish Inquisition, to the mildest, which is social ostracism. Persecution cannot prevent independent thinking. It cannot prevent even the expression of independent thought. For it is as true today as it was more than two thousand years ago that it is a safe venture to tell the truth one knows to benevolent and trustworthy acquaintances, or more precisely, to reasonable friends. Persecution cannot prevent even public expression of the heterodox truth, for a man of independent thought can utter his views in public and remain unharmed, provided he moves with circumspection. He can even utter them in print without incurring any danger, provided he is capable of writing between the lines" (pp. 23–24).

[12] "What is novel in Freud's view of the unconscious is his claim that our unconscious selves are not dumb, sullen, lurching brutes, but rather the intellectual peers of our conscious selves, possible conversational partners for those selves. . . . He helped us become increasingly ironic, playful, free, and inventive in our choice of self-descriptions. . . . The intellectual's increased ability to treat vocabularies as tools rather than mirrors—is Freud's major legacy. . . . He made it far more difficult than it was before to ask the question 'Which is my true self?' or 'What is human nature?' By letting us see that . . . there was nothing to be found save traces of accidental encounters, he left us able to tolerate the ambiguities that the religious and philosophical traditions had hoped to eliminate" (pp. 149, 155, 158).

autonomy, and the law. With circumspection which is indicative of ambivalence there is a discernable movement in our culture toward upholding the individual's right to determine the time and manner of his or her death, and to meet that desire to die with dignity (Loewenberg, 2000).

America's great social experiment with assisted dying is Oregon's Death with Dignity Act, which went into effect after a popular referendum in November 1997. After a hard fought and costly campaign, including appeals to the U.S. Supreme Court, the people of Oregon, by a margin of three to two, overwhelmingly voted to establish the right to assisted dying. The timing of the Oregon vote was propitious because it came on the heels of a Supreme Court decision urging the states to experiment with legislation and referenda. In his majority opinion in *Washington v. Glucksberg* (1997) Chief Justice Rehnquist held: "Throughout the nation, Americans are engaged in an earnest and profound debate about the morality, legality, and practicality of physician-assisted suicide. Our holding permits this debate to continue, as it should in a democratic society" (p. 2258). In an expression of judicial restraint, the court said, we will not do it—the states and the people must decide. Other states are now considering legislation modeled after Oregon's Death with Dignity Act. This is the kind of private yet political issue, analogous to birth control, abortion, homosexuality, and adultery, or a position on the sexual privacy and personal life of the president, on which the majority of Americans are more tolerant, rational, and mature in their personal values than are the legislators, the media, and the political class inside the Washington Beltway who issue pronouncements that do not accurately reflect public opinion. The stance people will take before a network camera, or what they will disclose on the record to a media interviewer, or a neighbor at church, is not necessarily what they will do in a voting booth on what they perceive to be a profoundly personal issue.

Let us set this important trend in contemporary American law and society in the context of psychoanalytic humanism and Sigmund Freud's position on assisted dying. As early as 1899, in his correspondence with Wilhelm Fliess forty years before his death, Freud (1887–1904) objected to what he termed

> one of the most aggravating features of our modern medicine. The art of deceiving a sick person is not exactly highly necessary. But what has the individual come to, how negligible must be the influence of the religion of science, which is supposed to have taken the place of the old religion, if one no longer dares to disclose that it is this or that man's turn to die? . . . I hope that when my time comes, I shall find someone who will treat me with greater respect and tell me when to be ready.

Freud unconsciously altered Shakespeare's *Henry IV* (Act V, Scene I) where Prince Hal tells Falstaff: "Why, thou owest God a death" to "You owe Nature a death." To this letter he added a postscript evoking his engagement with the

Stoic values of Hellenic culture: "I am deep in Burckhardt's *History of Greek Civilization.*"[13]

In 1928, on the recommendation of Marie Bonaparte, Freud engaged Max Schur as his private physician. He presented Schur with two conditions, first, "that he always be told the truth and nothing but the truth," and second, "when the time comes, you won't let me suffer torture unnecessarily" (Schur, 1972, p. 408). In 1939 Schur was in America, taking his New York State Medical Board examinations in the last week of June when Freud summoned him. He recrossed the Atlantic by ship in early July, arriving in London on July 8, 1939. When, on September 21, Freud took Schur's hand and said: "My dear Schur, you remember our first talk. You promised then not to leave me in the lurch when my time comes. Now it is nothing but torture and makes no sense anymore." Schur indicated he had not forgotten (Schur, 1972, p. 529). Freud thanked him and asked Schur to "talk it over with Anna, and if she thinks it's right, then make an end of it." Schur redeemed his promise, giving Freud three centigrams of morphine, which he repeated, and then gave him a final morphine injection the next day (Gay, 1988, pp. 739–740 n.). Freud never awoke. Currently there is a change in a Freudian direction taking place in American culture—we are catching up with Freud in our social and legal culture's attitude toward death and dying.

Altruism and self-sacrifice are conventionally regarded as "virtues." Yet in a post-Freudian world we know that altruism can also be a mask for self-centeredness, that unselfishness may be self-punishment, that kindness may conceal patronizing superiority, and that celibacy may be a flight from sex. We intuitively think of success and failure as binary opposites, and of crime and guilt as having a direct causal relationship: if you commit an infraction of the laws, and if you have an intact superego, you feel guilty. In a brilliant insight, which is clinically useful to every psychotherapist, Freud reversed the causal chain, standing common sense on its head, showing that there are also "criminals from a sense of guilt." Freud also demonstrated how people who are successful may at the threshold of achieving their triumph destroy their success (Freud, 1916, pp. 309–333). I will only allude to the White House careers of two of our recent U.S. presidents, Richard Nixon and Bill Clinton, which can be illuminated by the insight of Freud's model of "wrecked by success." Watergate came when Nixon was an unprecedented political winner. The Monica Lewinsky affair occurred at the moment of Clinton's greatest political triumph, when he had just defeated Newt Gingrich and the Congress in the budget fight that closed down the federal government.

---

[13] Freud to Fliess, February 6, 1899 (p. 376).

The world is still too often seen as functioning on simple polarities without the nuanced ambiguities that Freud has taught us are part of the complex multiple realities of human lives. We experience political elections in which the simplistic binary opposition of good and bad is the stuff of media spin, campaign rhetoric, and popular idealization and demonization of candidates. Our post-Freudian sense of politics is ironic—we know that the great liberators, such as Robespierre, Napoleon, and Lenin, may also become great tyrants.

Our world knows bereavement as involving the expression of positive and sentimental feelings of loss for the dead. Freud dissected the process of mourning to include the acceptance of ambivalence toward the dead and the recognition that when someone dies, someone else invariably gains from that death. In treating the "Rat Man," Freud postulated that the patient gained by the death of his childhood rival, his sister Katherine. Freud (1909) did not hesitate to interpret a potential gain in freedom and money to a patient from death of a living parent: "Hasn't it ever occurred to you that if your mother died you would be freed from all conflicts, since you would be able to marry?" (pp. 283–284).[14]

I illustrate these complexities of mourning with an account of a group consultation with the staff of a psychiatric hospital who had just been displaced because their building had been confiscated. As we went around the room in personal introductions, I noted that many of the staff members defined themselves as having trained with Nancy, a personally warm and empathic child psychiatrist, a flexible leader who made things happen, who had been an important mental health administrator and who had recently died of cancer. Bitter resentment and feelings of abandonment and betrayal by the state administration were expressed. A major complaint was that correspondence is not answered, staff phone calls get no call back. I could only share their puzzlement at the apparent lack of communicating skills and insensitivity of the "higher-ups."

In the next session I interpreted that there seemed to be a group fantasy that if only Nancy were still alive, she would have interceded and saved the day for the staff. Now she is not there and does not respond. I shared with the staff my sense of loss because I had known Nancy over decades and always found contact with her enriching and supportive. She had been a gifted facilitator. I too missed her now. I interpreted there is an ambivalence and resentment at the loss of even a gifted and inspiring leader. There are feelings of neglect, abandonment, and desertion. When leaders leave, they must be replaced, there are new career opportunities, and new possibilities open up for others. When the staff left, the current director kept me behind to tell me how "right-on" I had been. She was the youngest of the group and had been named hospital director over others who were senior to her in age and service. She pointed to where her resentful rivals had been

---

[14] Original record of the case.

sitting in the room. She complained that they do not function as a staff, and they individually go over her head to the state administration, rather than through channels. In addition to trying to keep things together in adverse circumstances, her major institutional problem was the envy of several of her staff. Now it was clear why the staff had not been getting responses to their communications from the state administration. Freud made us aware that "mourning" may also contain unrecognized feelings of aggression, competition, and triumph.

To turn to a case of binary "terrible simplification" in modern European history,[15] Daniel Goldhagen recently advanced the thesis that "racial eliminationist antisemitism was a sufficient cause, a sufficiently potent motivator, to lead Germans to kill Jews willingly" (Goldhagen, 1996, p. 417). It is hard to comprehend the wide acceptance with which this shrill and shallow argument about a whole people has been greeted, both here and in Germany.[16] How easily we accept the idea that any nation, in this case "the Germans," were governed by one base motivation. It is as though no one, including Freud, had ever demonstrated that apparently homogeneous personal and historical behaviors are the product of many and varied individual interests, perspectives, and motivations.[17]

Freud taught us how complex human motivation and conduct really are. He observed that anxiety is an affective state caused by the loss of security and predictability, the feelings of helplessness created in the first instance by "missing someone who is loved and longed for" (Freud, 1926, p. 136). What originated as "the felt loss of the object" brought about by "a separation from the mother" (p. 137), "the loss of love" (p. 143) becomes in sociohistorical terms the feelings of helplessness and hopelessness occasioned by the dislocation and humiliation of a lost war, the loss of security and self-respect in the mega-inflation, and the multiple losses of self-esteem consequent to the great depression (Loewenberg, 1995).

Consider what is a more intimate example, Freud's (1930) deconstruction of the antipodes of altruism and selfishness in his critique of the religious injunction to "Love thy neighbor as thyself":

A love that does not discriminate seems to me to forfeit a part of its own value, by doing an injustice to its object; and secondly, not all men are worthy of love [p. 102].

---

[15] Jacob Burckhardt in a prescient passage foresaw "the *terribles simplificateurs* who are going to descend upon poor old Europe" (Burckhardt to von Preen, July 24, 1889; cited in Dru, 1955, p. 220).

[16] See the critical essay by Fritz Stern, "The Past Distorted: The Goldhagen Controversy" (Stern, 1999, pp. 271–288).

[17] Fred Weinstein (1990) is especially good on this in his chapter, "The Heterogeneity Problem in Practice and Theory," pp. 47–82.

My love is something valuable to me which I ought not to throw away without reflection. It imposes duties on me for whose fulfilment I must be ready to make sacrifices. . . . Indeed I should be wrong to do so, for my love is valued by all my own people as a sign of my preferring them, and it is an injustice to them if I put a stranger on a par with them (pp. 109–110).

The commandment is impossible to fulfil; such an enormous inflation of love can only lower its value, not get rid of the difficulty. Civilization pays no attention at all to this; it merely admonishes us that the harder it is to obey the precept, the more meritorious it is to do so. But anyone who follows such a precept in present-day civilization only puts himself at a disadvantage *vis-à-vis* the person who disregards it [p. 143].

The time comes when each one of us has to give up as illusions the expectations which, in his youth, he pinned upon his fellow-men, and when he may learn how much difficulty and pain has been added to his life by their ill-will [p. 112].

Freud destabilized the innocent categories of inner and outer, the boundaries between society and psyche, of mental and social, substituting a dynamic interpenetration and absorption. We incorporate our whole society in our mind, behaviors of sexuality and gender, systems of reward and punishment, self-esteem and values. We also make our outer world by projecting the expectations, premises, and internal objects of the world we have within. Psychoanalytic feminists are insistent that bipolar antinomies cannot apply to gender; they stress, rather, the unique mixture of each of our subjective sensibilities.[18]

When Freud (1930) exposed the interactional psychodynamics of love, he left behind cant and sentimentality in demonstrating the functions of intimate intersubjective idealizations, identifications, and intrapsychic internalizations:

If I love someone, he must deserve it in some way. . . . He deserves it if he is so like me in important ways that I can love myself in him; and he deserves it if he is so much more perfect than myself that I can love my ideal of my own self in him. . . . But if he is a stranger to me and if he cannot attract me by any worth of his own or any significance that he may already have acquired for my emotional life, it will be hard for me to love him [p. 109].

Freud's work enables us to construct richer and more plausible narratives of our life—more plausible because they subsume *all* of the behaviors, thoughts, and fantasies of our life, including our censored asocial and sadistic, self-indul-

---

[18] "Subjectivity creates and re-creates, merges and separates, fantasy and reality, inner and outer, unconscious and conscious, felt past and felt present, each element in the pair helping to constitute and give meaning and resonance to the other. Both in the psychoanalytic and in the cultural approach, we hold in abeyance any universal claim about the content of what is thought or felt: the content of that subjectivity or process cannot be universalized" (cited in Chodorow, 1999, pp. 76–77).

gent and self-deceptive, mean-spirited and self-destructive patterns of conduct, as well as our loving, self-less, and courageous actions. Freud's thought is profoundly subversive and liberating in supplying the best approach we have to irrationality in our lives and in the world, and the best answer we have to the oldest, yet the most acutely contemporary, political problem of the 21st century, how to reconcile order that is not oppression with freedom that is not license.

References

Abraham, H. & Freud, E. (1965), *A Psychoanalytic Dialogue: The Letters of Sigmund Freud and Karl Abraham*. New York: Basic Books.

Chodorow, N. (1999), *The Power of Feelings: Personal Meaning in Psychoanalysis, Gender, and Culture*. New Haven, CT: Yale University Press.

Dru, A., ed. & trans. (1955), *The Letters of Jacob Burckhardt*. New York: Pantheon.

Falzeder, E. & Brabant, E., eds. (1996), *The Correspondence of Sigmund Freud and Sándor Ferenczi, 1914–1919, Vol 2*, trans. P. T. Hoffer. New York: Basic Books.

Freud, E. (1960), *Letters of Sigmund Freud*. New York: Basic Books.

Freud, S. (1887–1904), *Briefe an Wilhelm Fliess 1887–1904*, ed. J. Masson. Frankfurt: Fischer Verlag, 1986.

—————— (1900), Interpretation of dreams. *Standard Edition*, 4 & 5. London: Hogarth Press, 1953.

—————— (1905a), Fragment of an analysis of a case of hysteria. *Standard Edition*, 7:7–122. London: Hogarth Press, 1953.

—————— (1905b), Three essays on the theory of sexuality. *Standard Edition*, 7:130–243. London: Hogarth Press, 1953.

—————— (1909), Notes upon a case of obsessional neurosis. *Standard Edition*, 10:153–318. London: Hogarth Press, 1955.

—————— (1910), Leonardo da Vinci and a memory of his childhood. *Standard Edition*, 11:63–137. London: Hogarth Press, 1957.

—————— (1915), Thoughts for the times on war and death. *Standard Edition*, 14:273–302. London: Hogarth Press, 1957.

—————— (1916), Some characters met with in psycho-analytic work: II & III. *Standard Edition*, 14:316–333. London: Hogarth Press, 1957.

—————— (1916–1917), Introductory lectures on psycho-analysis: Part III. General theory of the neuroses. *Standard Edition*, 16:243–463. London: Hogarth Press, 1963.

—————— (1926), Inhibitions, symptoms and anxiety [1925]. *Standard Edition*, 20:87–175. London: Hogarth Press, 1959.

—————— (1930), Civilization and its discontents [1929]. *Standard Edition*, 21:64–145. London: Hogarth Press, 1961.

Gay, P. (1988), *Freud: A Life for Our Time*. New York: Norton.

Goldhagen, D. (1996), *Hitler's Willing Executioners: Ordinary Germans and the Holocaust*. New York: Alfred A. Knopf.

Jones, E. (1955), *The Life and Work of Sigmund Freud: Years of Maturity, 1901–1919*. New York: Basic Books.

Kant, I. (1784), What is enlightenment? In: *The Philosophy of Kant*, ed. C. J. Friedrich. New York: Random House, 1993, pp. 145–153.

Loewenberg, P. (1995), *Fantasy and Reality in History*. New York: Oxford University Press, pp. 155–171.

—— (2000), A stoic death: Sigmund Freud, Max Schur, and assisted dying in contemporary America. In: *Enlightenment, Passion, Modernity*, ed. M. S. Micale & R. L. Dietle. Stanford, CA: Stanford University Press, pp. 360–376.

Poovey, M. (1998), *A History of the Modern Fact: Problems of Knowledge in the Sciences of Wealth and Society*. Chicago: University of Chicago Press.

Rorty, R. (1991), *Essays on Heidegger and Others Philosophical Papers, Vol. 2*. Cambridge, England: Cambridge University Press.

Schur, M. (1972), *Freud Living and Dying*. New York: International Universities Press.

Stern, F. (1999), *Einstein's German World*. Princeton, NJ: Princeton University Press.

Strauss, L. (1952), *Persecution and the Art of Writing*. Glencoe, IL: Free Press.

Washington v. Glucksberg (1997), 117 *S. Ct.* 2258, Renquist, CJ, for the majority.

Weber, M. (1925), *Essays in Sociology*, ed. & trans. H. H. Gerth & C. W. Mills. New York: Oxford University Press, 1946.

Weinstein, F. (1990), *History and Theory after the Fall: An Essay on Interpretation*. Chicago: University of Chicago Press.

III

FREUD'S IMPACT
IN SPECIFIC AREAS

Freud's Impact on Therapeutic Work with Children

BENJAMIN GARBER

Freud's influence on the understanding of infantile sexuality and the development of the child has been well documented in the psychoanalytic and popular literature, as has his influence on therapeutic work with adults. Freud's influence on therapeutic work with children, however, has not been fully appreciated. It is generally accepted that the first psychoanalytic therapy of a child was the analysis of Little Hans. The purpose of this essay is twofold: (1) to trace the impact of Freud's contributions on what is currently considered the optimum therapeutic approach to children; and (2) to frame the analysis of Little Hans in its historical context.

In "Analysis of a Phobia in a Five-Year-Old Boy," Freud (1909) described the course of the illness and recovery of a young patient. Freud reported the development and resolution of Hans's phobia. The therapy was conducted by the father. On a sometimes daily basis, the father talked with Freud about his son's difficulties and reported his conversations with his son. In the course of these talks, Freud instructed him in how to understand and handle the case. Freud only saw the boy once during the treatment.

At age three, Hans was showing a rather lively interest in that part of his body he called his "widdler." His thirst for knowledge was inseparable from his sexual curiosity, which was focused on his parents' "widdlers." At age three and a half, two traumatic events occurred: his mother threatened him with castration because he was masturbating, and his sister was born. At age five, he had an anxiety dream that his mother was gone, and as a result, his affection for his mother intensified. Hans would come to his mother's bed in the morning to be caressed by her, in defiance of his father's wishes. He became afraid of horses because they had big "widdlers."

After an attack of influenza, his fear of horses increased so much that he refused to go out. The immediate precipitating event of the phobia was the fall

133

of a big horse. At Freud's direction, the father interpreted that—just as he had witnessed the horse do—Hans wished that his father would fall down and be dead. Then Hans would take the father's place with the mother. The falling horse represented not only the dying father but also the mother in childbirth. The anxiety in the phobia was explained as being due to the repression of Hans's aggressive propensities. As a result of the analysis, Hans recovered. He ceased to be afraid of horses and was able to leave the house and to maintain a better relationship with his father.

Freud's touching and empathic description of a frightened little patient's initial restricted and anxious state, his final triumphant fantasy, and his recovery reflected the new conception of the child as an individual. This recognition went far beyond the knowledge of the day (Glenn, 1980).

When Freud undertook the treatment of Little Hans via his father, he probably did not set out to develop a treatment technique for children. Rather, he wanted to see if the material provided by a child of that age would confirm his theory of infantile sexuality and the origin of neurotic symptoms (Etchegoyen, 1988). Having reconstructed many significant events from the early life of his adult patients (Freud, 1905), Freud turned to children and adolescents to confirm his findings. The therapy proved effective in removing Little Hans's phobic symptoms, and it also gave support to Freud's theory that the sexual impulses of children determine their neurotic symptoms. This analysis, in a fortuitous manner, paved the way for the development of child analysis by Hermine Hug-Hellmuth, Anna Freud, and Melanie Klein.

This case was the beginning and the essence of what today constitutes child analysis. Although its impact on the field has been recognized, its specific and definitive influence on those child analysts who came after has not been delineated. Although the originality of the case has been appreciated, it has not been considered a model of child analytic technique. The case of Little Hans is often alluded to as a curiosity or an artifact whereas the real pioneers of child analysis are Hug-Hellmuth, Anna Freud, and Klein. There are valid reasons why this clinical material is seen as lacking analytic purity. Freud's main purpose in describing the analysis of Little Hans was not to demonstrate that children can be analyzed, but rather to present support for his theory of infantile sexuality. Also the analysis was conducted by the father and not by Freud himself. Consequently it was not considered a pure or bona fide analysis. A third reason was Freud's involvement with the family; important information was withheld, either because he did not wish to betray confidences or because he had blind spots about the parents, especially in regard to Little Hans's mother, who had been his patient. The mother was patently seductive and destructive in her behavior toward the boy, yet Freud downplayed the significance of her actions.

Freud accomplished two things with this case. First he led the father in the difficult analytic task of helping the child resolve his Oedipus complex and castration anxiety. Second, he allowed himself to listen and be led by the child, who provided valuable information about infantile sexuality. Freud was able to empathize with the child at his developmental level and simultaneously to stand back and to look at the material from the perspective of a concerned and interested adult. Such a basic approach is the essence of therapeutic work with children.

The general lines of treatment based on the father's reported observations were laid down by Freud (1909) and carried out by the father:

> [T]he special knowledge by means of which he was able to interpret the remarks made by his five-year-old son was indispensable, and without it the technical difficulties in the way of conducting a psycho-analysis upon so young a child would have been insuperable [p. 5].

When Hug-Hellmuth (1921) initiated the practice of child analysis in 1915, she introduced new techniques, including drawing and playing, which offered the child an easier way of expressing his or her fantasies. Even as she helped to develop the field of child analysis, she impeded its growth by imposing the following restrictions: interpretations should be used sparingly, and analysis should not be used with children younger than eight. She also believed that child analyses could be only partially successful. Her anxiety and tentativeness were based on the concern that analysis would unleash the basic impulses of the child, robbing the child of his or her innocence. Throughout the development of child analysis, there has been a search for an optimum technique that would allow children to overcome the obstacles blocking the path to analytic work.

The application of psychoanalysis to children came relatively late. Almost twenty years elapsed between Freud's case report of Little Hans and the burgeoning of child psychoanalysis as a specialized discipline. The debate over adapting psychoanalysis to meet the needs of the child oscillated between two poles represented by Anna Freud and Melanie Klein, and their followers. It is my contention that, while this debate raged in England and other countries, Sigmund Freud's contributions were pushed into the background.

Klein and her followers claimed that, although there were differences between them and their opponents, their work was a development and an extension of psychoanalytic knowledge based on Freud's theory and postulations. Klein claimed that she employed the same method Freud used with Little Hans while adding the use of play. Another difference was that she dealt directly with the child and had minimal contact with parents. She retained the instinctual theory and the basic relationship of psychology to the biological core of the human organism. Consequently she believed herself to be the "true Freudian" in her therapeutic approach to children.

Klein followed in the steps of Hug-Hellmuth who made use of toys and drawings to establish communication with the child, allowing him or her to express fantasies. In that regard she enlarged on Freud's technique with Little Hans, which consisted primarily of verbalization. By introducing these new elements into the analysis, she was able to enrich the child's productions and explore a variety of ways of gaining access to the child's unconscious.

Klein (see Smirnoff, 1971) made a number of other significant contributions, which were similar to Freud's original work but differed from it in important ways. She equated the play of the child with the free association of the adult. She emphasized the child's fantasy life, which was expressed via drawings and play. She felt that a transference neurosis occurs in children just the way it does in adults. She posited a developmental timetable that was not the same as Freud's; hers focused on the early development of the Oedipus complex and the super-ego. She did not rely on the parents but expected the child to establish his or her own independent relationship with the analyst. Klein felt that the real surroundings played a subordinate role as compared with the importance taken on by the intersubjective conflict. By making use of the transference and by recommending verbal interpretations of unconscious fantasies through the transference, Klein staked out a position for child analysis that is close to that of so-called classical psychoanalysis.

Klein's work subsequently influenced the school of object relations theorists in England and in the United States (Grotstein, 1996). Such gifted clinicians as Bowlby, Fairbairn, and Winnicott in England and Jacobson and Mahler in the United States extended Freud's original ideas and elaborated on them with an emphasis on understanding children in the first three years of life. These individuals studied infant development and, in doing so, emphasized theories of infantile dependency rather than theories of infantile sexuality. They spoke more of nurture than of instinctual drives. In spite of such deviations, they were strongly influenced by Freud's concepts of the ego ideal, the superego, the Oedipus complex, and the role of aggression.

Anna Freud (1946), in her seminal volume *The Psychoanalytic Treatment of Children*, was more intent on delineating her differences with Klein than on tracing the changes in technique since the publication of "Little Hans." She indicated that, ever since the publication of this work, child analysis as a therapeutic method had a stormy career. There is hardly a point that has remained uncontested or that has not, at some time or other, led to controversy. Anna Freud questioned the child's ability to free associate and doubted the child's ability to form a transference neurosis. She also championed educational procedures in the work with children by adding an introductory phase to the analytic process. She felt that free association might provoke the child's aggressive trends.

Anna Freud depended on parental input because the child's relationship with the parents persists during the course of the analysis. In that regard she was close to her father's position in his work with Little Hans. Her eventual emphasis on analyzing defenses with children is also similar to her father's approach. Although she never deviated from the instinctual-drive theory, she paid more attention than had her father to the child's defenses and the child's adaptation to his or her environment. The more recent formulations of self psychology (Kohut, 1971) also focused on parental behavior, specifically on empathy for the child, or the lack thereof, as crucial both in normal development and in psychopathology. These controversies between the two giants of child analysis—Anna Freud and Melanie Klein—often obscured the contributions of others and interfered with a more robust development of the field.

In spite of Sigmund Freud's one-dimensional technique, child analysis began with his undertaking of the case of Little Hans. He used the case to illustrate his ideas on infantile sexuality and to document the oedipal phase of psychosexual development. It also served to demonstrate the value of psychoanalytic developmental formulations in understanding and ameliorating neurotic symptoms.

Although the primary value of the case rests on its elaboration and support of a developmental framework of infantile sexuality it also has a bearing on ego psychology, psychoanalytic developmental theory, and principles of technique in child analysis.

For the clinician who works with children, the case of Little Hans is valuable because of two basic elements: it is a method of eliciting meaningful clinical data from a child and a developmental framework whereby these data can be organized in a useful manner. Freud's technique via the father evolved as he worked with the material presented by the child. At first, Freud suggested reassurance that the fear of horses was nonsense, and he urged the father to educate and enlighten Little Hans about sexuality. These reassurances led to some improvement, albeit temporary.

The next step was to get Hans to stop his masturbatory activity because that was considered the source of the problem; however, that also was ineffective. It was only then that the father, with Freud's guidance, engaged the boy in an active questioning and interpretative interaction that ultimately resulted in substantial improvement. Freud's understanding of this interaction evolved into a psychoanalytic approach with children. Applying the same principles to the child that he found to be effective with his adult patients, he used dreams and slips of the tongue as clues about what was current in the child's unconscious. By adapting the adult-oriented principles to the child, he demonstrated appreciation and respect for the child's intellect, psychological-mindedness, and capacity for insight. He urged patience because a single accurate interpretation does not result in the cure of a neurosis: a period of working through is needed before one can see results in a child or in an adult.

With children it is often the preceding and subsequent behavior rather than the words that confirm the accuracy of an intervention. The child's ability to respond to an accurate intervention by acknowledging its accuracy is limited, as the child is fearful of having his mind read or being too agreeable or compliant. Consequently an immediate denial may be followed by behavior that confirms the correctness of the interpretation.

In the analysis of children, as in that of adults, there may be prolonged periods without apparent progress. Patience is essential. For example, Hans's father would at times press too hard and force his preconceived ideas on the child. Freud cautioned the father not to ask too many questions and to allow the material to unfold at its own pace. In children, as in adults, there is a continuity to the analytic process. What emerges from the unconscious is related to what preceded it and what follows it. It is up to the analyst to see these connections and not be distracted by the child's incidental verbalizations.

With children, the birth of a sibling can be a significant precipitant and stimulus for psychopathology. The sense of being displaced and the parental reaction to the new infant may be important contributors to neuroses in some children. Because verbal confirmation is not always available in therapeutic work with children, the therapist may be compelled to make an educated guess or to use his intuition to determine what is significant.

From the beginning Freud responded to Hans with a sense of fondness but, more importantly, with respect. He appreciated his precocity, openness, honesty, and cooperation, as well as his ability to make use of psychoanalytic insights. It is this stance vis-à-vis the patient that contributed to the therapeutic alliance and the merging of the father and Freud into an effective therapeutic instrument. There is ample evidence that Freud had a special fondness for Little Hans; he makes frequent references to the child's intellect, precocity, and lively disposition. There are also implications that children are smarter than we give them credit for being, and that they know and understand much more than we realize. Although it was important for Freud to be a step ahead of Hans, at times the child was ahead of him. The case offers evidence that the use of interpretations helped to make the unconscious conscious and hence, in this regard, work with the child was similar to analytic work with adults.

These are some of the salient technical points that elevated analytic work with children to the same level and status as analytic work with adults. It became apparent that this was more than just an artifact or a curiosity; rather, it became a clinical method that not only illuminates the process of development but also can alleviate the suffering of children.

Freud's development of a method of working with children went beyond theory building and technique. In addition to the creation of child analysis, there were important child-rearing issues that emerged from Freud's work with Little Hans. Although these were not definitively stated, they were implied in his work with the child. Freud's approach advocated greater honesty in the parent-child relationship.

Parents were expected to take a reasonable approach when dealing with the child's masturbatory activity. Castration threats and other restraints were shown to be ineffective and potentially harmful to the child. Some intermediate approach between the extremes of punishment and threats and total permissiveness was indicated.

Freud advocated that children should be educated about sexuality at an early age, and this education should continue throughout childhood. The problem with sexual education in the schools was that it needed to be suppressive of the child's impulses but not so suppressive as to contribute to the formation of neuroses (Freud, 1907).

He cautioned that children should not be allowed to sleep in the parental bed, as it was too stimulating and seductive. Parental modesty in front of their children was necessary as a part of normal development, because otherwise the child is vulnerable to overstimulation, which can contribute to the formation of neuroses. Ultimately, what Freud championed with these suggestions was the child's right to obtain the knowledge necessary for optimum development.

To what extent these insights had an impact on child-rearing practices is beyond the scope of this study. There is, however, ample evidence that experts on child-rearing, such as Benjamin Spock, were influenced by Freud's ideas. Because of Freud, many parents have become aware of the child as a human being with an unconscious and sexuality.

Although the case of Little Hans is useful and rich, an evaluation of it from our current point of view, now that we have had decades of experience with child analysis, finds several problems (Joseph, 1990). Freud maintained a powerful connection with the parents of Little Hans. The mother was his former patient, and the father had been a member of the psychoanalytic inner circle for a number of years (Frankiel, 1992). Freud had engaged in child guidance with the parents from the time that Hans was a baby; consequently he became a powerful figure not only with the parents but also with the child. When the father became stymied in his therapeutic efforts, the boy suggested that they contact the Professor. As a result the parents and child developed an idealizing positive transference to the all-powerful "Professor."

It may be argued that, because of Freud's position in the family, he overlooked certain noxious elements in the external environment. For example he minimized the effect of the mother's seductive and destructive behavior toward the child. Nevertheless, on balance, his powerful connection with the parents was a significant factor in the child's improvement. During his one encounter with Freud, Hans was able to tell Freud, in the father's presence, that the latter was not always the benign and controlled figure he presented to the outside world. That very morning he had smacked Hans, a fact that the father had hidden or repressed. This communication established that the boy's fears were not entirely without foundation. Hans left the interview with his self-esteem elevated and with the conviction that the Professor was on his side. His ego had been strengthened, and this helped him master his anxieties.

In therapeutic work with children, it has been established that in order for the child analyst to be successful, it is essential to have a therapeutic alliance not only with the child but also with the parents. Freud sensed this, and that might be one of the reasons he allowed the father to do the therapeutic work. Rather than blame the parents for the child's problems, Freud wisely used them as allies and partners in his efforts to help the child. In any treatment undertaken with children, it is necessary to involve the parents in order for the therapy to be effective. Most parents have a deep interest in helping the suffering child by being actively involved rather than by being passive bystanders in the process. Officially, advice to parents of the child in analysis is frowned upon; yet for any therapy to be successful the parents need to be given something by the analyst to enlist them as allies in the work with the child. The parents also need understanding, empathy, a sense of hopefulness, and the reassurance that they are capable of being competent parents.

Hans seemed to relate to his father and to Freud in a trusting and open way. Usually he responded to their questions with candor, even when he allowed his death wishes to be detected (Silverman, 1980). Freud gave an accurate and vivid description of the kind of working alliance that is commonly found in the work with oedipal children. It is impressive how quickly such youngsters accept help once the analyst has demonstrated his genuine concern for their well-being. One can indeed form a working alliance with the child provided that the parents are supportive of the treatment. Hans's response to Freud is evidence that a child does not necessarily avoid therapy but is capable of becoming an active participant in the process.

Hans emerges from Freud's narrative as a charming, energetic, spontaneous, and engaging little boy. Not unlike many other bright and precocious children, he came up with spontaneous insights into the workings of the mind. When his father tried to discourage him from masturbating and pointed out that he still wanted to do it, Hans responded, "but wanting is not doing and doing is not wanting." This would be a profound distinction even for an adult to make. Freud believed it was essential for the father to be the primary figure in the treatment of Little Hans; however, after the field began to develop, he recognized that therapists other than family members were capable of carrying out the therapy.

The treatment technique that Freud used in this case has been described as psychoanalytic psychotherapy (as opposed to psychoanalysis) because the material was not always allowed to evolve spontaneously. The treatment has also been described as family therapy because Freud used the father as the primary therapist and because it caused a shift in the family equilibrium. Hans became closer to his father and formed a new relationship with him. The father became his friend and helper, facilitating ego and superego development. This new relationship gave Hans the strength to cope with and to counteract the mother's seductive behavior.

Freud, in his role of supervisor and overseer, also served as an auxiliary superego for Hans's parents. He helped them to restrain the overstimulating behavior which had fanned the little boy's oedipal strivings. Most child analysts probably perform this function (Silverman, 1980). Based on Freud's previous therapy of the mother and his supervision of the father, however, he had a far greater impact on the family organization than most child analysts have today. Consequently, one would wonder to what extent Hans's symptoms improved as a result of the intrafamilial shifts and to what extent they were affected by the analytic process of interpretation and working through. This question, however, is at the bottom of every child analysis and therapy. Even today, with our greater sophistication about therapeutic efforts with children, the confusion about what constitutes child psychoanalysis as opposed to child therapy is ever present.

One of the potential problems in doing therapy via the parent is that the parent may continue to make interpretations to the child after the analysis has ended. Such parental activity may lead to the child's resentment and his resistance to such interventions. Today parents who have been in analysis or are familiar with psychoanalytic principles may make interpretations to their children in an unsympathetic way. In supervising Hans's treatment, Freud did not establish a clear distinction between the parents' educative role and the analytic physician's interpretive function. Even today this confusion has not been resolved as therapists may educate while educators do therapy (Glenn, 1980). At one time education was considered a vital part of the analytic process; however, with time it was felt that optimally child analysis should be carried out without educative methods. Although plausible in theory, in practice this is not always possible.

From his work with the patient called the Wolf Man (Freud, 1918), Freud concluded that every neurosis of an adult is built upon a neurosis that occurred in childhood. The childhood neurosis, however, may not have been severe enough to be recognized as such. This theoretical and clinical construct forced adult analysts to pay more attention to the child and consequently more attention to clinical work with children. This was another way in which Freud had an indirect impact on clinical work with children.

In his "New Introductory Lectures," Freud (1933) had no misgivings about applying analytic treatment to children who either exhibited neurotic symptoms or were on the road to the development of an unfavorable characterological pattern. He felt that the child was a favorable subject for analytic therapy and that the results were thorough and lasting. This impression may have been based partly on the follow-up of Hans, whom he saw as a stable, capable, and competent young man. He argued, however, that the technique of treatment of adults had to be altered for the child. The method of free association did not go far with the child, and transference played a different role, as the parents were still involved. The internal resistances of the adult were replaced in the child by external difficulties, and the parents may become an interference in the analysis and may also need psychoanalytic guidance.

The method of the first child analysis took the form of an intellectual game of hide-and-seek. Little Hans was encouraged to ask questions of his parents, as well as of other adults. In turn, this opened the way for counterquestions by his father (Garrison, 1978). Success was likely once the "game" caught the boy's attention, curiosity, and enthusiasm. One may wonder, however, why neither Freud nor the father considered using play as an adjunct to the treatment, because drawings had some use in the process. It may well be that culturally it was not functional or appropriate for men to engage small children in play. Perhaps playing with children was seen as a threat to the man's position in the family or his manliness and as the responsibility of women. This may be a partial explanation of why women developed play therapy and why almost all of the early child analysts were women.

Freud's application of adult analytic principles to the treatment of the child was limited by his lack of experience with children. Even though the treatment in some ways consisted of a judicious combination of child psychotherapy and parental advice, it was still a breakthrough that offered neurotic children the potential for relief from suffering. From these promising beginnings, child analysis emerged as a potent therapeutic procedure. Child analysis sprang from adult analysis; now we have come full circle, as experience with children has had a profound impact on analytic stance in work with adults.

In this day and age, when a pill is deemed an appropriate cure for what ails most children, psychoanalysis and psychoanalytically informed therapies are able to offer children an alternative: a better understanding of themselves and others.

References

Etchegoyen, R. H. (1988), The analysis of Little Hans and the theory of sexuality. *Internat. J. Psycho-Anal.*, 15:37–44.

Frankiel, R. V. (1992), Analyzed and unanalyzed themes in the treatment of Little Hans. *Internat. Rev. Psycho-Anal.*, 19:323–334.

Freud, A. (1946), *The Psychoanalytical Treatment of Children*. London: Imago Publishing.

Freud, S. (1905), Three essays on the theory of sexuality. *Standard Edition*, 7:130–243. London: Hogarth Press, 1953.

——— (1907), The sexual enlightenment of children. *Standard Edition*, 9:129–139. London: Hogarth Press, 1959.

——— (1909), Analysis of a phobia in a five-year-old boy. *Standard Edition*, 10:5–149. London: Hogarth Press, 1955.

——— (1918), From the history of an infantile neurosis. *Standard Edition*, 17:7–122. London: Hogarth Press, 1955.

——— (1933), New introductory lectures on psychoanalysis: Explanations, applications and orientation. *Standard Edition*, 22:136–157. London: Hogarth Press, 1955.

Garrison, M. (1978), A new look at Little Hans. *Psychoanal. Rev.*, 65:523–532.

Glenn, L. (1980), Freud's advice to Hans's father: The first supervisory sessions. In: *Freud and His Patients*, ed. M. Kanzer & J. Glenn. New York: Aronson, pp. 121–127.

Grotstein, J. (1996), Object relations theory. In: *Textbook of Psychoanalysis*, ed. E. Nersessian & R. Kopff. Washington, DC: American Psychiatric Press.

Hug–Hellmuth, H. (1921), On the technique of child analysis. *Internat. J. Psycho-Anal.*, 2:281–305.

Joseph, D. I. (1990), Preoedipal factors in Little Hans. *J. Amer. Acad. Psychoanal.*, 18:206–222.

Kohut, H. (1971), *The Analysis of the Self*. New York: International Universities Press.

Silverman, M. (1980), A fresh look at the case of Little Hans. In: *Freud and His Patients*, ed. M. Kanzer & J. Glenn. New York: Aronson, pp. 95–120.

Smirnoff, V. (1971), *The Scope of Child Analysis*. New York: International Universities Press.

Freud's Impact on Marriage and the Family

JACK L. GRALLER

To grasp the scope of Freud's work it is crucial to understand the psychology of the family in the Victorian era in the second half of the nineteenth century. Medical science before the 1800s was primitive, and most doctors believed that a person's health was determined by shifts in the balance of bodily fluids called humors. Some even thought that illness, physical or mental, meant that people who were ill were haunted by spirits or cursed by God.

For a brief time Freud experimented with hypnosis to try to understand that the workings of the mind might cause physical symptoms. Then he developed his own simple but ingenious technique, which he called free association. He found that if his patients talked randomly about whatever came to mind that certain ideas evolved that would reveal thoughts, feelings, and conflicts of which the patients were unaware. Freud began to apply some of this technique to himself. He discovered that dreams were similar to symptoms and free associations and that they too revealed, in symbolic form, hidden meanings that resided outside of consciousness. His close attention to the unconscious ideas and feelings in himself and in his patients led to a theory that many repressed childhood memories had sexual meaning. Most people assumed that a person's sexual life began at puberty when the body became sexually mature. Freud challenged this assumption and proposed that sexuality was a critical part of a child's development *before* the onset of puberty.

Many of Freud's patients claimed to have memories of being sexually seduced in their childhood by an adult of the opposite sex. From these observations Freud developed a theory that neurotic disorders were caused by these sexual experiences. As he examined more patients, however, he came to believe that such stories were usually only fantasies. Like dreams they were the fulfillment of unconscious wishes. Through self-analysis he had discovered his own sexual desires, and that suggested that he went through a similar phase of development. Freud named this constellation the Oedipus complex (named for Oedipus,

145

the mythical king in ancient Greece), where a child's unconscious wish for the parent's love of the opposite sex is combined with wishes of hurting or killing the parent of the same sex. The Oedipus complex represents only one aspect of infantile sexuality. In addition, he identified other stages of development. In the first, the oral stage, children derive pleasure from eating; in the anal stage, children derive pleasure from controlling their bowels; and in the genital or oedipal stage, children become aware of their bodies and their sexual organs. These stages are followed by the latency period when the child's intellectual and emotional development takes priority over sexual urges. Each of these stages contributes to a person's sexual identity.

The Dynamics of the Family

Until the last decade of the 19th century, science did not scrutinize the ways a family functioned psychologically. Sanctioned by religion and tradition, the family had a constant, unchanging structure, with each of its members fulfilling a role thrust upon him or her by the tenets of cultural expectations.

The emotional structure of the Victorian patriarchal family was comprised of the father/husband, who was assumed to be strong and active, providing for his wife and children not only the means of livelihood, but also love and protection as the means of emotional security. The mother/wife, connected with her husband in a lasting marriage, was assumed to accept this arrangement as the prerequisite for her happiness, which in turn enabled her to love her children with tender, unwavering motherliness. The children, raised in a spirit of respect toward an authority figure (who might at times delegate his authority to the mother), accepted the authority in devotion and gratefulness until they became parents themselves and acted in their turn the same way toward their children. *Therefore*, it was *revolutionary* when Freud and his followers began to methodically study the boiling cauldron of emotions beneath the static-appearing, smooth ideological surface of the patriarchal Victorian family.

With the discovery of the Oedipus Complex, Freud began to appreciate the triangular dynamics of the family. The steady interaction between these various family members describes a dynamic, fluid, changing system that partially determines the personality development of the child (Benedek, 1973). The family unit is a closely knit organism thriving on the delicate balance of its emotional currents, which continually must be reestablished in its adjustment to everyday occurrences. A macroscopic example is the manner in which a family changes decisively when one or several of its members separate from it. Such separation disturbs the existing balance, mobilizes the psychological trends, and exposes the original conflicts, which usually receded into the background through the usual adjustments of living. A microscopic example would be the way a child intuits changes in affect in his/her parents. This is commonly encountered when parents think they have a secret, for example, a divorce or decision to have another child, only to discover later that their child has sensed or known about the "secret" weeks before it was discussed.

Freud's Discoveries

Freud began a revolutionary new way of conceptualizing individual personality development and the method by which members of a family affect each other. His discoveries started a new understanding of personality development within the family or triangle. He deserves credit for describing the fact that there is a hidden psychology between family members, and that the unique blend of spouse personalities, healthy or neurotic, affects the child's mental life. His discovery of the unconscious was pivotal. He was able to demonstrate the existence of the unconscious by understanding the symbolism contained in symptoms, dreams, slips of the tongue, parapraxes, and the way patients had wishes and fantasies about their analyst which he called *transference reactions*. Therefore, the residual oral-anal-oedipal themes in parents influence the psychology between parents and child.

There are several mechanisms that contribute to transference formation, namely displacement and projection. Displacement is the basic mechanism of the classic transference paradigm in which an object representation (person in the patient's childhood), derived from any level or combination of levels of the subject's developmental experience, is *displaced* onto the new object (person in the here and now) in the therapeutic relationship. The effects of the past are imposed on the new object, namely the analyst, so that now they are invested with the affective burdens and connotations that were inherent in the old object relationship in the person's childhood (Wolman, 1996). Displacement is the basic mechanism for libidinally based transferences, both positive and negative, and describes how feelings are transferred from an important person from the past to a person in the present. By and large, displacement transferences play a dominant role in neurotic disorders. Projection tends to play a more prominent role in the formation of transferences in more primitive character pathology. The effect of the projective or externalizing transference is to make the therapist represent a part of the patient's own self-organization, thus projecting something from *inside* the patient onto the therapist or others. An example might be an angry person, physically abused in childhood, who imagines (projects) that others will attack him. Later, in describing transference for those in psychoanalysis, Freud used the term "transference neurosis" to designate the revival, under certain specific conditions, of the infantile neurosis[1] in the analytic situation.

---

[1] The term utilized by Freud to designate the revival, for patients in psychoanalysis, of their childhood neurosis. The successful interpretation and management of the transference neurosis gives the patient insight into this current edition of his/her neurosis and also leads to insight into the first edition, the infantile neurosis.

Freud modified the scientific method to develop the psychoanalytic method—
to uncover the content of one's unconscious in an optimal environment (the psychoanalytic situation), using an analytic instrument (our capacity for hovering
attention, carefully listening for affect-laden data in complicated symbolic communication to be passed through the analyst's well-trained self-knowledge). The
analyst deciphers this information and provides insight by way of interpretation.

Freud was a role model for those who followed him, exuding a tenacious
objectivity and curiosity, practicing his analytic detective work with empathy
and benevolent skepticism. He showed mature strength and courage in standing
up to his critics whether they came from the lay public, religious groups, other
physicians, or his competitive colleagues. He kept working, accumulating knowledge and writing, simultaneously testing and modifying his theories, in spite of
severe health problems and external trauma (i.e., the war years).

Freud was a pioneer, a trailblazer, who endured and established a solid base
of theory and practice upon which others might build. Because of the naïve
medical beliefs of the times and the rigid Victorian family structure, he was even
more of a giant who endured and succeeded in spite of severe criticism.

The Rise of Psychoanalytic Theory and Practice, and the Near Death of Family Dynamic Theory

Freud was able to deepen his understanding of personality by discounting the
rigid Victorian structure of the family and doubting that archaic explanations for
neuroses were caused by humors or immorality. By relentlessly studying his
subjects and his own neurotic symptoms, he was able to challenge Victorian
explanations. Gradually he was able to invent a psychoanalytic method to study
the contents and workings of the unconscious. These were revealed in patient's
relationships, symptoms, parapraxes, jokes, fantasies, dreams, and transference
reactions and led him to hypothesize the basic drives of love and sex, aggression
and dependency.

Freud's explanations in the late 1800s suggested that the family members
were responsible for the pathology in children. His early hypothesis stated that
parents or other adults were actually molesting children. He called this the seduction theory. He further theorized that the trauma of that seduction was repressed and later was precipitated by subsequent related events, which, when
analyzed, uncovered the original incestuous behavior by the adult.

This particular hypothesis was a crucial step in Freud's brilliant discovery of
the unconscious and its contents. It was discarded when he later realized that the
alleged seductions were most often fantasies, wishes, and fears that are universally present and unconscious in all of us. So, at this exciting historical moment,
he not only demonstrated that there was an unconscious, but also that the unconscious contents included infantile sexuality with the various stages of psycho-

sexual development—oral, anal, genital, oedipal, and latency. At this moment Freud integrated all of this information to create psychoanalysis, and unfortunately this had a devastating impact on the development of a family dynamic theory.

The seduction theory mostly *criticized fathers*[2] in an era when patriarchal families were the norm. His intention was to explain the unconscious workings of the mind, but this theory set the tone for blaming parents as the cause of their children's psychopathology. Much later non-Freudian therapists *blamed mothers*[3] for their child's psychopathology, often an unfair indictment that encouraged blaming rather than understanding the parent's role in the child's problem and therefore suggesting treatment (Arieti, 1959). The early anger at his theories and inadvertent accusation of parents was the beginning of the anger and skepticism at many of his theories. Even though he reconsidered and discarded the seduction theory, his followers and defenders persisted in one way or another to blame parents. The blame even grew into the shame or social stigma of many illnesses other than neuroses, such as schizophrenia, mental retardation, and epilepsy.

The development of transference theory propelled parents into further blame. Negative transferences were accepted by analysts as the *bad* part of analysands, the gratifying positive transference reactions as the *good* part. Implicitly, negative transference was traceable back to the way in which parents either overindulged or deprived their child, a further criticism of the parents who were unenlightened due to their own unconscious factors. For the most part, the parents of his patients often felt ambushed by Freud and his followers, as they had no idea that they were making either errors of omission or commission in their child-rearing practices. They were simply parenting in the Victorian style described earlier.[4]

In summary, as psychoanalysis was launched at the turn of the century, and has continued to progress up to the present, family theory went into a negative growth or blame period from 1900 until the 1950s when it began to develop as a separate viable theory and therapy.

---

[2] My conclusion is that the seduction theory implies that either the parents were incestuously involved or neglected to protect their children from other adults.

[3] Lidz, for example, describes the role of the parents with severe psychopathology. He generalizes that mothers are often domineering, nagging, and hostile, and their husbands are weak and dependent, thus implying the ideology of the psychopathology in severe character disorders or schizophrenics.

[4] The assumption is that Freud was able to develop his theories at an unacceptable moment in time, as he was fascinated and immersed in discovering the cure for mental illness. Because of that very specific focused goal, he did not have some other important issues in sight. For example, he missed the treatment of the parents and later even the psychology of women.

Studying personality by way of the psychoanalytic method was an enormous discovery that deepened our understanding of development. It established the mental health movement and then psychoanalysis as a scientific theory, research tool, and form of treatment. It provided insights into the infrastructure of the psychological development of personality that led us to understand unconscious motivation (why we think and behave the way we do). Many professionals were able to make use of the new discoveries and theories and were able to expand and generate constructive use of this evolving science and treatment form.

Freud's theories are still the organizing principles of our field. Unfortunately some who wrap their professional identity around a particular belief system are unwilling to accept criticism or change. Freudianism in its most orthodox form is rigid; in its least orthodox form it is fluid and open to objective study of other's ideas and concepts. Application of the scientific method provides a chance to further expand either a portion of theory or technique by studying and understanding new and different ideas. Then one may question these ideas, use them in trial and error experimentation, and then include or discard them based on the results.

Freud (1917) did not see at that time that the interplay that caused the child's psychopathology needed the application of the diagnostic psychoanalytic method for the parents. By seeing parents as contaminants, it suggested that they were not neurotic and operating out of their unconscious, but were behaving badly and could volitionally stop their neurotic behavior without insight. Parents were meddlesome, bad, or relentless and were expected to *stop* their behavior rather than be patients who needed insight to change. In addition, the best and brightest therapists were attracted to psychoanalysis and psychology and paid little attention to the parents' pathology. The child psychology movement started to address this problem, specifically the child-guidance approach that explained the psychology of the children to parents and guided them into healthier interactions with their children. Not until after World War II did some analysts begin to turn their attention to theories and treatment needs of the family, and specifically to the couple or parents.

The Emergence of Marital and Family Theory and Practice

Freud's influence on marriage and family theory was both direct and indirect. The direct influence is limited and can be seen in specific schools of family therapy that draw explicitly on psychoanalytic concepts and incorporate at least some notion of unconscious processes. In contrast, the indirect influence is far more persuasive and yet harder to articulate. The Freudian concepts occur at what almost might be thought of as an unconscious level, and permeates almost every school of family therapy. This indirect influence may be thought of as the intellectual zeitgeist from which family therapy emerged, or the ground from which family therapy grew. Freud, and a number of the key concepts that he articulated, provided the context for the development of family therapy.

Direct Influences

The direct influence of Freud's work can be seen clearly in the work of many early family theoreticians[5] such as Ackerman (1958), Bowen (1978), Boszormenyi-Nagy and Urlich (1981), Framo (1992), Paul and Paul (1975), and currently Graller (1981), Sander (1979), Erlich, Zilbach and Solomon (1997), and Lansky and Morrison (1997). It also may be found in the work of more contemporary family therapists (Scharff and Scharff, 1991), who have explicitly articulated an object relations theory of family therapy. In addition, direct influences may be seen in the ideas of other contemporary work of integrative therapists, such as Pinsof (1995), and Wachtel (1997). These theoreticians have retained many core psychoanalytic concepts, primarily belief in the unconscious processes, such as projections and transference.

Indirect Influences

Freud, more than any other theorist, opened up the psychosocial interior of the family as a subject of scientific and clinical inquiry. His work pointed directly at the child's early experience in his or her family, as the primary determinant of his or her adult psychology. With concepts such as transference, he asserted, in fact, that much of adult experience is forever filtered through the lens of the early childhood experience, so that most adult relationships echo, if not totally reflect, the child's early experience with his or her caregivers. The family was at the heart of Freud's theories of human development.

Beyond his general contribution of pointing to the family as the crucible of personality and neurosis, four aspects of Freud's work play particularly critical roles in establishing the ground from which family therapy emerged: (1) the concept of the unconscious; (2) the Oedipus complex; (3) the exploration of the role of sexual experience or fantasy in early childhood in shaping personality and neurosis, particularly the so-called hysterical or conversion neuroses; and (4) the transference (as explained earlier in the process of displacing and projecting feelings onto the therapist or another person). Although Freud tended to reify the notion of the unconscious as a place or entity (a concept that has been and still is unacceptable to many family therapists), his more general emphasis on mental processes that occurred *outside of awareness* was revolutionary. Virtually every form of family therapy attempts to increase each family member's awareness of what he or she feels, thinks, and/or relates to each other, which is basically a process of making that which is unconscious available to consciousness. It is an unarticulated tenet of virtually every form of family therapy that

---

[5] A description of each theorist's work is beyond the scope of this essay as this could lead to an extensive review that would emphasize others' impact on marriage and family, rather than Freud. This is a sampling, not an entire list of theoreticians.

family members do not consciously understand their dynamics, so that much of family experience occurs unconsciously and repetitively.

Freud's proposal of the Oedipus complex as a critical developmental phase articulated what has become a central theme of family systems theory as the fundamentally triadic nature of family experience. The Oedipus complex refers to the issues and struggles involved in the child's reorganization of his or her sexuality (affection) and aggression (assertiveness) in regard to parental figures by five or six years of age. The brilliant insight in this theory was the idea that the child is not just interacting with his or her mother (an idea that unfortunately came to dominate later schools of psychoanalysis), but that the father is critical to psychological development, as well. Going even further, it is not just the child's relationships with mother or father, but the triad (or triangle[6]) of relationships that matters. In other words this theory was *systemic* in that it implied that each of the dyadic relationships (each of the pairs) in the triad influences every other.

The family systems pioneers were diverse and clever in the ways in which they uncovered the unconscious (for instance psychodrama and how people act out that which was unconscious). They saw dynamic patterns in couples and families in vivo (saw arguments and disagreements unfold in therapy sessions), so that they obtained different information from that of individual analysis. Couples in analytically oriented marital therapy often bring seemingly unimportant arguments into the sessions, and the therapist can begin to see that regardless of content, their system of dealing with many issues is competitive and conflictual, the flip side of sharing and compromising. Those analytically informed therapists who use systems theory help the couple discuss and reasonably resolve their issues, and help both spouses become empathic with each other. If they do go deeper, the therapist is able to help them discuss and possibly discover that this is a learned behavior that one or both spouses experienced, as their parents had bickered in a similar way. The more analytic the therapist, the more one searches for other roots of conflict by exploring *childhood* feelings and experiences (for example, residual or unresolved oedipal losses and sibling rivalry issues). In the actual experience in psychoanalytically oriented marital therapy, the session becomes an arena for therapists to see and hear a portion of the neurosis in each spouse. An example of an old trauma might be that an older brother was punished when he did not relinquish a toy to a younger sibling. He was then traumatized in that his parents punished him by sending him to his room. He was deprived of his parents and was also deprived of the toy. As the love from his mother or father was withdrawn from him, he was then left in an angry, deprived, depressed position. This pattern might be acted out later, as this child becomes an adult and has his own children.

---

[6] Triad and triangle are used interchangeably.

Some of the anti-analytic pioneers were disenfranchised Freudians who had analytic or partial analytic training. Some had established analytic careers, but were also well versed in the psychotherapy movement of understanding the value of bringing insight and understanding to a family. Still others worked diligently to integrate Freudian theory and marital and family systems theory. In the early 1980s, a small group of analysts began to meet to study this integration problem. The original 15 or so members came from larger cities, were faculty members of their local institutes, and had emerged as accepted members of the psychoanalytic community with a subspecialty interest in marital and family theory and practice. I was the Chicago member of this group and a founding member as well. This subgroup of analysts had a different mission, to understand personality development on an individual basis, *along with* how the combustion of two personalities, the parents with residual neurotic psychopathology, unconsciously formed the nucleus of neurotic conflicts in their children. The goal was to bring insight to those with neurotic patterns that emerged in psychoanalytic marital psychotherapy. If neurotic patterns could be understood and interpreted, it was hoped that the couple could be helped to alter the neurotic environment to a less neurotic one for their children and improve their marriage.

In the early 1980s, this group was perceived by some as anti-analytic, so that they met independent of the American Psychoanalytic Association annual meetings. Later they were accepted and included in a seminar setting as part of those annual scientific meetings.

The Psychoanalytic Understanding of Marriage

Many professionals have come to believe that the psychoanalytic study of marriage is an oxymoron. Freud's discovery of psychoanalysis was an analysis of the psyche (singular), so that, by definition, one cannot study the family per se in psychoanalysis. Thus, one can only use psychoanalytic concepts and adapt them extra-analytically to study the way a couple thinks, functions, and affects each other unconsciously. With license then to apply psychoanalytic terms and meanings to marriage and later to a family, I will attempt to explain my method of integrating the psychoanalytic understanding of marriages and later families.

To begin, the dynamic understanding of marriage informed by analytic ideas describes the interpersonal dynamics of the marital relationship, how a couple may psychologically fit together in both healthy and neurotic ways, and includes the spouse-to-spouse transferences (displacements and projections). It is important to allow for some flexibility in using the term transference, as there is a continuum of transference reactions that one may experience. In the most general way, as described earlier, a transference reaction is a displacement or projection onto another person. There can be transference reactions to those who are close to the patient but not intimates, such as bosses or friends. There are transference elements to authority figures such as a medical doctor, where feelings from the patient to the doctor are common, but the doctor is not open about his/her thoughts and feelings to the patient. This nonmutual kind of transference is very common in our society. There are then specific transferences to general therapists who have little interest or knowledge about the unconscious or transference. There are also specific transference reactions to an analyst or analytically orientated therapist, who uses the concept of transference as a way to demonstrate the patient's unconscious wishes. The interpretation of that transference reaction describes the current edition of the person's displacement of feelings within the framework of their neurosis onto the therapist. The last, but most comprehensive form of transference, would be the *transference neurosis*, the term Freud utilized to designate the revival under certain specific conditions of the infantile neurosis in the analytic situation.

The dynamic system changes as new life experience and the aging process influence the intrapsychic lives of the couple. Some of life's events can stimulate growth and maturation in one or both spouses, and some may trigger regression or maladaptive behavior in one or both as they live out their current lives (or edition of their residual unresolved conflicts with each other). The couple has opportunities to master such regressions, thus deepening the relationship. Some unmastered regressions can become core fixations in the course of a marriage, thus forming a *marital neurosis*. What I have labeled the *marital neurosis* is a *transference-neurosis-like* constellation that evolves in the marital relationship over time. It is not one of the earlier aforementioned superficial transferences, but is deeper and more intense because of the enduring quality of the relationship. Manifestations of a healthy or *nonneurotic fit* occur where spouses bond, work as a team, and successfully understand and manage the common regressions in the other spouse. In this process some couples demonstrate areas of a *neurotic* fit. These areas may be manifested by abnormal behavior patterns, lack of empathy, or conflict. The inability to negotiate these conflicted areas often leads to referrals for marital therapy. A study of these conflicts shows them to be loaded with powerful spouse-to-spouse transferences. The *marital neurosis* is the term that describes the development of this *unconscious transferential process in the marital* relationship.

Psychoanalytically oriented or informed marital psychotherapy[7] is an incredibly complex process as it involves the ability by the therapist to understand the individual dynamics of each spouse, and the signs and symptoms of marital neurotic conflicts as expressed in the marital neurosis. It requires group or system techniques to help couples feel comfortable enough to reveal themselves to the therapist and to their spouse. This usually involves private information, dreams, and fantasies. It also includes, along with the spouse-to-spouse and spouse-to-

---

[7] See "Adjunctive Marital Therapy: A Possible Solution to the Split Transference Problem," page ix in Graller (1981) for an extensive description.

therapist transferences, the many potential countertransference reactions, namely, the reactions that the therapist has to the individual and/or couple. This is especially important because in the early phase of marital therapy each spouse usually tries to position him or herself psychologically to be favored by the marital therapist.

The crucial goal is the successful understanding and interpretation of the marital neurosis in marital therapy. When one adds the genetic and dynamic roots of neurotic patterns explored in marital therapy and more comprehensively in psychoanalytic therapy, *this becomes a microscopic method of studying the marital neurosis.* It reveals the delicate balance of power between spouses. The analytically orientated marital psychotherapist has a chance to see the beginning of a pathway to study a symptom to its historical genetic roots. The more proficient we become as diagnosticians of the marital neurosis and all of its complexities, the more we are able to see the limits of analytically informed marital therapy and that some spouses need individual analytic referrals to deepen their understanding of their residual neurotic conflicts. In summary, this informed, customized, psychoanalytic marital psychotherapy is the *instrument* to study the marital neurosis and the subtleties of each spouse's projections and displacements onto the other. Obviously, if successfully analyzed, that insight has the potential to modify or change behavior.

The addition of the marital neurosis to psychoanalytic theory expands the theory of personality development to include the parents' neurotic psychopathology in the dynamic mix. Had Freud done that, parents of children in treatment might have more readily accepted entering treatment to understand how their residual problems affected their child's personality development. If the situation had involved a spouse in psychoanalysis, it would possibly be a more acceptable trend for the other spouse to consider diagnosis and treatment, because psychoanalysis would alter the neurotic reciprocal pathology in the couple.

In summary, the *psychoanalytic dynamic theory of marriage* describes the nature of the couple's attachment and explores each spouse's unresolved conflicts and vulnerabilities (Freud's fixation points) in genetic (early childhood), dynamic, and transferential terms. Close attention would be paid to how unresolved, earlier conflicts are enacted in the marital relationship. The microscopic field then to be studied in the marital evaluation would be the interpersonal transferential field. Once the marital neurosis or spouse-to-spouse transferential patterns are established, the couple's conflicts are frequently treatable in psychoanalytic marital treatment that spotlights the neurotic transference fit. If further individual treatment is necessary, referral may be made to another analyst.

Psychoanalytic Dynamic Theory of the Family

The psychoanalytic dynamic theory of the family focuses on the development of the marital neurosis plus the impact on the marital neurosis by the addition of a child. Most couples begin marriage with the ambitions and dreams to procreate. To love and be loved and to feel whole, to include becoming a parent, is an adult developmental phase that needs fulfillment. These issues are usually conscious themes in choosing a marital partner. Both spouses imagine how the other would fit their image of a coparent. This set of thoughts and feelings has a developmental path through courtship, engagement, and marriage. By then, most couples have shared information that influences the decision or timing of the first pregnancy. Anywhere along the way neurotic conflicts within the premarital and then marital couple might emerge depending upon what dormant issues lie within each partner. Similarly, unconscious potential conflicts might occur from the moment of the child's conception and throughout the child's development. The fantasies of most couples intensify soon after conception, triangular thinking begins to become a reality, and family dynamics are launched.

At any moment old conflicts might be revived. For example, a wife's memory of an early parent loss might be triggered by deciding a baby's name; a husband's memories of his mother's successive pregnancies and the birth of younger siblings could revive childhood anger at his parents that could be displaced onto his wife and children.

Spouses are forced to confront their feelings, fantasies, joys, and even anger once conception becomes actualized. The mastery of these regressions or visits to the past unresolved childhood issues are crucial to preserving the healthy marital fit that was hopefully developed before pregnancy. If a couple can deepen their love and maintain their intimacy, they become bonded at a deeper level. What follows should be a deepening evolution through time, as each developmental phase of the child progresses. Each phase has the potential to revive an earlier conflict or edition in one or both spouses.

The major *pivotal concept* is the understanding of the spouse-to-spouse transferences. If studied carefully using the method informed by core analytic ideas, one can see, especially in vivo, that the potential for a *marital neurosis exists in all couples.*

If the concept of the marital neurosis were used universally in the psychoanalytic community, then we would have an organizing principle and theoretical structure that would allow for categorization of *marital neuroses.* The organization and diagnosis would pave the way for the diagnosis and treatment in psychoanalytic terminology to complement individual dynamic psychoanalytic theory and practice. It would be fortunate if we could use the concept of *marital neurosis* as comfortably as *neurosis* in describing the potential in all patients to have residual childhood issues. Thus it is helpful, in my consideration of diagnosis, to think of the marital neurosis as the neurotic fit and the way the infantile neurosis is played out in the here and now. That way of thinking expands my understanding of the analysand and helps me anticipate extra-analytic impasses and split-off transferences (Graller et al., 2001).

The marital neurosis unfolds, or emerges, most clearly in analytically oriented marital psychotherapy, not necessarily in psychoanalysis. It is important not to argue about the dominant therapeutic or technical modality; if so, we miss the *basics* of how unconscious factors operate in marriage and later in the family. In its simplest form a triangle exists. How that triangle functions over time (through developmental phases, through aging and maturation, and through the traumas of our complicated society) can be understood transferentially (transference as the frame of reference) in psychoanalytic terms. It *is* appropriate to describe an oedipal family as one who has an oedipal child. This mere fact has the *potential* of reviving oedipal themes of parents' childhood experiences—repeating some unconscious neurotic patterns reflecting each spouse's unresolved oedipal issues. As couples lay down the new track of their child's life experiences, one hopes they will strive to give their children the healthiest of their nonneurotic affect and behavior. Awareness of one's neurotic tendencies, vulnerabilities, and childhood traumas allows for the optimal condition for understanding rather than acting out one's marital or family neurosis.

Summary and Conclusion

As we begin the 21st century, it is humbling to think of how farsighted Freud was and how towering and tumultuous were the events that engulfed his vision. Just as each new discovery is an improvement on the past, it also becomes an important way station along a developmental line to the future. Freud's discoveries began that developmental line in modern times. Every discovery of his has been carefully studied; some have been modified, and many remain the same.

Those who study the family as a focus in the twenty-first century use a current model that understands that psychological growth and development is an active dynamic process *throughout* life. This is a fluid, evolving process moving along a developmental pathway influenced (a) mostly by the closest relationships (family, close friends, mentors, children); (b) by the conditions that surround us (affluence, poverty, illness, wartime); and (c) by the emotional relationship of the current cast of characters that become important to us at any given time.

The *marital neurosis* and how it evolves over time determines the nature of the triangle when a child arrives. It is unfortunate that Freud or one of his followers did not appreciate the neurotic behavior in parents and important intimates. If so, he could have turned his genius to a systematic theory for family members in marriage. That would have begun the developmental line of marital and family theory and applied psychoanalytic adaptation to *complement* psychoanalysis.

Because marital and family theory did not develop on a parallel track with psychoanalysis, many different schools or theories emerged in the second half of the 20th century. It would be optimal to bring marital and family theory closer or more integrated into psychoanalytic theory. In our American Psychoanalytic Association group, we have seen trends develop that highlight that integration. For example, it is not unusual to treat a couple in psychoanalytic couples therapy while one or both spouses are in individual therapy or psychoanalysis. These concurrent therapies address not only the individual spouse neurosis, but also the marital neurosis. Furthermore, it is becoming more common to find that a marital neurosis is a major resistance to psychoanalysis proper, so that the marital therapy becomes imperative to resolve the resistance or impasse (Graller et al., 2001). With acceptance of the marital neurosis as an entity to be diagnosed and treated, couples therapists more frequently refer spouses for analysis during or after couples therapy, and analysts refer more couples for marital therapy.

Individual analysis by separate analysts and the concurrent psychoanalytic marital therapists often can provide a positive treatment outcome. Several analysts in collaboration bring more creative and synthetic power to the understanding of the individual and marital dynamics.

It is hoped that we can transpose our evolving sophistication to widen our scope in this field by developing leaders, scholars, and clinicians, who can embrace an increasingly complex understanding of the various levels of marital and family struggle and suffering (individual, interpersonal, communal, and cultural). If that leadership can collaborate and combine their resources, they will be able to find successful treatment solutions to the current psychopathological trends in marriages and families.

References

Ackerman, N. W. (1958), *The Psychodynamics of Family Life.* New York: Basic Books.

Arieti, S. (1959), *American Handbook of Psychiatry.* New York: Basic Books.

Benedek, T. (1973), *Psychoanalytic Investigations: Selected Papers.* New York: Crown Publishing, pp. 226–254.

Boszormenyi-Nagy, I. & Urlich, D. N. (1981), Contextual family therapy. In: *Handbook of Family Therapy*, ed. A. Gurman & D. Kriskern. New York: Brunner/Mazel, pp. 159–186.

Bowen, M. (1978), *Family Therapy in Clinical Practice.* Northvale, NJ: Aronson.

Erlich, F. M., Zilbach, J. & Solomon, L. (1997), The transference field and communication among therapists. *J. Amer. Acad. Psychoanal.*, 24:675–690.

Framo, J. L. (1992), *Family of Origin Therapy: An Intergenerational Approach.* New York: Brunner/Mazel.

Freud, S. (1917), Introductory lectures on psychoanalysis: Part III. *Standard Edition*, 16:243–464. London: Hogarth Press, 1963.

Graller, J. (1981), Adjunctive marital therapy: A possible solution to the split transference problem. *The Annual of Psychoanalysis*, 9:175–187. New York: International Universities Press.

———— Nielsen, A., Garber, B., Davison, L. G., Gable, L. & Seidenberg, H. (2001), Concurrent therapies: A model for collaboration between psychoanalysts and other therapists. *J. Amer. Psychoanal. Assn.,* 49:587–606.

Lansky, M. & Morrison, A. (1997), *The Widening Scope of Shame.* Hillsdale, NJ: The Analytic Press.

Paul, N. L. & Paul, B. B. (1975), *A Marital Puzzle: Transgenerational Analysis in Marital Counseling.* New York: W. W. Norton.

Pinsof, B. (1995), *Integrative Problem-Centered Therapy.* New York: Basic Books.

Sander, F. (1979), *Individual and Family Therapy.* New York: Aronson.

Scharff, D. E. & Scharff, J. (1991), *Object Relations Family Therapy.* Northvale, NJ: Aronson.

Wachtel, P. L. (1977), *Psychoanalysis, Behavior Therapy, and the Relational World.* Washington, DC: American Psychological Association.

Wolman, B. (1996), *Encyclopedia of Psychiatry, Psychology and Psychoanalysis.* New York: Henry Holt, pp. 584–589.

American Women Psychoanalysts 1911–1941

NELLIE L. THOMPSON

Many gifted and unusual women have been drawn to psychoanalysis. Indeed it can be argued that this fact constitutes one of the most significant elements of Freud's intellectual legacy: the creation of a theory and therapy that afforded women, as theorists and therapists, opportunities to undertake meaningful work among whose satisfactions was the knowledge that their theoretical and clinical investigations continually reshaped and refined psychoanalysis (Thompson, 1987). The contributions and lives of many first- and second-generation European women analysts—among them Lou Andreas-Salomé, Sabina Spielrein, Marie Bonaparte, Helene Deutsch, Anna Freud, Karen Horney, Melanie Klein, and Joan Riviere—have been the subject of both scholarly and popular interest.[1] By contrast, the lives and careers of American women analysts are not as well known or appreciated. This essay represents an initial contribution to rectifying this neglect by sketching in broad strokes a portrait of the 58 American women who became psychoanalysts between 1911 and 1941. A consideration of their institutional, clinical, and theoretical contributions will both encourage an appreciation of their individual achievements and demonstrate that psychoanalysis offered a wide range of women, with distinctive temperaments, interests, and talents, an opportunity to pursue gratifying work. Individual portraits encompassing the personal histories and careers of Helen Ross, Martha Wolfenstein, Elizabeth Zetzel, and Phyllis Greenacre illustrate this last point.

In the 30-year period from 1911 to 1941, there are three distinct, if overlapping, stages in the development of psychoanalysis in the United States. During

---

An early version of this essay was presented at the Western regional Psychoanalytic Conference on Psychoanalysis and Its Influence on 20th Century Culture, Skirball Cultural Center, Los Angeles, CA, April 7–9, 2000.

[1] See, for example, Livingstone (1984); Carotenuto (1982); Kerr (1993); Bertin (1982); Roazen (1985); Young-Bruehl (1988); Quinn (1987); Grosskurth (1986); Segal (1980); Hughes (1991); and Appignanesi and Forrester (1992).

the first period, 1911 to 1919, psychoanalytic societies are established in New York; Washington, DC; and Boston, and the American Psychoanalytic Association is founded. The second period, between 1920 and 1932, was one of reorganization for the societies, whose activities had been disrupted by the First World War. During these years American societies looked to Europe for organizational guidance, and many analysts traveled to Vienna, Berlin, London, and Budapest for personal analysis and training. The third phase, the years 1932 to 1941, heralded significant changes: American societies established their own training institutes and declared their independence from the standards of the International Psychoanalytical Association. Parallel with these events, there was a growing influx of emigré analysts to the United States. The outbreak of World War II interrupted these developments, and my survey ends at this point.

A Collective Portrait

During the years between 1911 and 1941, 58 American women joined the psychoanalytic movement. The majority, 51 out of 58, became psychoanalysts after 1920. By and large they were drawn to psychoanalysis in the mid-to-late 1920s and early 1930s. A significant number, 27 of the 58, received all or part of their psychoanalytic training abroad in Vienna, Berlin, Budapest, or London.

The careers of some of these individuals are very well documented, whereas for others only broad outlines of their careers are known. For the majority (48 of 58), it was possible to collect basic biographical and professional data. All but five had medical degrees, not a surprising finding given the medical requirement of American societies. Women psychoanalysts graduated from the top or very good medical schools, including Johns Hopkins, Rush in Chicago, Cornell, Columbia, Tufts, Stanford, and the Women's Medical College of Pennsylvania; and several attended medical school in London, Vienna, and Geneva.

Geographically the majority grew up in the Midwest or along the East Coast; a small number came from Colorado and California. Two were from Canada, and the families of two migrated from Russia when they were very young children. Socially their backgrounds are equally varied. Some women came from wealthy, privileged backgrounds, notably Dorothy Burlingham, Ruth Mack Brunswick, Viola Bernard, Muriel Gardiner, Edith B. Jackson, Mary O'Neil Hawkins, and Bettina Warburg. Equally some came from families that struggled to maintain themselves. These individuals, among them Helen Ross, Lucile Dooley, and Lillian Malcove, supported themselves from an early age.

The seven American women who became psychoanalysts before 1920 are an eclectic group. They include Lucile Dooley, Beatrice Hinkle, Josephine Jackson, Mary Isham, Marion Kenworthy, Mary O'Malley, and Edith Spaulding. Only two of them, Marion Kenworthy and Lucile Dooley, were to play prominent roles in the development of American psychoanalysis. Kenworthy's multifaceted career defies compression, but she is remembered today for her work training social workers and as the first woman president of the American Psychoanalytic Association. Dooley grew up in a deeply religious family in Tennessee and Kentucky and worked as a missionary school teacher in the South and for a short while in Japan before developing an interest in psychology. At the urging of L. Pierce Clark, she attended the 1909 Clark Conference and heard Freud deliver his famous lectures. After finishing medical school at Johns Hopkins, she traveled to Vienna in 1930 where she underwent an analysis with Ruth Mack Brunswick. Her experiences in Europe had a deep impact on her, both emotionally and intellectually, and upon her return to Washington, DC she became a leading training analyst in the Washington Psychoanalytic Society (Burton, 1998).

Beatrice Hinkle and Josephine Jackson, respectively, the first and second women members of the New York Psychoanalytic Society, pursued successful careers outside the psychoanalytic mainstream. Hinkle was born in 1875 in San Francisco, where she became the first woman public health doctor in the United States. During her tenure the city was struck by bubonic plague and she was impressed by how differently people responded to the disease. She began to practice suggestion, at the time a popular form of psychotherapy, and in 1905 she moved to New York. Hinkle's interest in psychoanalysis prompted her to travel to Europe. She attended the 1911 Weimar Congress and began an analysis with Jung. She returned to New York, joined the New York Psychoanalytic Society in 1911, but soon returned to Europe. By 1915 she was back in New York and reapplied to the New York Psychoanalytic Society, but was blackballed by four members, probably because of her Jungian sympathies. Hinkle's major work was *The Recreating of the Individual* (1923) where she developed her ideas on psychological types. Critical of Freud, she linked the psychological conflicts of women to their social and cultural position. Hinkle was also part of the New York feminist network, Heterodoxy, so named because the only requirement for membership was that a woman hold nonorthodox views on the position of women and social issues (Wittenstein, 1998). For many years Hinkle ran a small sanatorium, Smokey Hollow Lodge, in Connecticut. This establishment was memorialized by Nancy Hale (1957), a former patient of Hinkle's in her novel, *Heaven and Hardpan Farm*. Gently sardonic, the novel describes an establishment where extroverts are housed on one floor and introverts on another. Hinkle was one of the founders of the New York Jungian Institute in the 1930s and continued to play an important role in its activities until her death in 1953.

In 1913 Josephine Jackson was elected the second woman member of the New York Psychoanalytic Society. She is an intriguing figure because although she remained a member for nearly 20 years, she only attended one meeting of the society, and her name is virtually absent from accounts of the history of the early psychoanalytic movement in the United States (Thompson, 1998). In 1903 Jackson became the first woman to graduate from Rush Medical College of the University of Chicago. She moved to Pasadena, California, in 1904, and it was there that she began her career as a psychotherapist and psychoanalyst. It is likely that her interest in psychoanalysis developed before her move to California because two institutions she was associated with, Northwestern University Medical School and Rush Medical College, employed or trained several neurologists who were seriously interested in Freud's work.

Jackson built a thriving psychotherapy practice in Pasadena, and her establishment was described as a kind of psychotherapeutic boardinghouse. Not content to confine herself to presiding over this milieu, she also wrote books and articles and lectured, and in the late 1920s she published a newspaper column, *Guiding Your Life*. Jackson's books, written in the style of primers, make it easy to see why she was described by a colleague as a popular and gifted lecturer. Her first book was charmingly titled *Outwitting Our Nerves* (1921), although the title of her second, *Guiding Your Life* (1937), conveys a more accurate sense of the mixture of sympathetic listening and reeducation that inform her therapeutic approach. Jackson's appeal as a writer is confirmed by the sales figures for the first book, which reportedly sold 100,000 copies, a truly staggering figure when compared to William A. White's *Mechanisms of Character Formation* (1916) which sold 3810 copies, and A.A. Brill's *Psychoanalysis: Its Theories and Application* (1912) whose sales reached 8750 copies (Hale, 1971). In a curious twist of fate *Outwitting Our Nerves* played a minor role in the life of the distinguished writer V. S. Naipaul. His father in Trinidad, in an attempt to lift Naipaul's spirits when he was depressed and living alone in London in the early 1950s, sent him Jackson's book.

The careers of the women who became psychoanalysts after 1920 coincide with the institutionalization of American psychoanalysis. It is natural, therefore, to ask to what roles the women played in the institutional development. Nathan G. Hale Jr., in *The Rise and Crisis of Psychoanalysis in the United States* (1995), devotes a chapter to those young Americans who sought training in Europe in the 1920s and 1930s and then returned home to wrest power from a generation of less well-trained older figures. He emphasizes, correctly I think, the element of generational conflict in the struggle to realize more rigorous training standards and to tighten the standards for selecting candidates. But all the examples he cites are men, notably Ives Hendricks in Boston and Lawrence Kubie and Bertram Lewin in New York. It is one thing to insist on higher standards, but another to design and implement criteria for realizing these standards. Many women, among them Sara Bonnett, Marie Briehl, Lydia Dawes, Joan Fleming, Phyllis Greenacre, Susanna Haigh, Lillian Malcove, May Romm, Helen Ross, Helen Tartakoff, Lucia Tower, and Elizabeth Zetzel, who held positions as training analysts, supervisors, and teachers, played important roles on educational and curriculum committees in transforming the selection and education of candidates during the 1940s and 1950s. At the local level, women also held various offices in societies and institutes, including ten who served as president of either their society or institute. On the national level, however, only one woman from this group (Marion Kenworthy) became president of the American Psychoanalytic Association, and only two (Joan Fleming and Sara Bonnett) chaired the Association's Board of Professional Standards. Although many women analysts wrote influential papers and published regularly, they were underrepresented on the editorial boards of the three major American journals *(The Psychoanalytic Quarterly, The Psychoanalytic Study of the Child,* and *The Journal of the American Psychoanalytic Association).* Three women—Phyllis Greenacre, Edith Jackson, and Ruth Mack Brunswick—served on the editorial board of *The Psychoanalytic Study of the Child* from its inception in 1945. Ruth Mack Brunswick was also on the board of *The Psychoanalytic Quarterly*, and Greenacre and Helen Vincent McLean served on the editorial board of *The Journal of the American Psychoanalytic Association* in the late 1950s. This underrepresentation remains to be explained.

Although the institutional influence and role of women analysts within the American psychoanalytic movement has been insufficiently explored, their stature outside psychoanalysis was considerable. For example, women analysts headed child guidance clinics in hospitals or social agencies (Florence Clothier, Eleanor Pavenstedt, Marian Putnam, Helen Ross), held hospital or university teaching positions (Lydia Dawes, Margaret W. Gerard, Edith Jackson), and acted as long-term consultants to clinics and social service agencies (Viola Bernard, Muriel Gardiner, Margaret W. Gerard, Marion Kenworthy, Margaret Powers). Thus we misread their power and influence if we restrict ourselves to considering only the psychoanalytic offices they held.

It is widely acknowledged in both oral tradition and various written accounts that women analysts were held in high repute for their clinical skills and valued as supervisors and teachers. Thus a woman analyst may have never held a position beyond that of training analyst, or even have written very much, yet have an immense reputation within the field. Lillian Malcove and Grace Abbate, members of the New York Psychoanalytic Society, and Helen Tartakoff of the Boston Psychoanalytic Society are excellent examples of this phenomenon. The fact that this kind of influence is difficult to measure should not deter us from devising ways to read the record for it. Of equal interest is the conception women held of psychoanalysis as a theory and technique. The question here is: What exactly did they see themselves as preserving, distilling, and extending in their roles as teachers and supervisors?

Setting aside the complexities that arise when trying to reconstruct the institutional roles of women analysts, it is possible to delineate their intellectual achievements and in so doing to appreciate the remarkable and diverse nature of the careers that women psychoanalysts created for themselves. In the rest of this essay, the careers of four individuals with very different personal histories and intellectual gifts illustrate how women forged distinctive and fulfilling careers both as clinicians and psychoanalytic writers. These individuals are Helen Ross, Martha Wolfenstein, Elizabeth Zetzel, and Phyllis Greenacre.

Four Careers

Helen Ross

Helen Ross (1890–1978), one of the few American lay analysts, was for many years the administrative director of the Chicago Psychoanalytic Institute. She is also remembered as the coauthor, with Bert Lewin, of *Psychoanalytic Education in the United States* (1960). Ross was born in Missouri in 1890, one of seven children in a family that valued education. Her older brother supported her college education, and after her own graduation in 1911, she worked for five years as a school teacher to enable her younger siblings to continue their education. During this period she augmented her income by teaching English to immigrants in a Jewish settlement night school in Kansas City. She writes that under the tutelage of Jacob Billikopf she learned a great deal about social problems, and traced her later interest in social work to this experience (Ross, 1945). In 1916 she began graduate work in sociology and economics at Bryn Mawr and the following year was awarded the Susan B. Anthony Memorial Fellowship. She gave up her graduate studies, however, at the urging of Pauline Goldmark, one of the famous Goldmark sisters, whose sister Alice was married to Supreme Court Justice Louis Brandeis, to accept a job as a field agent for the U.S. Railroad Administration, whose women's division was headed by Pauline Goldmark. For two years she traveled all over the United States, investigating the working conditions of women working on the railroads and, she emphasized in a memoir, making sure they were getting equal pay for equal work. In 1920 she went to London to study at the London School of Economics. Beginning in 1914 she and an older sister had established a summer camp for girls in Michigan, and she writes that the constant contact with "the everyday problems of normal children" sharpened her interest in human behavior and made her eager to deepen her understanding of personality development. This led her to an interest in psychoanalysis, and in 1929, at the urging of Franz Alexander who had recently arrived in Chicago, she went to Vienna. There she was analyzed by Helene Deutsch and began a lifelong friendship and collaboration with Anna Freud. After returning to Chicago in 1934, she began a private practice and acted as a consultant to a number of social agencies. For many years she also wrote a newspaper column, *About Our Children,* for the *Chicago Sun-Times.* Autobiographical fragments she left behind and the recollections of colleagues and friends after her death leave the vivid impression of an adventurous woman, a doer in every sense of the word, whose analytic career was a platform for conveying in clear and intelligent language the insights of psychoanalysis to teachers, social workers, and parents. Her curiosity and social conscience took her from Missouri and Kansas to Bryn Mawr and field work, insuring that working women were being treated fairly on the railroads. From there she went to London and Vienna, where she found her vocation in one of the most vibrant intellectual movements of the twentieth century.

Martha Wolfenstein

Martha Wolfenstein (1911–1976), also a lay analyst, earned an M.A. in psychology and a Ph.D. in aesthetics from Columbia University. Unlike Ross, she was not a member of a society belonging to the American Psychoanalytic Association, but nonetheless was a widely admired teacher and supervisor in New York. Wolfenstein wrote three classic essays on childhood bereavement: "How Is Mourning Possible?" (1966a); "Loss, Rage, and Repetition" (1969); and "The Image of the Lost Parent"(1973). Her mother died when she was a child, and there is a history of parental (maternal) loss extending back several generations in her family. Ellen Handler Spitz, the psychoanalytically trained art historian, has written insightfully about this history and its role in Wolfenstein's work, and in particular how it shaped her study of the Belgium painter René Magritte (Spitz, 1985, 1998). Wolfenstein also wrote a powerful study, "Goya's Dining Room" (1966b). In explicating the psychological fantasies revealed in Goya's paintings, she argues that for this artist the loss of his hearing was linked to the earlier losses, in their infancy, of all but one of his five children. Themes of grief, rage, and sexual guilt are linked to the horrifying images that characterize the paintings that Goya painted after his illness in 1792.

Less well known, but deserving of wider appreciation, are Wolfenstein's books on film (Wolfenstein and Leites, 1950), children's humor (1954), and catastrophic events (1957). She also wrote a group of less well known essays whose subjects become the prism for illuminating the origins and vicissitudes of cultural values and attitudes. Two of these essays are especially notable because they exemplify how psychoanalytically informed observation can illuminate the mutually reinforcing bonds of individual experience and cultural values. The first essay explores the behavior of parents and children in the park and the second scrutinizes government publications on child care.

The first, "French Parents Take Their Children to the Park" (1954), followed two trips to Paris that Wolfenstein made in 1947 and 1953 as a member of the Columbia University Project Research in Contemporary Cultures which was led by the anthropologists Ruth Benedict and Margaret Mead. She begins by noting that in the park French children do not leave their parents to play with other children in a communal area. French parents do not appear eager to have their children play with others, "showing little of the usual eagerness of American parents that their children should make friends and be a success with their age mates" (1954, p. 100). French children quickly learn that displays of physical aggression are not permissible, and verbal disputes are substituted.

These observations lead to a broader and quite far-reaching analysis. For the French, childhood and adulthood are two very distinct conditions. One consequence is that the emotions of the child do not seem very serious, and French adults are likely to be detached in the face of the child's distress (p. 111). Americans, by contrast, do not recognize a sharp cleavage between childhood and adulthood. For example, to be able to play with children is a highly valued capacity. In France, childhood is a long and difficult preparation for adult life and in particular schoolchildren are subjected to the hard regime preparatory to taking the dreaded *bachot*, a rite of passage to which youth are subjected by their elders. Wolfenstein writes that the relation between childhood and adulthood is almost the complete opposite in the two cultures. In America, childhood is regarded as very nearly an ideal time, an end in itself; adults feel nostalgic for their childhood. Adulthood is a ceaseless round of work and getting ahead, and the enjoyment of immediate sensuous pleasures is nearly lacking. With the French, it seems to be the other way around. It is in adulthood that the possibility of living in the moment is achieved; sensuous pleasures are an end in themselves. Concern with such pleasures and ingenuity in achieving them are persistent themes of adult life (p. 116).

"Fun Morality: An Analysis of Recent American Child-Training Literature" is based on Wolfenstein's (1951) close reading of publications of the U.S. Department of Labor Children's Bureau, in particular, the Infant Care Bulletins of three periods: 1914–1921, 1929–1938, and 1942–1945. A close examination of bulletins published in 1914 and the early 1940s leads to an account of the emergence of "fun morality." Between 1914 and the early 1940s, the conception of the child's basic impulses undergoes a startling transformation. In 1914 the infant is depicted as being endowed with dangerous, strong impulses manifested in autoerotic, masturbatory, and thumb-sucking behavior. The child fiercely rebels if these impulses are interfered with, and the mother must be ceaselessly vigilant against the child's sinful nature. By the early 1940s, in contrast, the baby has been transformed into a creature of almost complete harmlessness. The intense and concentrated impulses of the past have disappeared, and have become diffuse and moderate in character. The baby's play with him or herself is now seen as expressing interest in exploring his or her world.

In this recent period, Wolfenstein (1951) finds parenthood has become a major source of enjoyment for both parents. "The parents are promised that having children will keep them together, keep them young, and give them fun and happiness" (p. 173). Enjoyment, happiness, and fun now permeate all activities with the child. The message is clear: parents ought to enjoy their children. Wolfenstein cogently remarks that:

> When a mother is told that most mothers enjoy nursing, she may wonder what is wrong with her in case she does not. Her self-evaluation can no longer be based entirely on whether she is doing the right and necessary things but becomes involved with nuances of feeling which are not under voluntary control. Fun has become not only permissible but required, and this requirement has a special quality different from the obligations of the older morality [pp. 173–174].

Wolfenstein links this changing conception of human impulses, which is accompanied by an altered evaluation of play and fun, as signaling a profound moral transformation. Instead of being suspect, if not taboo, fun has become obligatory. Instead of feeling guilty of having too much fun, one is inclined to feel ashamed if one does not have enough of it. The boundaries between work and play are being increasingly breached by this changing conception of the nature of the self.

Elizabeth Zetzel

Elizabeth Zetzel (1907–1970) was born in New York but received her medical education at the University of London. She began her analytic training in the 1930s at the British Psychoanalytic Society where her analyst was Ernest Jones. In a short memoir describing the years between 1936 and 1938, Zetzel (1969) recalled with pleasure her exposure to the work of Melanie Klein and her followers, Joan Riviere and Susan Isaacs. She credits D. W. Winnicott, however, with most influencing her subsequent work because he was "fully alive to the importance of the real mother-child relationship. . . . My first awareness of the importance of early object relations was attributable to my opportunity to work in his Clinic at Paddington Green Hospital" (p. 718).

Zetzel returned to the United States in 1949 and became a member of the Boston Psychoanalytic Society, where she was a leading training analyst and teacher. She was a prolific writer and her essays include contributions to psychoanalytic technique—her name is practically synonymous with the term "therapeutic alliance"—and to the psychodynamics of hysteria and depression. But equally as important as her original contributions to the psychoanalytic literature was her sympathetic interest in the work of Melanie Klein. In an astute and generous obituary written after Klein's death, Zetzel (1961) decried the fact that many contemporary analysts still remain unfamiliar with Klein's work:

> [F]ailure to acknowledge her contribution is so prevalent that papers on infantile development and early responses to separation and loss typically omit

detailed reference to her concept of the depressive position, to her recognition of the positive functions of early anxiety, and to her formulations concerning the role of symbol formation in the learning process [p. 422].

At the same time, Zetzel was deeply skeptical of the theoretical reconstructions that Klein posited in her writings. She also chided Klein and her followers for failing to acknowledge the work of other analysts, notably Anna Freud, Willi Hoffer, Rene Spitz, Phyllis Greenacre, and Ernst Kris, whose findings on early psychic development were convergent with their discoveries.

Zetzel's (1961) efforts to rectify the situation she described in her obituary of Melanie Klein began with her return to the United States. At a meeting of the American Psychoanalytic Association, Zetzel (1951) presented a paper urging her American colleagues to recognize the value of Klein's clinical findings. In 1954 Edith Jacobson invited Zetzel to present a paper to the New York Psychoanalytic Society on Klein's work.[2] In February 1955 Zetzel presented the paper, "An Approach to the Relation between Concept and Content in Psychoanalytic Theory (with special reference to the work of Melanie Klein and her followers)," which was discussed by Heinz Hartmann, Rudolph Loewenstein, Bertram Lewin, Phyllis Greenacre, and Margaret Mahler. The discussants were knowledgeable about Klein's clinical findings, but skeptical of her theorizing. Phyllis Greenacre's comments alluded to conversations she had had with Zetzel about Klein's findings and exhibited a serious interest in them.

Zetzel's advocacy of Klein's work has significant implications for the development of psychoanalytic theory in the United States. Conventionally psychoanalytic theory in America in the 1950s is portrayed as dominated by the variant of theory called ego psychology. But Zetzel's writings on Klein and her followers, and her extended contacts with other analysts interested in preoedipal development, notably Edith Jacobson and Phyllis Greenacre, suggest a more fluid and complex state of affairs. In other words, among a group of influential psychoanalytic thinkers, there was a sophisticated awareness of Klein's work and a recognition that her clinical discoveries should be considered in their own work.

Phyllis Greenacre

Phyllis Greenacre (1894–1989) was born in Chicago and after finishing medical school in 1916 moved to Baltimore where she was an intern and resident at the

---

[2] In June 1954, Jacobson, then president of the New York Psychoanalytic Society, wrote to Zetzel: "Do you still remember our nice little chat during the last midwinter meeting in New York? If you do, you may also remember that we both agreed on the necessity of informing our young American colleagues about Melanie Klein's work. . . . Do you think you could read a paper pertinent to the Kleinian ideas?" (Jacobson, 1954).

Henry Phipps Clinic at The Johns Hopkins Hospital under the great Swiss-American psychiatrist Adolf Meyer. In the late 1920s, she moved to New York and in 1932 began psychoanalytic training at the New York Psychoanalytic Institute. Among American analysts whose careers were established in the 1930s and 1940s only one other, that of Bertram Lewin, matches hers in terms of clinical and theoretical creativity. Greenacre's essays were engaging, stimulating, and insightful when first written, and remain so. Particularly noteworthy are her studies of creativity, fetishism, the creative individual, and infant development. Two aspects of her work and career deserve serious study: her clinical researches and the emergence of her long preoccupation with creativity and the creative individual. In turn, they each speak to a larger question in the history of psychoanalysis that has been unjustly neglected: How do we account for creative theoretical innovation that is not characterized by dissent and schism?

Greenacre's first psychoanalytic essay, "The Predisposition to Anxiety" (1941), and a companion paper, "The Biological Economy of Birth" (1945) were not well received at the time because they were regarded by many as excessively speculative, and were criticized for their exploration of the preverbal stages of infancy. Undeterred by this reception Greenacre continued to explore with imagination and empathy the inextricably linked physical and psychological maturational vicissitudes of the infant and young child. Her clinical approach rested upon her conviction of the importance of reconstruction and screen memories in analysis. She reported (1971) that she watched patients as devotedly as she listened to them because nonverbal communications—weeping, sweating, muscle cramps, blushing, sudden hoarseness—constitute the body's reporting in its own language. In her view such nonverbal communications may be representative of experiences which have never heretofore been verbalized, or they may be representations of childhood experiences which were at such an emotional pitch as to preclude clear verbalized thinking, that is, communication with the self, even when speech had been reasonably established (p. xxiv). In a later defense of reconstruction and screen memories in analytic work, Greenacre (1980) cited Freud's precepts regarding their importance in clinical psychoanalysis. She notes that he wrote an explicit statement regarding the efficacy of reconstruction in 1938 shortly before his death. She also makes an interesting observation on why reconstruction fell out of favor for so many years. She observes that "the prolonged period of mourning for a lost leader" was accompanied by an "increased clinging to those metapsychological perspectives which had been his last gift before the war had forced emigration." She goes on to write that an apparent expansion in the intellectual framework of analysis was accompanied by a somewhat reactionary tightening in the teaching of technique. "The precise interpretation began to takes the place of reconstructive interest" (p. 39).

It is clear from Greenacre's writings that she felt free to explore not only Freud's legacy but also the work of other analysts, for example, the writings of

Willi Hoffer, Heinz Hartmann, Ernst Kris, and D. W. Winnicott. This openness to the thinking of others, while at the same time pursuing her own interests, is one of the most attractive features of her work. Such responsiveness also served to continually renew her own creativity.

In 1953 there is an important shift in Greenacre's work with the publication of "Certain Relationships between Fetishism and the Faulty Development of the Body Image." Henceforth she returns again and again to explorations of the problems of fetishism, early ego development, and the creative individual. Greenacre's observations that fetishism and allied conditions were frequently accompanied by feelings of change in body size, together with a tendency to individualize and personalize different body parts, was accompanied by an awareness that such descriptions were frequently found in fairy tales and folklore, unusually so in Lewis Carroll's Alice books and in Jonathan Swift's *Gulliver's Travels*. These insights led to her 1955 book, *Swift and Carroll*, a rich and absorbing biographical study of the two men in relation to their preoccupation with and insight into these particular phenomena. This book remains an exemplary and outstanding work of applied analysis. In studying writers and artists for what their lives and creations may reveal about complex clinical phenomena, Greenacre was continuing a rich line of psychoanalytic research begun by Freud (1910) with his study of Leonardo da Vinci.

In 1957 Greenacre published her first theoretical essay on creativity, "The Childhood of the Artist: Libidinal Phase Development and Giftedness." She described the (potentially) gifted infant as unusually responsive to both external and internal stimuli; possessing a capacity to see and capture relationships; and having an enhanced capacity for symbolization and continual access to primary process thinking. This essay contains her famous characterization of the gifted individual as engaged in a "love affair with the world." It should perhaps be noted that citations of this phrase often omit her observation that this love affair may also present itself conversely as a colossal disappointment in the world (p. 490). Nonetheless Greenacre believed that "for the potentially gifted infant the primary object which stimulates certain sensory responses to it is invested with a greater field of related experiences than would be true for the infant of lesser endowment" (pp. 489–490). This love affair with the world has often been considered to reflect narcissism, whereas in Greenacre's view it is really more of a collective relationship. In this connection she notes that gifted children may solve their oedipal problems less decisively than others. Thus she stressed the importance of the family romance in creative individuals, a theme elaborated in "The Family Romance of the Artist" (1958), and in her book, *The Quest for the Father: A Study of the Darwin-Butler Controversy, as a Contribution to the Understanding of the Creative Individual* (1963).

Two other important points Greenacre makes in her 1957 essay concern the nature of the artistic creation and the role of aggression. Concerning the former Greenacre (1957) observes:

It seems unlikely that the artistic performance or creative product is ever undertaken purely for the gratification of the self, but . . . there is always some fantasy of a collective audience or recipient. . . . The artistic product has rather universally the character of a love gift, to be brought as near perfection as possible and to be presented with pride and misgiving [p. 490].

She also proposed a theory of aggression as *initially* a manifestation of a positive developmental force, a positive response by the infant to the vicissitudes of its earliest experiences, both frustrating and gratifying.

What inspired this long and rich phase of Greenacre's work, which begins with her 1953 essay, when she was 59 and had already published many notable contributions? She directly links this phase of her work to her meeting Ernst Kris in 1941. Greenacre (1971) later recalled that she was "soon launched into a discussion concerning *Alice in Wonderland*. It was a little eerie as I found myself stating, with a lively interest, observations and opinions that I did not know I had. It was Kris's great talent to stimulate and liberate people in this way" (p. xxvii). In "The Family Romance of the Artist," written in Kris's memory, Greenacre (1958) elaborated on the importance of their meeting.

The subject of creativity had not previously been in the arena of my clinical research interests and I had never expected to tackle it. Perhaps I was intimidated by a latent interest which might become too engrossing. At any rate, it was through the stimulation—even the persistent prodding—of the late Ernst Kris that my concern with the subject was brought into the daylight. Now I am grateful for this gift—surprising to me at the time and hesitatingly accepted [p. 505].

Her relationship with Kris is a valuable reminder that friendships among and between analysts can have an enormous impact on the emergence of new developments. Friends and colleagues and, by extension, societies may foment and sustain an environment (or boundaries) within which an individual's curiosity and imagination can flourish. But with the exception of Freud's relationships with Fliess, Ferenczi, and perhaps Abraham, their role has perhaps not been sufficiently appreciated or examined. Support and acceptance were important to Greenacre, who was very aware of herself as working alone.

Greenacre notes that the creative product is always intended for a particular recipient or collective audience. Perhaps if we can understand what response Greenacre sought to evoke we might better appreciate why some analysts arouse such excitement and insight in their readers. In other words an analyst's style, the capacity to use written or oral language to help the reader experience a new and meaningful insight, seems to be an important dimension of an analyst's creativity.

In addition, Greenacre's work and career is especially relevant to an important, but neglected, problem that confronts historians of psychoanalysis, the question of how to explain creative advance in theory and technique that does not follow from or end in schism. The history of innovation in psychoanalysis is all too often written as if it is synonymous with its recurring schisms (Thompson, 1995). Schisms can foster creativity, but they can also have negative consequences, especially when new groups re-create the rigidity they claim to be rebelling against or create a new one. In addition, many emergent creative and innovative ideas do not rise out of a context of institutional dissent, and their genesis requires as much attention and explanation as those that arise during schism. If the history of psychoanalysis focuses only on schisms as the basis of creativity, much is clearly lost. Phyllis Greenacre's work and career certainly illustrate this point. She is, however, only one member of an interesting and diverse group of analysts who managed to be creative and individualistic in their work and whose stimulus to creativity may have been of a similar order to hers. Such a group might include, for example, Bertram Lewin, Ella Freeman Sharpe, Martha Wolfenstein, D. W. Winnicott, and Marjorie Brierley. The history of psychoanalysis will remain incomplete, in my view, until the conditions that made their achievements possible are viewed as essential to our history as those that surround the recurrence of its schisms.

The work of Phyllis Greenacre, and the other analysts I have noted, offers us an opportunity to examine under what circumstances creative developments have occurred in psychoanalytic theory apart from periods of dissent and schism. In particular I would argue that there are two features of Greenacre's work and career that may be true for other figures like herself: a responsiveness to the ideas of others and a significant friendship that encourages and supports a latent interest.

In closing I want to make one observation about a tantalizing link between Greenacre's personal history and the nature of her psychoanalytic interests and the character of her writing. The latter is characterized by beautiful, evocative prose in the service of imaginative theoretical ideas, and sensitive, often tender, interpretation of clinical material. She uses language to create an atmosphere of intimacy that draws in the reader. This intimacy is perhaps a reflection of an archaic yearning or need to stimulate a response in her reader. The clarity of her writing is thrown into sharp relief by the unexpected appearance of words or phrases that underscore how excited and absorbed she is by her subject. Very often the subject is the intimate relationship between the physical and psychological maturational experiences of the infant and young child. As a young child, she wrote before she spoke. Apparently a speech impediment prevented her from speaking intelligibly before her sixth or seventh birthday, and she communicated by writing notes, having learned to read and write at the age of four (Kabcenell, 1990, p. 23). In her essay, "The Transitional Object and the Fetish with Special Reference to the Role of Illusion" (1970), she writes: "Speech is the great creation of each infant's life, and he leaves his individual stamp in many ways on its ultimate fullest achievement" (p. 349). Greenacre also, to our great and lasting benefit, left her individual stamp on the language and thought of psychoanalysis.

Conclusions

At the beginning of this essay I noted that psychoanalysis in America attracted a diverse group of richly talented women between 1911 and 1941. These women sought and exercised considerable influence and power within societies and institutes as teachers, supervisors, training analysts, and members of curriculum and educational committees. Psychoanalysis, as a theory and profession, afforded them work that was emotionally engrossing and intellectually deeply satisfying, and their clinical and theoretical publications enriched, modified, and extended psychoanalytic theory in important ways.

The brief sketches of the careers of Helen Ross, Martha Wolfenstein, Elisabeth Zetzel, and Phyllis Greenacre have illustrated the point that psychoanalysis, as a theory and profession, allowed them to make contributions that reflected their individual gifts. Thus, Helen Ross was an educator and administrator, who effectively reached out to the larger community through her newspaper column and her talks to parents, teachers, and child care workers. Martha Wolfenstein wrote on a sweeping range of cultural subjects with insight and sophistication, thereby demonstrating that applied analysis is a valuable part of the psychoanalytic canon. Elisabeth Zetzel's independence of mind supported her conviction that American analysts needed to heed Melanie Klein's clinical discoveries, and conversely her familiarity with American psychoanalytic thought enabled her to point out to Kleinians that they should be more receptive to the writings of American analysts that complemented their own findings. Finally, Phyllis Greenacre's brilliant originality of thought and expression is a testament to how psychoanalysis, as a theory and profession, could nurture and sustain individual creativity.

References

Appignanesi, L. & Forrester, J. (1992), *Freud's Women*. New York: Basic Books.

Bertin, C. (1982), *Marie Bonaparte*. New York: Harcourt Brace Jovanich.

Burton, K. (1998), Lucile Dooley, M.D. *Psychoanal. Rev.*, 85:51–73.

Carotenuto, A. (1982), *A Secret Symmetry: Sabina Spielrein between Jung and Freud*, trans. A. Pomerans, J. Shepley & K. Winston. New York: Pantheon Books.

Freud, S. (1910), Leonardo da Vinci and a memory of his childhood. *Standard Edition*, 10:59–137. London: Hogarth Press, 1957.

Greenacre, P. (1941), The predisposition to anxiety. In: *Trauma,Growth, and Personality*. New York: W. W. Norton, 1952, pp. 27–82.

———— (1945), The biological economy of birth. In: *Trauma, Growth, and Personality*. New York: W. W. Norton, 1952, pp. 3–26.

———— (1953), Certain relationships between fetishism and the faulty development of the body image. In: *Emotional Growth: Psychoanalytic Studies of the Gifted and a Great Variety of Other Individuals, Vol. I.* New York: International Universities Press, 1971, pp. 9–30.

———— (1955), *Swift and Carroll: A Psychoanalytic Study of Two Lives.* New York: International Universities Press.

———— (1957), The childhood of the artist: Libidinal phase development and giftedness. In: *Emotional Growth, Vol. II.* New York: International Universities Press, 1971, pp. 479–504.

———— (1958), The family romance of the artist. In: *Emotional Growth, Vol. II.* New York: International Universities Press, 1971, pp. 505–532.

———— (1963), *The Quest for the Father: A Study of the Darwin–Butler Controversy as a Contribution to the Understanding of the Creative Individual.* New York: International Universities Press.

———— (1970), The transitional object and the fetish: with special reference to the role of illusion. In: *Emotional Growth*, Vol. II. New York: International Universities Press, 1971, pp. 335–352.

———— (1971), Introduction. In: *Emotional Growth, Vol. I.* New York: International Universities Press, 1971, pp. xi–xxviii.

———— (1980), A historical sketch of the use and disuse of reconstruction. *Psychoanal. Study of the Child*, 35:35–40. New Haven, CT: Yale University Press.

Grosskurth, P. (1986), *Melanie Klein: Her World and Her Work.* New York: Knopf.

Hale, N. (1957), *Heaven and Hardpan Farm.* New York: Charles Scribner's Sons.

Hale, N. G., Jr. (1971), *Freud and the Americans; The Beginnings of Psychoanalysis in the United States, 1876–1917.* New York: Oxford University Press.

———— (1995), *The Rise and Crisis of Psychoanalysis in the United States: Freud and the Americans, 1917–1985.* New York: Oxford University Press.

Hinkle, B. (1923), *The Recreating of the Individual: A Study of Psychological Types and Their Relation to Psychoanalysis.* New York: Dodd, Mead.

Hughes, A., ed. (1991), *The Inner World and Joan Riviere, Collected Papers: 1920–1958.* London: Karnac Books.

Jacobson, E. (1954), An unpublished letter. In: Archives and Special Collections, A. A. Brill Library, The New York Psychoanalytic Institute, June 19.

Jackson, J. (1921), *Outwitting Our Nerves.* New York: Century.

———— (1937), *Guiding Your Life, with Psychology as a Key.* New York: D. Appleton-Century.

Kabcenell, R. (1990), Phyllis Greenacre: 1894–1989. *Amer. Psychoanal.*, 24:2.

Kerr, J. (1993), *A Most Dangerous Method—The Story of Jung, Freud, and Sabina Spielrein.* New York: Knopf.

Lewin, B. & Ross, H. (1960), *Psychoanalytic Education in the United States.* New York: W. W. Norton.

Livingstone, A. (1984), *Salome: Her Life and Work.* Mt. Kisco, NY: Moyer Bell.

Quinn, S. (1987), *A Mind of Her Own: The Life of Karen Horney.* New York: Summit.

Roazen, P. (1985), *Helene Deutsch.* Garden City, NY: Anchor Press/Doubleday.

Ross, H. (1945), An unpublished autobiographical memoir.

Segal, H. (1980), Melanie Klein. In: *Modern Masters,* ed. F. Kermode. New York: Viking Press.

Spitz, E. (1985), *Art and Psyche*. New Haven, CT: Yale University Press.
———— (1998), Martha Wolfenstein: Toward the severance of memory from hope. *Psychoanal. Rev.*, 85:105–115.
Thompson, N. (1987), Early women psychoanalysts. *Internat. Rev. Psycho-Anal.*, 14: 391–407.
———— (1995), Spaltungen in der psychoanalytischen bewegung Nordamerikas. In: *Spaltungen in der Geschichte der Psychoanalyse*, ed. H. Ludgers. Tubingen, Germany: Edition Diskord, pp. 205–218.
———— (1998), Josephine Jackson, M.D. *Psychoanal. Rev.*, 85:27–40.
Wittenstein, K. (1998), The feminist uses of psychoanalysis: Beatrice M. Hinkle and the foreshadowing of modern feminism in the United States. *J. Women's History*, 10: 38–62.
Wolfenstein, M. (1951), Fun morality: An analysis of recent American child-training literature. In: *Childhood in Contemporary Cultures*, ed. M. Mead & M. Wolfenstein. Chicago: University of Chicago Press, 1955, pp. 168–178.
———— (1954a), French parents take their children to the park. In: *Childhood in Contemporary Cultures*, ed. M. Mead & M. Wolfenstein. Chicago: University of Chicago Press, 1955, pp. 99–117.
———— (1954b), *Children's Humor*. Glencoe, IL: Free Press.
———— (1957), *Disaster*. Glencoe, IL: Free Press.
———— (1966a), How is mourning possible? *The Psychoanalytic Study of the Child*, 21:93–123. New Haven, CT: Yale University Press.
———— (1966b), Goya's dining room. *Psychoanal. Quart.*, 35:47–83.
———— (1969), Loss, rage, and repetition. *The Psychoanalytic Study of the Child*, 24:432–460. New Haven, CT: Yale University Press.
———— (1973), The image of the lost parent. *The Psychoanalytic Study of the Child*, 28:433–456. New Haven, CT: Yale University Press.
———— & Leites, N. (1950), *Movies*. Glencoe, IL: Free Press.
Young-Bruehl, E. (1988), *Anna Freud*. New York: Summit Books.
Zetzel, E. (1951), The depressive position. In: *Depressive Disorders*, ed. P. Greenacre. New York: International Universities Press, 1953, pp. 84–116.
———— (1955), An approach to the relation between concept and content in psychoanalytic theory: With special reference to the work of Melanie Klein and her followers. *The Psychoanalytic Study of the Child*, 11:99–121. New Haven, CT: Yale University Press, 1956.
———— (1961), Melanie Klein 1882–1960. *Psychoanal. Quart.*, 30:420–425.
———— (1969), 96 Gloucester Place: Some personal recollections. *Internat. J. Psycho-Anal.*, 50:717–719.

Childhood Sexuality after Freud: The Problem of Sex in Early Childhood Education

JOSEPH TOBIN

In this essay I discuss sense of three interrelated phenomena that in the past decade or so have swept through American early childhood education: (1) a "moral panic" about sexual abuse in preschools; (2) the prohibition of physical contact, both among children, and between children and their adult caretakers; and (3) the disappearance of psychoanalysis as a source of knowledge and a guide to good practice.

I sort out the causal links that tie these phenomena together. For readers who are psychoanalysts, one particular causal relation may tend to come to mind: Psychoanalysis for some reason fell from its position of influence in early childhood education, and once cut off from psychoanalytic knowledge as a source of rational thinking about sex, the field of early childhood education lost its bearings. This theory has the attractive features of being plausible, straightforward, and flattering to psychoanalysis. But I don't think it is true. Instead, drawing on Michel Foucault's "repressive hypothesis," I argue that the relationship between a rational, liberatory discourse such as psychoanalysis and such repressive practices as firing male teachers and prohibiting affectionate touch is much more complex, wrought, and paradoxical.

Before turning at the end of this essay to a discussion of the relationship that ties the decline of psychoanalysis to the rising hysteria over sexuality in preschool settings, I must first provide evidence of the phenomena. To do so I present two kinds of evidence, drawn from two studies I have conducted. The first is a review of 72 years of early childhood education textbooks, showing a decline in the influence of Freud and a shift in the presentation of sexual curiosity from a normal feature of childhood to a symptom of abuse. The second is a focus-group study of American early childhood educators' panicky responses to scenarios depicting sexuality in preschool settings.

Study One: The Disappearance of Psychoanalysis from Textbooks

To chart the rise and fall of psychoanalysis's fortunes in the field of American preschool education, I analyzed the contents of over 70 years of early childhood educational textbooks. My method was simple: I reviewed the tables of contents and the indexes and then the appropriate pages of all of the early childhood educational texts I could find in the Chicago Public Library's main branch, as well as at the University of Chicago's libraries. This search led me to 55 titles, ranging from 1927 through 1999. I will review this 72-year span of history by breaking it into three phases.

Phase one, which runs roughly from 1927 through 1940, is characterized by the explicit citation of psychoanalytic theory. Freud's new ideas are cited as a scientific source of knowledge, which nursery school educators should take into account as they grapple with the question of how best to deal with incidents of infantile sexuality. In books from this period, it is not uncommon to find direct quotes from *The New Introductory Lectures, Three Contributions to the Theory of Sex* and *A General Introduction to Psychoanalysis*. The main lesson early childhood educators of this era took from Freud is that repressive responses to young children's fledgling expressions of sexual curiosity are likely to produce negative developmental sequelae. For example, in her 1920 book *Nursery School Education*, Grace Owens writes:

> What numbers of children have their development impeded and their tempers spoiled by their mothers' over-anxiety about furniture and clothes and respectability! We are just beginning to realize, largely through the work of Jung and Freud and other psychoanalysts, how great is the danger of the repression of the instincts and appetites—the dynamic forces of the mind—and how appalling are the disasters that result from it. It has shown beyond all doubt that a powerful impulse or emotion may not cease to exist when it is denied expression. It may be driven into the unconscious and find for itself surreptitious and indirect modes of expression. . . . The truth seems to be that the repression of any innate impulse which is sufficiently powerful may be the source of mental and moral inefficiency [p. 6].

Later in her book, Owens adds: "What the nursery school teacher can do is to prevent unnatural repression of primitive impulses. . . . The morality of a civilized community must not be imposed on the child by the wholesale suppression of his natural instincts" (p. 53). In his 1923 book *The Preschool Child From the Standpoint of Public Hygiene and Education*, Arnold Gesell, though like many of his contemporaries unwilling to endorse psychoanalysis in toto, nevertheless acknowledges the indispensability of the psychoanalytic stance on early experience:

> It is unnecessary to accept uncritically the doctrine and interpretations of psychoanalysis, but we are compelled to recognize the justice of an emphasis upon infancy in any dynamic or behavioristic type of psychology. We must at least subscribe to such a conservative statement as the following one from the well-known British psychiatrist Dr. Richard Rows: "Of special importance also are the experiences of childhood. An unhappy home or unjust treatment as a child may warp the development of the personality, lead to a lack of self-confidence, to the predominance of one emotional tendency, and so prevent that balanced equilibrium which will allow a rapid and suitable emotional reaction such as we may consider normal." Rows himself illustrates the truth of this by describing the case of a mentally ill woman in whom "the germ of her serious breakdown thirty years later was laid in her fifth and sixth years." In somewhat the same strain, Freud has said: "The little human being is frequently a finished product in his fourth or fifth year and only reveals gradually in later years what has long been ready within him" [p. 119].

In other publications of this era, we find less explicit traces of psychoanalytic reasoning and less liberal stances toward masturbation and other forms of childhood sexuality. But even in the less progressive writings of this between-the-wars era, masturbation and sex play are not seen as dangerous antecedents of degeneracy, as they were in child-rearing manuals of the nineteenth century, nor as signs of abuse, as they would come to be in child development books of the 1990s. Instead, early childhood educators of this era tended to recommend a matter-of-fact approach to childhood masturbation and sexual curiosity, as we can see in excerpts from Josephine Foster and Marion Mattson's 1929 *Nursery School Procedure* and 1939 *Nursery School Education*:

> A habit which distresses the mother and which appears from time to time in some members of any group of children is that of handling the genitals. As a general thing, the behavior occurs only at nap or at bedtime and the cause seems in almost every case to have been the accidental discovery that the activity resulted in a pleasurable sensation. The problem is one which, like thumb-sucking, is usually best met by the substitution of some other form of activity [1929, p. 167].

> Let us answer the child's questions of sex so simply that he understands what we say, so truthfully that he will not have later to unlearn what we are telling him today, and so unemotionally that he will not put undue importance upon the information, and above all so that he will not fail to ask for further information when he needs it [1939, pp. 74–75].

In *Nursery School Education* (1939), by Olive Wheeler and Irene Earl, we find another example of a commonsense approach to children's sexual curiosity, combined with an indirect reference to the psychoanalytic notion that repression of sexuality in childhood is a primary cause of adult unhappiness:

> Active curiosity concerning birth and sex may arise in young children, and, if so, should not be repressed. Questions asked should be dealt with frankly, and without tension or embarrassment—just as other questions are answered at this stage. Most of the difficulties which arise later can be traced back to the irrational attitudes of adults, many of whom attempt to hide in the darkness of a primitive taboo all the matter relating to sex and the creativeness of life [p. 38].

In the second phase of this history, the post–World War II era, citations of Freud and psychoanalysis become more rare in early childhood education textbooks but a generally relaxed and progressive stance toward childhood sexuality continues. For example, Marjorie Green and Elizabeth Woods wrote in *A Nursery School Handbook for Teachers and Parents* (1948) "Remember, childish sex play in itself will not harm your child, but wrong attitudes on your part may warp his future attitudes, and seriously impair his social adjustment" (p. 109). In her *Nursery School Guide*, Rhoda Kellogg (1949) echoes psychoanalytic reasoning without citing Freud, as she refers to the connection between repression and anxiety and as she links infantile sexual curiosity to intellectuality:

> Because children are scolded and punished for wetting, soiling, and masturbating, they come to think that certain parts or areas of the body are "bad," and this becomes a source of anxiety. . . . The inability of the adult to deal with the child's sexuality makes the child feel there are some things he must not reveal to anyone. Thus masturbating becomes a clandestine affair, and all sex interest must be repressed as much as possible. Since all learning processes thrive upon the individual's curiosity, the repressive type of sex education may have a very unfavorable influence upon the child's capacity to learn anything [p. 107].

This presentation of psychoanalytic perspectives without, as we found in the 1920s and 1930s, the citation of Freud or other psychoanalytic authors, suggests that psychoanalytic theory in this era had become integrated into the everyday consciousness of early childhood educators.

In early childhood educational textbooks of the 1950s and early 1960s, the emphasis in discussions of childhood sexuality begins to shift to the topic of gender formation, as we can see in an excerpt from Katherine Read's *The Nursery School: A Human Relationships Laboratory* (1950):

> A girl may not notice sex differences the first time that she uses a toilet beside a boy; but when she does notice a difference, she will usually want to watch

boys frequently as they urinate. . . . She may comment and ask questions. If she does, she will be helped by the teacher's casual acceptance of her comments. It may help her to have the teacher verbalize in some way as, "Bill has a penis. He stands up at the toilet. Boys stand up and girls sit down there." Psychiatrists tell us that an important factor in later sex adjustment is the acceptance of one's sex. In this situation it is usually easier for the boys to feel acceptance because they possess a penis. Many times a girl will try to imitate the boy by attempting to stand—with not very satisfactory results! . . . Some girls may need help in feeling that being a girl is desirable. The teacher may remark, "Mothers sit down, too" [p. 101].

In a similar vein, in a 1956 book on *The Education of Young Children*, D. E. M. Gardner writes:

Interest and pride in their own bodies, especially in their genital organs, are very normal in healthy children at this age. In earlier times, when the tendency was not recognized, children often suffered acutely by being severely reprimanded or punished for displaying their own bodies or showing curiosity in other children's. . . . If children are inclined to over-stimulate each other they are best helped . . . by the provision of other interests and the unobtrusive directing of the child's attention to other interesting play, in much of which the healthy and normal tendency, for example, of the little boy to glory in his masculinity or the little girl to emulate her mother can be sublimated. But the teacher should not be over-anxious to distract the child every time such interests are shown and should recognize that one of the values of the Nursery School is that small boys and girls have a natural opportunity of finding out about and accepting the differences between the sexes [pp. 75–76].

The emphasis on clarifying rather than challenging gender differences distinguishes this writing of the 1950s from the gender equity emphasis that is found in early childhood textbooks from the 1970s onward. I would speculate that the general social conservativism and the absence of critiques of patriarchy that are characteristic of American psychoanalysis contributed in the last quarter century or so to psychoanalysis' loss of influence in early childhood education, which, as a field of women's work, has an affinity with theories emphasizing gender equality.

Psychoanalysis enjoyed a return as an explicit discourse in early childhood educational textbooks of the 1970s, although this time it was Erik Erikson rather than Freud who was most widely cited. Erikson's *Childhood and Society*, first published in 1950, was reissued in a new, enlarged edition in 1964 which quickly became a staple of child development courses. I view Erikson's prominence in the child development and early childhood education curricula of the 1970s and 1980s as both a plus and minus for psychoanalytic influence in these fields. Textbook authors and readers found Erikson's psychosocial stages more palatable than Freud's schema of psychosexual development. Although Erikson saw himself as applying and amplifying rather than negating Freud's theories, by the time Erikson's formulations made it into early childhood education textbooks the effect was to dilute Freud's emphasis on the centrality of sexuality and to replace a focus on libidinal development with the development of the ego. Although the case studies in *Childhood and Society* are classically Freudian in their depiction of troubled children caught up in confusion over the functions and symbolism of their bodies and genitalia, the primary lesson early childhood educators took from Erikson's work was that the key developmental issues of early childhood are trust, autonomy, and initiative. The shift in early childhood education in the later half of the century from Freud's focus on sex to Erikson's on ego development parallels and anticipates the shift in psychoanalysis from drive to ego theory.

An example of the turning away from Freud and toward Erikson is Bettye Caldwell and Julius Richmond's 1974 essay in *The Formative Years: Principles of Early Childhood Education.* After briefly discussing Freud's notion of the oral, anal, and genital stages, Caldwell and Richmond write:

During the "oral period" in infancy, for example, it is thought the child develops feelings about accepting things and the mother's manner of giving them. Erikson (1950) has postulated that from the totality of experiences in this period, the individual develops a basic sense of trust in people—or else a lack of trust which hampers his ensuing development [p. 51].

After presenting similarly Eriksonian takes on the anal and genital stages, the authors conclude:

There is growing recognition among psychoanalytic investigators that the application of knowledge gained from psychoanalysis in preventive efforts must be approached cautiously. The objective of psychoanalytic investigations as stated by Erikson (1950) a decade ago [n.b. actually, twenty-five years ago, at the time their essay was published] remains valid: "Psychoanalysis today is implementing the study of the ego, the core of the individual. It is shifting its emphasis from the concentrated study of the conditions which blunt and distort the individual ego to the study of the ego's roots in social organization" [p. 51].

In the 1970s, alongside the popularity of Erikson, object relations and attachment theorists became important figures in child development and early childhood education. Margaret Mahler's writing on separation, John Bowlby's and Mary Ainsworth's on attachment, and Rene Spitz's on hospitalism all had impacts on the field, indirectly if not directly. I would point out that early childhood education's infatuation with attachment theory in the 1970s was a bit paradoxical, as this theory was often used to suggest that young children are better off at home with their mothers than in institutional child care. Some psychoanalysts and psychoanalytically informed psychologists of this era (for example, Burton White, 1985a,b) took an openly critical stance toward out-of-home child care, pitting them against feminists who saw affordable child care as a crucial component of women's economic self-sufficiency and equality of opportunity (Hewlett, 1986).

The psychoanalytic turn toward a focus on attachment, the ego, and object relations had the virtue of making psychoanalysis more palatable to American early childhood educators, but at the cost of a loss of attention to sexuality. The psychoanalytically informed discussions of masturbation and sexual curiosity that could be found in early childhood education textbooks in the between-the-wars era became much rarer after 1960.

Another new direction in textbooks during the late 1970s and early 1980s was the addition of a feminist-informed discussion of the issues of gender formation and gender equity. Nancy Chodorow's (1978) pathbreaking feminist psychoanalytic take on gender development began to be cited in early childhood education within a few years after its publication. Unfortunately Chodorow is much less cited in the 1990s than she was in 1980s. But psychoanalytic feminism remains a fruitful intellectual source for research in early childhood educational issues in the future. A new breed of early childhood researchers (MacWilliam, 1996; Boldt, 1997; Silin, 1997; Tobin, 1997; Johnson, 2000) is drawing on the writings of Freud and Lacan and their leading postmodern feminist interpreters (e.g., Cixous, 1976; Irigaray, 1985; Butler, 1993; Grosz, 1994; Britzman, 1998) to rethink issues of gender formation and desire in the early childhood classroom. The writings of these "reconceptualizers" of early childhood education are slowly getting into textbooks and in other ways reaching practitioners.

By the mid 1980s, the issue of gender formation aside, discussions of sex had all but disappeared from early childhood education textbooks. It was to return to the textbooks in the late 1980s in a new visage: the specter of sexual abuse. A review of early childhood education textbooks of the past 15 years shows that when sexuality is mentioned at all, it is most often in the context of sexual danger. Masturbation and sexual play, no longer presented as natural features of early childhood, are discussed instead as possible indicators of abuse and precursors of sexual danger. From the 1920s through the 1950s, early childhood education textbooks warned of the mental health risks of repressing children's sexuality; in the 1990s the risk teachers are urged to keep in the forefront of their minds is children's sexual vulnerability. For example, in the 1987 edition of their book *Who Am I in the Lives of Children*, Feeney, Christenson, and Moravcik give this somber advice:

> It is part of your professional responsibility to learn to identify and report child abuse and neglect. . . . While sexual abuse most often occurs in the context of the family, it is by no means unheard of for a child to be sexually

abused by others with whom they have contact such as neighbors, friends, and–in some of the most tragic and publicized cases–their school staff members. Children and families can be given information that will help children to protect themselves from molestation. Schools can take steps to ensure security by having stringent staff screening policies. . . . Perhaps most important is that families and teachers learn to take seriously children's reports of abuse and that children learn how to report incidents to caring adults without fear of repercussions [p. 374].

In a 1988 textbook entitled *The Whole Child: Developmental Education for the Early Years*, following sensible discussions of masturbation and sexual curiosity in young children, Joanne Hendrick writes on sexual molestation:

> Children need to be empowered to protect themselves, too. They should be taught never to taken anything (typically candy) from any stranger and never to get in a car with strangers . . . they need to understand the difference between "good touching," such as snuggling and hugging, and "bad touching" that doesn't feel right. . . . They should be assured that their bodies belong to themselves, that its okay to say "No!" and that, no matter what the threat, they should tell their parents right away if anyone makes that kind of advance to them. In recent years a number of educational programs have become available that offer guidelines in such preventive kinds of instruction [p. 70].

The advice offered to early childhood practitioners by Feeney et al. (1929) to learn to identify sexual abuse and to take precautions to keep sexual predators off their staff and by Hendrick (1988) to teach children to protect themselves from sexual predators seems reasonable and necessary. But that it seems so is in large part a reflection of the concerns and anxieties of our time. The sexual vulnerability of young children is both an ongoing reality and a contemporary moral panic. The shift in textbooks from a focus on normal sexual development to sexual abuse and from caretaker–child intimacy to protecting children from adult predators has its costs. When early childhood educators refer uncritically in their textbook to unsubstantiated allegations of sexual abuse by preschool teachers, they are complicit in the public demonization of their own profession. And when these educators urge practitioners to teach children to defend themselves from sexual predators, they support a burgeoning industry of experts who, for a fee, teach sexual safety courses to children as young as three years old. As my colleague Richard Johnson (2000) points out, we don't trust young children to cross streets by themselves and yet we are now expecting them to deal with the confusion presented by an adult sexual predator.

The current status of discussions of sexuality in contemporary early childhood education textbooks can be summarized quite succinctly: Psychoanalytic perspectives have all but disappeared; "normal" infantile sexuality is rarely discussed; when sex is discussed, it is as a danger.

Study Two: Preschool Teachers'
Talk about Sexuality

As an early childhood educator concerned with what seemed to me to be a rising moral panic that was distorting practice in the field, in 1994 I launched a study of preschool teachers' attitudes toward sexuality. I assembled focus groups of preschool teachers to discuss a series of stories or "critical incidents," each of which dealt with a problematic issue involving young children, their teachers, and sex. I gathered these stories in seminars I taught to preservice and inservice preschool teachers and then rewrote the stories, removing confusing and idiosyncratic features, so that they would function effectively as projective devices, like Rorschach inkblots or TAT pictures. This study is based on 12 focus groups conducted in Durham, New Hampshire; Honolulu; and Chicago with teachers and directors from a variety of early childhood educational settings, including Head Start, Montessori, private, church-related, and university-attached preschools.

The focus-group discussions generally took about 90 minutes, with approximately 10 minutes spent discussing each of the eight stories. The 20 focus groups collectively produced over 1500 recorded comments, presenting me with a formidable task of analysis. I am not interested in psychoanalyzing the unconscious motivations and defense mechanisms of my informants as individuals. I used group discussions rather than individual interviews as a research method because my object of study is a public discourse rather than psychological conflicts of individuals. In my analyses of statements made in the focus-group discussions, I pay little attention to who said what and instead treat the discussions as collaboratively produced texts. Even where individuals take up sharply opposing positions, I think it most useful to think of their arguments as expressions of culturally shared conflicts and ambivalences.

My reading of the focus-group responses suggests a thesis: the core concerns contemporary Americans have about sexuality in preschool settings reflect the projection of larger social problems onto early childhood education. With a constituency composed chiefly of underpaid women, young children, and their preoccupied, anxious, and sometimes guilty parents, preschools are a vulnerable sector of society, lacking the power and voice to resist the projection of extraneous issues, interests, and concerns. In these discussions that took place in the mid 1990s, we find little trace of either the matter-of-factness or of the psychoanalytic insight that informed early childhood educators' attitudes toward sex earlier in the century. Nor is the reaction of contemporary educators to sexuality a throwback to the "masturbation leads to degeneracy" stance of the 19th century. Instead, as we shall see, the contemporary reactions of early childhood educators to sexuality are more intractable and insidious than the repression of the Victorian era.

The Symptomology of Endangered
and Dangerous Children

> Story 1: There's a four-year old girl in my group who runs up to the boys
> during free play and kisses them. And I don't mean just a peck on the cheek.
> She kisses them right on the lips. I was hoping the problem would kind of
> fade away, but now she's got some of the other girls doing the same thing.

In their discussions of several of the scenarios, informants used the logic and
language of medical symptomology. The little girls in these stories were seen as
having clinical conditions, conditions that should be referred to medical special-
ists. Many of the respondents associated kissing games with germs, contagion,
and sexually transmitted diseases. In nine of the 12 focus groups, germs came
up in the discussion. In three groups the mention of spreading germs through
kissing escalated to a discussion of sexually transmitted diseases. The most striking example of such a jump was this sequence of comments made by a group of
Honolulu early childhood-education graduate students in the spring of 1992:

Teacher A: I worry about germs. I'd tell them, "You can kiss on the cheek, but
            not on the mouth. You have yucky germs in your mouth."

Teacher B: I heard somewhere that actually you have lots more germs on your
            hands than in your mouth. You're more likely to get sick from shak-
            ing hands than from kissing.

Teacher A: We make the children wash their hands several times a day, but it's a
            constant battle. A lot of them just run in and out of the bathroom and
            pretend they washed their hands. Or they just stick one hand under
            the faucet and think their hands are clean.

Teacher B: That's why so many preschool children and teachers are sick. There
            are germs being spread all over the place because the kids have such
            bad hygiene. Someone did a study of germs in a preschool class-
            room using like an infrared device to show how the children spread
            germs, and germs were literally all over the place. The whole room
            was red in the picture.

Teacher C: It's scary, all the new germs out there they don't have medicines for.
            There's even resistance to the old germs that used to be handled by
            antibiotics. I was reading something the other day about how common
            herpes is, and that once you get it, it's almost impossible to get rid of
            it. I mean the kind of herpes you get in your mouth, on your lips.

Teacher D: With this whole Magic Johnson thing, you can't help but think about
            HIV.

Teacher B: But it's a myth that you can get AIDS by kissing.

Teacher D: Right, I know, but the whole safe sex and AIDS thing, and we have
            to be really careful. I just mean that somehow this story just brings
            to mind the whole thing with Magic and AIDS.

Teacher E: And now there's that book that says Wilt Chamberlin had sex with 30,000 different women!

Teacher D: You know how doctors and dentists and nurses have to wear rubber gloves with all their patients. I bet we'll be next. I can just see me putting on gloves to wipe the kids' noses and make their snacks.

Taken one by one, these comments are reasonable and unexceptional. But the conversation taken as whole follows the (il)logic of association, displacement, and substitution characteristic of dreams, hysterical symptoms, and moral panics. The conversation moves from children's kissing, to children's inconsistent hand washing, to children and teachers getting sick, to (oral) herpes, to AIDS, to sexual promiscuity and finally to teachers' need to wear rubber gloves. Topical jumps and shifts are characteristic of informal human communication, but the associative jumps in this conversation have a logic and directionality characteristic of an anxiety-driven, culturally shared hysteria in which a larger societal panic about adult sexuality and AIDS is projected onto the benign bodily contacts of young children.

This conversation gives us insight into the projective mechanisms that lead teachers to regard as dangerous a kissing game that in other times and contexts would be seen as benign. The conversation leaps from minor worry to apocalyptic disaster, from the common cold to the AIDS epidemic, from a little girl kissing several boys to a man having sex with 30,000 women. This is how moral panics work: by synecdoche (the substitution of parts for whole and wholes for parts) and the erasure of distinctions between dissimilar actors and actions. In this conversation the child's mouth becomes a synecdoche for the sexually vulnerable and dangerous adult body. Critical distinctions are erased between the sexuality of children and adults, as promiscuous kissing by a four-year-old girl is linked to Wilt Chamberlain's improbably prodigious sexual promiscuity. There are substitutions of the mouth for the genitals, of the relatively benign germs of the cold and the sore throat for the deadly viruses of sexually transmitted diseases, of the beginning (kissing as foreplay) and the end (sexual intercourse). In the leap from a little girl to Magic Johnson to Wilt Chamberlain to the gloved preschool teacher, we have a collapsing and confusion of perpetrator and victim and of guilt and innocence (guilty victims and innocent vectors) characteristic of the moral panic and projection surrounding AIDS.

Unnatural Female Desire

Story 2: Emily touches herself a lot. When she's excited, she keeps touching herself with one hand. During story time, she rubs her legs together, with a sort of far-off look in her eyes. Even at lunch, she'll have a hand in her pants sometimes. I don't mean she's doing it every minute, but it's not like it's only now and then, either.

Just as the focus group respondents turned the story of the kissing girl into a discussion of infectious disease, so they turned the story of the masturbating girl into a discussion of gynecological disorders. In all 12 of the focus groups, the most frequent explanation for the girl's activity was that she was scratching a vaginal itch:

- Could be a medical problem: rash, yeast infection, bladder infection.
- Vaginal irritation? Improper hygiene?
- Talk to parents. Maybe she has an infection.
- Irritating underwear.
- Suggest that parent take child to doctor to check for pinworms, yeast infection, and so forth.

Rather than discuss the story in terms of masturbation, most of the respondents perceived Emily as having an infection. By suspecting an infection, they avoid dealing with childhood sexuality. Instead of coming to terms with their feelings about masturbation in early childhood education settings, these respondents transform ordinary sexuality into a gynecological disorder.

In contrast to the majority of respondents who saw Emily's behavior as itch-related, a minority saw Emily as masturbating and were very concerned:

- I would worry about frequent masturbation.
- I would ask the teachers to keep a log: frequency, duration, times, pattern, intensity.
- Unloved? For attention? It's one of the telltale signs of abuse.
- Send her to a counselor for disclosure. You don't want to contaminate disclosure by talking to the girl first.
- Talk to her. Things about home, recent events, siblings, trips, anything out of the ordinary.

Clearly, at the heart of this concern is the sexual abuse of children. Disclosure, logs, telltale signs—this is the language of the courts and child protective services, of the legal and social work apparatus that battles child sex abuse.

If the story that provoked these reactions had been about a sexually abused girl, this language would make sense. But where did these respondents find indications of abuse? In the story of the masturbating girl, as in the story of the kissing girl, behaviors that a psychoanalytic perspective (not to mention experience and common sense) would suggest are typical of young children became danger signs to many of my respondents. In each of these stories, an expression of sexual desire by a young girl was marked as dangerous. The logic seems to be that, first, these girls were desired (abused), and this abuse in turn stimulated the release of unnatural, dangerous desires.

Girls masturbating and chasing and kissing boys are not strange or bizarre behaviors that should lead us in search for an explanation in trauma. Reading these stories as sagas of abuse and victimization works to demonize female sexuality. Female sexuality in our culture has long been under attack. Feminists in the 1970s and 1980s, challenging the notion that (good) girls and women are without desire, attempted to overturn the shame girls and women have been made to feel about their bodies and their desires. But in the 1990s, the moral panics surrounding pornography, AIDS, teen pregnancy, and sex abuse combined to reinvigorate the long-standing suspicion of female desire.

The Girls Who Knew Too Much

Story 3: The other day, two girls and a boy where playing "doctor." Actually, they were playing "delivery room." One girl, who was being the patient, lay on her back and said, "It's time for the baby." Then the other girl, who was the nurse, and the boy, who was the doctor, got ready to "deliver" the baby. I was watching from across the room. At first I was thinking this was cute, but then the nurse told the doctor, "Pull down her underpants so we can get the baby out," and that's just what they did. When they pulled her underpants down I could see that she had put a little baby-doll in her underpants and was now holding it between her legs. At that point I came over. The "nurse" told me, "Get away, we're birthing a baby," but I told the "patient" she had to put her underpants back on immediately.

It is not just children's sexual desire and pleasure but also their sexual knowledge that worries early childhood educators. If the focus-group discussions of the kissing and masturbation stories are classically Freudian in their hysterical conversion of tabooed desires to somatized symptoms and in their concern with female immodesty, reactions to the delivery room story are Lacanian in their anxiety about the interplay of knowledge, ignorance, and innocence. In several of the discussions, the conversation turned to the question of how these children knew so much:

- What graphic, vivid language they use!
- Too much maturity for kids of that age.
- Where did they get all this knowledge of where babies come from?
- I would question how these children would have such knowledge. I mean actual physical knowledge of the birthing process.
- Something about this gives me an uncomfortable feeling. These girls seem to know a bit too much for, how old does it say they are? Four years old?

Similar concerns were expressed in reactions to the kissing story: "She's too precocious. I would want to talk to this child's parents. I would want to know what's she seeing at home. Is there a baby-sitter who has a boyfriend? Is the child seeing adult sexual behavior? I would want to know where it's coming from, how she knows so much about kissing."

The core concern here is that excessive sexual knowledge is dangerous. This is knowledge in the old, biblical sense, the kind of knowledge that comes from eating forbidden fruit (or watching someone else do so). These girls who know how to play doctor too expertly are suspicious. Sexual knowledge is dangerous because it suggests a lack of innocence. These girls suffer from lack of a lack. In *Looking Awry: An Introduction to Jacques Lacan through Popular Culture*, Slavoj Žižek (1992) discusses the characters in Hitchcock films who are in danger because, by chance, they have come to know things they should not know. Children shouldn't know too much about kissing or the anatomical details of birth, much less of sexual intercourse. This knowing becomes dangerous to others but mostly to the child who knows and who for this reason comes under suspicion of needing treatment.

Panopticism: A Problem Posing as a Solution

> Story 4: We have three little toilets in a row in the bathroom, with no dividers in between. Sometimes, when they're all in use, some other kids are also in there, standing around waiting for a toilet or watching the kids on the toilet. Sometimes they even try to look from behind. They laugh and say, "I can see the doo-doo coming out." We try to shoo the watchers away, to give the kids who are going to the bathroom more privacy, but the kids on the toilet usually don't seem to mind the attention. The only time they really mind is when they have a b.m. and one of the other kids tries to flush the toilet.

We can see in the beliefs and practices of the contemporary American preschool a preoccupation with sightlines and other techniques for making young children constantly visible. Many respondents offered panopticism as a solution to the problems presented in the bathroom, sprinkler, and playing-doctor scenarios:

- I'd let the children know that I was watching. Usually, that's all it takes. Once they see that you are watching, they monitor their own behavior, and usually you don't even have to say anything.
- I'm much less worried about a game like this, which is going on in the dramatic play area, than I would be about the same thing happening behind a closed bathroom door.
- To catch problems before they get started the secret is to set up the room so you can see at a glance right into the dress up corner. We've totally reorganized our setup here to give us improved sightlines. Now, right here where we are sitting, if you stand up and turn around you can immediately see where everyone is and what they are doing.

Panopticism as a solution to children's sex play is not without its problems. For instance, in their discussions of how they would handle children's bathroom play, many American respondents found themselves caught between the urge to make the bathrooms visible and thus safe and the children's right to privacy and developmentally appropriate play:

Teacher A: I would set up a system to limit the number of children in the bathroom at one time. Children should learn that going to the bathroom is a private time, and that they shouldn't be following each other in there to watch.

Teacher B: But should the teachers be socializing the kids to think of the bathroom as private when the attitude toward privacy in this context is not logical? If privacy were really a concern, then the school should have put in dividers between the stalls.

Teacher C: What's needed here is more supervision, not dividers.

Teacher D: There's a natural curiosity that I don't want to turn off. To adults the bathroom is private, but to children it's a social time, especially for kids still learning to use the toilet. In the story the teacher didn't ask why the kids were bothered. Maybe the kids are upset that they don't get to flush the toilet themselves. If so, that's the kind of situation I'd let the children try to work out on their own.

A similar ambivalence came out in discussions of the playing-doctor story. Most of the respondents felt it was their responsibility, if not to break up the game, at least to keep an eye on it. But several respondents, concerned that their surveillance would change or inhibit this play, pointed out the irony that play which they would choose to ignore at home with their own children they feel compelled to interrupt as teachers of other people's children: "It would be totally different if you were the parent at home. You wouldn't blink. It would be nothing." "I would let it go at home, but in school, teachers are accountable." "For all I know my daughter plays doctor up in her room with her friends. That thought doesn't bother me a bit. But at school I don't have the luxury of thinking that way."

In each of these situations, we see teachers caught in the panoptic trap. Like prison guards, they hold the power of the panoptic gaze over their charges, but they know that they, too, are being scrutinized. Part of the genius of the Panopticon, or modern prison, invented by Jeremy Bentham in the eighteenth century is that it does not require constant vigilance: it is not necessary for a guard to be always watching, only for the inmates to know that the guard *could* at any moment be watching. Parents are rarely physically present to watch and pass judgment on their children's teachers. Nevertheless teachers are governed by the power of the parents' gaze. It is all the more intimidating to teachers that this gaze is indirect, refracted through the (often unreliable) reports children give their parents each night about what went on that day in school.

The paranoia and panopticism that are eroding the rights and pleasures of both children and teachers and making parents increasingly frantic are not being imposed from above by a central authority. For better or worse, governmental agencies in the United States play a very small role in the regulation and control of preschools. The panoptic gaze is not the all-seeing eye of Big Brother looking; it is something we are doing to ourselves and each other. Foucault teaches us to be aware of the diffuseness of power. Like the other repressive disciplinary practices Foucault describes, panopticism in early childhood education settings has come to seem so necessary, prudent, inevitable, and logical that we don't ask where it came from, nor do we question its costs.

Psychoanalysis versus the Forces of Antisexuality

In this essay I have chronicled the story of the declining influence in American early childhood education of psychoanalytic and especially of Freudian theory and I have provided evidence of the rising sexual panic that is sweeping through American preschools. I conclude by offering some speculations on connections between these phenomena.

As I mentioned at the start, one version of the relationship of psychoanalysis to sexuality in early childhood education would be to suggest that psychoanalysis burst on the scene at the dawn of the 20th century as an emancipatory discourse, with Freud's writings giving early childhood educators a startlingly new perspective on children's sexuality, a perspective that led to the temporary victory of enlightened insight and progressive practice over Victorian repression in preschool settings. In the second half of the century, psychoanalysis's influence in early childhood education, as in other social contexts, waned. The causes for this waning could be attributed to a variety of factors, including the withdrawal of psychoanalysts from the public sphere as they became increasingly oriented toward private practice (Freud's fear for psychoanalysis in business-oriented America); the not-to-be underestimated resiliency of fundamentalism and anti-intellectualism in American life; the decline of psychoanalysis' influence on related fields, beginning with psychiatry, which became increasingly biochemical, and with psychology, which became increasingly behavioral and then cognitive; the increasing control over the mental health system seized by the insurance and managed care industries unwilling to pay for long-term treatment; and the gradual shift from Freud's focus on libidinal dynamics to a focus on ego functions and the self, a shift that made psychoanalysis more abstract, less glamorous and compelling, and less easily distinguishable from a proliferating array of self-actualization and self-improvement therapies and discourses that circulate in contemporary American society.

This story of the decline of psychoanalytic influence, a decline caused by its inherent flaws and bungling and by the power and ruthlessness of its enemies, leads to finger-pointing and prevents us from seeing the bigger picture. Rather than bemoaning psychoanalysis' fate as a flawed, fallen hero, defeated by the forces of repression and anti-intellectuality, I suggest we see the relationship between psychoanalysis and the forces of antisexuality in early childhood education in more complex terms. As Foucault teaches us in *Discipline and Punish* (1979) and *The History of Sexuality* (1981), the repression and the acceptance of sexuality are paired positions that need and fuel each other. Foucault challenges us to consider the possibility that the aggressive, century-long battle psychoanalysis has waged against the forces of sexual ignorance and repression may have had the paradoxical effect of strengthening and in some cases even creating its opposition. As a result sexuality in early childhood education's postpsychoanalytic era is more rigorously and ruthlessly controlled than it was in the prepsychoanalytic era, when children's sexual activities and curiosity were often overlooked or seen, simply, as naughty or sinful.

I have no desire to rehash arguments about the relationship of psychoanalysis to the sexual abuse of children. For the record I find Jeffrey Masson's (1984) accusations ludicrous. But a Foucauldian perspective compels me to point out that the current panic over the sexual abuse of children, a panic that is distorting practice in early childhood education and reducing the quality of the lives of children (without protecting children in any meaningful way), could never have come about had there been no such thing as psychoanalysis. Although the conclusions reached by the children's sexual abuse lobby are not widely shared by psychoanalysts, the moral panic about abuse is built on a foundation of psychoanalytic principles, including infantile sexuality, the importance of the first five years of life in character formation, repressed memory, and the psychodynamics of perversion. Foucault argues that by making the sexuality of children visible and categorizing and naming the stages of infantile sexuality, psychoanalysis made possible ever greater control of this sexuality. Childhood sexual activity, which adults once could ignore, or, when it came to their attention, which they could simply order to stop, is now marked and named as a category of deviance that we cannot not look at and attempt to control. We've lost our ability to not see childhood sexuality.

I illustrate this point and close this essay with two stories, cautionary tales from the late 1950s, a point in time when the tide may have begun to turn in the struggle of psychoanalysis to inform and influence our society's understanding of childhood sexuality.

Story One

In the focus-group discussions I conducted with teachers, many of the informants reflected positively on how children's sexuality was handled in the past, in phrases such as "We didn't used to have to worry about . . ."; "We no longer have the luxury of . . ."; "When we were growing up it was different . . ."; and "When I was a kid . . .":

> When I was a kid, my Mom didn't work so I didn't go to nursery school every day. I must have been four or five, and there were tons of kids on my block, and we'd gather in my garage. I remember being the doctor, and making some little boys from next door—they must have been younger than me, maybe three-years-old or so—I remember making them line up and I was the doctor and they were the patients and I'd call out, "Next patient." And when they came over to me I'd pretend to take their temperatures and give them a shot, but really the point of the game was to pull down their pants. Didn't everyone play games like that? My mother was probably in the house, cooking or watching T.V. I'd like kids to have the chance for that kind of sex play. But as a teacher, there is absolutely no way I can look the other way and let kids play doctor in my classroom. Do I sound hypocritical?

Conservative Americans who would like to see a return to the patriarchal family relations of the 1950s portray postwar mothers as constantly available to their young children, supervising their every move. But what if the secret of motherhood in the 1950s was not middle-class mothers' constant attention but their *inattention*? I have memories of playing with my brothers and my friends, and with their sisters and brothers, playing in each other's basements, bedrooms, garages, and in the ravines behind our houses, playing doctor, having peeing contests, telling doo-doo jokes, all while our mothers were cooking, doing laundry, running off to the store. Apparently our mothers did not feel they had to know where we were or what we were doing each minute of the day. It's not that our mothers were intentionally choosing not to supervise us because they wanted to make sure we would have opportunities to play doctor and kissing games, or because they were philosophically opposed to panopticism as a parenting technique. The sociospatial norms governing mothers and children in the suburbs at the time just didn't call for surveillance. Teachers in this era similarly felt permission from society to not keep children constantly in their view, to not intervene in kissing games, and to not read children's sexual curiosity as a potential symptom of abuse. This permission enjoyed by parents and teachers in this era to not police childhood sexuality was the result less of psychoanalytic teaching than of the absence of a riled up opposition to children's sexuality and of an atmosphere of sexual panic.

Story Two

My father, who is a psychoanalyst, recently reminded me of an event he participated in some forty years ago. At that time a Chicago textbook company invited

our school district to be a pilot site for an innovative, psychoanalytically informed sex education curriculum, a curriculum that would include not just reproduction and sexually transmitted diseases, but also masturbation and which
would begin, not in the junior-high school years, but in kindergarten. To debate
this proposal, the school board appointed a task force which included teachers,
parents, psychiatrists, pediatricians, and members of the clergy. My father, pleased
that a progressive sex education curriculum was on the agenda, and drawing on
his psychoanalytic expertise and the status that he assumed this expertise would
carry in this context (for who at the gathering could claim to know more about
children and sex than psychoanalysts?) went to the meeting with great optimism.
He spoke enthusiastically, praising the curriculum, and particularly the inclu-
sion of masturbation, which he argued should be taught matter-of-factly and
nonjudgmentally and congratulating the teachers and the school board for their
willingness to overcome the forces of sexual ignorance and repression. Alas, his
well-intentioned and theoretically sophisticated but politically naïve presentation ended up having a counterproductive result—by articulating so clearly how
masturbation could and should be taught in school and by praising the educators
for standing up to repression, he managed to stimulate and provoke the opposition. Teachers and school board members who had come to the meeting hoping
to finesse the adoption of the new textbooks cringed as my father put forward
his honest and bold vision for sexual education, for they understood something
he did not: direct attacks on sexual ignorance and repression and open discussions of childhood sexuality end up strengthening and mobilizing the opposition. Following my father's presentation, as the rabbis and ministers and other
conservatives in attendance seized on what he said and asked teachers if they
were indeed planning to promote masturbation and talk openly about sexual
pleasure with the children of the community, teachers ran for cover, school board
members retreated, and the new sexual education curriculum was tabled.

Psychoanalysts will have to become much more savvy if they hope to regain
a voice in the early childhood curriculum.

References

Boldt, G. (1997), Sexist and heterosexist responses to gender bending. In: *Making a
    Place for Pleasure in Early Childhood Education*, ed. J. Tobin. New Haven, CT:
    Yale University Press.
Britzman, D. (1998), *Lost Subjects, Contested Objects*. New York: State University of
    New York Press.
Butler, J. (1993), *Bodies That Matter*. London: Routledge.
Caldwell, B. & Richmond, J. (1974), The impact of theories of child development. In:
    The Formative Years, ed. S. Coopersmith & R. Feldman, Los Angeles: University
    of California Press.

Chodorow, N. (1978), *The Reproduction of Mothering*. Berkeley: University of California Press.

Cixous, H. (1976), The laugh of the Medusa. *Signs*, 1:875–899.

Erikson, E. (1950), *Childhood and Society*. New York: W. W. Norton.

Feeney, S., Christenson, D. & Moravcik, E. (1987), *Who Am I in the Lives of Children*. Columbus, OH: Charles E. Merrill.

Foster, J. & Mattson, M. (1929), *Nursery School Procedure*. New York: D. Appleton.

———— (1939), *Nursery School Education*. New York: D. Appleton.

Foucault, M. (1979), *Discipline and Punish: The Birth of the Prison*, trans. A. Sheridan. New York: Vintage.

———— (1981), *The History of Sexuality, Vol. 1*. London: Penguin.

Gardner, D. (1956), *The Education of Young Children*. London: Methuen.

Gesell, A. (1923), *The Preschool Child from the Standpoint of Public Hygiene and Education*. Boston: Houghton.

Green, M. & Woods, E. (1948), *A Nursery School Handbook for Teachers and Parents*, Sierra Madre, CA: Sierra Madre Community Nursery School Association.

Grosz, E. (1994), *Volatile Bodies*. Bloomington: Indiana University Press.

Hendrick, J. (1988), *The Whole Child: Developmental Education for the Early Years*. Englewood Cliffs, NJ: Prentice-Hall.

Hewlett, S. (1986), *A Lesser Life*. New York: Warner Books.

Irigaray, L. (1985), *This Sex Which Is Not One*. Ithaca, NY: Cornell University Press.

Johnson, R. (2000), *Hands Off!* New York: Peter Lang.

Kellogg, R. (1949), *Nursery School Guide*, Boston: Houghton Mifflin.

MacWilliam, E. (1996), Touch subjects: A risky inquiry into pedagogical pleasure. *Brit. Educ. Res. J.*, 22:305–317.

Masson, J. (1984), *The Assault on Truth*. New York: Farrar, Straus & Giroux.

Owens, G. (1920), *Nursery School Education*. New York: E. P. Dutton.

Read, K. (1950), *The Nursery School: A Human Relationships Laboratory*. Philadelphia: W. B. Saunders.

Silin, J. (1997), The pervert in the classroom. In: *Making a Place for Pleasure in Early Childhood Education*, ed. J. Tobin. New Haven, CT: Yale University Press.

Tobin, J. (1997), *Making a Place for Pleasure in Early Childhood Education*. New Haven, CT: Yale University Press.

Wheeler, O. & Earl, I. (1939), *Nursery School Education*. London: University of London Press.

White, B. (1985a), Foreward. In: *The Child Care Crisis*, ed. F. Maynard. Ontario, Canada: Penguin Books.

———— (1985b), *The First Three Years of Life*. Englewood Cliffs, NJ: Prentice-Hall.

Žižek, S. (1992), *Looking Awry: An Introduction to Jacques Lacan Through Popular Culture*. Cambridge, MA: MIT Press.

IV

FREUD'S IMPACT ON
HUMANISTIC STUDIES

Freud in Time: Psychoanalysis and Literary Criticism in the New Century

PAUL J. EMMETT

WILLIAM VEEDER

Love is a long close scrutiny.
—John Hawkes

Sigmund Freud, characteristically, did not go gentle into the 21st century. The 1990s visited upon the man and his ideas a virulence of critique that exceeded in its range and publicity anything he encountered in his professional life. In addition to ongoing opposition to Freud's theories, there have been highly personal attacks on his ethics and basic probity. Especially since Freud's partisans have addressed these attacks frequently and cogently, we as literary critics will forego filial piety and will, instead, pose a core question: what of Freud's legacy remains viable for humanistic studies? What tools for analysis, and what truths about motivation and desire, will foster literary criticism in the new century?

In posing the question this way, we are entering into a debate that psychoanalysts have staged, often acrimoniously, for more than 30 years, a debate over what they call the two Freuds. On the one hand, Freud is the scientist, the researcher-theorist-metaphysician whose Newtonian-Darwinian orientation prompted him to insist that psychoanalysis *is* a science. On the other hand, Freud is the reader, the clinician-exegete-mythmaker whose masterpieces include the books on dreams and parapraxes and jokes, the case histories, and the incidental studies of verbal and visual texts. This debate within psychoanalysis has serious import for literary criticism, as two partisans of Freud-the-reader establish. Michel de Certeau in France and Roy Schafer in America make arguments against Freud's metapsychology that highlight Freud's persisting usefulness for the humanities, and for students of fiction especially. De Certeau (1986) reminds us of Freud's admission in 1895 that his " 'histories of the ill ones' (*Krankengeschichte*) read like novels (*Novellen*)." Freud finds indispensable to treating hysteria "a detailed description (*Darstellung*) of mental processes such as we are accustomed to find in the works of poets (*Dichter*)" (p. 19). Freud's achievement, for de Certeau, is that he transcends "science" and achieves "fiction." He acknowledges the data that theory cannot account for, the unique elements of a patient's case that scientific rules would dismiss as fanciful or ignore as irrelevant. Producing narrative rather than reproducing schema, "he . . . thus substitutes for 'objective' discourse . . . a discourse that adopts the form of a 'fiction' (if by 'fiction' we understand a text that openly declares its relation to the singular place of its production)—to the particular situation of each analysand" (p. 6).

Also commited to the analysand's specific vicissitudes, Roy Schafer's (1976) espousal of Freud-the-reader has proven attractive to literary critics because it emphasizes "language." Schafer focuses on "disclaimed actions" (p. 130). Like characters in fiction, patients are "engaged in contradictory or paradoxical actions" (p. 135) which are often revealed in verbal slips. "The slip is not a disrupted action; it is a special kind of action in which two courses of action are taken up simultaneously" (p. 131). Thus Schafer, like de Certeau, emphasizes how any particular narrative exceeds in its richness any theory we might apply to it. Whether we call this richness overdetermination, or latency, or, in Lacanian/Derridean parlance, the *supplement,* the basic admonition of Freud-the-reader is our bedrock. "There is often a passage in even the most thoroughly interpreted dream which has to be left obscure. . . . This is the dream's navel, the spot where it reaches down into the unknown" (Freud, 1900, p. 525).

Freud's admonition is especially germane for literary criticism today. By the 1990s, our profession had reacted so severely against New Criticism's exclusively textual focus that contextual study was all the rage, and close analysis was quickly becoming a lost art. We believe that, in the new century, extreme antiformalism will give way to two more moderate, fostering attitudes toward reading. On the one hand, contextualists will come to see close analysis as an ally rather than an enemy. Close analysis will generate complexities that enrich contextual discussions both by revealing the limitations of ideology (including the contextualist's own) and by problematizing that reductive mining of texts for "themes" which happens now all too often. On the other hand, close analysis will provide readers of every stripe with exquisite pleasure, the pleasure of discovering and appreciating textual richnesses. Genius in play. What limited New Criticism was not only its anticontextualism but also its failure to live up to its own billing. We agree with Peter Brooks (1987) agreeing with Geoffrey Hartman that "the trouble with Anglo-American formalism was that it wasn't formalist enough" (p. 337). We have chosen for our epigraph the words of the contemporary novelist John Hawkes (1961) because they define our ideal of literary-critical relations. "Love is a long close scrutiny" (pp. 8–9). For us as critics, love of textual intricacy generates the long scrutiny of close analysis and produces intense delight. This delight we want to share with the readers of our essay. (Spatial constraints prevent us from also assaying the other pleasure we've defined in this paragraph, the pleasure of moving out from textual to contextual analyses.) Before doing so, however, we need to make one more general point.

Much of what Freud can teach us today about psychology and reading he found in the novels of his contemporaries and their predecessors. "In their knowledge of the mind they are far in advance of us everyday people, for they draw upon sources which have not yet opened up for science" (1907, p. 8). This is the Freud whom de Certeau values, the Freud who knew the limits of his "science." "[Creative artists] know a whole host of things . . . of which our philosophy has not let us dream" (p. 8). The very ambiance of Freud's formative 1890s is alive with "psychoanalytic" thought. In *What Maisie Knew* (1898), for example, Henry James' heroine knows "the art of not thinking singly" (p. 189). Able "to read the spoken in the unspoken" (p. 205), Maisie knows that "everything had something behind it" (p. 54). She is indeed "a young person with a sharpened sense for latent meanings" (p. 189). Half a century earlier, Nathaniel Hawthorne's narrator in "Roger Malvin's Burial" (1832a) could say of his protagonist, Reuben Bourne, "unable to penetrate the secret places of his soul where his motives lay hidden, he believed that a supernatural voice had called him onward" (p. 356). Clearly Hawthorne knew about the unconsciousness, suppression, and self-deception. Now that we know, Fredrick Crews (1966) and other critics have brought Freud to Hawthorne with promising results. But they have yet to penetrate the secret place of Hawthorne's text where Reuben Bourne's motives still lie hidden. Who, for that matter, thinks that any of us, Freud, friends or foes, have plucked the heart out of Hamlet's mystery?

To indicate how Freud can foster readerly pleasure in the new century, we study the enduring features of his legacy—first his techniques, then his concepts. In the process we advance an overall argument. We believe readers should take seriously what Freud theorized but hedged about, what he practiced, though only at his best: literary texts can, and should, be read as we read dreams. Our argument is shaped by several factors particular to the occasion that has evoked it. Because we are writing to general readers rather than to professional literary critics, we forego footnotes and other scholarly apparatus; restrict ourselves to texts in English; focus on fiction of the nineteenth and twentieth centuries, both recognized masterpieces and major achievements that either have been unfairly forgotten (such as Harriet Prescott Spofford's "Circumstance") or have not yet been accorded their full due (such as John Hawkes's *The Lime Twig,* 1961, and Bharati Mukherjee's *Jasmine,* 1989). Finally, we want to acknowledge a substantial debt—to the many students of criticism and theorists of psychoanalysis whom we draw upon but have no space to cite individually.

The Legacy Techniques

The Interpretation of Dreams (1900) is where Freud teaches us how to read, to parse the stylistic techniques of the unconscious. Here Freud establishes that texts—be they dreams or "literature"—are multileveled structures where the manifest is a distorted presentation of the latent. Techniques for distorting are manifold, the most prominent being displacement, condensation, and overdetermination. The trick is to reverse the process in order to understand the unconscious content that is struggling to—and not to—be revealed. Displacement is "a transferring of psychical intensities" (p. 308); the affect associated with one object at the latent level is transferred to another object at the manifest. We can begin to reverse this process, as Freud does, by paying close attention to inappropriate affects. To take a seemingly straightforward example: Can anyone hate felines as much as Poe's narrator in "The Black Cat"? When he attempts to axe the cat and ends up axing his wife, we suspect that the answer is "no." The rage and loathing that the narrator cannot admit to feeling for his wife are displaced onto the cat which was her "great favorite" (p. 854). Simple: a psychoallegory of suppressed rage. So straightforward a logic is what has caused "Freudian" analysis to be dismissed by many readers as "reductive." The most famous Poe Freudian, Marie Bonaparte, uses displaced hatred in "The Black Cat" to read the animal as "a totem of Poe's [phallic] mother." But nothing more. Simple. Problems of jargon and biography aside, if Freud at his best shows us anything, it's that nothing is simple, and nothing is nothing more. The very fact that Bonaparte says cat = Phallic Mother, whereas we've already seen that cat = wife, indicates that displacement is not, in itself, a reductive technique. We're not done when we find *a* source for an affect, because displacement often operates along with the second technique of distortion, condensation, where a manifest element has multiple latent associations. The narrator's cat is, in fact, associated with wife, and mother, and Phallic Mother, and women, and the threat of gender fusion. Because the cat has these multiple associations, when the husband blinds the cat, his motives, and his story, are masked through the third technique of distortion, overdetermination, where a manifest action has several causes. To interpret the causes here, we must again turn to Freud because blinding is *the* Freudian representation of castration. The narrator blinds the cat in order to castrate the Phallic Mother, his wife, and all women, and he does so to escape the threat of gender fusion.

This is still too simple. We can read "The Black Cat" as a tale of suppressed misogyny—fear and hatred of the feminine, and of the female within—but, though the story is just that, just that is exactly what it isn't. To enter further into Poe's complications, we could repeat the circuit of displacement, condensation, overdetermination. The narrator doesn't displace just rage onto the cat; he also displaces tenderness. The cat that makes a "cry . . . like . . . a child" (p. 859) and clamors up the narrator's "dress" to his "breast" (p. 855) is condensed into more than wife, mother, and female. It is also the child he has never had, and the child he has never been (his distant, bizarre parents give him pets rather than hugs). Thus when the narrator makes his overdetermined attack on the cat's vision, he himself isn't so determined: he cuts out only one eye. Moreover, although our first reading of the cat—involving misogyny and rage against mother and the female within—was decidedly "masculine," our second reading—with "dress . . . breast" and the longing to be maternally nurturant and protective—is "feminine." Freud knew that texts were distorted because they presented feminine and masculine, two antithetical readings simultaneously. He told us that another technique of distortion was, in effect, bisexuality. He told us, but we didn't listen so well. Twentieth-century psychoanalytic critics have tended to emphasize displacement, condensation, and overdetermination at the expense of other methods of distortion, and other methods of reading—especially juxtaposition, verbal play, absurdity, and associative patterns.

What Freud (1900) says about dreams—"whenever they show two elements close together, this guarantees that there is some specifically intimate connection between what corresponded to them among the dream thoughts" (p. 349)—is true of literature too. Juxtaposition suggests latent connection. So when the narrator of "The Black Cat" ends one paragraph by telling us that the cat "became immediately a great favorite of my wife" (Poe, 1843, p. 854) and then begins the next paragraph with "For my own part, I soon found a dislike to it arising within me," we realize the "intimate connection" here is causality. He dislikes the cat *because* it—and not he—is his wife's favorite.

Juxtaposition is so powerful a technique that it can operate across, through, punctuation, in order to reveal latent desires (even as the unconscious itself recognizes no "no"). In *Frankenstein,* for example, Victor insists he's being a devoted bridegroom when he leaves Elizabeth alone in their honeymoon bedroom while he searches for the monster; but that Victor is in fact abandoning his new wife to the violent rage which he feels toward her and which the monster embodies is revealed if we read across periods and with an eye to juxtaposition.

> I resolved that I would sell my life dearly, and not relax the impending conflict until my life, or that of my adversary, were *extinguished. Elizabeth. . . .*
> I earnestly entreated her to retire, resolving not to join her until I had obtained some knowledge as to the situation of *my enemy. She . . .* [Shelley, 1818, p. 192; emphasis added].

Elizabeth's earlier anger at Victor's abandonment of her and the family is expressed through similarly juxtaposed sentences. "I am rewarded for any [familial] exertions by seeing none but *happy, kind faces around me. Since you left us*" (p. 243; emphasis added). Similarly, in "The Yellow Wallpaper" (Gilman, 1892), the young mother in her postpartum depression can admit to a need for distance from her baby son, but she can only reveal through unconscious juxtaposition how dehumanizing her anger toward him is. "I *cannot* be with *him, it* makes me so nervous" (p. 6). And in *Wuthering Heights,* the faux-misanthrope Lockwood signals his infatuated desire to be the truly misanthropic Heathcliff when he introduces himself. "I announced my name. 'Mr. Heathcliff?' " (E. Brontë, p. 3).

Verbal play, Freud tells us, recurs in dreams and texts to bridge manifest and latent. Dictional puns, of course, but also syntactic puns, plus bilingual play, anagrams, neologisms, ambiguities, naming, figures of speech, and verbal sounds. That readers of the 21st century need to heed that Freud's emphasis on language play is evident when we realize that a crucial pun in the most famous sentence of "Bartleby the Scrivener" (Melville, 1855) has been missed by every critic who's published on Bartleby's strange behavior: " 'I prefer not to.' " Bartleby's refrain becomes less perplexing when we realize that this man who lives behind a screen and dies in the fetal position has a latent drive to symbiotic fusion. He would, indeed, prefer not *two!* Likewise the narrator of "The Black Cat." What he prefers and fears is suggested through a network of intricate puns. When he awakens to "the hot breath of the thing upon [his] face," and feels a weight "incumbent" on his heart, under which the good within "succumbed" (Poe, p. 856), there is an intimation of *incubus* and *succubus* which confirms both that the "thing" on his heart is more than a cat and that his obsessions are bisexual. The fact that he calls it "Night-mare" emphasizes the cat's maternal quality by enlisting another pun. The narrator initially tells us that he will present "a series of mere household events" (p. 849), but we soon wonder how blinding a cat and axing a wife can be "mere"—unless we know Freud and French. *Mère* as mother emphasizes how thoroughly the maternal permeates the narrator's household and all "mere household" events.

Puns involving syntax rather than diction are rarely studied by critics, but they are a specialty of Freud's and indicate latent depths throughout great fiction. The postpartum mother in "The Yellow Wallpaper" (Gilman, 1892), for example, intends to announce her heroic determination to save her baby son from having to sleep in the house's horrid "nursery": "I can stand it so much easier than a baby" (p. 11). Her syntax, however, reveals her latent loathing. "I can stand it so much easier than a baby can stand it" screens "I can stand it so much easier than I can stand a baby." The surfacing of love rather than hate is signaled through syntax in "Bartleby": " 'If you do not go away from these premises before night, I shall feel bound—indeed, I *am* bound—to—to—to quit the premises!' " (Melville, 1855, p. 30). Eventually the narrator completes his syntax: "bound to quit." The desire *not* to quit delays him repeatedly, however: ". . . bound . . . I am bound . . . to—to—to . . ." *almost* manages to express his repressed desire to be bound to Bartleby. *He* prefers *two!* In "The Cask of Amontillado" (Poe, 1846), Montressor greets his victim with the words: " 'My dear Fortunato, you are luckily met. How remarkably well you are looking to-day.

But I have received a pipe of Amontillado, and I have my doubts'" (p. 1257). This moment's dramatic importance might distract us from the oddness of Poe's syntax. Why "but"? In what way is Montressor's possession of Amontillado *opposed to* Fortunato's handsome appearance? "But" is, we believe, the sole surfacing of a repressed desire that runs counter to the victimization that Montressor plans for Fortunato. Thus love and hate battle in Montressor's psyche. He seems to be thinking, "How remarkably well you are looking today. But I *cannot let my attraction to your person and patrician manliness distract me from my plan to kill you. So I'll spring the trap.* I have received a pipe of Amontillado." The surfacing of political, as opposed to erotic, content can also be signaled by syntactic play. In James's *The Turn of the Screw* (1884), a handsome patrician does violence to a poor parson's daughter by subjecting her to the impact of his elegant willfulness. "He struck her, inevitably, as gallant and splendid" (p. 152). Place the adverb at the end or beginning of the sentence, and the syntax loses most of its force because it no longer represents what it presents, no longer manifests the iron fist beneath the velvet glove of patriarchy.

Names are another way that latent desire surfaces. Inspired by Freud's wonderful work with dream-distorted proper names ("Hearsing," "Hollthorn") and trick words ("Autodidasker," "Auf Geseres"), we are attentive to writers' wit. Flannery O'Connor (1988), for example, reveals her Bible salesman's phallic insecurity when he adopts the alias Manly Pointer; Vladimir Nabokov (1955) inserts himself into *Lolita* by naming a character anagrammatically Vivian Darkbloom; Hawthorne (1832b) reveals the limitations of materialist science in "The Birthmark" when he gives to the scientist's helper the palindromic name Aminadab, Bad Anima; and Edgar Allan Poe (1839) in "The Fall of the House of Usher" suggests the androgynous fusion of brother and sister in their very surname—us/she/he/her. Henry James plays with names more extensively in "In the Cage" (1898). The handsome soldier who captivates ladies of every class is, according to the critics, christened with an appropriately phallic name: Captain Everard as ever hard. But the name is not Ever*h*ard. James (who delights in outré names—Ulick Moreen, Fanny Assingham!) has emphatically omitted the "h," the letter that portrays most graphically the two-part structure of the male genital. Missing his "h," Everard is eventually revealed as castrate. "'Don't you know, dear, that he has nothing?'" the infatuated heroine of the novella is told (1898, p. 262). "'Nothing?' It was hard to see him in such a light.'" Hard is just what he is not, because his enamorata, Lady Bradeen, has all the power. "'What does he bring [to their marriage]? Think what she has. And then, love, his debts.'" The phallic one is indeed the woman. "'So she just nailed him?'" the heroine emphasizes. "'She just nailed him'" (p. 265).

Names, like syntax, can enact the very theme they announce. Woman's place in patriarchy, for example, "*Catherine Earnshaw . . . Catherine Heathcliff . . . Catherine Linton.*" The three identities of Heathcliff's beloved in *Wuthering*

Heights (E. Brontë, p. 15) signal woman's fate as an object of exchange among men. This appropriative process is dramatized emphatically in the name games of great postcolonialist novels. *Wide Sargasso Sea*'s retelling of *Jane Eyre* scrutinizes what Jane (and Charlotte Brontë?) took on faith—the name of the mad woman in the attic. "'Bertha is not my name,'" Rochester is told by the Caribbean woman whose real name is Antoinette. "'You are trying to make me someone else, calling me by another name'" (Rhys, 1966, p. 147). The Brontë-Rhys genealogy is then carried on by Mukherjee (1989) in *Jasmine*. "I am Jane with my very own Mr. Rochester" (p. 210), says the Hindu heroine as she redeploys near the end of the novel a motif she sounded soon after she arrived in Iowa and met her second husband. "Bud calls me Jane. Me Bud, you Jane. I didn't get it at first. He kids. Calamity Jane. Jane as in Jane Russell, not Jane as in Plain Jane. But Plain Jane is all I want to be. Plain Jane is a role, like any other" (p. 22). It's not this easy, of course, and not only because of the difficulty of fitting into a new culture. Back in India the heroine's first husband also wanted to reshape her identity (and change her name, Jyoti), like Pygmalion. "How much of Professor Higgins there was in my husband. He wanted to . . . make me a new kind of city woman. To break off the past he gave me a new name: Jasmine . . . Jyoti, Jasmine: I shuttled between identities" (p. 70). Nor does she object. "'All right,' I said, 'if you want me to have a new life, I want it, too'" (p. 81). When he proceeds to imagine them forming a business, "'Vijh & Wife,' my husband said from deep inside my embrace. 'Maybe even Vijh & Vijh'" (p. 81), she again agrees. "'I can't live without you,' I said" (p. 85). Nor does she change when she first reaches America and rejects Virginia Woolf's ideal. "They thought I wanted a room of my own" (p. 165). Mukherjee is thus not glib about the relationship between identity and naming. To what extent were the name-changing men in fact evoking selves inherent in Jyoti-Jasmine-Jane? "How many more shapes are in me, how many more selves, how many more husbands?" she wonders (p. 190), shortly before abandoning Bud-Rochester and heading off with Taylor who "didn't want me to change. . . . I changed because I wanted to. . . . I bloomed from a diffident alien with forged documents into adventurous Jase" (p. 190).

With absurdity, Freud (1900) may seem narrow when he restricts manifest-level absurdity in dreams to implying latent criticism or ridicule (pp. 434–435), but he is surely correct that "dreams . . . are most profound when they seem most crazy" (p. 444). In texts generally, manifest absurdity points us to latent desire. It is absurd for King Lear to disinherit and banish his favorite daughter just because she declines to flatter him. What besides momentary disappointment is driving the old man? It's absurd for Victor Frankenstein to misread the monster's words, "'*I will be with you on your wedding-night!*' Such was my sentence" (Shelley, 1818, pp. 185–186). How can Victor miss the pun on "my sentence"? How can he assume *he* will be killed—when the monster is obviously threatening to slay Victor's bride, Elizabeth, because Frankenstein had refused to create a mate for the monster? Victor *wants* Elizabeth dead. His repressed desire sur-faces enough to block his recognition of the "sentence" pun—and thus of the monster's intention. Absurd, maybe, but lethally effective. Like the rationaliza-tions of the narrator of "The Black Cat" are absurdly comic—but still shaped by latent forces. After his house burns down on the night he hangs the first cat in the garden, he finds one wall standing. Graven on it in white bas relief is the figure of the hanged cat. His explanation? Someone who'd noticed the fire from the garden had cut the dead cat down and thrown it through his window to wake him up. "The falling of the other walls had compressed the victim of my cruelty into the substance of the freshly-spread plaster" (Poe, 1843, p. 853). Absurdity demands attention, but, even attentive, even directed to the latent, we find it difficult to get beyond the fairly obvious fact that the narrator is either dishonest or psychotic—until we attend to patterns and recognize a Freudian slip: "Freshly-spread plaster"? The narrator has never talked of remodeling. He has, however, revealed a penchant for entombing—wife and second cat—that constitutes a pattern. Manifest penchant gives way to latent obsession, an obsession with en-tombing that at least here, early in the tale, the narrator can suppress. His latent obsession takes us to mother, child, womb, tomb, and beyond, but it all started with absurdity and patterns.

Patterns are emphasized by Freud (1900) who insists that finding manifest parallels to replace suppressed latent parallels constitutes "no inconsiderable part of the dream-work" (p. 320). Although Freud himself tended to spend more time on condensation, displacement, and overdetermination, his recognition of the importance of patterns is especially instructive for literary criticism today because the profession's obsession with themes and contexts ignores a basic fact about all great art—a fact insisted upon by John Hawkes when speaking about his own work. "Related or corresponding event, recurring image and recurring action, these constitute the essential substance or meaningful density of my writ-ing" (Enck, 1964, p. 149).

In "The Black Cat," as we have seen, recurrence of both forms and contents tells the latent story. Cats, entombings, hangings—all repeat. The narrator blinds the cat, then "blindly" abandons himself (Poe, 1843, p. 856); he refers to his "bosom" three times in the last two pages; and, he tellingly associates the writ-ing process with the blinding process by lamenting, "I shudder while I pen the damnable atrocity" (p. 851) as he recalls cutting out the cat's eye with a "pen-knife." And then there's the "meres." This word and its variants appear six times in "The Black Cat," whereas in, say, "Hop-Frog," a story of the same length, there are none. Even a quick glance at a few of the "meres" in "The Black Cat" suggests how meaningfully dense the recurrence is. The narrator laments "the paltry friendship and gossamer fidelity of mere Man" (p. 850); the white gal-lows on the cat's breast is "the merest chi*mera*" (p. 855; emphasis added); and the bravado that compels the narrator to expose his crime begins as "mere frenzy"

(p. 858). Mother is never manifest, but in latent depths she is everywhere: unfaithful and masculine, lethal and monstrous, frantic and compelling.

It is recurrence that leads us to her, recurrence that structures "The Black Cat." Wherever there's meaningful density, there's recurrence. But for us, recurrence is more than a structural strategy and a road to the latent. Recurrence plays a key role in future Freud because it will ultimately allow critics to do what we now explore—reading literary texts as we do dreams. This is important because even though many theorists emphasize the parallels between dream and literature, when it comes right down to it, when it comes to parallel readings, they all hedge. And, in his theorizing, Freud is one of the hedgers. In practice he once again leads the way, but let's start with theory.

Seven years after "The Interpretation of Dreams" (1900), Freud writes "Delusions and Dreams in Jensen's *Gradiva*" (1907) to show that dreams in literature can be interpreted with the same techniques that he'd developed for "real" dreams. Along the way, Freud (1907) presents the reason for hedging, for not analyzing all literature like dreams.

> Are we perhaps under an obligation to replace . . . each separate piece of the manifest content of the dream [in *Gradiva*] by unconscious thoughts? Strictly speaking, yes; if we were interpreting a dream that had really been dreamt, we could not avoid that duty. But in that case, too, the dreamer would have to give us the most copious explanations. Clearly we cannot carry out this requirement in the case of the author's creation; nevertheless, we shall not overlook the fact that we have not yet submitted the main content of the dream to the process of interpretation or translation [p. 60].

We can't read dreams in literature—the rest of the century will say, we can't read literature itself—like actual dreams because *clearly* literature doesn't provide the dreamer's "copious explanations." We can't do it, but with a quick "nevertheless" Freud goes on to do just that. He reads dreams in *Gradiva,* usually "each separate piece," *exactly* like dreams in life. And he takes on more than he imagines because clearly neither *Gradiva's* dreams nor *Gradiva* itself have an actual dreamer to make those personal associations, those "copious explanations," which are so essential to Freudian dream theory. Texts don't have dreamers. The way Freud circumvents this problem—in practice, not in theory—is instructive. Analyzing a dream of the main character, Norbert Hanold, Freud says, "[S]ince . . . we cannot question Hanold . . . we may very tentatively put our own associations in place of his" (p. 73). This is what Freud *says,* but when it comes to doing, he demonstrates, skillfully, and not so very tentatively, that if we use, *not* our associations, but *the associations of the text,* we can read textual dream like literal dream. Freud's analysis of Hanold's dreams in *Gradiva* attend to their displacements, condensations, and overdeterminations; he even finds a bilingual pun, showing us that "[s]omewhere in the sun Gradiva is sitting" indicates that unconsciously Hanold knows she's staying at the Allegro de *Sole* (p. 77). But all this comes while Freud confronts the text's associations. He shows that Gradiva catching lizards in the text's dream is like her father catching lizards in the text; that Gradiva's slipping lizard-like through narrow gaps associates her with the lizard in the dream; and that a lady colleague in dream is much like the "famous" Eimer in text because they have similar lines. Patterns. Characters, actions, images in the dreams reverberate with associations from the nondream portions of the text. Dream and nondream are commingled: condensations work with elements of each, displacements go from one to another, and overdeterminations contain both. The nondream portions are just as deep, just as subtle, just as layered as dream: the real "Eimer," for example, is one of the men whose role is taken over by dream women, but his surname has subtle feminine associations—eimer/bucket, ei/ovum, mer/sea—which suggest that the name of the father has been taken over too. In the very midst of working with Hanold's dreams, Freud (1907) says, "[O]ur author . . . never introduces a single idle or unintentional feature into his *story*" (p. 68; emphasis added), and his Freudian slip says it all. It's not just the density of dream that demands Freud's reading. Freud knew what Joyce and Kafka would dramatize: because you can't ultimately differentiate between textual dream and textual nondream anyway, they must be read the same way, and with the help of the associations *of the text,* they can be.

Indeed, we can't read latent levels *without* the associations of the text. In Hawkes's *The Lime Twig* (1961), William Hencher "pulled open the door and there was the hallway dry and dark as ever . . . the one faint bulb swinging round and round on its cord. But our boxes were burning" (p. 14). Hencher can never discover how the boxes caught fire, but we can. There are only two other swinging lights in *The Lime Twig,* and both swing round the head of the underworld boss, Larry. Once Hencher's swinging bulb takes us to Larry, once we know that Larry is the arsonist, we can then begin to explore latent motives. Earlier we said that Reuben Bourne's motives still "lay hidden"; now it's important to note that most critics haven't been able to explore hidden motivation here because they haven't been able to follow the patterns that show something is amiss. When Reuben goes on the hunting trip that will end with his "accidentally" shooting his son, "his devious course kept him in the vicinity of the encampment" (p. 355), but we don't know how devious this course is until we recall that his son has just left, promising "not to quit the vicinity of the encampment" (p. 354). Actually we don't *have* to recall, because when Cyrus is shot we're reminded: "[his mother] was aroused by the report of a gun in the vicinity of the encampment" (p. 358). Until we read the patterns, we can't begin to ask why this father would *want* to kill his son or *why* this mother would be aroused by it.

The indistinguishability of dream and text becomes more evident when we study another type of recurrence. In *Frankenstein* (Shelley, 1818), as in other intense narratives, characters hide behind reversal of affect. We've touched on one instance already, where, after the creature's "'I'll be with you on your wedding night,'" Frankenstein takes his new bride to isolated Evian for a honeymoon, "earnestly entreat[s] her to retire, resolving not to join her" (p. 192)—only to discover, as anyone but Victor could have foreseen, his "beloved girl" (p. 180) is no more. The creature "consummate[s] his crimes" (p. 186), and we're left to determine whether Frankenstein is nefarious or naive. If there is any doubt, "Evian" puts it to rest: the palindromic reverse of "naive" emphasizes that at the latent level it's all the reverse of naïve, the reverse of Victor's asserted adoration. We can proceed to explore Victor's motives for wanting the creature to do away with Elizabeth—his referring to her as "[his mother's] favorite" (p. 28), suggests jealousy; the sexual connotations of "join" and "consummate" suggest impotence. But, again, we can't get far beneath the manifest level until we know what Victor has done and that his affects can't be trusted.

And reversals of affect recur. Robert Walton's "love" for his sister—"[his] dear, excellent, Margaret" (p. 12)—is as vexed as Victor's love for Elizabeth. The ambiguity that persists throughout Walton's letters haunts the first line of *Frankenstein.* "You will rejoice to hear that no disaster has accompanied the commencement of an enterprise which you have regarded with such evil forebodings" (p. 9). The difference between "evil forebodings" and "forebodings of evil" is about as significant as the juxtaposition that comes right after the very next time Walton mentions evil. "I have no friend, Margaret" (p. 13). The defending reaction formation, "dear excellent Margaret," is almost de rigueur because Walton, like Victor Frankenstein, can't face up. And they're not alone. Alphonse Frankenstein memorializes his best friend and his wife, who is also his best friend's daughter, in a living room picture—of his wife *kneeling at her father's deathbed.* But he can never say that he likes seeing his best friend dead and his wife bereft. Elizabeth herself, when the servant, Justine Moritz, is on trial for her life, rushes to save the poor innocent, whom she, of course, loves dearly. But Elizabeth defends with the likes of "she appeared to me the most amiable and benevolent of human creatures . . . notwithstanding all the evidence produced against her, I believe and rely on her perfect innocence" (p. 80). Little wonder that her oration is received with "a murmur . . . not in favor of poor Justine" (p. 80). Elizabeth is not a defense attorney; she's more of a defended attorney. She sees Justine as a "great favorite" of both her mother and brother (p. 60), but she can't see her own jealousies. Like all the rest of the characters, Elizabeth uses reversal of affect to hide from her darker affects, because darker affects lead to darker motives, and darker motives lead to the darkest self-incriminations.

One of the ways that *Frankenstein* stresses the similarity of dream and waking life is by having Victor's dream begin with a reversal of affect. "I thought I saw Elizabeth in the bloom of health, walking in the streets of Ingolstadt. Delighted and surprised, I embraced her" (p. 53). We might give him "surprised," but by now we know enough to see through "delighted"; after all, this is the young man who has just spent five years hiding out in Ingolstadt without ever going home to see "beloved" Elizabeth. But reversal of affect is not the only Freudian technique in both *Frankenstein*'s dream and daily life. This dream continues with another reversal of affect and with what Freud calls a transformation.

> [B]ut just as I imprinted the first kiss on her lips, they became livid with the hue of death; her features appeared to change and I thought that I held the corpse of my dead mother in my arms; a shroud enveloped her form, and I saw the grave-worms crawling in the folds of the flannel. I started from my sleep with horror; a cold dew covered my forehead, my teeth chattered, and every limb became convulsed; when, by the dim and yellow light of the moon, as it forced its way through the window shutters, I beheld the wretch—the miserable monster whom I had created [p. 53].

In dream, Elizabeth is transformed into mother; at the moment of waking, the site of mother is filled by the monster, who in the next paragraph is compared with "a mummy again endued with animation" (p. 53). In both dreaming and waking states, Freud's assertion that manifest transformations represent latent causality can help us because mother does, in fact, "cause" both Elizabeth and the monster. Of course it is all overdetermined, but at one level, Victor's relationship with Elizabeth, his "more than sister," is quasi-incestuous, a displaced version of the oedipal relationship he longs for. At another level the creature, "the mummy endued with animation," is a displaced version of the dead mommy Victor longs to reanimate. Once we see this, it can help us realize that Victor's "horror" is in fact the fulfillment of a wish oedipal and matricidal. After all we know the patterns, and they say that in dream life, waking life, and the nebulous life in between, *Frankenstein* is structured on reversal of affect.

Well . . . not exactly all of *Frankenstein*. The story that the creature tells, his life story that he narrates to Victor, has *no* striking reversal of affect. Mary Shelley goes out of her way to avoid transformations and displacements, verbal play and symbols—to excise distortions. The creature's story is what it is and that's all that it is. You can sample anywhere.

> I gradually saw plainly the clear stream that supplied me with drink and the trees that shaded me with their foliage. I was delighted when I first discovered that a pleasant sound, which often saluted my ears, proceeded from the throats of the little winged animals who had often intercepted the light from my eyes. I began also to observe, with great accuracy, the forms that surrounded me and to perceive the boundaries of the radiant roof of light which canopied me. Sometimes I tried to imitate the pleasant songs of the birds but was unable. Sometimes I wished to express my sensations in my own mode, but the uncouth and inarticulate sounds which broke from me frightened me into silence again [pp. 98–99].

The creature says what he means and means what he says. He says, ominously, but directly, "I will be with you on your honeymoon": it's only Victor who introduces the ambiguity that begins with the pun on "sentence." Whenever *any* of the other characters says anything, we have to think it over. Victor refuses to make a female for the creature because that might lead to a horde of baby creatures—*that* would be thought on. But think as we might on the creature's words, we're not going anywhere: there's very little to undistort. There are no hidden motives; indeed the creature uses the word "motive" twice: "I endeavor[ed] to discover the motives . . . I longed to discover the motives" (pp. 105, 109). And this is one pattern that *isn't* repeated. The other characters in *Frankenstein* don't try hard enough to discover motives; they're all too busy hiding from their own motives and hiding from themselves. Only the creature can face up. Just as he quickly learns the dual nature of fire, "How strange, I thought, that the same cause should produce such opposite effects" (p. 99), so too he learns, and accepts, the dual nature of his self. "The feelings of kindness and gentleness which I had entertained but a few moments before gave place to a hellish rage and gnashing teeth" (p. 138). Elizabeth doesn't do much teeth gnashing because she suppresses her rage; like all the other characters here, with the single exception of Victor who needs to hate his creature, Elizabeth needs to see herself loving all God's children, loving all God's children as Justine Moritz hangs. Only the creature has no suppressions, no distortions, and no unconscious *because* he alone has had no infancy. "No father had watched my infant days, no mother had blessed me with smiles and caresses" (p. 117). But Mary Shelley knows what Sigmund Freud makes a cornerstone of his psychology: father's watchings and mother's caresses come at a high price. The creature, born full grown, misses smiles and caresses, but he also misses the anxieties of infantile sexuality, the longings and loathings, failings and frustrations that initiate repression which, in turn, create the unconscious.

Victor Frankenstein too talks of smiles and caresses. "My mother's tender caresses and my father's smile of benevolent pleasure while regarding me are my first recollections. I was their plaything and their idol, and something better—their child, their innocent and helpless creature" (p. 234). But his language resonates—"plaything," "idol," "helpless," *"creature."* The language of his creature, who never was a creature of infancy, neither resonates *nor fascinates*. It is what it is and that *is* all that it is. The creature is boring. His story is more than enough to make us truly appreciate how much fun—later we will say "forepleasure"—Freudian reading has brought to literature. The creature's portion of *Frankenstein* is neither the meaningfully dense literature that Hawkes (1964) talks about above nor the "significant literature" that he discusses in another context. "Fear of the unknown, fear of sexual destruction at the hands of the father, fear of annihilation at the hands of absolute authority, infantile desire for the security and sublimity of the mother's love—these components of the familiar oedipal situation as defined by Freud are to be found in significant literature through the ages" (pp. 519–20).

Although Hawkes's quotation emphasizes much of what we've seen, such as the importance of the infantile to literature, it also suggests that we should look further at latent contents. But before we do let's stay with form a bit longer because there is something else going on here. When Hawkes talks about the content of literature, he defers to Freud; but when he talks about form on page 13, Freud doesn't even get a footnote. This is indicative of an all too popular notion, put much more directly by Jean-Michel Rey (1977): "[T]here is in Freud an astounding failure to recognize the formal work of which literature is capable, the power that a fictional text can deploy for representation, the syntactic and symantic transformations of which fiction is the locus" (p. 310). Throughout the 20th century, critics, the more recent the more virulent, have taken Freud to task for ignoring the formal in literature, and though there are some grounds for this attack, the problem is that there is in most of these critics an astounding failure to recognize the formal work of which Freud's dream theory is capable. Yes, Freud (1914) himself told us that "the subject-matter of works of art has a stronger attraction . . . than their formal and technical qualities" (p. 211). Yes, his brief analyses of *Hamlet* and *Oedipus* reflect this proclivity. And yes, at times Freud does seem a bit naïve regarding literature. "To discover [the author's] intention . . . I must first discover the meaning and content of what is represented in his work; I must, in other words, be able to *interpret* it" (p. 212). The suggestion here that we can discover *the* meaning and *the* intention, *the* interpretation, recalls Freud's suggestion that dreams in *Gradiva* demand his intricate techniques, whereas literary texts really do not. There is, it seems, some truth in Rey's (1977) assertion that "Freud never really takes into account the different degrees of veiling that the literary text is capable of" (p. 316). But before we start bashing Freud with the likes of the intentional fallacy and his "formal disclaimer," let's remember the Freud of dreams, jokes, and the uncanny, the Freud who demonstrates and advocates the importance of the formal. Let's remember the Freud of *Gradiva* who, despite his theory, utilizes his dream techniques on nondream fiction with results both impressive and formal. As we go on into the new century, let's remember that whatever Freud's own priorities, he gave us in "The Interpretation of Dreams" the methodology to deal with *any* degree of veiling that a literary text is capable of. Once we see that the text can give us as many associations as the dreamer can—through repetitions and elaborations, reversals and echoes, along with what Rey calls syntactic and symatic transformations—then we can see that Freud has given to the 21st century the methodology for interrogating the text and discovering meaning through and *in* form.

The formal parallels between dream and literature speak, moreover, to more than reading; they can help us with theories of literature and creativity. Again because of spatial constraints we will just glance at a few possibilities. Jack Spector (1973) begins *The Aesthetics of Freud* by conceding that "[e]ssential questions implicit in a psychoanalysis of art remain—and perhaps must remain—wholly or partially unanswered: How does form evolve from its origins in the chaotic unconscious, and how does it provide us with its pleasures and satisfactions?" (p. vii). And while Freud's direct confrontations with questions of form are neither frequent nor particularly optimistic, we've seen that Freud (1925) often does more than he says. He says "[psychoanalysis can't] explain the means by which the artist works—artistic technique" (p. 65), but we've seen that, as he says this, he's presenting concepts that will ultimately suggest that the creative work is like the dream work, the artistic technique like the techniques of dream distortion. These suggestions can, in turn, begin to answer Spector's perplexing questions about form, when we consider them in light of Freud's own most perplexing—and most discussed–reference to formal aesthetics. In "Creative Writers and Day-Dreaming," Freud (1908) discusses how creative writers escape the repulsiveness inherent in day dreams.

> The essential *ars poetica* lies in the technique of overcoming the feeling of repulsion in us which is undoubtedly connected with the barriers that rise between each single ego and the others. We can guess two of the methods used by this technique. The writer softens the character of his egoistic daydream by altering and disguising it, and he bribes us by the purely formal— that is, aesthetic—yield of pleasure which he offers us in the presentation of his phantasies. We give the name of an *incentive bonus,* or a *fore-pleasure*, to a yield of pleasure such as this, which is offered to us so as to make possible the release of still greater pleasure arising from deeper psychical sources [p. 153].

Previous critics have pondered this passage or dismissed it, but we can refine it because our work with dream suggests that writers use Freud's techniques of distortion to soften, alter, and disguise, *and* our work with the creature's somewhat tedious narrative suggests that these very techniques—the condensations and juxtapositions, puns and verbal ambiguities missing in the creature's story— are essential to the text's formal yield of pleasure. So, how does literature assume form? Literature assumes form as dream does: the writer, consciously or unconsciously, utilizes Freud's techniques of distortion to both disguise *and* shape materials from his "chaotic" unconscious. How does form provide pleasure? As readers consciously or unconsciously reverse the disguising and shaping process, their pleasures are largely epistemophilic. We penetrate formal techniques, expose the latent, come to know.

Of course this isn't simple in any sense. We can't really come to consummate knowledge because we can't penetrate *all* the distortions, we can't trace all the reverberations. Freud's navel of the dream, the place where analysis can't reach, is yet another concept applicable to literature as well as dream. We'll never come to know fully, but do we need to? Do we even want to? If we completely reversed the distorting process, we'd be back to daydream and that's repulsive. Part of the pleasure is in the struggle, the glimpse, the text tease. Textual foreplay is pleasurable in and of itself. So Freud's suggestions that fore-pleasure is there only "to make possible a release of greater pleasure arising from deeper psychical sources," only to keep us going until we come to know the text's psychic depths, is misdirective, another privileging of comprehensibility over complexity and content over form. But Freud's situating the formal in the realm of the erotic is *most* directive. How quickly our own discussion of form moved to the sexual: expose, penetrate . . . know. How quickly we turned away from knowing and revisited the pleasures of textual foreplay, the pleasures that did not lead to consummation. The techniques of distortion that conceal as they reveal, the repetitions that force us backward and forward in the text, keeping us from the *petite* and the symbolic deaths of climax, ending, and knowledge, these are— like epistemophilia itself—the pleasures of the perverse. These are the pleasures that "Creative Writers and Daydreaming" can't handle because Freud's emphasis on the climactic moment here recognizes forepleasure only in the genital realm of consummate knowing. If, however, we move to Freud's "Three Essays on the Theory of Sexuality" (1905a), where he locates forepleasure in the pregenital, we might be able to read the formal foreplay that we've associated with Freud's techniques of distortion in light of the perverse; we might be able to work with the meaningful pleasures of frustrated meanings to learn about the readers' epistemophelia and the writers' creativity. The forms that reveal and conceal, which seem to work both with the pleasure principle as they provide limited meanings *and* beyond the pleasure principle as they provide limitless frustrations might help us to develop an erotics of form that could call into question the boundaries between perversion and normalcy, genital and pregenital, pleasure and beyond.

It's not just Freud's theories of sexuality and perversion, of life and death, that can help us develop an erotics of form. Freud knows that literature breaks down boundaries. But as with most of his insights into literature, he doesn't elaborate much, so let's go back to "Creative Writers and Day-Dreaming" to recall how suggestive Freud's own language can be, how much it does and how much it leaves to be done. Freud insists that "the essential *ars poetica* lies in the technique of overcoming the feeling of [day-dream's] repulsion in us"; then he casually adds "which is undoubtedly connected with the barriers that rise between each single ego and the others." So, with what almost appears a throwaway line, Freud implies that creative texts break down the boundaries between self and others, and, because he moves right to form, he also implies that this breaking down of boundaries has to do with more than content, with more than, say, the writer tapping into universal fantasies.

It has to do with form. And this too would be thought on: how can form break down the barriers between author and reader? We could begin by saying that familiar forms, be they sonnets or haiku, like familiar fantasies, help bridge the gap between selves, but the answer here must be overdetermined because barriers separating selves and structured on *repulsion* seem too formidable to be dissolved by iambic pentameter or seventeen syllables. Like many of the "casual" insights that Freud has with creativity, this seems worth pursuing—especially in light of our discussions of Freud's techniques which all implicitly suggested the relevance of breaking boundaries. Reading through punctuation breaks down boundaries; bisexual distortions question the distinction between male and female; repetitions bring life and death a bit closer; and figurations associate signifiers with signifiers and signifieds with signifieds. Manifest/latent, dream/reality, love/hate—our texts are texts of fusion. And just as Freud's techniques of distortion, in various ways and to various degrees, bring two's closer to one's, so too our confrontations with these distortions, our pleasures of the text, combine what Barthes (1975) calls "an oedipal pleasure, to denude, to know, to learn the origin and the end" (p. 10) and what Freud (1905b) calls the preoedipal verbal pleasure of foreplay (pp. 137–138). Puns and patterns are paradigmatic. With Poe's "The Black Cat" (1843), we've seen that the narrator's repetitions of "mere" unite household events, gossamer fidelity, white gallows, chimera, and frenzy, whereas "mere" itself unites mere, mirror, and mother. "The Black Cat" emphasizes one final union, for if the narrator's forms are fusional, so is his fantasy. The narrator who entombs cats and wife and buries mother in "mere" betrays himself in "a mere frenzy" to die tomorrow and, presumably, to be buried soon after. *To* be buried. He turns himself in so that he can be buried with and in mother, and the fusion that he craves comes with and in form as Poe uses fusion to break down the barriers between form and content.

Theorists both literary and psychoanalytic have recently moved toward Poe's concerns, and, some would say, away from Freud's, as they stress the relevance of this preoedipal fusion. Joyce McDougall (1995) in the *The Many Faces of Eros* is representative. Following Freud, she begins by associating creative writing with play, then moves on to show that the creative writer, like Winnicott's baby during "primary creativity," "seeks to *recreate,* in hallucinatory fashion, the lost fusion with the maternal universe" (p. 54). Although this would certainly explain why the formal techniques of creative writing are fusional, it wouldn't explain why they're Freudian. But we've seen that they are, and this in itself suggests that Freud can help with *au courant* literary theory. Indeed, Freud's discussions of both jokes and the uncanny speak directly and profoundly to the issues of form and fusion. Freud (1905b) stresses that repetition structures both jokes and the uncanny, so that we're lead to "a rediscovery of the familiar" (p. 128). In "The 'Uncanny,'" it's even a familiar place: "mother's genitals or her body" (1919, p. 245) trigger the uncanny effect. "To some people the idea of being buried alive by mistake is the most uncanny thing of all. And yet psycho-analysis has taught us that this terrifying phantasy is only a transformation of another phantasy, . . . the phantasy, I mean, of intra-uterine existence" (p. 244). If this takes us to Poe, Freud's explanation of how writers re-create such un-canny phantasies with techniques such as doubling takes us to McDougall. "They are harking-back to particular phases in the evolution of the self-regarding feel-ing, a regression to a time where the ego had not yet marked itself off sharply from the external world and from other people" (Freud, 1919, p. 236). And "Jokes and Their Relation to the Unconscious" takes us directly to formal foreplay, as Freud (1905b) shows how the texts of jokes—with techniques such as *unifica-tion*—take us back to when a child "is learning . . . his mother-tongue" (p. 125), back to "pleasurable effects, which arise from a repetition of what is similar, a rediscovery of what is familiar, similarity of sound, etc." (p. 128). Just when it gets aggressively innovative—similarity of sounds causing textual infantile plea-sures—Freud stops. Readers might wish that he had gone on, just as we might wish that he had written the study of the aesthetics of the uncanny that he called for at the end of his essay on the psychology of the uncanny or suggested *how* texts give fore-pleasure. But he didn't. And now, nearly a century later, Freud's provocative "etc." and his unanswered call and question linger, suggesting the potential insights that Freudian theory can some day bring to literary theory.

The Legacy: Concepts and Figurations

"Freud's inconspicuous discovery of the unconscious mind at the end of the nineteenth century bids fair to be the defining moment in the intellectual life of the twentieth." Norman Holland's speculation in 1964 has proven prescient (p. 3). Freud's core concepts and their figural representations did indeed become basic to how the twentieth century saw itself, that is, the unconscious and its structure, infantile sexuality, repetition compulsion, and the oral-anal-genital-oedipal phases of maturation. At issue for literary criticism in the twenty-first century is not the continued relevance of these concepts but their adaptation and development. Spatial restrictions require us to focus on a single feature of this ongoing process: the Oedipus.

Freud as a nineteenth-century, Viennese, Jewish, professional man tended to emphasize both the oedipal over the preoedipal and male desire over female within the Oedipus. Various later twentieth-century factors suggest, however, that the millennium is the time of mother and the preoedipal. The resurgence of feminism in the 1960s, the emergence of the Object Relations school of psycho-analysis in the 1970s and 1980s, and the convergence of these forces in the 1980s and 1990s (especially in the work of Chodorow, Benjamin, Suleiman, Kaplan) require and enable us to rethink both the oedipal structure and preoedipal desire in light of the mother.

The Oedipus came as a shock to Western culture. Beneath manifest orthodoxy lay heterodox desire: the beloved son desires his sire's death and his
mother's bed. The shock has worn off by the twenty-first century. But maybe it
shouldn't have. Suppose—in addition to being a shocking revelation—the Oedipus was also a reaction formation. Suppose the latent level of incestuous-patricidal
desire hid a still darker secret. Fear of the mother. Suppose the Oedipus was—
ultimately—a way of explaining and thus controlling not just the son but *her*?
Dracula ends:

> Seven years ago we all went through the flames; and the happiness of some of
> us since then is, we think, well worth the pain we endured. It is an added joy
> to Mina and me that our boy's birthday is the same day as that on which
> Quincey Morris died. His mother holds, I know, the secret belief that some of
> our brave friend's sprit passed into him. . . . In the summer of this year we
> made a journey to Transylvania. . . . Van Helsing summed it [the question of
> proof of what happened] all up as he said, with our boy on his knee:—
>
> "We want no proofs; we ask none to believe us! This boy will some day
> know what a brave and gallant woman his mother is. Already he knows her
> sweetness and loving care; later on he will understand how some men so
> loved her, that they did dare much for her sake" [Stoker, 1897, pp. 485–486].

Wife-mother Mina never gets in a word. She cannot even hold her son. She is so
absorbed into the relentless "we" that readers cannot determine whether she was
included when *we* returned to Transylvania (would she have taken a child so
young on a journey so arduous, or have left him back home for so long?). She
has "secret beliefs," but these are not *secret* because her husband blabs them to
everyone constituting the group and reading the novel. Finally, and most co-
optive, Mina is encased in a narrative. Although it is patently untrue that Van
Helsing's "Army of Light" worked its wonders chiefly on her behalf, his fiction
retells the St. George myth. Woman, so long as she remains helpless, receives
the service of manly men. Mina of course has been anything but helpless in
Dracula: As the New Woman she's mastered the new technologies of typewriter
and dictaphone and shorthand; she's also replicated on her forehead the "scar"
of Dracula, as well as ingesting his blood and sustaining telepathic communication with him. No wonder this woman needs to be reinscribed into the old tale of
male devotion and female quiescence, and no wonder that her son is held by the
senior patriarch. In this boy's veins flow the blood of all the Army of Light—
and Dracula too! Has Mina transmitted into the heart of patriarchy's future the
contagion that Dracula could not effect personally? Is woman—and the oedipal
triangle which she constitutes with Jonathan and little Quincy—the true villain
of *Dracula*? Confine her at all cost!

Literature, with its large female readership and brilliant women practitioners,
has freed and explored female desire throughout the 19th and 20th centuries. We

have space to explore, even briefly, only two aspects of the feminine. One is woman's role within the Oedipus. In 1858, the brightest new star in America's literary firmament, Harriet Prescott (Spofford, 1859), opens her masterpiece, "Circumstance," by positioning a frontier wife-mother as a paradigmatic True Woman: returning home through the twilight forest to her husband and baby son after nursing an invalid all day. Suddenly she is snatched up into a tall tree by a monster called the Indian Devil. The tale ends with a reunion of mother-father-baby son that allows for a "comic" interpretation, a reaffirmation of the oedipal triangle. Any such simple affirmation of orthodox values and stereotypes would ignore, however, all the heterodox emotions that surface during the dark night of this Everywoman (she has no name). She in fact occupies all three positions of the Oedipus as she reveals what orthodoxy refused to acknowledge in the wife-mother role—a (no doubt unconscious) distaste for every component of the nuclear family, for baby, husband, and self.

The distasteful aspects of all three figures are embodied in the monster, whose overdetermined nature is signaled by the heroine's "wondering lest his name of Indian Devil might not be his true name" (p. 87). This makes no sense on the manifest level: *Who cares* what a monster is *called* at such a terrifying moment? The heroine's wonderment suggests that the monster's role is identificatory, projective: for her, his names are baby, husband, self. As baby the monster is soothed by her singing. "Still the beast lay with closed eyes. . . . Once a half-whine of enjoyment escaped him—he fawned his fearful head upon her. . . . His long sharp claws were caught in her clothing, he worried them sagaciously a little, then, finding that ineffectual to free them, he commenced licking her" (pp. 86, 90). Attachment so tactile is exacerbated by an orality so intense that it suggests the horror a nursing mother can feel during lactation, her experience of being literally devoured. "The torrent of his breath prepared her for his feast as the anaconda slimes his prey" (p. 88). The monster becomes husband as his behavior becomes phallic. Although the wife's prettiest vision represents her husband as ideally androgynous—"cleaning his gun, with one foot on the [cradle's] green wooden rundle" (pp. 86–87)—latent antagonism finds expression in the monster's "holding her in his great lithe embrace . . . his eyes glaring through all the darkness like balls of red fire" (p. 86). Focusing on the sharp claws, she fears penetration, "the fierce plunge of those weapons" (p. 86). Her worries seem well founded, for when the charm of her music wanes, the monster, growing more aggressive, disentangles his "fettered member" (p. 88). Probably strangest and most revealing are the ways in which the monster bodies forth the heroine herself, her self-hate. It's understandable that, confronting ferocious teeth and claws, she feels horror at imagining "the long strips of living flesh torn from her bones, the agony" (p. 86), but it's surely odd that she goes on to specify "the agony" as "the quivering disgust, itself a worst agony." How can disgust be an agony worse than evisceration? And why would she feel disgust at her body assaulted without provocation? An answer suggests itself when she, projectively, calls the monster "this living lump of appetites" (p. 89). She insists that dying by fire is superior because it "is not to be known by the strength of our lower natures let loose." Disgust at her own animal nature takes on a decidedly sexual cast as "his tongue retouched her arm. Again her lips opened by instinct" (p. 86).

Despite charges that it is reductively apolitical, the Oedipus can in fact help us understand female desires when they are shaped by cultural as well as domestic forces (slavery, for example). "124 (Bluestone Road, the haunted house where the heroine, Sethe, lives with her mother-in-law and her daughter, in *Beloved*] was spiteful." *Beloved* (Morrison, 1987) opens without a "three": not 123, but 124. Human development—from grandiose self, to mother–child dyad, to oedipal triangle, and on to the four that Freud called the number of completion—was especially difficult under slavery because the slave-owner's prime concern was to break the black family, to prevent "three" from happening. A breeding pair; then a mother–child dyad: two but not three: no family. "A house with two stories" (p. 47) is how Morrison characterizes 124 Bluestone Road. Will her own novel constitute the third story, the tale of a woman achieving an oedipal family after the grandiose and dyadic stages have been left behind? "'You lucky. You got three left'" (p. 5). What Baby Suggs lauds expressly is the fact that Sethe has three children left from her slave years, but, more important, what Sethe has left is the possibility of a *true* family, of forming a permanent union with a man now that she is safely in Ohio and can solidify three-ness by having a baby in sanctioned wedlock with him.

Another possibility (once her two slave-born sons flee) is that Paul D can adopt Sethe's daughter, Denver, and the three can form their own family. "The three of them, Sethe, Denver, and Paul D, breathed to the same beat" (pp. 18–19). Paul D's very efforts undercut our hopes, however. "'I got two dollars. Me and you and Denver gonna spend every penny of it [at the fair]'" (p. 46). *Two* dollars, *three* people. Going to the fair, "they were not holding hands, but their shadows were. . . . All three of them were gliding over the dust holding hands. . . . Maybe he was right [thinks Sethe]. A life. . . . all the time the three shadows that shot out of their feet to the left of their hands" (p. 47). Shadows, but not substance. "Up and down the lumberyard fence old roses were dying. The sawyer . . . had planted them twelve years ago" (p. 47). The rose cannot get beyond 1–2 to 1–2–3, and neither can Paul D. Slavery has so damaged his sense of manliness that "he didn't believe he could live with a woman—any woman—for over two out of three months" (p. 40). Two, not three. Sethe, also damaged severely by slavery, has, in turn, other plans. Instead of having a child with Paul D, she replaces him with her baby-come-back, Beloved. "Hearing the three of them [Sethe, Beloved, Denver] laughing at something he wasn't in on" (p. 132), Paul D is doomed as Sethe attempts to form another type of threesome, a matriarchal family. "Walking back through the woods, Sethe put her arm around each girl at her side. Both of them had an arm around her waist. . . . Obviously the three hand-holding shadows she had seen on the road were not Paul D, Denver and herself [Sethe ruminates], but 'us three.' The three holding on to each other skating the night before; the three sipping flavored milk" (pp. 175, 182). This matriarchal family fares no better than an adoptive family, however. The female threesome soon breaks down into two and one, as the voracious baby Beloved devours the abject mother, and Denver is left alone.

Sethe and Paul D never make it to three, to marriage and a baby. The depredations of slavery prove too great; more than an Emancipation Proclamation and a bloody war are needed to heal psyches so savaged. "Freeing yourself was one thing; claiming ownership of that freed self was another" (p. 95). What Sethe does manage with Paul D is reunion. Numbers again are crucial. Having wounded Sethe to the core by indicting her as a beast for killing her children—"'you got two feet, Sethe, not four'" (p. 165)—Paul D returns to minister to the damaged woman, to face the number two. " 'Is it all right, Sethe, if I heat up some water?' 'And count my feet?' He steps closer. 'Rub your feet'" (p. 272). And thereby find strength in what remains behind. Oedipal analysis, analysis in light of the developmental role of three, is thus capable of social and political, as well as domestic insights. The Oedipus can help us recognize both what is missing, thereby indicting a racist society, and what is achieved, thereby attesting to the value of a true union of any kind.

Moving from the oedipal to the preoedipal, we can address the role of the feminine in terrors that Freud tended to underplay and that literature features insistently. Immediately we must establish what is at stake here: "Mother" in the preoedipal terrors of adults is a figure of *fantasy*. We are therefore not analyzing here the "reconstructed maternal image" to which feminists such as Marianne Hirsch (1986) and Julia Kristeva (1980) have given considerable attention. We are analyzing the fantasies of characters, chiefly male, who are battling imagoes recurring from early childhood. The destructive Kleinian (1946) mother, for example, is encountered by poor Maisie as she's drawn to "her mother's breast, where, amid a wilderness of trinkets, she felt as if she had been suddenly thrust, with a smash of glass, into a jeweler's shop-front, but only to be as suddenly ejected" (James, 1897, p. 124). Bad Breast indeed. The expressly *oral* threat posed by the Kleinian mother is dramatized in Stevenson's *Jekyll and Hyde* (1886) when the doctor's desperate need for a chemical to complete his potion prompts a note to the pharmacist. "'For God's sake . . . send me some of the old.'" The response announced by Jekyll's butler? "'The man at Maw's was main angry'" (p. 66).

This old Ma who's the main man (and angry all the time) is embodied in the figure of the Phallic Mother. Her virtually mythic status is suggested in the "Rip Van Winkle" myth (Irving, 1818) of "the old squaw spirit, said to be their [the Indians'] mother" who "hung up the new moons in the skies and cut up the old ones into stars. In times of draught, if properly propitiated" she would send rain, but "if displeased . . . she would brew up clouds black as ink, sitting in the midst of them like a bottle-bellied spider, in the midst of its web; and when the clouds broke, woe betide the valleys!" (p. 54). The fluid indispensable to life becomes a weapon of death in the castrating hands of the timeless woman who cuts up "the old ones" and remains alone and invincible. Her real-life counterpart is Juliana Bordereau in James's (1888) *The Aspern Papers.* "I felt her look at me with great penetration" (p. 61), observes the nameless narrator who is particu-larly disconcerted because "the old woman remained impenetrable" (p. 62) to him. Surveying the "impenetrable regions" of her palazzo, "I looked at the place with my heart beating as I had known it to do in dentists' parlours" (p. 55). What occurred in Victorian dentist parlors was, of course, tooth extraction; the castra-tion that the narrator feels here recurs both when his friend says of Juliana and her niece "'they'll get all your money'" (p. 70) and when he himself experience's Juliana "extracting gold from me" (p. 92). Where the Phallic Mother gets her penis is explained to King Lear (Shakespeare, 1607) by the Fool. "Thou gav'st them [Goneril and Regan] the rod, and put'st down thine own breeches" (I.4.164–165). After Goneril later castrates Gloucester ("Naughty lady, / These hairs which thou dost ravish from my chin / Will quicken and accuse thee" [III.7.36–38]), Lear confuses his emasculate friend with his phallic daughter. "Goneril with a white beard!" (IV.6.96).

How to defend against such feminine puissance is a steady preoccupation of fiction's males. A few, like Heathcliff, have the personal force to join 'em since you can't beat 'em. Unlike the faux-misanthrope Lockwood who's terrified by "the canine mother, who had left her nursery . . . her lips curled up, and her white teeth watering for a snatch" (p. 5), Heathcliff thrills to nature's violence and dies baring his "white teeth" (p. 254). Most men are less hardy, however. They defend against the fantasy Mother either by resisting or by replacing her. The narrator in *The Aspern Papers,* for example, resists by trying to castrate Juliana through projection. First, imagining that her green eyeshade "created the presumption of some ghastly death's-head lurking behind it" (p. 60), he replaces her penetrating gaze not only by an image replete with multiple orifices but also by a patriarchal stereotype—woman=death. Obviously ineffective, he soon re-fers to the eyeshade as a "mysterious bandage" (p. 91). How can an eyeshade be a *bandage*? By the logic of reaction formation. What bandages cover are wounds, and "wound" is how woman's genitals are traditionally characterized—as cut and scar, absence. He further attempts to emasculate Juliana by pelting her with images of detumescence ("shriveled . . . shrunken . . . withered . . . impotent . . . spent"). But, sticks and stones . . .

Males are no more effective when they attempt to resist other incarnations of the All-Powerful Mother. Two extremes—the Overstimulating and the Aloof Mothers—evoke comparable strategies from sons named Paul in Doctorow's

The Book of Daniel (1971) and Lawrence's "The Rocking-Horse Winner" (1933). "Shameless by design," Doctorow's Paul says of his provocative mother, "I remember the hair around her slit, sparse and uneven" (p. 37). His reprisal? "I took my mother my blue tin of pennies and gave them to her: there was about eighty cents. She cried and hugged me as I knew she would. I wanted to see her cry. I wanted her to hug me. I wanted her to experience the poignancy of the moment I had planned" (p. 147). Of course this moment of control cannot erase Paul's rage and sexual obsession; he will proceed to brand his wife's naked bottom with a cigarette lighter and to ogle his sister's naked body as she lies dying. Only the ordeal of writing *The Book of Daniel* will begin to heal his wounds by giving him at least some control over the past. Paul in Lawrence's story also craves control. His aloof mother "paid no attention to his assertion [that God tells him things]. This angered him somewhat, and made him want to compel her attention. He went off by himself, vaguely, in a childish way, seeking for the clue to 'luck.' Absorbed, taking no heed of other people, he went about with a sort of stealth" (pp. 150–151). Although "absorbed" obviously indicates self-absorption, a deeper read of Paul's dilemma reveals that his mother's aloofness means he's paradoxically absorbed in her. "'I wouldn't worry, mother, if I were you.' 'If you were me and I were you,' said his mother, I wonder what we *should* do!'" (p. 162). Death, not control, is Paul's fate, as two becomes one and hence zero for the son absorbed.

Another thing that males can do is to switch strategies. Instead of resisting Mother, they can attempt to replace her—by assuming the role of the nurturant father. Neglected by critics (Ruddick's *Maternal Thinking,* 1989, is a useful exception), this masculine figuration of the "feminine" is fertile ground for psychoanalytic inquiry in the new century. Despite the enormous authority of the Cult of True Womanhood, the century that produced Sigmund Freud knew that woman was not *indispensable* to domesticity. We encounter male-centered home spaces, for example, on shipboard, not only in a homoerotic tale such as Melville's *Billy Budd* where the sailors build for their darling top-foreman a little chest to hold his clothes. Even an insistently heterosexual novel such as *Frankenstein,* where Mary Shelley establishes unambiguously that the traditional, woman-centered home is superior to the destructive wanderings of Prometheans like Victor, we find a nautical domesticity. "We [sailors] . . . restored him to animation by rubbing him with brandy, and forcing him to swallow a small quantity. As soon as he shewed signs of life, we wrapped him in blankets, and placed him near the chimney of the kitchen stove" (p. 20). Closer to home, Sir Claude in *What Maisie Knew* (James, 1897) rejects woman's role as domestic angel but delights Maisie by his nurturant instincts (to say nothing of the big cake he brings her!). "'I'm not an angel—I'm an old grandmother,' Sir Claude declared. 'I like babies—I always did. If we go smash I shall look for a place as a responsible nurse.' Maisie, in her charmed mood, drank in an imputation" (p. 74).

Probably the Victorian period's amplest representation of the Nurturant Male appears in *Jane Eyre* (Brontë, 1847). Before Rochester even enters the novel, we readers enter with Jane into the domesticity he has fostered. "A glow suffused both it [the hall at Thornfield] and the lower steps of the staircase. This ruddy shine issued from the great dining-room, whose two-leaved door stood open, and showed a genial fire in the grate, glancing on marble hearth and brass fire-irons, and revealing purple draperies and polished furniture, in the most pleasant radiance" (p. 133). The man himself proves bountifully nurturant to Jane. "There was ever in Mr. Rochester (so at last I thought) such a wealth of the power of communicating happiness, that to taste but of the crumbs he scattered to stray and stranger birds like me, was to feast genially" (p. 275). The revelation of Bertha forces Jane to withdraw her promise to marry Rochester but does not alter her need for his nurturance. "'Do you think I can stay to become nothing to you? Do you think I am an automaton?—a machine without feelings? and can bear to have my morsel of bread snatched from my lips, and my drop of living water dashed from my cup?'" (p. 284). The enduring quality of such nurturance means that hope remains for their union, of course, even when Rochester tells Adele that she must go to school without Jane:

> ". . . for I am to take mademoiselle to the moon, and there I shall seek a cave in one of the white valleys among the volcano tops, and mademoiselle shall live there with me, and only me."
> "She will have nothing to eat: you will starve her," observed Adele.
> "I shall gather manna for her every morning and night" [p. 299].

Essential to Brontë's figuration of the Nurturant Male is her representation of the phallus. Brocklehurst, the benefactor of Lowood School, is characterized by Jane as "a black pillar! such, at least, appeared to me, at first sight, the straight, narrow, sable-clad shape standing erect on the rug: the grim face at the top was like a carved mask, placed above the shaft by way of capital" (p. 40); St. John Rivers, her erstwhile suitor, is "a steadfast bulwark for great interests to rest upon; but, at the fireside, too often a cold cumbrous column" (p. 438). Critics who have noticed these phallic attributes have not tended to connect them to nurturance. Brocklehurst starves the Lowood girls under his care; Rivers rudely reads in silence at the family dining table. Hypermasculinity untempered by the feminine signals castration, not puissance. Brocklehurst is inescapably tied to his mother, and Rivers cannot offer Jane a marriage where passion goes beyond devotion to missionary labors. The same is true of women. Miss Ingram and her mother arrive at Thornfield to lay siege to Rochester's heart, but attentive readers feel no worry for Jane. The mother is "very erect" with "a double chin, disappearing into a throat like a pillar . . . the chin was sustained by the same principle [pride], in a position of almost preternatural erectness" (p. 195); and the daughter, having bossed around the servants ("'Go!' ejaculated Miss Ingram"), "rose solemnly: 'I go first,' she said, in a tone which might have befitted the leader of a forlorn hope, mounting a breach in the van of his men" (pp. 217, 218). Jane is a better fit for Rochester.

Prepared to walk from the inn to Thornfield for the first time, she specifies that "my muff and umbrella lie on the table" (p. 108). *En route,* we find her "sheltering my hands in my muff" (p. 127). What's happened to the umbrella? Surely so poor a girl would not have left behind a possession especially valuable in rainy England. The question becomes immediately germane when Rochester injures himself falling from his horse and asks Jane for assistance. "'You have no umbrella that I can use as a stick?' 'No.' . . . He laid a heavy hand on my shoulder, and leaning on me with some stress, limped to his horse. . . . [After helping him mount] I took up my muff and walked on" (p. 131). Although Jane had initially seemed ideally androgynous with her masculine umbrella and her feminine muff, she needs no phallic prosthesis when support is required of her. The paramount Victorian image of male-female union—the ivy wrapped around the supporting oaktree—is reversed in Jane's scene with Rochester. He, unlike the grotesquely phallic Brocklehurst and Rivers, is manly enough to forego the male role and cling like ivy to a woman who, unlike the grotesquely masculine Blanche Ingram, is capable of assuming the male role of support when required. Rochester's capacity to function as the Nurturant Male depends precisely on this androgynous balance of gender traits.

Fiction also stages, however, the failure of this Nurturant Figure. Sometimes the male simply isn't up to the role. Pap in *Huckleberry Finn* (Twain, 1885) is marked as feminine, not only by his long hair, but also by his name which means breast (as "Pappa" or "Pop" would not). Pap cannot nurture Huck, however, because he is orally needy himself. "Pap . . . got drunk and went a-blowing around and cussing and whooping and carrying on; and he kept it up all over town, with a tin pan, till most midnight; then they jailed him" (p. 26). Pap acts out here his need for home, for food in his tin pan and a roof over his head. He finds his own Nurturant Father in "the new judge [who] said he was going to make a man of him. So he took him into his own house, and dressed him up clean and nice, and had him to breakfast and dinner and supper with the family, and was just old pie to him, so to speak" (p. 26). Old pie indeed. In fact the nurturant judge is doing for the father what Widow Douglas has already done for the son: clothes, food, religion. Pap reacts as Huck did: he escapes out the window. The difference is that Pap returns to his alcoholism, as do the other males in the novel who might nurture Huck. "The king sneaked into the wigwam, and took to his bottle for comfort" (p. 264). Pap's death sums up Huck's dilemma. His naked body lies dead in the floating house where "there were two old dirty calico dresses, and a sun-bonnet, and some women's under-clothes, hanging against the wall, and some men's clothing too" (p. 61). Whatever happened in this scene of androgyny gone bad, Pap's nakedness indicates his inability to fit into either masculine or feminine role, let alone combine them. His son is thus left needy and bereft. "And there was a bottle that had milk in it and it had a rag stopper for a baby to suck. We took the bottle, but it was broke" (p. 62).

A different type of failure of male nurturance is staged in "Rip Van Winkle." Rip's flight from his phallic wife's sharp tongue leads him deep into the forest of dream where repressed desire surfaces. "Rip now felt a strange apprehension stealing over him; he looked anxiously in the same direction [as the voice] and perceived a strange figure slowly toiling up the rocks, and bending under the weight of something he carried on his back" (p. 43). The Good Breast. "He bore on his shoulder a stout keg that seemed full of liquor" (p. 44). Joining a male cohort organized around oral gratification ("they quaffed the liquor in profound silence" [p. 45]), Rip seems to have realized his repressed desire. "He was naturally a thirsty soul and was soon tempted to repeat the draft. One taste provoked another." How can it be, then, that when he awakes, "Rip felt famished" (p. 46). He goes on to stipulate, "famished for his breakfast," but psychologically it's another story. Unlike Jane Eyre who homes in on what she needs, and Huck who at least seeks for what he needs, Rip has fled from what he can't handle. Rather than regression in the service of the ego, Rip has practiced denial. Thus the depression that he's felt every day is reencountered in his male cohort. "They maintained the gravest faces, and were, withal, the most melancholy party of pleasure he had ever witnessed" (p. 45). To indicate that flight from woman is no way to deal with the Terrifying Mother, Irving stages the male pleasure party within a womb. "Passing through the ravine, they came to a hollow, like a small amphitheater" (p. 44). Rip goes back to town, but cannot return to face his true problem because Dame Van Winkle is dead. Alcoholism, as in *Huckleberry Finn*, is the males' only solution. "'It is a common wish of all henpecked husbands in the neighborhood, when life hangs heavy on their hands, that they might have a quieting draft out of Rip Van Winkle's flagon" (p. 53). The word "quieting"— instead of "quiet"—is terrifying. Quiescence, not maturation, is the only hope for those who follow Rip Van Winkle rather than Sigmund Freud. They relisten compulsively to Rip's unexamined narrative, rather than risking the talking cure and eventually hearing their own truth.

Coda

Fathers in "Rip Van Winkle" have poison in their mouths and ears. Like Hamlet's father. We turn now to *Hamlet* (Shakespeare, 1603) for several reasons. It is the text most implicated in the Oedipus and in the movement from oedipal to preoedipal; fusion is the fantasy of Hamlet and *Hamlet*. As such the play allows us to draw together much that we've said in this essay about Freud's techniques and contents. Finally we indicate, one last time, how Freud can contribute to the humanities in the new century. We offer a fresh answer to the most frequently asked question in *Hamlet* criticism and, possibly, in all literary criticism. Why does Hamlet hesitate to kill the king?

Freud's discovery that Hamlet puts off killing Claudius because he has unconsciously identified with Claudius killing his father and sleeping with his mother may well be, as Holland (1964) suggests, "this century's most distinctive contribution to Shakespeare criticism" (p. 165). Directed by Freud to the play's unconscious desires, we want to begin with one desire that he did not explore—the issue of male nurturance. If Hamlet's father is the "rouser" (I.4.8) that Claudius is, if Hamlet too is surrounded by orally needy fathers, male nurturing would certainly seem to be an issue in Shakespeare's play. Although we might suspect that King Hamlet was a drinker when Prince Hamlet indicts Danes for drinking, even though he himself was "to the manner born" (I.4.15), the actual proof that Hamlet sees his father as orally needy comes with recurrence. Hamlet compares the Danes' drinking with a particular fault in men, which he, in turn, compares with "some vicious mole of nature" (1.4.24); he then calls his father's ghost "old mole" (1.5.161). Although we ultimately see that this mole *is* both vicious and of nature, the initial problem is that, as we have seen with Huck and Pap, orally needy fathers tend to produce orally needy sons. And with Hamlet's vision, albeit disguised and softened, of feeding on his dead father, we must suspect he's one of them.

Hamlet: A man may fish with the worm that hath eat of a king, and eat of the fish
         that hath fed of the worm.
King: What dost thou mean by this?
Hamlet: Nothing but to show you how a king may go through the guts of a beggar.
                                       (IV.3.27–31)

At this point in *Hamlet,* there is only one dead king, and with Hamlet saying to Rosencrantz "[b]eggar I am" (II.2.269), there's one and only one beggar, a beggar most anxious to envision himself feeding on his father's corpse.

We follow the repetitions and we learn. But we don't have to *learn* that eating of father is not exactly male nurturing. The problem is that where nurturing fails, devouring lurks. *Hamlet*'s orally needy fathers are in one sense just ravenous mouths, and Hamlet, himself an oral beggar, becomes devouring in order to nurture and defend himself and to punish the inadequate nurturer—just as Melanie Klein (1935) theorizes in her paranoid-schizoid model of archaic fantasizing. Some of this is presented fairly directly; early in the play, another father, Polonius, is imaged into a mouth (1.2.28); later Hamlet cautions that Claudius "keeps [Rosencrantz and Guildenstern] . . . like an ape, in the corner of his jaw, first mouthed, to be last swallowed" (IV.2.17–19). But the oral battle between father and son is more "airy." Defended and disguised, it is presented, tellingly and ironically, through repetitions of "air"—the very element that many cultures have contrasted with Mother Earth and associated with the male principle. One of the first things we learn about King Hamlet's ghost is that "it is as the air, invulnerable" (I.1.146); in Gertrude's closet the ghost is "the incorporeal air" (IV.4.119). Incorporeal but dangerous. When Hamlet goes out looking for his father's ghost, the very first thing we hear is Hamlet's "the air bites shrewdly; it is very cold" and Horatio's confirmation, "It is a nipping and eager air" (I.4.1–2). Hamlet's oral retaliation comes later. "I eat the air, promised-crammed. You cannot feed capons so" (III.2.90–91). The castration implicit in Hamlet being a capon tells the story. You can't feed on air *and you shouldn't*. Recourse to nurturing fathers itself suggests two problems: traditionally mothers should provide nutrition and fathers should provide phallic identification. Hamlet, feeling castrated, has problems with the breast and problems with the phallus. His awareness of the latter is shown by one last piece of the air puzzle. To Polonius's question, "Will you walk out of the air, my lord," Hamlet responds "Into my grave?" (II.2.204–205). If you can't be with father, you're with mother. If father can't provide differentiation, you're fused with and thus lost in the maternal. Dead.

Hamlet's latent awareness of his problems with the breast is shown in an imputation, manifestly directed at Osric. "He did comply with his dug before he sucked it. Thus has he, and many more of the same bevy that I know the drossy age dotes on, only got the tune of the time . . . and do but blow them to their trial—the bubbles are out" (V.2.179–185). That this is projection, that it's latently directed at Hamlet himself, is emphasized by the fact that in all of Shakespeare there's only one other person who "complies"—Hamlet (II.2.263). This unique repetition establishes his latent similarity to Osric—the prince too complies with mother's breast. "*Thus*" he remains a frivolous complier, of the bevy that, as he says of *himself,* "[is] pigeon-livered and lack[s]" (II.2.562). He can't win. He complies with the breast and he still ends up pigeon-livered, lacking, *and* hungry.

He'd better comply: mother is hungry too. Nurturing problems know no gender. The very first craving we hear of is Gertrude's as Hamlet recollects the "good" times when mother and father were together. "Why, she would hang on him as if increase of appetite had grown by what it fed on" (I.2.143–145). The context shows that the queen's appetite is a threat at both the genital and the oral levels; the complicated syntax—how can "increase" *grow?*—shows that the threat is considerable. It certainly seems to take some of the bite out of the nipping air; in fact, if we look closer, we see that in both Hamlet's fantasy and *Hamlet*'s fantasy the maternal threat is everywhere—not even the father and son's oral battle ground is exempt. Even if Hamlet eats of the fish that ate of the worm that ate of the king, he's two displacements too late. As with Polonius who is, as Hamlet says, "At supper. Not where he eats but where he is eaten" (IV.3.17–19), the worm has first dibs. And Hamlet, after twice calling Gertrude "lady," doesn't soften the displaced associations of the worm much. He insists that the graveyard corpses are now "my Lady Worm's" (V.1.82). Mother is the conqueror worm. Even the father's bite is associated with the shrew: the air bites shrewdly. Mother's appetite has fed on father, and in Hamlet's eyes, she has devoured father. That's why even the father's bite is maternal, and that's why King Hamlet is indeed a mole of *nature*. And, because Freud's theories of preoedipal identification show that you are what you eat, that's why Gertrude, my Lady Worm, is another phallic mother. "Gertrude" means spear-maiden, so it's no surprise that one of the first things she's called is "imperial jointress" (I.2.9). Hamlet tries to see his father as Hercules (I.2.153), but it's just overcompensation. Father is neither Hercules nor mountain, so even though Hamlet asks Gertrude, "could you, on this far mountain leave to feed, and batten on this moor?" (III.4.66–67), he knows that the answer is yes. Mother feeds on everything, moor and mountain, so Hamlet will always be both orally and genitally bereft.

In one sense that's not so bad because there's a pull on Hamlet both more powerful and more primal than oral and genital desires. Hamlet, one of the biggest punsters in all of literature, longs for more than verbal fusion. He is so anxious to conflate "out of the air" and "into the grave" because he's so anxious to be in, what Horatio calls, very early, "the womb of the earth" (I.1.137). And Polonius's response to "into my grave" is straight on. "How pregnant sometimes his replies are! A happiness that often madness hits on" (II.2.106–108). Indeed. Pregnancy is the happiness that Hamlet's madness is *based* on. That's why it's "*mere* madness"! Right after Hamlet jumps into Ophelia's grave, Gertrude concludes, "This is mere madness; and thus a while his fit will work on him. Anon as patient as the female dove when that her golden couplets are disclosed, his silence will sit drooping" (V.1.271–275). Hamlet in Ophelia's grave, the implicit link between the fit and the pregnant dove, and "mere madness"—all suggest that symbiotic/lethal fusion, womb/tomb, is somewhere near the heart of Hamlet's mystery.

But not just Hamlet's. Osric might have his "crib . . . stand at the King's mess" (V.2.87–88), but we've seen that even a nurturing father couldn't help, "This lapwing [who] runs away with his shell on his head" (V.2.178). Before Osric complies with the dug, he complies with the womb, the shell he can never quite escape. There's also Ophelia who, though without a mother, retains her individuality for the first three acts with her father's help. But when Polonius dies, she immediately goes the route of mere madness. From fantasizing about a phallic lover with his "cockle hat and staff" (IV.5.25), she plunges most rapidly "to muddy death" (IV.7.182), obliterating and fusional. In the water there's a telling moment as she floats for a second "like a creature native and undued / Unto that element" (IV.7.178–179). Ophelia who carries with her a garland of dead man's fingers, "That liberal shepherds give a grosser name" (IV.7.169), has rapidly *disintegrated* into a "creature" of Hamlet's world, where "Things rank and gross in nature/Possess it merely" (I.1.136–137). Neither father's fingers nor father's cock can save her now because she is drawn back to her "*native element*."

Freud's theory of repetition compulsion can be helpful here, both with the repetitions that explode through the text—"mere," "gross"—*and* with the lethal drive to repeat symbiotic fusion that lurks in the text's depths. Even Hamlet's dead father, Horatio suggests, wanders in search of lost "treasure in the womb of the earth" (I.1.167). But Horatio can't verbalize the fact that the lost treasure is the womb itself; Laertes comes closer the very next time "treasure" is used. "[Don't] your chaste treasure open" (I.3.31) he insists, cautioning Ophelia against Hamlet's advances, as recurrence again takes *us* to the treasures of the text. And what a treasure this is, because the suggestion that King Hamlet himself is seeking the lost womb lets us provide a new answer to the most frequently asked question in all of literature: Why doesn't Hamlet do it? Why doesn't he kill Claudius right away? Why? Because he *wants* his father's ghost to wander; he doesn't want to lay him to rest in the womb of the earth. Freudian technique along with Freud's original insight into Shakespeare's text allows us to say that Hamlet's oedipal jealousy is actually a displaced form of symbiotic jealousy. He doesn't want father—or anyone else but himself—inside mother. In both Hamlet and *Hamlet,* this is the primal jealousy. This is why Hamlet hides Polonius's body. This is why Ophelia weeps, not only because father's dead, but because "they would lay him in the cold ground" (IV.5.69–70). This is why Laertes jumps into Ophelia's grave with "Hold off the earth" (V.1.236). And this is why Hamlet doesn't do it.

But Hamlet *does* do it; he does kill Claudius. And, if our theory is correct, critics are wrong that Hamlet can act only because his mother is dead. Because fusion in death seems to be his fantasy, Hamlet's symbiotic jealousies should still prevent him from sending Claudius to mother. But he can, and as he pours the poisoned drink down Claudius's throat, he even calls our attention to it. "Is thy union there? / Follow my mother" (V.2.314-315). To see what's going on, we must go back again to Hamlet's encounter with Osric where a radically different note is, ever so indirectly, first sounded.

Hamlet: What's [Laertes'] weapon?
Osric: Rapier and dagger.
Hamlet: That's two of his weapons. (V.2.140–142)

This is the first time Hamlet insists on two, and though it might not seem like much, it's a long way from "father and mother is man and wife, man and wife is one flesh, and so [you, father, are] my mother" (IV.3.50–51). It's also significant that Hamlet insists on difference with respect to Laertes' weapon, because Laertes' "weapon" is what thrusts Hamlet out of the pregenital world of fusion and orality. Laertes is "full of most excellent differences" (V.2.107); without a mother, "his semblance is his mirror" (V.2.118)—not his mere. He is a man of action, the most phallic male in the play, the man whom Hamlet has practiced sword fighting to emulate, and his challenge, with its promise of macho penetrations and consequent incorporations, allows Hamlet to step up, to insist on two. When it comes time for the actual touché, Hamlet is able to refuse the cup proffered by both father *and* mother, to move beyond both oral *and* fusional—"in the cup of union" (V.2.261). Hamlet now intuits that drink and union are poison, and though the foil is poisoned too, it's at least in the realm of genitality and individuality. So after Hamlet is penetrated by Laertes, he forces Claudius to drink of the cup that he himself has been able to get beyond. "Drink of this potion. Is thy union here? / Follow my mother" (V.2.314–315). Then six lines later there's a repetition that emphasizes why he can say this: he tells Laertes, "I follow thee," then bids the "wretched queen, adieu!" (V.2.321–324). Laertes has given Hamlet the image of masculinity that allows him to escape the realm of the mother. Hamlet's last words "the rest is silence" (V.2.347) and Horatio's echo "not from his mouth" (V.2.361) enforce the fact that Hamlet has moved beyond the oral.

It might seem that we ourselves have moved beyond preoedipal textual foreplay to consummation and completion, but remember this *is* "significant literature." Remember that though Laertes has moved beyond mother in Hamlet's fantasy, we can't help but hear the "mere" in "his semblance is his mirror," just as we can't help noting that Laertes is in Ophelia's grave even before Hamlet is. Remember that Hamlet refuses his mother's drink with "I dare not drink yet, madam—by and by" (V.2.283) *and* that "by and by" was when he will come to his mother's chamber (III.2.378). Remember one last repetition. Eighteen lines after Horatio seems to cap it all off with "not from his mouth," he somewhat surprisingly makes an assertion that is as latently regressive as it is manifestly progressive; he tells Fortinbras that he'll hear of Hamlet's election "from his mouth" (V.2.381). So it would seem that instead of consummation and completion we're still in the realm of foreplay and frustration. This is where we should be. All great texts are like the dreams that inspired Freud's "navel" metaphor: all have passages that must "be left obscure." Mystery prevails, even as Freud-the-reader outlasts Freud-the-scientist. The long close scrutiny is what we finally enjoy most, even as we move beyond "meaning" to wonder, beyond schema and ideology to the navel that evokes mother and the origins we can neither reach down to nor forget.

References

Barthes, R. (1975), *The Pleasure of the Text*. New York: Hill & Wang.
Benjamin, J. (1995), *Like Subjects, Love Objects*. New Haven, CT: Yale University Press.
Brontë, C. (1847), *Jane Eyre*. New York: Oxford University Press, 1996.
Brontë, E. (1847), *Wuthering Heights*. New York: W. W. Norton, 1990.

Brooks, P. (1987), The idea of psychoanalytic criticism. *Critical Inq.,* 13:334–348.

Chodorow, N. (1978), *The Reproduction of Mothering.* Berkeley: University of California Press.

Crews, F. (1966), *The Sins of the Fathers.* New York: Oxford University Press.

de Certeau, M. (1986), *Heterologies,* trans. B. Massumi. Minneapolis, MN: University of Minnesota Press.

Doctorow, E. (1971), *The Book of Daniel.* New York: Random House.

Enck, J. (1964), John Hawkes: An interview. *Wisconsin Studies in Contemporary Literature,* 6:140–155.

Freud, S. (1900), The interpretation of dreams. *Standard Edition,* 4 & 5. London: Hogarth Press, 1953.

———— (1905a), Three essays on the theory of sexuality. *Standard Edition,* 7:130–243. London: Hogarth Press, 1953.

———— (1905b), Jokes and their relation to the unconscious. *Standard Edition,* 8:9–236. London: Hogarth Press, 1960.

———— (1907), Delusions and dreams in Jensen's *Gradiva. Standard Edition,* 9:7–95. London: Hogarth Press, 1959.

———— (1908), Creative writers and day-dreaming. *Standard Edition,* 9:141–153. London: Hogarth Press, 1959.

———— (1913), The Moses of Michelangelo. *Standard Edition,* 13:211–238. London: Hogarth Press, 1958.

———— (1919), The "uncanny": Parts I, II & III. *Standard Edition,* 17:217–256 London: Hogarth Press, 1955.

———— (1925), An autobiographical study [1924]. *Standard Edition,* 20:7–74. London: Hogarth Press, 1959.

Gilman, C. (1898), The yellow wallpaper. In: *The Charlotte Perkins Gilman Reader.* New York: Pantheon Books, 1980, pp. 3–20.

Hawkes, J. (1961), *The Lime Twig.* New York: New Directions Books.

———— (1964), Imagination, fantasy, dream. In: *The Personal Voice,* ed. A. J. Guerard, M. B. Guerard, J. Hawkes & C. Rosenfield. Philadelphia: Lippincott, pp. 519–525.

Hawthorne, N. (1832a), Roger Malvin's burial. In: *Centenary Edition of the Works of Nathaniel Hawthorne, Vol. 10.* Columbus: Ohio State University Press, 1974, pp. 337–360.

———— (1832b), The birthmark. In: *Centenary Edition of the Works of Nathaniel Hawthorne, Vol. 10.* Columbus: Ohio State University Press, 1974, pp. 36–56.

Hirsch, M. (1989), *The Mother/Daughter Plot.* Bloomington: Indiana University Press.

Holland, N. (1964), *Psychoanalysis and Shakespeare.* New York: McGraw-Hill.

Irving, W. (1818), Rip Van Winkle. In: *The Sketch Book.* New York: New American Library, 1981, pp. 37–55.

James, H. (1888), *The Aspern Papers and the Turn of the Screw.* New York: Penguin Books, 1986.

———— (1897), *What Maisie Knew.* New York: Penguin, 1985.

———— (1898), In the cage. In: *Henry James: Eight Tales from the Major Phase,* ed. M. D. Zabel. New York: W. W. Norton, 1958, pp. 174–266.

Kaplan, L. (1991), *Female Perversions.* New York:. Basic Books.

Klein, M. (1935), A contribution to the psychogenesis of manic depressive states. In: *The Writings of Melanie Klein, Vol. 1*. New York: Macmillan,1975, pp. 262–289.
——— (1946), Notes on some schizoid mechanisms. In: *The Writings of Melanie Klein, Vol. 3*. New York: Macmillan, 1975, pp. 3–24.
Kristeva, J. (1980), *Desire in Language*, ed. L. Roudiez (trans T. Gora, A. Jargine & L. Roudiez). New York: Columbia University Press.
Lawrence, D. (1933), The rocking-horse winner. In: *The Portable D. H. Lawrence*. New York: Viking, 1946, pp. 147–166.
McDougall, J. (1995), *The Many Faces of Eros*. New York: W. W. Norton.
Melville, H. (1855), Bartleby the scrivener. In: *The Portable Melville*. New York: Viking, 1952, pp. 465–512.
——— (1924), *Typee and Billy Budd*. New York: E. P. Dutton, 1958.
Morrison, T. (1987), *Beloved*. New York: New American Library.
Mukherjee, B. (1989), *Jasmine*. New York: Random House.
Nabokov, V. (1955), *Lolita*. New York: Berkley Books.
O'Connor, F. (1988), Good country people. In: *Collected Works*. New York: New American Library.
Poe, E. (1839), The fall of the house of Usher. In: *The Collected Works of Edgar Allan Poe, Vol. 2*, ed. T. O. Mabbott. Cambridge, MA: Belknap, 1978.
——— (1843), The black cat. In: *The Collected Works of Edgar Allan Poe, Vol. 3*, ed. T. O. Mabbott. Cambridge, MA: Belknap, 1978.
——— (1846), The cask of Amontillado. In: *The Collected Works of Edgar Allan Poe, Vol. 3*, ed. T. O. Mabbott. Cambridge, MA: Belknap, 1978.
Rey, J-M. (1977), "Freud's writing on writing." In: *Literature and Psychoanalysis*, ed. S. Felman. Baltimore, MD: Johns Hopkins University Press, pp. 310–328.
Rhys, J. (1966), *Wide Sargasso Sea*. New York: W. W. Norton.
Ruddick, S. (1989), *Maternal Thinking: Toward a Politics of Peace*. Boston: Beacon Press.
Schafer, R. (1976), *A New Language of Psychoanalysis*. New Haven, CT: Yale University Press.
Shakespeare, W. (1603), *Hamlet*. In: *William Shakespeare: The Complete Works*, ed. A. Harbage. Baltimore, MD: Penguin, 1969, pp. 930–976.
——— (1607), *King Lear*. In: *William Shakespeare: The Complete Works*, ed. A. Harbage. Baltimore, MD: Penguin, 1969, pp. 1060–1106.
Shelley, M. (1818), *Frankenstein*. Chicago: University of Chicago Press, 1974.
Spector, J. (1973), *The Aesthetics of Freud*. New York: Praeger.
Spofford, H. (1859), Circumstance. In: *The Amber Gods and Other Stories*, ed. A. Bendixen. New Brunswick, NJ: Rutgers University Press, 1989, pp. 84–96.
Stevenson, R. (1886), *The Strange Case of Dr. Jekyll and Mr. Hyde and Other Stories*. New York: Penguin, 1979, pp. 27–97.
Stoker, B. (1897), *Dracula*. New York: Penguin, 1993.
Suleiman, S. (1990), *Subversive Intent*. Cambridge, MA: Harvard University Press.
Twain, M. (1885), *Adventures of Huckleberry Finn*, ed. W. Blair & V. Fischer. Berkeley: University of California Press.

The Impact of Psychoanalysis
on the American Cinema

GLEN O. GABBARD

Claude Chabrol, the highly respected French film director, once explained why he collaborated with a psychoanalyst on one of his films: "It's very hard, when you deal with characters, not to use the Freudian grid, because the Freudian grid is composed of signs that also apply to the cinema" (Feinstein, 1996, p. 82). Indeed, since the birth of psychoanalysis, which closely coincided with the birth of the cinema, the two fields have been closely linked. As early as 1900, a writer would describe his psychotic episode in terms of the "magic lantern" effects of the nickelodeons (Schneider, 1985). In fact, the Lumiere brothers first invented a rudimentary film projector in 1895, the same year that "Studies on Hysteria" by Breuer and Freud appeared.

Many early filmmakers recognized the close resemblance between film imagery and the work of dreams. In 1931 the American film industry was already being called a "dream factory" (Ehrenburg, 1931).

The first work, though, that seriously applied psychology to the study of the cinema was written by Harvard psychologist Hugo Munsterberg in 1916. He argued that "the photoplay" can more or less replicate the mechanisms of the mind in a way that is more convincing than typical narrative forms in storytelling. This long-standing marriage, though, between psychoanalysis and the movies was not in any way facilitated by Sigmund Freud. Freud appeared to have nothing but contempt for the cinema as an art form and showed little interest in the development of movies during his lifetime (Sklarew, 1999).

Samuel Goldwyn, legendary Hollywood producer, approached Freud in 1925 with an offer he hoped that the founder of psychoanalysis could not refuse. He offered him a $100,000 fee to consult on the film he was planning to shoot about famous love stories throughout history. Freud responded curtly and dismissively to the offer, and *The New York Times* of January 24, 1925, carried the following headline: "Freud Rebuffs Goldwyn: Viennese Psychoanalyst Is Not Interested in Motion Picture Offer" (Sklarew, 1999, p. 1244).

Not all of Freud's colleagues looked at film with a jaundiced eye. Karl Abraham and Hanns Sachs consulted with the Austrian director G. W. Pabst on a remarkable 1926 film about psychoanalysis, *Geheimnisse der Seele* (the English translation is usually *Secrets of a Soul*). The film has long amazed analysts at its capacity to depict condensation, displacement, symbolic representation, and other aspects of Freud's dream work with compelling accuracy. The protagonist in the film, a Viennese chemist, is cured of a knife phobia and impotence through dream interpretation by a psychoanalyst.

Abraham actually died before the film was finished, and Sachs ended up serving as the primary consultant to Pabst. However, prior to Abraham's death, Freud corresponded with him about his skepticism concerning the ability of the cinema to represent psychoanalytic constructs such as repression (Sklarew, 1999). Since this first foray into the role of the psychoanalyst as a "technical advisor" to a filmmaker, many other analysts have also consulted to the film industry, often with far less auspicious results (Farber and Green, 1993; Gabbard, 2000).

When psychoanalysis began to sweep the culture in the 1940s and 1950s, experimental filmmakers, such as Maya Deren and Stan Brakhage, adapted primary process thinking and other unconscious mechanisms in their work. These creative artists appeared to be more interested in psychoanalytic *form* than *content*.

Focusing only on early experimental directors, however, would be misleading. Mainstream Hollywood cinema has been suffused with psychoanalytic ideas for decades. Even summer popcorn movies marketed to the masses, such as Jan de Bont's 1996 *Twister*, have appropriated psychoanalytic ideas to enhance their narrative form. Helen Hunt, the protagonist in *Twister*, plays a scientist who chases tornadoes with a fervor that seems driven by unconscious forces. Through a flashback the audience learns early on that the Helen Hunt character lost her father to a tornado when she was a child. Hence the drivenness is explained by the familiar psychoanalytic construct of active mastery over passively experienced trauma. In her efforts to master the mysteries of tornadoes, she will somehow overcome her childhood trauma and work through her grief at the loss of her father.

The French critic Marc Vernet (1975) once commented, "The great contribution of psychoanalysis has been to provide a new alibi for the structure of the American narrative film" (p. 233). A movie like *Twister,* or Alfred Hitchcock's 1964 film *Marnie,* does not actually have a psychoanalytic or psychotherapeutic scene to facilitate the psychoanalytic understanding of the protagonist, but nevertheless incorporates unconscious motivation in the narrative. Another major impact that psychoanalysis has had on the American cinema, however, is the introduction of analysts[1] as useful plot devices in the screenplay itself.

---

[1] In this communication I use the term *analyst* generically to refer to all mental health professionals who appear in the movies. Hollywood has always had trouble making distinctions among analysts, psychiatrists, psychologists, social workers, and assorted alienists, mesmerists, and quacks.

Analyst as Plot Device

In the 1999 remake of *The Thomas Crown Affair*, Pierce Brosnon stars as a suave art thief who is a billionaire jet-setter and a remarkably successful womanizer. Periodically throughout the film, however, he settles down a bit for sessions with his psychotherapist (played by Faye Dunaway), and the audience sees a more thoughtful, reflective side of him.

In the 1971 Arthur Hiller film *The Hospital*, George C. Scott plays a burned-out physician who early in the picture visits a psychiatrist. Although the psychiatrist is not actually a psychotherapist but rather a colleague, he is used in the same way. The George C. Scott character explains his bitter disillusionment with his family, his career, and his life in general. The audience learns from this scene that he is contemplating suicide. The psychiatrist is a completely insignificant character and is only there as a listener.

These two films that use psychotherapists as plot devices are typical of many others. In a novel the author can use a first-person or omniscient narrator to describe the private thoughts and feelings of the protagonist. A narrative voice-over in a film, though, does not usually work effectively. Audiences today experience such techniques as "hokey" or a throwback to the films of yesteryear. Hence the protagonist visits a therapist instead. The therapists used in this way are often "faceless," with no real identity or character and no other role within the film.

Mental health professionals are not only used as sounding boards, however. In the classic Alfred Hitchcock film *Psycho* (1960), a forensic psychiatrist (Simon Oakland) is brought in at the end of the film to provide a comprehensive psychodynamic formulation that explains why Norman Bates (Anthony Perkins) dressed as his dead mother and killed the beautiful guest (Janet Leigh) at the Bates Motel. Psychoanalytic explanations, then, can tie up loose ends of the plot and make sense out of chaotic aspects of human behavior.

In science fiction and horror movies, psychiatrists and psychoanalysts often appear in the role of the "rationalist foil," who scoffs at supernatural explanations for bizarre and fantastic events (Gabbard and Gabbard, 1999). A suave psychiatrist played by Tom Conway in Jacques Tourneur's *Cat People* (1942) finds it preposterous that Simone Simon can actually turn into a panther. In *Terminator 2: Judgment Day* (1991), the box office hit directed by James Cameron, the psychiatrist in charge of the hospital treatment of Linda Hamilton regards as delusional her belief that visitors from the future are trying to kill her. The scrupulously rational and earthbound work of psychiatrists and psychoanalysts makes them ideal foils for the generic conceit of the unknown, the unseen, and the unimagined. Many rationalist foils pay for their skepticism with their lives. They may also be useful for comic purposes, as in the Harold Ramis film *Groundhog Day* (1993), when Bill Murray tries to explain to his befuddled therapist that he is trapped in time and must live the same day over and over again.

To say that filmmakers have found psychoanalysts, psychotherapists, and other mental health professionals as useful characters to introduce into the narrative of a film is an understatement. When we published our first edition of *Psychiatry and the Cinema* (Gabbard and Gabbard, 1987), we were able to identify approximately 250 theatrically released American films that had some form of psychotherapist or psychotherapist-like figure at work. We excluded all television movies and all foreign films to make the number manageable in one lifetime. We also excluded a large number of pornographic films in which the appearance of a psychotherapist was included for "socially redeeming value."

When the second edition of the book appeared 12 years later (Gabbard and Gabbard, 1999), we had compiled a list of nearly 450 theatrically released American films. At the very least, then, Hollywood is fascinated with what psychoanalysts and psychotherapists do. Having made this observation, I should also clarify that what analysts and therapists are seen doing in movies generally bears little or no relationship to what happens in psychoanalysis and psychotherapy in the real world.

Cinematic Mythology

American films operate in well-established mythic narratives that are part of fixed genres that audiences expect to see when they cough up $9 or $10 at the box office. In a romantic comedy, for example, boy meets girl, boy loses girl, and boy ultimately gets girl by the end of the film. So in Marshall Brickman's *Lovesick* (1983), a romantic comedy featuring an analyst and patient in the starring roles, this generic convention must be fulfilled even though the "boy" is an analyst and the "girl" is a patient. The needs of the genre far outweigh any interest the filmmakers may have in accurate portrayals of psychoanalytic treatment. At the end of the film, the analyst played by Dudley Moore must give up his profession and disregard what is portrayed as a highly restrictive and unreasonable ethics code so he can stroll off into the moonlight with his patient (Elizabeth McGovern).

Similarly, when an analyst and patient are featured in a musical such as Fred Astaire and Ginger Rogers in the 1938 film *Carefree* directed by Mark Sandrich, certain conventions must be carried out. The analyst (Fred Astaire) and the patient (Ginger Rogers) happen to be at the same black-tie ball. The analytic couple begin to dance, and the analyst performs the traditional coaxing, arm-waving gestures of the showbiz hypnotist as part of the choreography of the scene. After all, if you cast Fred and Ginger, you'd better have them dance!

The depictions of psychoanalysts or psychotherapists often reflect the sociohistorical *zeitgeist* as well. In films of the 1930s and 1940s, psychoanalysts were often depicted as eccentric buffoons complete with pince-nez, goatees, a vaudeville version of a Viennese accent, and a penchant for spouting jargon at the drop of a hat. In films such as *Bringing Up Baby* (1938) or *Mr. Deeds Goes to Town* (1936), these buffoonish psychiatrists are juxtaposed with conventional Hollywood leading men such as Gary Cooper and Cary Grant. The mythology in such films is clear: psychoanalysis, an experience-distant European import, is basically useless. Its practitioners are more disturbed than their patients, and all that is needed to solve most social or psychological problems is common sense and down-home values of God, Mother, and apple pie.

There was a brief golden age of psychoanalysts in American cinema. From approximately 1957 to 1963, psychoanalysis had profoundly influenced the culture, and actors, directors, producers, and screenwriters were lining up at the analyst's office for their turn on the couch. During this brief period, we counted 22 films with consistently idealized portraits of psychotherapists or psychoanalysts (Gabbard and Gabbard, 1999). Films like *The Three Faces of Eve* (1957), *Psycho* (1960), *Splendor in the Grass* (1961), and *Pressure Point* (1962) show magnificent healers at work. Some of these films engage in extraordinary flights of fantasy about the mode of therapeutic action of psychoanalytic therapy. In *The Three Faces of Eve*, the therapist played by Lee J. Cobb helps his patient (Joanne Woodward) de-repress a traumatic childhood memory involving an episode when she was forced to kiss her dead grandmother. The film suggests that remembering this one episode of childhood trauma leads to the complete integration of the three alters characteristic of her multiple personality disorder.

Here we see another form of mythology, that is, the "cathartic cure" (Gabbard and Gabbard 1999), which is used repeatedly throughout the history of American film. Over and over again, audiences have been exposed to patients who are cured after they have recovered a traumatic memory and gone through a highly emotional abreaction with the assistance of an extraordinarily empathic therapist or analyst. The cathartic cure is highly dramatic, moving, and keeps the audience on the edge of their seats. We can easily understand the appeal of this convention to screenwriters. If a camera were placed in the office of a real-life psychoanalyst and an actual session was filmed, the audience would be bored out of their minds and would probably demand their money back because the "action" would be extraordinarily nondramatic.

What is ironic about the depictions of cathartic cures is that they depict Freud's technique as it was in 1895, forever frozen in time, preserved on celluloid. Even though Freud abandoned this type of cathartic abreaction as the mode of therapeutic action before the turn of the century, the technique is alive and well in the cinema. Even some of the Freud-bashers and critics of psychoanalysis, however, continue to discredit psychoanalytically oriented treatment based on this model of the recovery of repressed traumatic memories so often depicted in film. One can only speculate about the influence of this cinematic mythology on the public's understanding of psychoanalytic treatment.

After the golden age of therapists in the movies, the image rapidly began to deteriorate. Beginning in 1964, about the same time that the Berkeley free-speech movement and the anti–Vietnam War movement were launched, psychoanalysis began to be regarded as an establishment force that served as a repressive agent of society. This motif continued throughout the 1970s in such films as *One Flew Over the Cuckoo's Nest* (1975) and *Harold and Maude* (1971). A marvelous example of this depiction occurs in the latter film when teenager Harold (Bud Cort) wants to marry octogenarian Maude (Ruth Gordon). Director Hal Ashby sets up three consecutive scenes in which establishment authorities try to talk him out of his plan to marry a woman old enough to be his grandmother. First the audience sees an army general who speaks to Harold from his desk under an official portrait of Richard Nixon. The third scene in the sequence involves a sexually obsessed priest who admonishes Harold while a picture of the pope appears on the wall behind him. The middle scene shows a psychoanalyst sitting beneath a portrait of Freud as he intones: "A very common neurosis, particularly in this society, whereby the male child wishes to sleep with his mother. Of course, what puzzles me, Harold, is that you want to sleep with your grandmother." In this sequence Freud and psychoanalysis are seen as part of a system that demands blind conformity to an obsolete and sterile set of social norms (Gabbard and Gabbard, 1999).

In the 1980s and 1990s, the depictions of therapists continue with the same stereotypes, most of which are negative. There are occasional exceptions such as *I Never Promised You a Rose Garden* (1977), *Ordinary People* (1980), and *Good Will Hunting* (1997). In the latter film, much like the 1999 Harold Ramis movie, *Analyze This*, the psychotherapy depicted is preposterous, but the message of the film is that psychotherapy is helpful.

The films of Woody Allen have been major contributors to the decline and fall of the cinematic analyst. In his early films, like the 1971 *Bananas*, the analyst is simply a faceless audience to whom Allen delivers comic monologues from the couch. In later films, such as *Annie Hall* (1977) and *Stardust Memories* (1980), analysts are both ineffectual and buffoonish. There was a brief period in the mid to late 1980s when therapists were seen by Allen as helpful and were not lampooned in the usual manner. In the 1985 *Hannah and Her Sisters*, Michael Caine's character is clearly helped by a therapist, and in the 1988 *Another Woman*, the protagonist (Gena Rowlands) eavesdrops on entirely competent sessions of psychotherapy. In the 1990s, however, Allen's view of psychoanalysis became increasingly vitriolic. In the 1997 *Deconstructing Harry*, Harry Block (played by Allen) tells one of his therapists that he's had six different treaters and nothing has changed. In this same film, Harry ultimately marries one of his analysts. Kirstie Alley, the outspokenly antipsychiatry scientologist, was cast by Allen in the role of this analyst. Following their marriage, the Alley character discovers that her husband is having an affair with one of her patients. This discovery is made prior to the beginning of an analytic session, and she stomps out of the session to explode in anger at her husband. Her patient lies frozen on the couch as he hears her let loose with a long string of obscenities in her rage. When she returns to the consulting room, she tries to conduct the analysis while popping Prozac.

Kirstie Alley was interviewed about her character in a December 11, 1997, article in *USA Today*. She made the following observations:

> I don't like psychiatry. And I don't believe it works. And I believe psychiatrists are neurotic or psychotic, for the most part. I wanted to play her that way, and Woody just totally let me do it. I said, "I want to be taking Prozac or drugs during the session with her patient." I wanted to show that this woman is so twerked out that she has to take drugs too. She takes her own medicine. So he said, "Yeah! That's a good idea" [cited in Grinfeld, 1998, p. 1].

This revealing passage sheds a good deal of light on the depths to which Allen's view of psychoanalytic treatment has sunk.

Perhaps the most unvarying form of cinematic mythology involves films in which a female analyst or therapist treats a male patient. From Alfred Hitchcock's *Spellbound* (1945) up through films of the 1990s, such as *The Prince of Tides* (1991), *Mr. Jones* (1993), and *Twelve Monkeys* (1995), women therapists are consistently depicted as incapable of managing their countertransference and falling madly in love with their handsome male patients. Remarkably unchanged by the feminist movement, these depictions typically involve a role reversal where the woman therapist is actually cured by the male patient. Her work is generally shown to be a neurotically based solution to problems in her love life.

This stereotype is in keeping with the way women in general have been depicted in American film. Film scholar Jeanine Basinger (1993) studied the "women's films" of the 1930s, 1940s, and 1950s, and she concluded that cinematic mythology insists on a rather rigid portrayal of women in society. Basinger points out that American films always indicate that marriage and motherhood are the correct choices. They may show women settling the frontier, dodging bullets, running a newspaper, or chairing a meeting in a corporate boardroom, but as Basinger observes, "These movies don't say that women can't do these things, only that if they do, they'll be tripped up by love" (p. 452).

So it is with women psychoanalysts. They may be competent when treating female patients, as in *I Never Promised You a Rose Garden* (1977) and *Agnes of God* (1985), but if they treat a male patient, they are rapidly deprofessionalized, swept off their feet by countertransference love, and frequently drawn into unethical love affairs with their patients (even though the films themselves rarely comment on the ethics of the situation). In fact, out of over 400 American films we studied, we could only find two in which a woman therapist effectively treats a male patient. In these two films, *Private Worlds* (1935) and *Last Embrace* (1979), the actual treatment of the male patient by the female therapist occupies less than five seconds of screen time and is entirely peripheral to the major thrust of the narrative. By contrast, there are many films in which the successful treatment of a female patient by a male therapist is the major storyline.

Psychoanalytic Film Criticism

Psychoanalysis has also had a major impact on film scholarship. Academic departments of film studies have appropriated psychoanalytic thinking to understand and illuminate meanings in film and to elucidate the relationship between the spectator and the movie that takes place in a darkened theater. Wolfenstein and Leites (1950) inaugurated modern psychoanalytic film criticism in the 1950s, when they stressed that a psychological study of film could be every bit as productive as Freud's applied analytic efforts with Ibsen, Shakespeare, and Sophocles. In the same decade, the French periodical, *Cahiers du Cinéma*, appropriated Italian semiotics in addition to the ideas of the French psychoanalyst Jacques Lacan and the deconstructionist Jacques Derrida. What followed was the development of an entire field of psychoanalytically informed film scholarship appearing in other periodicals such as the British journal *Screen* and the American journal *Camera Obscura*.

In the ensuing decades, a number of time-honored methodologies of psychoanalytic approaches to film have been established (Gabbard, 1997). One of these approaches is the explication of underlying cultural mythology. Approaching Hollywood producers as cultural anthropologists, scholars such as Robert Ray (1985) have argued that filmmakers articulate the cultural mythology of the era, particularly regarding wished-for transformations of fundamental human conflicts or contradictions.

A second methodology is to consider the film as a reflection of the filmmaker's unconscious. Biographical material and quotations from the *auteur* are used as replacements for free associations of an analysand in a clinical process, and the film is seen as an outgrowth of the filmmaker's intrapsychic conflicts and early history.

Psychoanalytically informed film scholars may also regard films as depicting specific developmental crises. The 1946 French masterpiece, *Beauty and the Beast*, for example, could be regarded as Cocteau's story of how an adolescent girl successfully comes to grips with male genitality (Gabbard, 1997).

Numerous psychoanalytic writers (Kawin, 1978; Kinder, 1980; Everwein, 1984; Sklarew, 1999) have examined films from the standpoint of what they have in common with dreams. Indeed, a number of films cannot be understood unless they are viewed as dreams subject to displacement, condensation, and the other dream mechanisms. Only by understanding psychoanalytic dream work can the meaning of the film be revealed.

One of the most popular methodologies has been the analysis of spectatorship. The approaches derived from the works of Derrida and Lacan have stressed how the perspective of the spectator may be critical in understanding how a film works. Christian Metz (1982) has been particularly influential in drawing links between voyeurism and the "gaze" of the audience viewing a film.

A final approach to psychoanalytic film criticism that is more ambivalently viewed by film scholars is the analysis of a character in the narrative. Freud (1916) certainly used this technique in his understanding of Rebecca in Ibsen's *Rosmersholm*. In more recent years, this methodology has undergone a good deal of criticism. Many film scholars argue that the characters in a film are not analysands in a psychoanalytic process, and a greater emphasis should be placed on the *function* of a character in the narrative rather than on that character's underlying motivations for behavior.

Concluding Comments

This brief overview of the impact psychoanalysis has had on American film probably does not do justice to the way that movies and psychoanalytic thinking have become inextricably intertwined in our culture. The term *flashbacks*, so often used to describe patients with posttraumatic stress disorder, was actually lifted directly from cinematic language and appropriated by the mental health professions (Turim, 1989). Even the low-brow genres of slasher horror movies and science fiction films have generated a whole field of psychoanalytic scholarship. Indeed, Noel Carroll (1981) once commented that psychoanalysis is "more or less the *lingua franca* of the horror film and thus the privileged critical tool for discussing the genre" (p. 16). Thus the Frankenstein monster can be viewed as the projectively disavowed sexuality and aggression of the constricted and rigid scientist, Dr. Frankenstein. The cult classic *Alien* (1979) by Ridley Scott can be understood as a depiction of the Kleinian paranoid–schizoid position (Gabbard and Gabbard, 1999). Television film critics repeatedly refer to "Freudian" subtexts in films they are reviewing.

Patients who go to the movies compare the therapy they see on the great silver screen with the therapy they are receiving in their therapist's office. Patients commonly ask their therapist, "Why won't you hypnotize me and try to recover a repressed traumatic memory?" Although audiences know at one level that what they see in the movies is not an accurate reflection of reality, they are caught up in the cultural mythology depicted in the cinema and develop an unconscious storehouse of images that are highly influential.

We probably cannot expect filmmakers to take into account the opinions of analysts about the way cinematic analysts should be portrayed. To people in the industry, moviemaking is a business that is designed to entertain and bring people into the theater. Like other artists, they owe no debt to reality. We can content ourselves with the fact that there is tremendous interest in what we do, and to paraphrase Oscar Wilde, the only thing worse than being portrayed negatively in movies is not being portrayed at all.

References

Basinger, J. (1993), *A Woman's View: How Hollywood Spoke to Women, 1930–1960.* New York: Knopf.

Breuer, J. & Freud, S. (1893–1895), Studies on hysteria. *Standard Edition,* 2:1–311. London: Hogarth Press, 1955.

Carroll, N. (1981), Nightmare and the horror film: The symbolic biology of fantastic beings. *Film Quarterly,* 34:16–25.

Ehrenburg, I. (1931), *Die Traumfabriki Chronik des Films.* Berlin: Malik.

Everwein, R. E. (1984), *Film and the Dream Screen.* Princeton, NJ: Princeton University Press.

Farber, S. & Green, M. (1993), *Hollywood on the Couch: A Candid Look at the Overheated Love Affair Between Psychiatrists and Moviemakers.* New York: William Morrow.

Feinstein, H. (1996), Killer instincts: Director Claude Chabrol finds madness in his method. *Village Voice,* December 24, p. 82.

Freud, S. (1916), Some character types met with in psycho-analytic work. *Standard Edition,* 14:311–333. London: Hogarth Press, 1963.

Gabbard, G. O. (1997), The psychoanalyst at the movies. *Internat. J. Psycho-Anal.,* 78:429–434.

——— (1999), *Psychiatry and the Cinema: Second Edition.* Washington, DC: American Psychiatric Press.

——— (2000), Consultation to tinsel town. *Amer. Psychoanal.,* 34:17, 21.

——— & Gabbard, G. K. (1987), *Psychiatry and the Cinema.* Washington, DC: American Psychiatric Press.

Grinfeld, M. (1998), Psychiatry and mental illness: Are they mass media targets? *Psychiatric Times,* 15 March (3):1.

Kawin, B. (1978), *Mindscreen: Bergman, Godard, and First-Person Film.* Princeton, NJ: Princeton University Press.

Kinder, M. (1980), The adaptation of cinematic dreams. *Dreamworks,* 1:54–68.

Metz, C. (1982), *The Imaginary Signifier: Psychoanalysis and the Cinema,* trans. C. Britton & A. Williams. Bloomington: Indiana University Press.

Munsterberg, H. (1916), *The Film: A Psychological Study.* New York: Dover, 1970.

Ray, R. B. (1985), *A Certain Tendency of the Hollywood Cinema, 1930–1980.* Princeton, NJ: Princeton University Press.

Schneider, I. (1985), The psychiatrist in the movies: The first 50 years. In: *The Psychoanalytic Study of Literature,* ed. J. Reppen & M. Charney. Hillsdale, NJ: The Analytic Press, pp. 53–67.

Sklarew, B. (1999), Freud in film: Encounters in the *weltgeist. J. Amer. Pyschoanal. Assn.,* 47:1239–1247.

Turim, M. (1989), *Flashbacks in Film: Memory and History.* New York: Routledge.

Vernet, M. (1975), Freud: Effects *speciaex/mise en scene:USA. Communications,* 23:223–234.

Wolfenstein, M. & Leites, N. (1950), *Movies: A Psychological Study.* Glencoe, IL: Free Press.

Freud and the Human Sciences

PAUL MEYER

"What we employed you to find out is why people take him [Freud] so seriously" (see Figure 1). What the detective finds is that the language, concepts, and categories of psychoanalysis are not just attributes of our everyday contemporary cultural experience but are *internal* to such experience itself. That is to say, in the words of the savvy detective, buying into the conceptual foundations of psychoanalysis does not require an explicit affirmation of principles but is instead inextricably bound up with our perceptions of ourselves, of others, and of things in the world ("frankly I don't give a damn, but facts are facts and ids are unconscious"). It is not just that psychoanalysis has become part of our culture (an anthropological claim that one might make about any number of things that we spend a significant amount of time talking about). Instead, Freud's redescription of the subject and its relation to a set of social or historical formations should be conceived as having achieved a kind of formal systematic coherence that has both set up completely new laws for the production of statements in the human sciences and become an indispensable cultural form.

Consider briefly the following passage from a popular late twentieth century divination book on the interpretation of dreams:

> Taking the dream journey has always made a significant difference in peoples' lives. We can live at the surface or we can go very deeply into our experience to find meaning. To live at the surface is to participate in life without any reflection, having babies, turning out productive work, worrying about issues. . . . These experiences are real. No one can doubt them, but at the same time they often appear reenacted in dreams. This we call the inner life, as contrasted with the outer life . . . Reality is where we go from potential to actual. In Dreamwork we bring the potential inherent in the symbol to life. This grounds the symbolic experience in the everyday concrete world. . . . Dreams always tell the truth about what is really going on inside you [Kaplan-Williams, 1997, pp. 1, 32, 44].

Psychoanalysis at the center of the everyday

Figure 1. *From Freud for Beginners* by Richard Osborne (New York: Writers and Readers Publishing, 1993). Reprinted with permission of the publisher.

I invoke such a passage because it both nicely captures the pop-appropriation of Freudian theory in the modern world and is disconcertingly similar to a particular reading of Freud that has become entrenched within the Anglo-American psychoanalytic community.

Specifically, there are two centrally important kinds of relations pointed to in such an everyday perspective: (1) The "truth" of any inquiry into man reveals itself through the deciphering of symbols and signs that serve as the grounds for an absolute hermeneutic. Moreover, the site of symbolization is taken to reside metaphorically within the human body; the unconscious a shriveled up organ that resides in that inner location once occupied by the soul. Flipping through a random dream divination book, one is likely to encounter a specific technique for dream decipherment, techniques for training attention on unconscious content within oneself, and a canon of Jungian symbols that are given in a concrete schematized fashion. (2) The manifest, or our everyday conscious productive experience, is made *intelligible* only by an appeal to the latency of the symbolic world. The "true" (or authentic) self is given only by the series of mirrorings and translations between the symbolic and the non-reflective (by the reenactment of the "outer" life in the "inner" life). More important, there is a certain reduction of the unconscious, as the site of symbolization, to a *hidden* meaning, a reduction that aligns the Freudian discovery with both the old hermeneutics of a soul and a new humanism. Such are the implications of the pop-reading of Freud.

Two simple questions arise that we should ask ourselves despite their seeming triviality and the seeming self-evidence of their answers. First, why is it that the truth of man is unlocked in the symbol (that very truth of man that was once unlocked in the soul and later unlocked in the cogito)? Trying to answer the question without invoking the language, concepts, or techniques of psychoanalysis is no easy thing. I think in fact that it is a conceptually impossible kind of thing to do given the internal relationship between psychoanalysis and symbolization in the modern world. Second, and more interesting, can we form a self-conception and a conception of the world that is outside of the language, concepts, or techniques of psychoanalysis? Of course we can give a physiological, chemical, or theological conception that is immune to the psychoanalytic invasion. But once we enter into the domain of the human sciences, such a project is difficult to articulate.

It is precisely in the domain of the human sciences that I want to situate my discussion of Freud in order to understand the Freudian reconstitution of the human sciences as a transformation in methodological and epistemological models that inserts the problem of the unconscious into the heart of the project of knowing man in such a way that the two become inextricably interrelated.[1] By

---

[1] When I speak of psychoanalysis generally, I am speaking primarily of Freud since we should say that the *conceptual space* of psychoanalytic thought has not expanded or transformed appreciably beyond his texts. All of psychoanalysis still exists within the experience and technology of desire that is distinctly Freudian in its boundaries and conceptualizations.

the human sciences, I mean most simply the body of knowledge, and the techniques of investigation, that take man as a finite empirical entity—the human sciences as such are not an investigation into human nature but an analysis of the laws by which certain possibilities for living, speaking, or being are opened up. That is, the kind of analysis the human sciences claim to do is an analysis of the position of the subject (or group of subjects) in a set of formally related rules that define the field of knowledge or the epistemological field from which the subject speaks or acts.

To be more specific, we can say that the conceptual space of the human sciences was first opened by Kant's banishment of the infinite, and of a science or philosophy of the soul. It is in this space that man as a finite living being becomes something that is an object of knowledge, an object immersed in a network of relations that define his strategic possibilities.[2] But if it is Kant who clears away the space, then it is Freud who furnishes it as we know it today. As Michel Foucault (1970) notes, psychoanalysis becomes coextensive with the analytic of the finite whose possibility Kant establishes:

> Psychoanalysis stands as close as possible, in fact, to that critical function which, as we have seen, exists within all the human sciences. In setting itself the task of making the discourse of the unconscious speak through consciousness, psychoanalysis is advancing in the direction of that fundamental region in which the relations of representation and finitude come into play [p. 374].

It is the union of the finite and the representational that Freud articulates most vividly in the "Project for a Scientific Psychology" and "Beyond the Pleasure Principle" where we are presented with the language and models of repetition, identification, mastery, and the circuitous working out of the exigencies of life (a working out that is nothing less than the attempt to reconcile the demands of the representational and the fact of finitude). From such elementary configuration, we get the Freudian recoding of the symbolic function in "The Interpretation of Dreams," the reorganization of the space of desire in "Three Essays on the Theory of Sexuality," and the reconstitution of power relations in "Totem and Taboo."

In raising issues about the place of the Freudian project in the methodology and epistemology of the human sciences, my discussion is aligned closely with the writing of Foucault, and indirectly with the work of Arnold Davidson. I think Foucault provides a unique and persuasive perspective on both how to situate

---

[2] Indeed, this is how Foucault (1970) conceives not only a Kantian revolution but also a corresponding revolution in biology, economics, and philology. As a result of the revolution, man becomes a being such that the contents of his knowledge reveal themselves as "exterior to himself, and older than his own birth." Such contents "anticipate him, overhang him with all their solidarity, and traverse him as though he was merely an object of nature, a face doomed to be erased in the course of history. Man's finitude is heralded in the positivity of knowledge."

psychoanalysis as a historically objectified formation and how to understand the Freudian contribution to the modern world in terms of what Davidson (1988) calls "an epistemologically central constitutive new style of reasoning" that "is a set of concepts linked together by specifiable rules that determine what statements can and cannot be made with the concepts" (p. 42). Understanding Freud in the context of the human sciences is an understanding of how Freud opens up a new set of conceptual possibilities and a new set of formally related statements through opening up the domain of the unconscious. The challenge posed to the human sciences is how is Freud to be appropriated as providing the conceptual foundations for new types of investigations. In the domain of the historical sciences, that is also to pose a question like the one posed by the French school known as *la novelle histoire,* or the Ecole des Annales, that takes as the starting point of a history the new techniques and new objects of modern investigation for the sake of a critique of conventional history. The question then is, what are the techniques, concepts, and objects whose possibility Freud establishes in opening up the space of an unconscious and how are those techniques, concepts, and objects deployed by the human sciences? Of course when we speak of the unconscious in the domain of the human sciences, we are speaking of it both as an object of investigation that reveals the relations of signification and as a model for interpretation that specifies a technique (the technique of the analyst or the structural anthropologist).

That is not of course to say that the human sciences appropriate or internalize any single element or set of elements from Freud's theory (nor is it to say that they appropriate Freud faithfully or correctly), but instead it is to say that Freud founds a particular kind of discursive practice with a kind of coherence and mobility that has become internal to any kind of hermeneutics of man whatsoever. At least this is how Foucault (1969a) describes the Freudian contribution in his essay "What Is an Author":

> When I speak of Marx or Freud as founders of discursivity, I mean that they made possible not only a certain number of analogies but also (and equally important) a certain number of differences. They have created a possibility for something other than their discourse, yet something belonging to what they founded . . . the initiation of a discursive practice is heterogeneous in its subsequent transformations. To expand a type of discursivity such as founded by Freud is not to give it a formal generality it would not have permitted at the outset but, rather, to open it up to a certain number of possible applications [pp. 218–219].

It is what we might call the polymorphous nature of the Freudian contribution that allows psychoanalysis to exist at the gravitational center of our contemporary experience of man. That is, the question we should be asking is how it is that psychoanalysis as both a clinical practice and a body of theory becomes linked up through a network of relations to other seemingly disparate practices to form the colossal machinery from the production of a new orthodoxy (in the literal sense of true opinion or true belief). The centrality of psychoanalysis in our experience is not merely the centrality of psychoanalysis as a clinical practice or a body of autonomous theory but more important a polymorphous dispersion and appropriation of that theory as a popular cultural form, a hermeneutics, a sociology, a psychology, and an anthropology in the broadest sense of the term as an *Ethos Anthropos*. What is universally appropriated by the human sciences, however, is the space and problematic of the unconscious, or, the Lacanian problem of the discourse of the other that reveals the rules, structures, and laws in which the subject is situated—rules, structures, and laws that are not the subject's own and elude its consciousness.[3] To know man is no longer to try to decode his

---

[3] Since I repeatedly invoke the figure of Foucault as providing a persuasive example of how to historically describe the psychoanalytic *episteme,* a more general word needs to be said in passing on Foucault's attitude toward the Freudian figure. We can read Foucault's historical epistemology as concerned with a twofold problem that arises in the domain of history. The first and more localized problem is how can we do a history of psychoanalysis from within psychoanalysis, using its very rules for the production and appropriation of statements? The second and more dangerous/pervasive problem is how can we specify a level of analysis at all that allows the historian to get *outside* of the sway of a psychoanalytic style of interpretation, outside of an age of psychoanalysis, in describing noncontemporary historical phenomena? That is, how can we cleanse history from the human sciences and at the same time specify a methodology for the historian that allows him to get outside the figure of Freud? Both levels of epistemological and methodological problems are clearly present in the work of Foucault when faced with the question "What to do with Freud?" In cataloguing the series of statements made by Foucault regarding the figures of Freud and psychoanalysis in general, one cannot help but be struck by the pervasive uneasiness that underlies them. Sometimes Foucault wants to credit Freud with ushering in a scientific and ethical revolution grounded in freeing the subject from the psychoanatomical gaze of 19th-century psychology, undermining the psychoethical category of the pathologically abnormal by effecting a rupture with the psychology of Charcot, Jackson, Krafft-Ebing, and others. At other times Foucault wants to resist Freud as continuous with the psychiatric practices of his predecessors in terms of providing both a new medium for the mystification of the subject, the medium of unconscious symbolization, and reconstituting the doctor/patient relationship according to a new disciplinary dynamic (the confessional of the analyst/analysand). Sometimes Foucault wants to see psychoanalysis as opening up a new space for history that is not the linear unified history of the conscious speaking subject. At other times, Foucault wants to see psychoanalysis as inciting a new *teleos* and a new way to write a continuous history based on a model that has invaded the human sciences and philosophical discourse (a model that inserts or reinserts the psyche into human sciences). Sometimes, as in the first part of *Mental Illness and Psychology,* Foucault wants to do psychoanalysis from within psychoanalysis, to offer positive prescriptions for the future and direction of psychoanalysis. At other times, as in *The Archaeology of Knowledge,* Foucault wants to get outside the sway of the psychoanalytic style of interpretation, to treat psychoanalysis as a historically objectified formation. Sometimes Foucault seems to want to resist speaking of Freud altogether. At other times Foucault seems inescapably drawn to him insofar as he is at the center of our contemporary cultural episteme, insofar as psychoanalysis establishes our rules for the production of statements, organizes our perceptual field, configures how we think of the subject, and generally orients our attention toward social and interpersonal space.

individuality or spirit, to analyze his intentions, to peer within the abyssal depth of his soul, but to systematically describe the anonymous conditions that open up certain possibilities for him by virtue of his existence as a swimmer in a sea of signs.

It is in *The Interpretation of Dreams* that we can most clearly see the conceptual space of the unconscious unfolding, the space that becomes so internal to the constitution of the human sciences that we cannot, as subjects living within that space, simply think or talk our way out of it. As Foucault (1965) notes first in his essay "Philosophy and Psychology":

> The simple discovery of the unconscious is not an addition of domains: it is not an extension of psychology, it is actually the appropriation, by psychology, of most of the domains of the human sciences covered—so that one can say that, starting with Freud, all the human sciences became, in one way or another, sciences of the psyche. And the old realism à la Emile Durkheim . . . appears to me unthinkable now [p. 252].

Later in *The Order of Things* (1970) he continues:

> On the horizon of any human science, there is the project of bringing man's consciousness back to its real conditions, of restoring it to the contents and forms that brought it into being, and elude us within it; this is why the problem of the unconscious—its possibility, status, mode of existence, the means of knowing it and of bringing it to light—is not simply a problem within the human sciences . . . it is a problem that is ultimately coextensive with their very existence [p. 362].

That is, in the establishment of a new space of the unconscious, a new set of rules for the production and relations of statements emerges, rules that constitute a new model for the analysis of social formations, discourses, and epistemological structures in the human sciences.

The Episteme, the Unconscious, and the Subject of Knowledge

We may say thus that Freud, in founding a discursive practice that has become central in the general system of the formation, transformation, and transmission of statements in the human sciences since the late nineteenth century, incited a radical transformation of the modern *episteme*. Before entering into this role in detail, I want to lay two ways of understanding the *episteme* on the table—that of Lacan and Nietzsche, which give the *episteme,* in a most succinct fashion, its general characteristics:

> It isn't easy to wrap things up. That's because our *episteme* has made so much progress that it is evidently constituted completely differently from Socrates'

(articulated in the *Meno*). Nevertheless, it would be wrong not to realize that, even based on the model of experimental science, the modern *episteme*, as in Socrates' time, consists essentially in a certain coherence of discourse. It is simply a matter of knowing what this coherence means, what kind of bond it involves [Lacan, 1955a, p. 17].

Nietzsche (1873) provides an account of the production of truth through the formal, relational coherence of the *episteme:*

A mobile army of metaphors, metonyms, and anthropomorphisms—in short a sum of human relations, which have been enhanced, transposed, and embellished poetically and rhetorically and which after long use seem firm, canonical, and obligatory to a people [pp. 46–47].

Using Lacan's formulation of the *episteme*, we should say of Freud that he provides a new group of rules that makes possible a new coherence of discourse and provides a new set of objects, concepts, and theories of scientific discourse that center around the anthropological problem of finitude that Kant opens up. Moreover, if we take the *episteme* to be knowledge bounded by a formal coherence that is given by a set of relations in the production of truth, then the task of the historian or the human scientist in general can be seen as an attempt to articulate the boundaries, relations, and rules of the *episteme*—to uncover the logic by which discourses are related. Or, we can ask the question that Foucault (1969b) in proposing to do a *synchronic analysis* asks: "in order for a change to be able to be obtained, what are the other changes that must also be present in the field of contemporaneity?" (pp. 823–824). What conditions, structures, or relations need to be present for an epistemic change from one state of affairs to another to occur?

In order to provide an understanding of such rules as they pertain to the emergence of a psychoanalytic style of reasoning, we need to understand what it is that Freud overturns. We can say that for a period up to the Kantian turn in the nineteenth century, the *episteme* was constituted by a particular set of rules for interpretation that centered around a science of the soul of man—with a corresponding set of metaphorical relations that posed the question of man in terms of the language of the infinite and established the conditions for the possibility for a certain set of statements to be made about man that revolved around a Cartesian picture of the domain of the mental. Such is of course the picture that Kant overturns.

It is, however, between Kant's clearing of space and Freud's appearance that we see emerge a new set of laws for the coherence of discourse concerning man founded on a new kind of pervasive *realism* embodied in what Davidson (1990) calls in his essay "Closing up the Corpses" a new psychiatric style of reasoning. We need only look to Durkheim's conception of the individual and society as opposed kinds of *substances*, or more importantly for my purposes, to the psychophysiology embodied in Krafft-Ebing's (1969) *Psychopathia Sexualis* for evidence of the quasi-anatomical treatment of the natural subject by the human sciences. As Davidson points out, in the works of Krafft-Ebing and his contemporaries, we find a systematic concern for a picture of the "normal" as applied to the sexual instinct (where object and instinct are naturally unified), an attempt to enumerate the categories of sexual perversity, and a cataloging of functional diseases—with an accompanying anatamo-clinical gaze that tries to link the categories and conceptualizations of the subject to a rigorous and detailed account of anatomical and physiological processes.

It is precisely this functional understanding of the psyche as finding expression in the anatomical processes of the body that Freud quite literally inverts through dissociating mental and organic pathology. The body now forms part of the psyche, or at least forms part of the experience of the psyche. More generally, at the level of the epistemological field, we can describe a twofold transformation in the human sciences precipitated by Freud. There emerges a new hermeneutics that is no longer grounded in the natural unity of the individual but instead now centers around the unconscious as a concept that inserts the problem of otherness into human experience—and there simultaneously emerge new techniques for deciphering the meaning of the speaking subject, a meaning that the subject is consciously unaware of, through the symbolic mediation of the unconscious (meaning grounded in the concepts of repetitions, drives, wishes, fantasies).

We need, however, to distinguish between two fundamentally distinct ways the unconscious is appropriated by the human sciences. According to the first model, the model that is latent in the passage on dream divination and that is adopted by most American analysts, sociologists, psychologists, and anthropologists, the unconscious is nothing but a psychological concept. That is, the unconscious is coextensive with the speaking subject, metaphorically residing in some principle of mindedness or agency (circumscribed schematically within the confines of the individual actor). In this context the old psychology as a science of the soul persists, with the soul replaced by the unconscious as an anthropomorphic inner faculty through which meaning can be divined. Deployed in the arena of the human sciences as a whole, this reading of Freud is taken to provide a new tool to *interpret* historical or anthropological data, unify various discontinuous events, privilege individual agency in history, and provide a new narrative basis for a science of man as a totality-in-process, as a working out or a working through. That is, Freud provides under this gloss a new *teleos*.

On the other hand, I want to invoke the model of the unconscious adopted by the loose tripartite alliance of Lacan, Lévi-Strauss, and Foucault in order to understand in a more concrete fashion the appropriation of the space of the unconscious as a logical concept, structured like a language, by the human sciences.

Under this reading what Freud opens up is not a science of the speaking subject, not a new humanism, but instead the possibility of a science or analytic of man that seeks to describe the rules or structures that the subject makes its way into (the unconscious is not a spirit that underlies, animates, and drives the individual as an internal organ might do). The linguistic model of the unconscious, the model for the language-like signifying system of the unconscious (borrowed from Saussure and the structuralist school), is what we are by now familiar with in the work of Lacan (1957):

> As my title suggests, beyond this "speech," what the psychoanalytic experience discovers in the unconscious is the whole structure of language. . . . But how are we to take letter here (the agency of the letter in the unconscious)? Quite simply, literally. By "letter" I designate that material support that concrete discourse borrows from language. . . . This simple definition assumes that language is not to be confused with the various psychical and somatic functions that serve it in the speaking subject—primarily because language and its structure exist prior to the moment at which each subject . . . makes his entry into it [pp. 147–148].

That is, the unconscious operates according to the sorts of laws and logical relations that we find in the domain of a structural linguistics that seeks to describe the sets of relations among elements, relations that exist independently of and prior to the entry of the subject into them. According to this model, the subject plays a role in a network of symbols that represents, organizes, and structures the field of its possibilities independently of the subject's existence. The Lacanian task specified for the human sciences is thus precisely a description of the field of strategic possibilities opened and closed by the configuration of the symbolic universe.

Or, to use the example Lacan (1955b) gives in the "Purloined Letter," the aim is to describe the space the subject inhabits in a network of related structures where the position one takes within the structure determines the subject's possibilities for acting, speaking, or being a certain way ("thus the tale of the purloined letter signifies that there's nothing in destiny, or causality, which can be defined as a function of existence" [p. 199]).

Transferred into the realm of anthropology, we see an analogous space internalized by Lévi-Strauss's (1958) methodology:

> If as we believe to be the case, the unconscious activity of the mind consists in imposing forms upon content, and if these forms are fundamentally the same for all minds—ancient and modern, primitive and civilized (as the study of the symbolic function, expressed in language, so strikingly indicates)—it is *necessary and sufficient* to grasp the unconscious structure underlying each institution and each custom, in order to obtain a principle of interpretation valid for other institutions and other customs [p. 21].

Again we have the space of the unconscious as the space of logical relations, the kind of relations that for instance establish connections between the different elements of a myth (the temporal or causal relations that can be established logically). As in Lacan's "Purloined Letter," the subject inhabits a space in a network of logically related structures (like the elementary structure of kinship) where the position one takes within the structure determines one's possibilities for acting, speaking, or being a certain way.

In order to bring out the logical character of the Lacanian unconscious in a clearer way, we can consider what Foucault (1970) says in the preface to the English edition of *The Order of Things* about the possibility of a *positive unconscious* of knowledge:

> What I would like to do, however, is to reveal a *positive* unconscious of knowledge: a level that eludes the consciousness of the scientist and yet is part of scientific discourse, instead of disputing its validity and seeking to diminish its scientific nature. . . . It is these rules of formation, which were never formulated in their own right, but are to be found only in widely differing theories, concepts, and objects of study, that I have tried to reveal, by isolating, as their specific locus, a level that I have called, somewhat arbitrarily perhaps, archaeological [p. xi].

We can understand this unconscious as providing the conditions under which what is written could be written, an "unconscious not of the speaking subject but of the thing said" (Foucault, 1968, p. 309). The unconscious of the thing said immediately disqualifies itself from being bound up with the idea of a subject, with a psychology. This positive unconscious is the site of what Foucault terms the *historical a priori* that he defines as the group of rules that make possible a discursive practice and hence the objects, concepts, and theories of scientific discourse (see Davidson, 1997, p. 7). That is, this unconscious reveals the logically related rules that condition the appearance of discursive events and places such events in relation with other events in a practice. The language and field of the positive unconscious, like Lacan's unconscious, is not psychological but logical, revealing the logical relations (or rules) that condition the appearance of discursive events and place such events in relation with other events to form what Foucault terms a discursive practice.

Both Lacan and Foucault are thus interested in describing the position of the subject (understood as distinct from the individual) in a system of rules that constitute an unconscious that is prior to and noncoextensive with the speaking subject. It is precisely in this project that we find the conditions for the possibility of the cluster of concepts that Freud opens up and Lacan gives voice to, namely, the concepts of the *anonymous*, the *exterior*, and the *other*. As Foucault, Lacan, and Lévi-Strauss understand, the unconscious is not, as we are accustomed to believe, a new space of depth that is equivalent with a new interiority, but on the contrary, it is a new space of exteriority—a region that carries with it a new possibility for getting outside a psychological subjectivity—for dissociating man from his knowledge, his consciousness, and his language (see Foucault, 1969c; Davidson, 1977). The unconscious, or the space of the unconscious, is as such not a tool to get inside man as *Homo Natura*, but to specify a level of access in the human sciences that makes the problem of man a nonissue (man is now the anonymous subject and not the individual of the humanist or the curious quasi-Cartesian being of the pop-Freudian). The locus of attention is now, in the case of Foucault the historian, the practice, the statement, the archive, and the *episteme*, as anonymous historical configurations. In the case of Lacan, the locus of attention is the anonymous symbol and network of symbols that are always outside of the subject, that the subject confronts as other. And in the case of Lévi-Strauss and the anthropologists, the locus of attention is now *the structure* that overhangs, shadows, and outlines the subject.

It is this *anonymous other* that is embodied in the discourse (as a formally related ensemble of signs), the symbol, and the structure that reconfigures the human sciences after Freud. In the words of Foucault (1970):

> The unthought (whatever name we give it) is not lodged in man like a shriveled-up nature or a stratified history; it is, in relation to man, the Other: the Other that is not only a brother but a twin, born, not of man, nor in man, but beside him and at the same time, in an identical newness, in an unavoidable duality. This obscure space so readily interpreted as an abyssal region in man's nature, or as a uniquely impregnable fortress in history, is linked to him in an entirely different way; it is both exterior to him and indispensable to him; in one sense, the shadow cast by man as he emerged in the field of knowledge; in another, the blind stain by which it is possible to know him [p. 326].

So we have in a condensed form the presentation of this space, the space of an unconscious, in which the other, the exterior, and the anonymous reside. We have the images of the shadow, the blind stain, the other as twin, and we should add the mirror, as providing the limiting conditions for the field of man's possibilities—conditions in which the thinking, speaking, breathing subject disappears. This is the field of the limit into which man enters as a character in "The Purloined Letter" where the position of the subject can be assigned by describing the series of signs, structures, and relations that must be present in order for a subject to act or speak in a certain way.

However, whereas Lacan, the linguistics, and Lévi-Strauss are concerned with mapping out the formal possibilities of language and the language of the unconscious, Foucault (1968) locates his attention in the historical question of how it is that a certain statement came to appear, "to determine its conditions of existence, to fix its limits as accurately as possible, to establish its correlations with other statements with which it may be linked, and to show what other forms of articulation it excludes" (p. 307). When Foucault claims to be looking for the conditions for the appearance (the task of the historian) rather than the conditions for the possibility (the task of the linguist, the analytic philosopher, and the analyst) of the statement, he is looking to describe how actual utterances and inscriptions exist in coherent interaction with one another. So Foucault revises the lesson of "The Purloined Letter" toward an analysis of what position the subject must take in a set of historically instantiated relations that allow that subject to utter a specific statement at a specific time and place.

This is also a question of the role, status, and priority of the symbol, as a particular species of *sign*, in the unconscious. For Lacan (1955b), "the human order is characterized by the fact that the symbolic function intervenes at every moment and at every stage of its existence" (p. 29), where this symbolic function and order is from its start marked by a universal character. Our forms of living, speaking, and being are provided by the interplay of logically related symbols that form a dialectic structure that is always already complete, and that we are hence always already inside of. It is this totality of the symbolic universe that forms the basis for the project of analyzing/interpreting the position of the subject with reference to this *latent* order of things.

Now Foucault is of course also concerned with the existence, interplay, and relations of signs. But these are not the latent signs of Lacan's symbolic universe, nor do they form a totality that is a key for the decipherment of the meaning of the statement (nor are they a schematized key to unlocking meaning like we find in Jung). Rather they are the signs that are inscribed in discourse itself, in the statement or discourse as a group of signs that have a concrete application or arrangement in time and space. The relations of statements, or the relations of groups of signs that are absolute and nongeneralizable in their ensemble, like what we find in a discursive practice or formation, are then not the secret, invisible, latently animating relations of the symbolic universe. Instead they are the relations that exist in historical practices. They are the rules that govern such practices and that define the field of operation of the practice. That is also, in the context of the unconscious, to say that whereas the psychoanalytic unconscious is limitless and timeless, the positive unconscious of knowledge is limited by the historically instantiated utterances whose rules it contains (rules that are derived from the association of the signs of discourse, or, the analysis of the coexistence of different discourses).

In his 1955 lecture, "Freud, Hegel, and the Machine," Lacan poses the following question: Is psychoanalysis a humanism? (see Lacan 1955c, p. 67). Now we might try to answer this question in two fundamentally different ways. First, we might look to Freud's writings themselves as an autonomous body of theory and try to see if there is a humanistic spirit latent—a spirit that would restore man to his classical position as the rational measure of all things. Or, we might as I have attempted to do, take psychoanalysis as a historically objectified formation that has been appropriated, transformed, and transmitted by the human sciences, in order to see how psychoanalysis has changed the topography in the project of knowing man—to see how Freud incites a change in our modern *episteme* through providing a new set of logically related structures, rules, or laws in the human sciences that define the subject in terms of the symbols and signs in which it participates but is unaware of. It is through taking this second approach that we can I think see quite clearly Freud's contribution in freeing the human sciences from a humanism—a contribution reflected in Lacan's attempt to liberate psychoanalysis from its Anglo-American instantiation as a *new humanism* (from the ego psychologists among others); in Foucault's proposed attempt to free history, and perhaps philosophy, from a new humanistic slumber; and in Lévi-Strauss's attempt to free anthropology from the humanist and realist strains of thought found in Durkheim. In short we may say that what we find with the onset of Freud is not just the centrality of the unconscious in the human sciences, but the centrality of a new language and discourse in this age of psychoanalysis—an anonymous language and discourse in which the subject realizes its possibilities and the human sciences realize their subject.

References

Davidson, A. (1988), Freud's "Three Essays." In: *The Trial(s) of Psychoanalysis*, ed. F. Meltzer. Chicago: University of Chicago Press.
——— (1990), Closing up the Corpses. In: *Meaning and Method: Essays in Honor of Hillary Putnam*, ed. G. Boolos. Cambridge, MA: Harvard University Press.
Foucault, M. (1965), Philosophy and psychology. In: *Aesthetics, Method, and Epistemology: Essential Works of Foucault (1954–1984), Vol. 2*, ed. M. Foucault, J. D. Foubion & P. Rabinow (trans. R. Hurley). New York: New Press, 1988.
——— (1968), On the archaeology of the sciences. In: *Aesthetics, Method, and Epistemology: Essential Works of Foucault (1954–1984), Vol. 2*, ed. M. Foucault, J. D. Fabion & P. Rabinow (trans. R. Hurley). New York: New Press, 1988.
——— (1969a), What is an author? In: *Aesthetics, Method, and Epistemology: Essential Works of Foucault (1954–1984), Vol. 2*, ed. M. Foucault, J. D. Foubion & P. Rabinow (trans. R. Hurley). New York: New Press, 1998.
——— (1969b), Linguistique et sciences sociales. In: *Foucault and His Interlocutors*. Chicago: University of Chicago Press, p. 11.
——— (1969c), Nietzsche, Freud, and Marx. In: *Aesthetics, Method, and Epistemology: Essential Works of Foucault (1954–1984), Vol. 2*, ed. M. Foucault, J. D. Fabion & P. Rabinow (trans. R. Hurley). New York: New Press, 1988, p. 275.
——— (1970), *The Order of Things: An Archaeology of the Human Sciences*. New York: Vintage Books.
——— (1997), Structures and strategies of discourse. In: *Foucault and His Interlocutors*. Chicago: University of Chicago Press.
Kaplan-Williams, S. (1997), *Elements of Dreamwork*. New York: Element Books, pp. 1, 32, 44.

Krafft-Ebing, R. (1969), *Psychopathia Sexualis: The Case Histories,* 12th ed., trans. F. S. Klef. New York: Bantam.

Lacan, J. (1955a), Knowledge, truth, opinion. In: *The Seminars of Jacques Lacan: Book II.* New York: Norton, 1988.

——— (1955b), The purloined letter. In: *The Seminars of Jacques Lacan: Book II.* New York: Norton, 1988.

——— (1955c), Freud, Hegel, and the machine. In: *The Seminars of Jacques Lacan: Book II.* New York: Norton, 1988.

——— (1957), The agency of the letter in the unconscious. In: *Ecrits.* New York: Norton, 1977.

Lévi-Strauss, C. (1958), *Structural Anthropology.* New York: Basic Books, 1963.

Nietzsche, F. W. (1873), On truth and lie in an extra-moral sense. In: *The Viking Portable Nietzsche,* ed. W. Kaufmann. New York: Penguin Books, 1954.

Osborne, R. (1993), *Freud for Beginners.* New York: Writers and Readers Publishing, pp. 165–168.

The Humanity of the Gods:
The Past and Future of Freud's
Psychoanalytic Interpretation of Religion

Shortly after the publication of Sigmund Freud's "The Future of an Illusion" (1927), the poet T. S. Eliot (1929) gave it a negative review, emphatically stating, "it has little to do with the past or the present of religion, and nothing, so far as I can see, with its future" (p. 350). Eliot could not have been more mistaken. Indeed, a case can be made that no single thinker—not Marx, not Gandhi, not Billy Graham, not Pope John XXIII—has had a greater impact on the 20th century understanding of religion than Freud.

Freud's ideas have undoubtedly played a central animating role in the academic study of religion. But they have influenced religion outside the classroom as well. The popularization in literature and in film of Freudian theories about the human psyche, about sexuality, guilt, and the unconscious have played a transforming role in the way in which most of us in the modern Western world have come to think about the nature of the religious life. When atheists dismiss religion as a "crutch," they are recapitulating in a terse shorthand form one level of a far more complex argument that Freud himself made about the function of religious beliefs and practices. Yet, curiously, even though Freud was an atheist, his views have also shaped the understanding of religion within faith communities decisively, especially among Jews and Christians. Prominent theologians have drawn on Freud's insights to deepen their own analyses of belief (Homans, 1970). Freudian ideas have made their way into Christian and Jewish culture through books, sermons, and new models of pastoral care. Finally, perhaps it was inevitable—as religious belief has grown increasingly personalistic or individualistic over the course of the twentieth century—that the psychology of religion would become a part of popular religious culture. In any case Freud has found a prominent place among both atheists and believers not only in the

263

understanding but also in the making of the religious life in the latter half of the twentieth century.

Religion was, of course, one of Freud's major concerns, a cultural riddle he explored with indefatigable creativity and curiosity. An heir of the Enlightenment, Freud came to believe it possible to illuminate the irrational and unconscious dimensions of religious beliefs, rituals, and symbols with the bright lights of reason and science. As a consequence he became convinced early on that his psychoanalytic project not only offered hope to individuals who suffered from an array of debilitating neuroses but also an explanation for apparently irrational dimensions of cultural life, of which religion was, in Freud's view, an egregious example. Thus, by the time of his death in London in September 1939, he had left behind, in addition to his astonishingly original works that came to serve as the inaugural texts in psychoanalytic theory, a significant body of writings on the cultural and psychological origins of religious belief, ritual, and symbols. "The Future of an Illusion" (1927) was only one of nearly a dozen significant texts Freud devoted to this subject. Thus it is useful to think, as the French philosopher Michel Foucault has done, of Freud not merely as an "author," but rather as "a founder of discursivity" or what we might more prosaically call a "founder of a conversation." Such founders, Foucault has argued, are not merely "authors of their own works"; to the contrary, "they have produced something else: the possibilities and the rules for formations of other texts" (1984, p. 114). And, indeed, Freud's texts on religion have proven extremely useful for practitioners in a variety of disciplines. This does not mean that scholars continue to accept all of Freud's premises (though a certain dogmatism did haunt some of Freud's earlier followers) but rather that they have found it useful to pursue Freud's insights into the relation of the human psyche to religious beliefs and practices. But neither those who stand outside nor those who stand within religious traditions have held the original terms of Freud's equation static. Freud's texts have proven classic and influential precisely because they have created the conditions for an ongoing and intense conversation about the nature of religious phenomena. It is a conversation by no means confined to psychoanalysis, finding participants among philosophers, historians, literary scholars, feminists, and postmodernists of many stripes. Indeed, it is a conversation that has spilled over— through novels and films—into our popular culture. What Freud himself would think about such a discussion is not clear. What is plain is that the participants in this conversation have continued to find it useful, when thinking about religion, to think about Freud.

By religion, Freud meant patriarchal faith and, above all, Judaism and Christianity, though, as we shall see, students of religion have continued to expand Freud's insights to include a consideration of other faith traditions, as well as phenomena such as mysticism from which Freud himself turned away. Freud's particular preoccupations, however, were not surprising. Judaism and Christianity were the twin ghosts that haunted his life and from which his psychoanalytic project was, at least in part, an effort in intellectual and moral exorcism. Scholars have made much in recent years of the religiocultural context of Freud's Vienna in which a conservative Catholic Church often fanned the flames of popular anti-Semitic policies that would eventually culminate in Nazism (Schorske, 1979; McGrath, 1986; Gay, 1988; Gilman, 1993). To a significant extent, this context explains the polemical, antireligious tone of much of Freud's writing on this theme. Moreover—and this is a point to which I return—the realities of Nazism and the horrors of the Holocaust in particular did much to propel Freud's ideas on religion to center stage in academic and theological settings for the balance of the twentieth century.

Freud, of course, was a committed atheist, a self-described "godless Jew," one who placed his faith in science and rationality; and it would be from the scientific methods he developed both in his own self-analysis and in his clinical works that Freud drew in his nearly tireless efforts to lay bare the function of religion both in the lives of individuals and in the histories of culture generally (Gay, 1987). To be sure, he was not the first writer to offer a secular interpretation of religious beliefs and practices. To the contrary, he drew on an important Enlightenment tradition that included Voltaire, Diderot, and Hume. Most scholars acknowledge that Freud's insights into religion significantly deepened the theoretical discussion of the nature and origin of religious beliefs, practices, and symbols. Freud asked new questions. And, although very few psychoanalysts or theorists today would accept all the specifics of Freud's own answers to the questions he posed, they nonetheless continue to find the framework he constructed a meaningful one. As we shall see, they have expanded and rethought Freud's own arguments in quite radical ways, especially in the overlapping wakes of feminist theory and postmodernism. Nonetheless there is no question that Freud's ideas on religion, now nearly a century after he first began publishing on this theme, continue to serve as a deep reservoir upon which many still draw in order to clarify the emotional sway religion still has (and perhaps always shall have) over human culture.

The Psychoanalytic Interpretation of Religion—the Past

"If cattle and horses had hands, horses would draw the forms of gods like horses, and cattle like cattle." The idea that religious beliefs are a projection of human experience is, as this fragment from the Eleatic philosopher Xenophanes (late sixth–early fifth century B.C.E.) demonstrates, an ancient one (p. 67). Freud's theory continued this tradition; indeed, in one of his earliest assertions on the matter, Freud (1901) observed that religion "*is nothing but psychology projected into the external world. . . .* One could venture to explain in this way the myths of paradise and the fall of man, of God, of good and evil, of immortality and so on" (pp. 258–259). God had not created man, Freud argued; rather man had created God. Much of Freud's lifework was to be directed toward unmasking what he saw as the illusory nature of religious beliefs and practices.

Freud, however, was not merely reiterating the ancient hypothesis that humans are the creators of their own divinities. In fact Freud offered an original and compelling interpretation of the origins of the gods. He did so by linking his discussion of religion and culture to a new model of the human psyche—a model that stressed the crucial and formative role of childhood in the shaping of individual and universal personhood.

The key notion in Freud's understanding of the human person lay, as is well known, in his new interpretation of both the origins and the functions of the unconscious, a series of insights that, as the other contributions in this volume show, have fundamentally transformed our modern understanding of art, politics, society, and the individual. As the eminent historian Peter Gay (1999) has recently observed, "today we all speak Freud." To Freud the unconscious was a complex realm of primal wishes, eternal desires, and aggressive drives. Nonetheless the psyche was not only a cauldron of erotic and aggressive instincts but also a locus of restraint—with the ego and the superego both charged with managing antisocial desires in order to make communal life possible. Ultimately it was out of these conflicting forces—engaged in a continuous dialectical process—that religion would develop on both a cultural and an individual level.

Freud's explanation for the construction of the unconscious was developed in what most observers, especially in light of the emergence of feminist theory, now view as a gendered narrative that he was to make famous. In this narrative, Freud placed special emphasis on the growing desire a boy, usually beginning in his second or third year, feels for his mother, a desire that is generally frustrated by the boy's seemingly indomitable rival for his mother's affection, the father. Ultimately the boy internalizes the cultural prohibitions against incest, as well as other common social rules. He does this by *becoming* his father. This conflict—that part of the family romance that Freud aptly called the Oedipus complex from its striking similarities to the Greek legend in which the king Oedipus murdered his father (albeit unwittingly) to sleep with his mother—would come to form the core of Freud's theory of the psyche and indeed of culture in general. As he himself put it, the oedipal theory is the "immortal master-thesis of psychoanalysis" (1900, p. 453). Crucially, it accounted for the dual nature of the self as a psychic bundle of desires and prohibitions—a duality that could manifest itself in the most diverse ways.

Certainly, Freud's theory of the psyche was at the core of his works on religion. In perhaps his most widely read work on this subject, "The Future of an Illusion" (the work T. S. Eliot dismissed), Freud underscored the fact that human life, even in adulthood, remains precarious and fragile. As a result, religion, in Freud's view, look on the emotional function of providing solace in a broken world—a world haunted by natural calamities, disease, and, above all, "the painful riddle of death" (1927, p. 15). Against cruel Nature, religion provided the illusion of protection. Religion, from this perspective, was an expression of a wish: namely, the child's wish that his father protect him, one of the "oldest, strongest and most urgent wishes of mankind" (1927, p. 30). The Jewish hope for or the Christian belief in a Messiah might be understood largely from this perspective, as might the Catholic devotion to the particular saints, who are believed to offer protection (Balmary, 1986; Carroll, 1986). The anxieties that adult life brings, therefore, call to the surface the desire for protection that the individual first experiences as a helpless child. It is this anxiety that explains the deep emotional appeal of the idea of a protective divinity who, in some sense, benevolently oversees human life—an idea that many scholars, accepting Freud's universalizing claims about human nature in general and the Oedipus complex in particular, have found manifest in faiths as diverse as Hinduism and various forms of animism (Ortigues and Ortigues, 1966; Kurtz, 1992).

By the time Freud came to publish "Civilization and Its Discontents" (1930), however, his views on religion had undergone an important modification. No longer satisfied with the word "illusion" to describe religion, Freud now termed it a "delusion." That is, he no longer regarded religion as the attempt to fulfill an infantile wish; rather, he believed religion constituted an attempt to escape reality. "A special importance," Freud wrote, "attaches to the case in which this attempt to procure a certainty of happiness and a protection against suffering through a delusional remoulding of reality is made by a considerable number of people in common." He then poignantly added, "the religions of mankind must be classed among the mass delusions of this kind" (1930, p. 81).

On this view, religion was, Freud suggested, a kind of group psychosis. Indeed, the dominant tone of "Civilization and Its Discontents" is pessimism. Here Freud seems to have abandoned his earlier view that science could deliver human beings from their illusion. But "Civilization and Its Discontents" also offers a further insight into Freud's view of the psychoanalytic study of religion. As Freud (1930) noted in the opening section of the book, his friend the French novelist Romain Rolland (1866–1944) had written him that, though he concurred with Freud's conclusions in "The Future of an Illusion," he believed that Freud had not "properly appreciated the true source of religious sentiments" (p. 64). Rolland then described this source as an "oceanic feeling," a feeling he claimed to experience constantly. But again Freud saw this "feeling," which he viewed as a kind of mystical impulse, as illusory. Its source, he believed, lay in the period psychoanalysts refer to as primary narcissism, when a newborn intuits no boundaries between him- or herself and the world. Because it was defined by a strong sense of oneness with the universe, mysticism, from this perspective, was explained by the survival of primary narcissism in the adult. In recent years Jeffrey Maoussieff Masson (1980) and William Parsons (1999) have extended

Freud's description of the oceanic feeling into considerations of sacred Indian texts and other forms of mysticism.

Freud, however, tellingly refused to see religion as an expression of primary narcissism. He remained convinced that the Oedipus complex was the defining origin of religious belief. "The derivation of religious needs from the infant's helplessness and the longing for the father aroused by it seems to me incontrovertible," Freud wrote, "especially since the feeling is not simply prolonged from childhood days, but is permanently sustained by fear of the superior powers of Fate" (1930, p. 72). Once again Freud's analysis was consistently patriarchal and oedipal, with all the aggressive impulses this implies. In the end Freud could make no room for an analysis of mysticism or other reconciliatory and communal dimensions of religious beliefs and practices. His was a story of fathers and sons, of struggle, domination, and authority. It was a theory that seems now, in retrospect, incomplete as feminist scholars in particular turn their attention to mothers and daughters and to the preoedipal experience as perhaps equally decisive in the formation of religious beliefs and practices.

To solve the riddle of religious belief, Freud also needed a historical and an anthropological account, because the analysis of the origins of the beliefs of individuals required also an analysis of the origins of religion in general. He turned to this problem first in another of his major cultural texts, "Totem and Taboo" (1913). This was Freud's first major cultural interpretation of religion— a work that, at its core, was a highly imaginative narrative of the passage from barbarism to civilization. Like many of his contemporaries, perhaps most especially Emile Durkheim and Robertson Smith, Freud believed that totemism constituted the elementary or inaugural form of religious belief. Thus, like them, Freud believed that if he could solve the riddle of the origins of totemism, he would be able to offer an explanation of the origins of religious belief in general. Again, as in his other works on religion, Freud drew a sharp distinction between what the participants themselves believed they were doing (their own manifest or phenomenological account) and what psychoanalysis could actually disclose about their practices. As he observed, "[t]here is no sense in asking savages to tell us the real reason for their prohibitions—the origins of taboo. It follows from our postulates that they cannot answer, since the real reason must be 'unconscious'" (1913, p. 31).

Significantly, the narrative Freud developed in "Totem and Taboo" paralleled on a cultural level the narrative he had developed to explain the Oedipus complex on a personal level. This is not surprising, because Freud was convinced that societies developed in much the same way as individuals. Freud shared, after all, his contemporaries' view that "ontogeny recapitulates phylogeny"— that the development of the individual contains within it a coded history of the development of the species (Preus, 1987, p. 181; Jonte-Pace, 1997, p. 250). Thus totemism could be viewed as a kind of oedipal struggle writ large. Rather than the struggle between one son and his father, Freud viewed totemism as an outgrowth of the struggle between a "primal" father and his sons. In Freud's view the primal father monopolized all the women. The sons, driven by their sexual desire, overthrew the father, killed him, and then devoured him. But desire is only one dimension of the psyche; other dimensions include repression and guilt. Thus, the sons, overcome by guilt, determined to "resurrect" the father as a clan totem—a sacred figure essential to clan ritual and law, with particular prohibitions against murder and incest. "[The totem] confesses," Freud wrote, "with a frankness that could hardly be excelled, to the fact that the object of the act of sacrifice has always been the same—namely what is now worshipped as God, that is to say, the father" (1913, p. 151). On such a scaffolding, Freudian theorists of religion have been able to develop a psychoanalytic interpretation of the Catholic mass, because a ritual such as the Eucharist would be envisioned by Freud as a repetition of this primal crime, "a fresh elimination of the father, a repetition of the guilty deed" (1913, p. 155).

This story, a form of imaginative anthropology that was fashionable at the beginning of the 19th century in the works of such scholars as Robertson Smith and James G. Frazer, derives its importance in contemporary psychoanalysis not from its accuracy as history but rather from its striking parallels to Freud's Oedipus theory, which, in this text, Freud has extended from the individual to the culture as a whole (Lang, 1911; Paul, 1991). As in his best-known "cultural texts" "The Future of an Illusion" and "Civilization and Its Discontents," so in this work, Freud offered a powerful reading of religion as an expression of the collisions that take place between eros and thanatos, sex and death, desire and power. Recently the Canadian scholar James J. DiCenso, drawing on the psychoanalytic theories of Jacques Lacan and Julia Kristeva, has made a compelling case that Freud's views on this subject need to be "de-literalized," and he makes the useful suggestion that we read Freud not for the historical accuracy of his text, stressing instead its importance for unraveling, for example, the central role of trauma (in this case the killing of the primal father) in the shaping of collective memory (DiCenso, 1999). In either case, religion, in Freud's view, was an expression of fundamental divisions within the psyche. Thus, here as elsewhere in his writings, we might best interpret Freud as a master of a reductive theory, one that continuously argued for both the consoling and the repressive function of religious beliefs and practices to a humanity that was, given its roots in nature and biology as well as its embeddedness in countervailing cultural forces, forever at war with itself. For Freud, there was no ultimate reconciliation possible. This was the great illusion of Christianity, which Freud observed in the hostility of Christian culture to Judaism in Vienna, where he had first developed his career and where he had lived from his young adulthood until the *Anschluss* by the Nazis of Austria made his flight to England, just before his death, inevitable.

No single Freudian cultural text has received as much attention in recent years as Freud's "Moses and Monotheism" (1939), Freud's last work and one that picks up on many of the themes of "Totem and Taboo" (Yerushalmi, 1991; Paul, 1996; Bernstein, 1998). Freud's ostensible concern in this text was to offer an explanation of monotheism. In his view, Yahweh, the God of the Jews, was at heart a reflection of a mountain deity, which in turn was a reflection of the primal father. Essentially Freud develops his argument for the princely origins of Moses, an Egyptian, who turned to the Jews after he was disappointed by his own people. This Moses was a harsh ruler who was murdered by the Jews—an act not unlike the sons' killing of the father of the primal horde in "Totem and Taboo." Eventually the Jews' remorse led them to invest Moses with the role of their founder, even claiming that Yahweh had long been his God.

Scholars continue to find Freud's discussion of Judaism in "Moses and Monotheism" to be of great significance. Indeed, in this unruly and disjointed discussion, begun in Austria and completed in England, Freud presents us with the ethical (but strict) and intelligent leader Moses. Moses represents a form of abstract philosophical wisdom possessed of a moral code almost as rigorous and demanding as Kant's. For Freud, Moses is the embodiment of the rational authority of science that, as we have seen, he praised in "The Future of an Illusion." In short, Freud's understanding of Moses was precisely the opposite of the magical, credulous, nonsensical beliefs (including a fundamental strain of anti-Semitism) that infused the Viennese Catholicism of his day.

Although Freud never wrote at length on the subject of religious symbols, a semiotics is in fact implicit in his work, and both psychoanalysts and scholars in religious studies have turned to Freud's masterpiece "The Interpretation of Dreams" (1900) as Freud's definitive text on symbol interpretation. Freud's discussion of dreams makes clear his assumption that dream symbols are initially deceptive and misleading. In the critical distinction between manifest and latent content, he propounds a theory in which remembered aspects of the dream—its manifest aspects—and the impulses and desires that are only represented in the most enigmatic way—its latent aspects—represent two levels of dream life. The symbols, in the surface analysis of the dream, are thus disguises with which we hide from ourselves the intense passions that drive our interior lives and our relationships with one another. Acknowledging these passions would put one face-to-face with oneself, forcing one to admit the depths of one's hostility to parents and siblings, primitive greed, and narcissism. In other words Freud viewed symbols as concealing something. This contrasts with conventional religious paradigms that focus on the revelatory aspects of symbols: symbols as providing a glimpse of the ideal social order such as the kingdom of God, or as representing the divine power to comfort and heal, or as intimations of hope in dark times.

Psychoanalytic Interpretations
of Religion—The Future

In "Civilization and its Discontents," Freud wrote that religious beliefs are "so patently infantile, so foreign to reality, that to anyone with a friendly attitude to humanity it is painful to think that the great majority of mortals will never be able to rise above this view of life" (1930, p. 74). In a profound sense, Freud knew that psychoanalysis would never free the great majority of men and women from their illusions, though there is no question but that both he and his earlier followers placed considerable faith in psychoanalysis as a movement that could at least lead the better educated away from the hold that religious beliefs had over them. But I doubt he could have foreseen either the enormously fruitful afterlife of his ideas in general nor the rich array of approaches to religion that his own seminal explorations made possible.

The explanation for the power of Freud's views has many sources. To a large degree, the Holocaust seemed a terrible confirmation of Freud's worst fears about human nature. If Nietzsche had pronounced God dead in the nineteenth century, the Holocaust appeared to verify God's death in the twentieth. Those who had already, in the wake of the Enlightenment, rejected the idea of a benevolent deity if not the idea of a divinity altogether, saw in the policies of Hitler horrific evidence of the profound irrationality of religion. Religion was, it seemed clear, a mask civilization had worn over aggression. Once again the children (the Christians) had killed their fathers (the Jews). But Jewish and Christian theologians who continue to adhere to their faith also turned to Freud. Although they rejected his atheism, they nonetheless acknowledged that his insights had great value for their religious communities. Above all, they came to believe it essential for believers to pay greater attention than ever before to those dimensions of their beliefs that could result in harm to self or to community. They developed new theologies and new modalities of pastoral care that attempted to address the shortcomings of Christianity and Judaism, as well as to bring the two faiths into new forms of dialogue with one another.

One of the most insightful proponents of this position is the philosopher Paul Ricoeur. In his impressive interpretation of Freud's importance for the interpretation of religious symbols, Ricoeur calls Freud one of the great "masters of suspicion" (1974). In particular Freud's critique constitutes a fundamental challenge for Christians. A failure to take Freud's insights into account, Ricoeur argues, will result in a faith characterized by the childish naïveté of idealized, simple, and literal forms. Believers must be able—and this argument was especially important after the Holocaust—to confront the many sadistic and aggressive forms religion can take. Only by doing so and by taking Freud's critique seriously, Ricoeur continued, could believers achieve a form of "second naïveté": a sophisticated, adult, reflective affirmation of religious symbols that never lets go of a necessary, corrective suspicion.

Although the shadow of the Holocaust has continued to render Freud's insights into religion especially compelling, another dimension of 20th-century life has also played a key role in ensuring Freud an important legacy. Twentieth-century faith has, in ways almost unimaginable in more traditional societies, been an expression of an unprecedented and almost unrestricted individualism (Bellah et al., 1985). Certainly religious belief remains communitarian in many settings, but, by and large, both Americans and Europeans have come to see faith in increasingly individualistic terms. Religion, therefore, has come to lend itself to increasingly psychological explanations, among which Freud's own contribution has been, in my view, the most compelling. In all fairness, there-fore, it was not only Freud's insights nor merely the formation of psychoanalytic societies that saw it largely as their mission to preserve Freud's legacy, but also specific political and cultural developments over the last 60 years that have fo-cused the attention of psychoanalysts, theologians, sociologists, psychologists, and scholars in religious studies on Freud. But how might we best understand Freud's legacy?

There have been two highly significant shifts in the psychoanalytic approach to religion over the last generation. The first involves recognition that Freud's theory was primarily a theory about men, about authority, and about patriarchy. Within this context the emphasis on the Oedipus complex made perfect sense. Precisely because of Freud's emphasis on male development, feminist theorists were at first hesitant to make use of Freud. But, once again, Freud's theories have proven adaptable, and feminism has constituted one of the liveliest arenas for the discussion of Freud's ideas in the last 20 years. Although many feminist writers in the 1970s were extremely critical of Freud, Juliet Mitchell, in her groundbreaking book *Psychoanalysis and Feminism*, produced a compelling ar-gument that feminists need Freud to understand patriarchy (1974).

The marriage of psychoanalytic feminism and religious studies, in turn, has produced some important contributions to both disciplines. In her *Freud on Femininity and Faith*, for example, Judith van Herik (1982) has teased out of Freud's work a crucial addition to our understanding of Freud's relation to Judaism and Chris-tianity (1982). Van Herik's scrupulous reading of Freud, most particularly "Moses and Monotheism," has led her to argue that Freud equated Christianity with femi-ninity and fulfillment; at the same time, he equated Judaism with masculinity and renunciation. Although many commentators have assumed that all Freud's work on religion addressed religion in a general and nonspecific sense, van Herik has shown us that Christianity and Judaism ultimately become separated in Freud's mind, with Christianity representing weak, infantilizing femininity. Chris-tianity is surpassed by its precursor, which renounced idols and magic to make possible the stern monotheism that eschewed childlike religion with the demand-ing and abstract Mosaic form of belief. Sander Gilman, in his masterful *Freud, Race, and Gender*, has addressed this topic from a historical perspective (1993). He demonstrates that the European stereotype of the Jew included images of the Jew as feminized. In "Moses and Monotheism," Freud responds to this stereotype by depicting—albeit in code—Christians as the feminized ones, with Jews possessing the more masculine attributes. This emphasis is transparent in the German title: *Der Mann Moses und die monotheistische Religion.*

Feminist psychoanalytic theory has also drawn on the work of the mother-centered British object relations theorists. To a large degree, object relations theory itself took form early on in the work of Melanie Klein and was then decisively advanced by a number of others, including Donald Winnicott (Hughes, 1989). Essentially Klein and Winnicott, still working within a Freudian framework, laid the foundations for an exploration of the infant's experience in relation to her mother. This retrieval in turn has proven extremely useful to a reinterpreting of religious experience from the perspective of infancy—a process that scholars have come to call "the turn to the mother." This methodological reorientation resembles that of feminist theologians, many of whom present the image of God as mother. These scholars have developed powerful ways of critiquing the inherently patriarchal character of Christianity and Judaism—most evident perhaps in their shared depiction of God as male (Daley, 1973; Ruether, 1983; McFague, 1987). Object relations theory, in short, has significant affinities with the emergence of a feminist theology by making it possible to question the notion that God must be a projection of the father. Indeed both theologians and psychoanalysts have come to argue that one's conception of deity can be tied up with many different kinds of object relations—including, most obviously, the following: son-mother, daughter-father, daughter-mother. They conclude that, if these other significant relationships are taken seriously, then the psychoanalytic study of religion can become far more inclusive in its understanding of religion (Rizzuto, 1979; Ross and Ross, 1983; Rabb, 2000), and even be able, psychoanalytically, to account for various forms of goddess worship (including veneration of the Virgin Mary). This framework has allowed psychoanalytic thinkers such as Sudhir Kakar to apply the psychoanalytic study of religion cross-culturally—in Kakar's case to apply psychoanalysis to Hinduism, in which mothers and goddesses are without doubt closely intertwined (Kakar, 1981). Ironically Freud, despite his preference for masculine and oedipal categories in his analysis of the psyche, has proven to be, in the words of Gail Rubin, a "feminist manqué."

The second major shift has been the "linguistic turn." In psychoanalysis this change has been associated primarily with the teachings of Jacques Lacan whose work might be read as a brilliant, extended commentary on Freud. Indeed, Lacan (whose seminars drew enormous crowds of academics and intellectuals together in Paris for some 20 years) played perhaps the single most important role in developing Freudian thought in postwar France. Yet, ironically, his views, which actually led to his expulsion from the French psychoanalytic society, famously shifted the terms of psychoanalysis from history and biology to language, perhaps best captured in Lacan's celebrated observation that "the unconscious is structured like a language" (1978, p. 20). Lacan's ideas are complex, but his emphasis on language has important implications for the study of religion (Raschke, 1997). We see this, in particular, in the Lacanian notion that the symbolic (the stage at which the infant enters language) develops as the child separates from his or her mother (Lacan, 1977, 1978). Thus language is always an expression of an absence, or a lack, and the means through which humans seek to reintegrate themselves into a greater whole. In a similar vein, religious language might be seen as a desire to restore the original unity the child experiences in his or her preoedipal or presymbolic (i.e., prelinguistic) stage.

Yet the most innovative thought in the psychoanalytic study of religion at the end of the twentieth century derives, as Diane Jonte-Pace has suggested in an insightful essay, from the work of the Bulgarian-French theorist Julia Kristeva (1997). As Jonte-Pace notes, Kristeva's work derives its importance largely from her synthesis of Freud, Lacan, and object-relations theory. And she has constructed works that are largely rewritings of Freud's religious essays in light of her new synthesis. Thus, just as her "Powers of Horror: An Essay on Abjection" (1982) is a rewriting of "Totem and Taboo," her *In the Beginning was Love: Psychoanalysis and Faith* (1987) revises "The Future of an Illusion," and her *Strangers to Ourselves* (1991) revisits "Civilization and its Discontents." Particularly exciting in Kristeva's work has been her refusal to reduce the human subject—what Lacan called the "speaking subject"—to a purely linguistic artifact. Thus her emphasis on the preoedipal is even more pronounced than Lacan's. Like Lacan, she sees the transition from this earlier stage to the symbolic as one of loss, mourning, absence, even trauma. But, like Winnicott, she never envisions the emerging self as an exclusively linguistic construction (or illusion). The prelinguistic experience of the maternal body (a source of comfort as well as of terror) becomes for Kristeva a central focus in her psychoanalytic interpretation of religion. Her work, therefore, offers an important synthesis of some of the richest ideas in psychoanalysis and now constitutes an essential point of departure for contemporary reflection on religious beliefs and practices within a psychoanalytic context.

Freud's legacy has, therefore, proven enormous. By the end of the century, an entirely new academic field devoted to the psychoanalytic study of religion had been erected on the basis of Freud's writings and the contributions of his followers. A recent and undoubtedly incomplete bibliography on the subject lists over 2000 titles (Beit-Hallami, 1996). Internet searches on the subject also turn up countless books, essays, articles, and web-pages. Thus, what began as a series of carefully controlled reflections by Freud on the origins of religious beliefs and practices in both individuals and societies has resulted in a rich array of explorations into the connection between the human and the divine, real or imagined. A psychoanalytic interpretation of religion (namely Freud's) has given birth to a numerous family of psychoanalytic *interpretations* of religious beliefs and practices. Moreover, within religious communities as well, Freud continues to animate significant discussions. The prominent Catholic theologian Hans Kung, for example, has grappled with Freud's legacy, retrieving those aspects that he believes essential for the revitalization of his faith (Kung, 1979). At the same time, pastoral psychology, though by no means exclusively Freudian, continues to draw on his ideas. As Kung himself has noted, "theologians and pastors are increasingly discovering today the critical potential of psychoanalysis for Church and theology" (1979, p. 100).

Yet it would be a mistake to assume that Freud's ideas on religion are confined to the high-brow discussions of scholars, psychoanalysts, and theologians. For scholars are also teachers, psychoanalysts work closely with their patients, and theologians inform the thought of clergy and, indirectly, their congregations. Freudian views on religion, that is, have come to be one of the fundamental dimensions in virtually all aspects of modern culture. It matters little whether we are believers. Critics of religion have found in Freud an important ally in a critique of everything from organized religion to individual convictions. At the same time, believers have found in Freud a guide to the complexity and the depth of the meaning of religious beliefs and practices on both an individual and a cultural level. This has been especially apparent in the proliferation of faith-based counseling centers in almost every sizeable community in the United States as well as in the proliferation of publications that draw on psychology to explain what is healthy, what less so in various forms of religious beliefs and practices. In a curious sense, therefore, Freud is a virtually inevitable part of our religious culture and our religious debates. He not only informs our most widespread assumptions about sexuality, aggression, guilt, and personality. The very force of his argument that it is we who have created the gods has rendered Freud one of the great architects of twentieth-century understandings of the relation of human beings to their deities, real and imagined. Finally, it is with no little irony that Freud, who famously described himself as a "godless Jew," has also brought forth some of the richest discussions of belief and theology within faith communities themselves. Our own cultural imagination would seem impoverished without Freud's insights into the humanity of the gods.

References

Balmary, M. (1986), *Le sacrifice intérdit: Freud et la bible*. Paris: Grasset.

Bellah, R. N., Madsen, R., Sullivan, W. M., Swidler, A. & Tipton, S. M. (1985), *Habits of the Heart: Individualism and Commitment in American Life*. Berkeley: University of California Press.

Beit-Hallahmi, B. (1996), *Psychoanalytic Studies of Religion: A Critical Assessment and Annotated Bibliography*. Westport, CT: Greenwood Press.

Bernstein, R. (1998), *Freud and the Legacy of Moses*. Cambridge: Cambridge University Press.

Carroll, M. P. (1986), *The Cult of the Virgin Mary: Psychological Origins*. Princeton. NJ: Princeton University Press.

Daley, M. (1973), *Beyond God the Father: Toward a Philosophy of Women's Liberation*. Boston: Beacon.

DiCenso, J. (1999), *The Other Freud: Religion, Culture, and Psychoanalysis*. London and New York: Routledge.

Eliot, T. S. (1929), Review of *The Future of an Illusion* by Sigmund Freud. *Criterion*, 8:350–353.

Foucault, M. (1984), What is an author? In: *The Foucault Reader*, ed. P. Rabinow. New York: Pantheon, pp. 101–120.

Freud, S. (1900), The interpretation of dreams. *Standard Edition*, 4 & 5. London: Hogarth Press, 1953.

———— (1901), The psychopathology of everyday life. *Standard Edition*, 6:1–290. London: Hogarth Press, 1960.

———— (1913), Totem and taboo. *Standard Edition*, 13:1–161. London: Hogarth Press, 1955.

———— (1927), The future of an illusion. *Standard Edition*, 21:5–56. London: Hogarth Press, 1961.

———— (1930), Civilization and its discontents. *Standard Edition*, 21:64–145 London: Hogarth Press, 1961.

————(1939), Moses and monotheism: Three essays [1934–38]. *Standard Edition*, 23:7–137. London: Hogarth Press, 1964.

Gay, P. (1987), *A Godless Jew: Freud, Atheism, and the Making of Psychoanalysis*. New Haven, CT: Yale University Press.

———— (1988), *Freud: A Life for Our Time*. New York: Norton.

———— (1999), Sigmund Freud. *Time*, March 29, pp. 38–41.

Gilman, S. L. (1993), *Freud, Race, and Gender*. Princeton, NJ: Princeton University Press.

Homans, P. (1970), *Theology after Freud*. Indianapolis, IN: Bobbs-Merrill.

Hughes, J. (1989), *Reshaping the Psychoanalytic Domain: The Work of Melanie Klein, W. R. D. Fairbairn, and D. W. Winnicott*. Berkeley: University of California Press.

Jonte-Pace, D. (1997), Julia Kristeva and the psychoanalytic study of religion: Rethinking Freud's texts. In: *Religion, Society, and Psychoanalysis*, ed. J. L. Jacobs & D. Capps. Boulder, CO: Westview Press.

Kakar, S. (1981), *The Inner World: A Psycho-analytic Study of Childhood and Society in India*. New York: Oxford.

Kristeva, J. (1982), *Powers of Horror: An Essay on Abjection*. New York: Columbia University Press.

———— (1987), *In the Beginning Was Love: Psychoanalysis and Faith*. New York: Columbia University Press.

———— (1991), *Strangers to Ourselves*. New York: Columbia University Press.

Kung, H. (1979), *Freud and the Problem of God*. New Haven, CT: Yale University Press.

Kurtz, S. N. (1992), *All the Mothers Are One: Hindu India and the Cultural Reshaping of Psychoanalysis*. New York: Columbia University Press.

Lacan, J. (1977), *Ecrits: A Selection.* New York: Norton.
———(1978), *The Four Fundamental Concepts of Psychoanalysis.* New York: Norton.
Lang, A. (1911), Totemism. In: *Encyclopaedia Britannica,* 27:79–91. Cambridge, UK: Cambridge University Press.
McFague, S. (1987), *Models of God: Theology for an Ecological, Nuclear Age.* Philadelphia: Fortress.
McGrath, W. J. (1986), *Freud's Discovery of Psychoanalysis.* Ithaca: Cornell University Press.
Masson, J. M. (1980), *The Oceanic Feeling. The Origins of the Religious Sentiment in Ancient India.* Dordrecht, Holland: D. Reidel.
Mitchell, J. (1974), *Psychoanalysis and Feminism.* New York: Pantheon.
Ortigues, M. C. & Ortigues, E. (1966), *Oedipe Africain.* Paris: Plon.
Parsons, W. B. (1999), *The Enigma of the Oceanic Feeling.* New York: Oxford University Press.
Paul, R. A. (1991), Freud's anthropology: A reading of the cultural books. In: *The Cambridge Companion to Freud,* ed. J. Neu. Cambridge: Cambridge University Press, pp. 267–286.
———(1996), *Moses and Civilization: The Meaning Behind Freud's Myth.* New Haven, CT: Yale University Press.
Preus, J. S. (1987), *Explaining Religion: Criticism and Theory from Bodin to Freud.* New Haven, CT: Yale University Press.
Raab, K. (2000), *When Women Become Priests: The Catholic Women's Ordination Debate.* New York: Columbia University Press.
Raschke, C. (1997), "God and Lacanian psychoanalysis: Towards a reconsideration of the discipline of religious studies." In: *Religion, Society, and Psychoanalysis: Readings in Contemporary Theory,* ed. J. Liebman & D. Capps. Boulder, CO: Westview.
Ricoeur, P. (1974), *Freud and Philosophy.* New Haven, CT: Yale University Press.
Rieff, P. (1966), *Freud: The Mind of the Moralist.* New York: Viking.
Rizzuto, A.-M., (1979), *The Birth of the Living God: A Psychoanalytic Study.* Chicago: University of Chicago Press.
Ross, M. E. & Ross, C. L. (1983), Mothers, infants, and the psychoanalytic study of ritual. *Signs: J. Women in Culture and Society,* 9:26–39.
Ruether, R. R. (1983), *Sexism and God-Talk: Toward a Feminist Theology.* Boston: Beacon Press.
Schorske, C. E. (1979), *Fin-de-siècle Vienna: Politics and Culture.* New York: Knopf.
van Herik, J. (1982), *Freud on Femininity and Faith.* Berkeley: University of California Press.
Xenophanes (n.d.), Fragment. In: *The First Philosophers of Greece,* ed. A. Fairbanks. London: Kegan Paul, Trench, Truebner, 1898.
Yerushalmi, Y. H. (1991), *Freud's Moses: Judaism Terminable and Interminable.* New Haven, CT: Yale University Press.

Psychoanalysis, Drama, and the Family: The Ever-Widening Scope

FRED M. SANDER

> . . . the purpose of playing, was and is, to hold
> as 'twere, the mirror up to nature;
> —Shakespeare, *Hamlet*

> *The doctor should be opaque to his patients
> and, like a mirror, should show them
> nothing but what is shown to him.*
> —Freud, "Recommendations to Physicians
> Practising Psycho-Analysis"

> . . . *both tragic drama and the best of
> psychoanalytic thinking are so rich that there is
> a mutual enhancement, a two-way dialogue.*
> —Bennett Simon, *Tragic Drama and the Family*

> *The softness of the boundary between inside
> and outside is a universal characteristic
> of living systems.*
> —Lewontin, *The Triple Helix*

"All the world's a stage," in Latin, *Totus mundus agit histrionem,* was inscribed at the original Globe Theater four hundred years ago. The word histrionic, from the Latin *histrio* meaning acting or story, has a different derivation from hysteria, that once mysterious emotional state of "acting ill," that Freud first explored

The author acknowledges Matthew von Unwerth, librarian of the New York Psychoanalytic Institute, for his help in locating bibliographic references, and Joelle Sander, Dr. John Pareja, and Dr. Morton Schatzman for their editorial suggestions.

en route to his discovery of the Unconscious. Hysteria is derived from the Greek *hysteros,* meaning uterus. The close association of histrionic and hysterical in our minds, and our nosology (Slavney, 1990, p. 78), even if etymologically co-incidental, serves as a starting point for this essay on how drama and psycho-analysis have mutually influenced one another from the earliest days when Freud first turned his attention to the dramatic nature of hysteria. Psychoanalysis, in its exquisite privateness, ultimately deals with family conflicts internalized and trans-formed by unconscious fantasies whereas drama, in its communal publicness, deals with family conflicts played out upon the stage. Each mirrors and reflects truths about the human condition from different points of view.

This essay is divided into five sections. The first section looks to the past and notes the links between drama and the origins of psychoanalysis; the second deals with the specific ways psychoanalytic thinking has contributed to our un-derstanding of drama. Subsequently I mention, in brief, the impact of psycho-analysis upon twentieth-century drama before reviewing how several theorists have seen the analytic process itself as a dramatic and/or narrative art. The con-cluding section looks to the future and ever-expanding scope of psychoanalysis.

While throwing light upon the complex nature of theater process, we keep in mind both Freud's (1928) acknowledgment, in his essay on Dostoyevski, that, "Before the problem of the creative artist analysis must, alas, lay down its arms" (p. 177) and Pirandello's (1925) similar observation, a few years earlier, in his introduction to *Six Characters in Search of an Author* that, "The mystery of artistic creation is the mystery of birth itself" (p. 364).

Throughout this essay we may also find ourselves concurring with Martin Bergmann's (1973) caveat that psychoanalytic studies of biography and litera-ture and, *I would add our case studies as well,* illuminate the ever-expanding nature of psychoanalytic theory more than the work or person being studied. Clearly our understanding is forever partial, always being refined, and deter-mined by our theories, biases, and our "psychic realities" (Arlow, 1981). Even though Freud's ideas were rooted in a century that believed in the modernist idea of our ability to know objective reality, his discovery of the power of "psy-chic reality" has contributed to our current postmodern questioning of that as-sumption, our current climate of pluralism, and the ever-changing psychoana-lytic landscape. Our clinical theories, increasingly pluralistic, mirror the com-plexity of life itself.

General Links between Psychoanalysis, Drama, and the Family

When Freud returned from Paris where he watched Charcot hypnotize hysterical patients in front of medical audiences in the amphitheater of the Salpêtrière, he and Breuer (Breuer and Freud, 1893–1895) described the cathartic treatment of patients with hysterical symptoms. Anna O., the patient most associated with the discovery of psychoanalysis, referred to her treatment as the "talking cure" as she revealed her "private theater" to Breuer. The original title of Arthur Miller's (1949) *Death of a Salesman* was, interestingly, "The Inside of His Head," and the form of his innovative drama, with its use of flashbacks, could be described as "psychoanalytic" in that past and present are so fluidly intertwined. The idea that the past emerges in the present, which Freud called "repetition compulsion," has been manifest in works of fiction as early as the Old Testament, where we learn that the sins of the fathers are visited upon subsequent generations of sons. In "Totem and Taboo," following the lead of Darwin (Ritvo, 1970), Freud speculated that the crime of patricide by the sons set in motion subsequent generations of oedipal conflict. A more recent example from drama, of the power of the past, can be found in O'Neill's (1974) last play, *A Moon for the Misbegotten*. James Tyrone, in his attempt at confessional catharsis, bemoaned, "There is no present or future—only the past happening over and over again—now you can't get away from it" (pp. 82–83). His attempt at catharsis in recalling his debauched behavior with a woman on the train which bore his mother's coffin was to no avail.

Freud was, at first, impressed by the idea of "cathartic cures" when each of Anna O.'s symptoms disappeared as she recalled the past traumas linked to them (Breuer and Freud, 1893–1895). However, Freud realized that his early cures were not permanent and he introduced the idea that psychoanalysis is rarely brief and requires "working through" (Freud, 1914; Sander, 1974; Brenner, 1987).

Twenty-five hundred years earlier, Aristotle wrote of catharsis in the theater. He suggested that the power of drama resided in the arousal and release of powerful emotions, such as fear and pity, in the audience. Binstock (1973) explored the overlap and differences in Freud's and Aristotle's formulations while emphasizing the limitations of catharsis in psychotherapy. In 1905, Freud, linking our reactions in the theater to our childhood experiences, eloquently expanded this Aristotelian idea of the power plays have on an audience:

being present . . . at a play does for adults what play does for children, whose hesitant hopes of being able to do what grown-up people do are in that way gratified. The spectator is a person . . . who has long been obliged to damp down, or rather displace, his ambition to stand . . . at the hub of world affairs; he longs to feel and to act and to arrange things according to his desires—in short, to be a hero. And the playwright and actor enable him to do this by allowing him *to identify himself* with a hero. They spare him something, too. For the spectator knows quite well that actual conduct such as this would be impossible for him without pains and sufferings and acute fears, which would almost cancel out the enjoyment. . . . Accordingly, his enjoyment is based on an illusion; that is to say, his suffering is mitigated by the certainty that firstly, it is someone other than himself who is acting and suffering on the stage [1905b, pp. 305–306].

Artaud (1970) wrote that "a real stage play upsets our sensual tranquility, releases our repressed subconscious" (p. 19). He also compared a successful play with a plague or mental epidemic communicable to the audience. Hamlet's staging of the play within a play, to catch the conscience of the king, is an apt example of such a process, dramatized upon the stage itself. Plato, St. Augustine, the English Puritans, and, more recently, government censors have tried to quarantine these artistic "pestilences" by suppressing them. Functioning as society's superego, they were and are the earliest and harshest critics of drama. They were and are the social and cultural correlates of Freud's early description of each individual's repression of his instinctual drives.

With this in mind I have occasionally prescribed attending a theater performance to resistant patients who may then see their persistent conflicts externalized on the stage. For example, I once recommended Shakespeare's *A Winter's Tale* to an oppositional couple where the wife threatened the dissolution of their marriage if she couldn't have a third child. Upon viewing the play, she saw Leontes' tyrannical treatment of his wife as similar to her single-mindedness, whereas her husband identified with Leontes becoming "mad" when his wife was pregnant with a second child (Sander, 1998).

Though religious systems evolved, in part, as a way of controlling our impulses, it was in temple rites dealing with the stages of life, from birth to the coming of age and death, that theater was born. In theaters, our modern secular communal temples, stories usually about families dealing with these stages of life continue to be enacted and stir us. In the prepsychoanalytic days when Freud saw hysteria as primarily dependent on genetic endowment, the cases he reported with Breuer nonetheless involved precipitants within the family and subsequently he traced hysterical illness to early repressed childhood traumas such as sexual seductions. In his now historic letter (#69) to Fliess (Freud, 1950), he abandoned this dramatic theory of the family origins of hysteria and soon after replaced it with the power of childhood sexual fantasies. Four centuries earlier Shakespeare reflected this nature-nurture controversy when he asked, "Is it in ourselves or in the stars that we are underlings?" Analysts have debated the relative weight of extra- and intrapsychic determinants of mental conflict these past hundred years. The associated blurred boundaries between reality and fantasy and the elusiveness of our perceptions in pursuit of the riddles of the human mind are at the core of both psychoanalysis and drama. Besides suspending disbelief via the power of our fantasies we also suspend belief in internal and external realities via denial and repression. The suspension of belief and the suspension of disbelief are paradoxically synonymous—a further testimony to the frequent confounding of fantasy and reality.

In the current hit play *Copenhagen,* Michael Frayn (1998) imagines the 1941 secret meeting of physicists Nils Bohr and Werner Heisenberg. Once mentor and student, respectively, they each, on opposite sides of the war, were presumably working on the atomic bomb. The play dramatizes, among other themes, Heisenberg's "uncertainty principle." At the level of quantum particles, the realities we study are altered in the process of observing them. Our interpersonal and intrapsychic worlds are all the more subject to such uncertainty. Michael Blakemore (2000), the director of the play, spoke of it as resembling an experiment where "the actors do their work and circle around the nucleus of a good text" upon whom the audience, encircling the stage "like a lot of photons, . . . shine the light of their attention. . . . Then something very strange happens: the thing you rehearsed . . . is put on the stage and a thousand pair of eyes hit it and alter it" (p. 20). The staging of the play, three actors in a circle, surrounded by the audience, here reflects its content. Actors and audience influence one another in complex and mysterious ways. Similarly, in recent years, analysts have begun to appreciate and study the many ways in which the patient and analyst affect one another beyond the classical transference-countertransference configurations (Stolorow, Brandchaft, and Atwood, 1987; Kantrowitz, 1996).

I turn now to the other early link of the origins of psychoanalysis to drama, the discovery of the Oedipus complex. Only three weeks after his abandoning the seduction theory, in another historic letter (#71) to Fliess, Freud (1950) revealed his discovery of the Oedipus complex. He cited both Sophocles' *Oedipus Rex* and Shakespeare's *Hamlet* as he put forward the universality of our sexual and aggressive drives toward our parents. "Auch bei mir" (In my case too [p. 265]), he wrote. In addition to his debt to Sophocles and Shakespeare, he also credited the philosophers Schopenhauer and Nietzsche and other literary figures for their intuitive understanding of what he systematized (1914, pp. 15–16). There are over 400 citations in the index of the *Standard Edition* dealing with works of art and literature to which Freud (1974) referred. Over 30 of these are plays and operas, including 15 of Shakespeare's plays (Holland, 1966). Tens of thousands of subsequent contributions over the past one hundred years illustrate the widening scope of analytic theory via its exploration of the arts. One major bibliographic source (Keill, 1982) reflects a fivefold increase to over 20,000 references between 1962 and 1980. At that rate the number should now be around 100,000. A review of psychoanalytic and psychological studies of Shakespeare's plays (Willbern, 1978) during just one decade (1964–1975) has over 300 references, and another review of articles on "Oedipus Rex" includes over 300 references (Edmunds and Ingber, 1977). A search on Amazon.com lists 79 books dealing with "The Oedipus Complex" in all languages.

Examination of Sophocles' Oedipus plays, since Freud's initial discovery, reflects the evolution and expansion of psychoanalytic theory from its initial reductionistic emphasis on every child's oedipal incestuous strivings to include the subsequent appreciation of the impact of the pre- and postoedipal years. Curiously it was after the death of Freud, the founding father of psychoanalysis, that a shift in emphasis toward mothers occurred. In the index to Freud's *Standard*

Edition (1974), the number of references to fathers are double those citing mothers. This ratio was reversed in the 1932–1966 index to the *Psychoanalytic Quarterly*. Balter's (1969) and Stewart's (1961) essays on the power of the preoedipal mother in Greek myths are but two of many such studies which demonstrate the widening scope of analytic theory. More recently Naiman (1992) discussed the early omission by Freud of Jocasta's role as the oedipal mother who knowingly fosters the incestuous mother-son relationship. Incest, as almost all human behavior, requires the complicity or collusion of others. Even after abandoning his seduction theory, Freud's (1905a) idea of "secondary gain" appreciated the external reinforcement of symptoms by the environment (p. 43). Object relations theorists' (Main, 1966; Zinner, 1976) descriptions of the role of mutual projective identification in families make it clear that primary and secondary gain are reciprocally reinforcing.

Others have also indicated that the environment, usually parents, are codeterminative, along with infantile intrapsychic fantasies in human development. For example, Ross (1982), while not minimizing the child's innate impulses, reminds us that infanticidal impulses of parents toward their children, usually repressed, are ever present. He reminds us that Laius, with Jocasta's compliance, abandoned Oedipus to exposure and death. The actuality of the killing of infants and children and its representation in myths and literature has been present from the beginning (Rank, 1932; Bergmann, 1992); from Abraham and Isaac, to Moses, to many other Greek myths, such as those surrounding Orestes, and Medea, to Macbeth (Calef, 1969) to *Who's Afraid of Virginia Woolf*. These ubiquitous, intergenerational familial conflicts have been the subject of many analytic investigations and led Simon (1988) to redefine tragedy as dealing with families in conflict ending in their (de)generation or dissolution. Rather than an individual hero's tragic flaw, it is the family's inability to regenerate itself, in Simon's view, that constitutes the *sine qua non* of tragedy. His focus on the family unit, a focus Lidz (1975) had already explored in *Hamlet,* relied upon a chorus of current psychoanalytic theorists who have expanded psychoanalytic theory by including an interpersonal perspective to complement our intrapsychic model.

With Freud's shift to intrapsychic conflict, the family dramas in which his patients were immersed receded in importance. As to their family members, Freud (1912) concluded that "I must confess myself utterly at a loss, and I have, in general, little faith in any individual treatment of them" (p. 120). The recent expansion into pluralistic theories has coincided with the widening application of psychoanalytic theory to the treatment of couples and families (Sander, 1979, 1998; Scharff, 1989, Graller, this volume). The expansion of theory and practice is limitless if one does not narrowly define psychoanalysis as a theory primarily applicable to "classical" analysis (Esman, 1998), a modality applicable, in fact, to a very small percentage of the population. Family treatment, on the other hand, still viewed with skepticism, represents a most underutilized modality with great scope given the number of patients whose neuroses are hidden by marital conflict. In this regard Freud (1919) wrote early on that "unhappy marriage and physical infirmity are the two things that most often supersede a neurosis" (p. 163).

Psychoanalytic Contributions to the Understanding of Theater Process

This section highlights the contributions of psychoanalytic theorists to the understanding of theater. Dramatic art is a collaborative process like no other. Like life, which it mirrors, it is multilayered, multidetermined, and unpredictable. The playwright conceives the play by imaginatively combining aspects of his inner life with the external historical-cultural materials at hand. The oedipal themes in *Oedipus Rex, Hamlet,* and *Death of a Salesman,* though illustrating the timelessness of these conflicts, also reflect the contexts within which they were written. For example, the Greeks could identify with the implacable role of fate in their lives. Shakespeare's audiences could identify with the individualism emergent in the Renaissance as Hamlet asks the question "To be or not to be?" In Miller's play an appreciation of intergenerational conflicts is seamlessly interwoven with social criticism of America's obsession with material success. Willy Loman's idealized older brother boasts to Willy's sons, "When I was seventeen, I walked into the jungle, and when I was twenty-one I walked out. *He laughs.* And by God I was rich" (Miller, 1949, p. 48). The author's creative efforts are then further elaborated by the input of producers, a director, actors, rehearsals, and many other contributors who bring the play to life. Just as Winnicott reminded us that there is no baby without a mother, Peter Brook (1968) insisted upon the indispensable role played by the audience in live theater. Actors tell us that live performances, before ever-changing audiences, differ from night to night. This distinguishes theater from most other arts. The audience, as a group, influences actors, and each audience member also reacts in subjective ways, as especially evidenced in those ambivalently perceived audience members, the reviewers, or critics.

The Playwright and the Text

The text of a play is born of the playwright's experience and imagination. Much analytic understanding has shed light on the connections between a playwright's life and the text. With some playwrights the connection is obvious. As Eric Bentley (1969) said somewhat critically of Eugene O'Neill: "he wrote the story of his ambivalence again and again and again; devoted his life to doing so; was able to live only by doing so" (p. 31). Nonetheless the variations from play to play are significant. For example, both *Anna Christie* and *A Moon for the Misbegotten* deal with a father, daughter, and suitor triangle. In the first play, Anna's father, Chris, who abandoned her in childhood, rages when she falls in love with Matt, the muscular coal stoker. Ironically, in the final scene, Chris and Matt end up going off to sea, leaving Anna abandoned again. In *Moon for the Misbegotten,* written 25 years later, Phil Hogan schemes to marry his daughter Josie off to their landlord, James Tyrone. In their inebriated and celibate night together, Josie nurses Tyrone as the Virgin Mother with her Christ child. Tyrone, with his corresponding self-destructive madonna/prostitute complex, leaves Josie to continue taking care of her father. Despite these manifest differences, they show how O'Neill's characters are, again and again, unable to resolve the oedipal triangle.

Philip Weissman's (1965) chapter on O'Neill examined how O'Neill's early play *Desire under the Elms* flowed from his repressed unconscious, whereas his later play, *Long Day's Journey into Night,* was consciously autobiographical. In the same book, Weissman also wrote a chapter showing the close connection between Shaw's *Pygmalion* and significant aspects of his childhood, which included the reworking of his mother's relationship with her voice teacher. The close connection between Pirandello's plays and his personal life has been noted by Kligerman (1962) and Wangh (1976) with special emphasis on the role of father-daughter incest and primal scene experiences. The most comprehensive psychoanalytic study of a playwright is Margaret Brenman-Gibson's (1981) psychohistorical biography of Clifford Odets. Written without the reductionism of so many clinical studies she follows Erikson's model of interweaving biography and history. At one point she quotes Odets as saying, "In making art one is free from inhibition and masking of emotions . . . and one becomes freely a man of action and all is possible" (p. 672), a process that complements Freud's observation, cited earlier, of the impact of a play upon the audience.

The analyses of texts to support evolving analytic theories are ubiquitous. I cite here an example of an author who puts forth two interpretations dealing with Oedipus before and after his self-blinding. In his book *Psychic Retreats,* John Steiner (1993) contrasts Oedipus in *Oedipus the King* and *Oedipus at Colonus* to illustrate two types of pathological "psychic retreats" from reality. In the first play, Oedipus "turns a blind eye" as a defense against anxiety and guilt, and in the second, when literally blind, he retreats to a state of omnipotence. Personality is here viewed as changing over time.

The multiplicity and variability of interpretations are even more pertinent when we turn to *Hamlet.* Solving the riddle of Hamlet has been the subject of endless interpretations, psychoanalytic and literary, over the past four centuries. I have elsewhere described how this interestingly parallels a process internal to the play itself where many of the other characters in the play give their personal perspectives on the etiology of Hamlet's "madness" (Sander, 1979).

This corresponds to our increasing appreciation of the complexity of human behavior which must take into account multiple levels, determinants, perspectives, and perceptions. Simon's (1988) observation that "both tragic drama and psychoanalytic thinking are so rich that there is a mutual enhancement, a two-way dialogue" (p. 10) sums it up well.

The Actor and Stage Fright

The text of a play is not the play. Only when the text is actualized by a company of actors, a director, lighting, scenic, sound and costume designers, and an audience, do we have a play. Let us start with the actor or acting. Acting is part of everyday life (Goffman, 1959) as are the symbolic masks we use to hide parts of ourselves (Grand, 1973). Our identifications early in life, unconscious and conscious, become part of our multiple selves as we interact with one another. Psychoanalytic literature is replete with how this manifests itself in development, in acting out, enactments, imposturing, creation of false selves, in as-if personalities, and in our varying gender, racial, ethnic, and generational roles. The world *is* a stage, and all of us are forever playing innumerable roles. Acting, as a profession, amplifies this ordinary human characteristic in the service of performances that entertain while making us aware of hidden parts of ourselves.

Fenichel (1946) was one of the first analysts to turn their attention to the psychology of acting. These analysts' essays are steeped in the drive language of early psychoanalysis with acting seen as involving the partial instinct of exhibitionism. They detail the role of castration anxiety, the need for applause, aggressive feelings, and guilt in relation to the audience. Weissman (1965) also emphasizes the importance of these impulses, especially exhibitionism, in a somewhat reductionistic and pathologizing way. Although the literature is replete with vignettes about actors, I came across only one detailed description of the analysis of an actor. Munro (1952) concluded that her patient's proclivity to "employ acting-out from an early age. . . . His capacity for internalization and identification allowed him to develop considerable empathy which, when united with his dramatic talents, enabled him to give vivid and alive performances on the stage" (p. 143).

More recent analytic contributions to this subject center on the ubiquitous and normative phenomenon of stage fright (Kaplan, 1969; Gabbard, 1979a, 1979b, 1983; Aaron, 1986). Gabbard (1979) emphasized that the underlying conflicts vary from person to person and that "the relative importance of any one conflict . . . is determined by the early childhood experience of the person under consideration" (p. 385). In a later contribution (1983), he draws parallels to the analytic situation, indicating that the actor and the patient may experience idealizing and mirroring transferences to the audience and the analyst, respectively. In a related article, Kaplan (1969) addresses stage fright in the actor about to face the audience. He emphasizes the actor's fear of a loss of poise. He also notes how the actor fears the audience's anger as a punishment for his playing out forbidden impulses. This leads him into a discussion of the imposter in whom stage fright rarely occurs.

Rather than the early analytic pathologizing tone, which focused on exhibitionistic impulses and disturbances in the sense of self, we might see acting as a form of "regression in the service of the ego" (Kris, 1952) and in the service of the performance. Rather than focusing on the pathogenic aspects of acting, we could as well ask whether most of us nonactors inhibit our own exhibitionistic impulses, while allowing others, as Freud suggested, to vicariously express them. Martin Wangh's (1962) description of this "evocation of a proxy" in everyday life is as relevant here as is Johnson and Szurek's (1952) description of a similar process of parents' unconsciously encouraging their children to enact antisocial impulses.

Aaron (1986), a former director and acting teacher, and now psychotherapist, in his book entitled *Stage Fright*, captures the intensity of both the intrapsychic and interpersonal forces at work in acting. He traces the development of the universal presence of stage fright from the early rehearsal phase when dependency upon the director is intense to the abrupt separation from the director after the dress rehearsal. He goes on to show that the transferences of the actor to director are replaced by complex and primitive transferences to the audience beginning on opening night. The transition from the rehearsing actor to the performing actor is fraught with anxiety from any number of childhood sources such as separation anxiety or fear of the audience's anger for his exhibitionistic impulses. To show the latent ambivalent bond between actor and audience, he cites (p. 101) Osborne's (1957) *The Entertainer* as a play illustrating the realized fear of an actor's failed performance. At the end of the play, Archie Rice, beaten and unsuccessful, addresses the audience with "You've been a good audience. Very good. A very *good* audience. Let me know where you're working tomorrow night—and I'll come and see you" (p. 89).

The Director

Aaron's (1986) study of stage fright begins with the director/actor relationship. In the rehearsal phase, the director as parent helps the actor create the role in the company setting which resembles a family. Stanislavski (1936) put it this way: "[O]ur type of creativeness is the conception and birth of a new being—the person in the part. It is a natural act similar to the birth of a human being" (p. 294). Opening night is, in fact, the delivery date of the play's birth. These dynamics have recently been dramatized in a new play by Nancy Hasty (2000) called *The Director*. The director in the play, trained in the methods of Grotowski, in his pursuit of artistic truth, perversely drives his actors to the brink of madness. His actor/children end up leaving him at the end of the play, and the play within the play is thus aborted. Weissman (1965) had already indicated, from his experience, that directors have a particular proclivity, through their oedipal identification with parental figures, to want to lead others. He reminds us of Freud's case study of "Little Hans," who, as a little boy, wanted a big "widdler" like his father, and later became a well-known opera director.

In a *New Yorker* profile by John Lahr (2000) Mike Nichols contrasts his work as a comedian with that as a director which illustrates this generational dynamic. Nichols saw the comedian as receiving immediate narcissistic gratification with each laugh while in the first fifteen minutes of directing *Barefoot in the Park* he had "a life changing revelation: the experience of taking care of others made him feel taken care of. 'I had a sense of enormous relief and joy that I had found a process that . . . allowed me to be my father and the group's father'" (p. 209).

Rehearsals

Aaron (1986) gives an example from a rehearsal of *The Death of a Salesman*: the actor playing Willy Loman had to be controlled by the director "when his body went rigid with rage. It turned out that the actor playing Willy, in hitting his son Biff, was coming too close to sadistic impulses toward his own father" (p. 90). This phenomenon of transference driven aspects in the rehearsal process has recently been explored by Nuetzel (1995), an analyst and part-time actor-director. His efforts along these lines included his (1999a) participant observation, while playing the part of Father Dewis in Sam Shepard's *Buried Child*. Janet Sonnenberg (1998), a professor of theater at MIT, while directing actors during rehearsals, utilizes dream induction, following a technique evolved by her Jungian collaborator, Robert Bosnak (1996), to help them reach less conscious levels.

The Critic

At the opening night, at a play's birth, the critics evaluate the production. As Weissman (1965) noted, the critic has particular skills that often are not creative ones. He suggests this may extend to the critic's personal life; a random sample of 14 well-known critics revealed that 12 of them were childless. He cites Kris's (1952) observations that the critic's response to an artist's work is a re-creation of a semblance of the artist's original experience. Weisman adds that the relationship to the artist may at times be rivalrous or fatherly. The relationship of the artistic community to the critic is highly ambivalent. Arthur Miller said he learned nothing from critics. Helen Hayes claimed that her stage fright disappeared when she stopped reading reviews. The audience, on the other hand, like would-be children, have a relationship that is often overly dependent upon the critic, seeking guidance on what plays to see or not see, as if the critic were actually objective. Vera Jiji (1988) studied the reviews of a number of critics of O'Neill's early plays to demonstrate the consistent biases critics often have. Over the last 10 years, I have led audience discussions of plays, as often as possible during the previews, to facilitate the audience members' trust of their own personal and varied reactions rather than those of the critics.

The Audience and the Architecture of the Theater

The changing nature of theater architecture and its relation to the audience has been the subject of a number of papers. Friedman (1953) has noted the essentially communal nature of Greek theater and the close relationship of actors, chorus, and audience. The elemental crimes of parricide and incest were enacted in harvest rituals to Dionysius, god of fertility. Plays took place on ground level, in broad daylight, in a circle with an altar at its center; feminine and masculine symbols thus combined. Friedman assumes a group psychology in relation to the actors that has changed over the past two millennia. The Roman amphitheater and the proscenium stage after the Renaissance distanced the players from the audience and led to a dilution of the communal nature of theater. Where he saw audiences as originally a communal group, a "band of brothers," he now sees them as an aggregate of individuals. Nonetheless, Freud, as mentioned earlier, emphasized the continuing identification of the audience members with the actions on the stage. Today, when the play is over, however, the audience disperses and no longer reworks the play as a group. The post-performance discussions that I lead through the New York psychoanalytic society counter this current trend and permit a communal reworking of the play. Such discussions give the audience a greater collective experience and also highlight the subjective nature of individual responses to the play. Our modern era's variable boundaries between the audience and performers has been extensively reviewed by Bennett (1990); the most permeable being the productions of the Living Theater where audience members and actors intermingle.

On the other hand, Kaplan's (1968) views differ from Friedman's by suggesting that psychologically theater architecture has "persisted virtually unchanged since antiquity" (p. 427). His study of the architecture of the theater takes as its starting point the relationship of body states to architecture. Relying on René Spitz's (1965) writings on the first year of life, Kaplan sees the theater, both then and now, as a primal cavity unconsciously and kinesthetically resonating with the oral stage of infant development when self and object are differentiating. He does not mention the earliest rituals associated with prehistoric cave drawings nor does he mention Winnicott, whose ideas of the transitional space between mother and infant, with the blurring of fantasy and reality and the indistinct boundaries between self and other, are played out in early development, in artistic and cultural arenas, as well as in the psychoanalytic setting.

This is currently evident at the new planetarium in New York City, an example of theater architecture where the ceiling is the stage. It shows a film of our solar system, its galaxy, and billions of other galaxies in an ever expanding universe. As these images are projected onto the ceiling of the large round auditorium, the audience is virtually enveloped. I have heard that small children attending this show often become frightened when the black holes in the universe give the impression of swallowing up the audience.

The current production of Michael Frayn's *Copenhagen* (1998), which deals with the birth of the atomic era, takes place on a stage with audience members encircling the actors. The actors play Werner Heisenberg, Niels Bohr, and his wife, an oedipal triangle colliding like atomic particles as they confront the implications of the recent discovery of atomic fission. The horror of incest and murder in the nuclear family played out in the original circular Greek theaters is here replaced by the horror of nuclear war that has threatened to envelop us these past 50 years.

The Influence of Psychoanalysis upon Drama

In Auden's (1940) oft-quoted poem "In Memory of Sigmund Freud," he sees Freud as having become a "whole climate of opinion." This is, of course, relevant to drama and film. The psychiatrist, often analyst, has became a stock character in 20th century drama and film (Siever, 1955; Gabbard and Gabbard, 1987), and psychoanalytic ideas and images have had a pervasive impact upon countless playwrights, plays, and movies in the 20th century. Lawrence Olivier apparently consulted Ernest Jones when preparing to perform the roles of both Hamlet and Othello. After Jones suggested the homosexual bond between Othello and Iago, Olivier, to underscore this dynamic, reportedly kissed Iago on the lips during rehearsals. The number of contributors to the theater who have acknowledged their debt to psychoanalytic ideas as well as their own personal treatments are scattered throughout newspapers, biographies, and magazines. Due to the confidential nature of psychoanalysis, however, it is impossible to calculate the number of artists who have benefitted.

In the past decade, a number of fictionalized aspects of psychoanalytic history were produced on stage. Willy Holtzman's (1998) *Sabina* reexplores the boundary violations in Jung's treatment of Sabina Speilrein, who later became a member of Freud's circle before dying in the Holocaust. Nicholas Wright (1995) in *Mrs. Klein* dramatizes Melanie Klein's preference for her protége, Paula Heiman, over her analyst daughter, Melitta Schmideberg, and Terry Johnson (1996) in *Hysteria* imagines Freud's last days in London before his death. In *Freud's Girls,* Dori Appel (2000) presents a feminist reading of Freud's treatment of Dora and Emma Ekstein as witnessed by an appalled chorus of

Anais Nin, Virginia Woolf, and Bertha Pappenheim (originally Breuer's patient, Anna O.).

Psychoanalysis as Dramatic and Narrative Art

From its beginnings, when Freud noted that his cases read more like novels than scientific reports, there have been debates on whether psychoanalysis was an objective science or humanistic art. Surely there is is no either/or answer to this, and when Freud first set the ground rules for psychoanalysis with the use of the couch, setting the time and number of sessions, the fee, and the prescription to "say everything that comes to mind," he was both a scientist observing the workings of the mind and also a quasi-director and audience of a "psychoanalytic drama" in which the analysand would, via evolving transferences, cast the analyst in various roles. Thus what Anna O. first called her theater of the mind was played out in the transference/countertransferences enacted in her treatment with Breuer. Although Freud did not elaborate on the theater metaphor, he did, while on his scientific path, in those early days, liken his work to a surgeon's. In the surgical theater of psychoanalysis, the transference laden roles assigned to him were interpreted and, in a sense, excised, thereby altering psychic structure ("Where id was there shall ego be").

Nuetzel (1999b) reviewed how later theorists (Winnicott, 1971; Loewald, 1975; Schafer, 1976; Spence, 1982; McDougall, 1985; and Modell, 1990) have all emphasized the dramatic and narrative nature of psychoanalysis as they relate to theater. Although Nuetzel prefers to keep the distinction between theater and life separate, he notes how Loewald (1975) viewed psychoanalysis as a dramatic art in which "[n]ot only is the psychoanalytic setting a stage, but the patient becomes playwright and actor, as the psychoanalyst becomes co-author, co-actor, and director. The patient gets top billing for writing and acting, but the analyst gets sole credit for directing. This is how patient and analyst play in a transitional state between fantasy and actuality" (p. 298).

Pierloot (1987) used Pirandello's *Six Characters in Search of an Author* without knowledge of Loewald's work to develop the idea of the analyst as author, coconstructor, or reconstructor of a more coherent narrative of the patient's past. This view resonates with the emphasis on narrative in the work of Schafer (1976) and Spence (1982). Edel's (1961) comparison of psychoanalysis and biography is also relevant here as is Rycroft's (1985) suggestion that the analyst functions as an "assistant autobiographer" (p. 193). Pedder (1977, 1979, 1992), relying heavily on the work of Winnicott, has drawn a number of parallels between theater and therapy, including the similarity between the role of the psychotherapist and theater director.

Drama critic Eric Bentley (1969) also reviewed similar resonances between theater and therapy in an illuminating essay written before Loewald's (1975) classic paper. Bentley began with a consideration of Moreno's (1946) use of psychodrama as a form of therapy and went on to cover a host of issues, including his sense of the similarity between psychoanalysis and theater. He wrote, "Psychoanalytic therapy is itself psychodramatic—up to a point. . . . At one point it specialized in the search for the early traumatic scene . . . reenacted, with the patient playing his childhood self and the analyst, for example, the hated father" (p. 331). Also relevant here are the contributions of child analysts to the role of play in child therapies where enactments in the office playground are the raw material for the interpretive work (Solnit, 1987). Kohut's (1971) work and, more recently, the burgeoning research on how mother and infant mirror and mimic one another's affects and behavior are relevant here.

As Winnicott (1971) noted, artistic and psychoanalytic contexts are potential intermediate spaces set apart from "the real world." In these artificial settings of the psychoanalytic situation and the stage, analyst and patient, audiences and actors explore deeper realities beneath our defensive masks, and below the manifest appearances of everyday life. This modern emphasis on our inevitable distortions of reality, our all-too-human subjectivity, is not new. Plato, in his "Allegory of the Cave," already noted our essentially subjective views when he illuminated how we mistake the shadows of reality for reality itself. Twentieth-century science has only objectified this notion, adding the humbling idea that we can *never* know "objective" reality fully. In the biological sciences (Lewontin, 2000) the boundaries of subsystems whether of DNA or of an individual are ever changing. Lewontin quotes Alexander Pope's simile in this regard. "Like following life thro' creatures you dissect, you lose it in the moment you detect." In physics Heisenberg's "Uncertainty Principle" and recently in psychoanalysis Modell (1990) reminds us that "there is no absolute reality to which distortions can be compared"; that "there are multiple levels of reality present in the therapeutic encounter which in turn lead to multiple paradoxes" (p. 25). This is especially true when we widen our scope from the original emphasis on the patient's psychology to the two-person psychoanalytic situation, and now further, to the complex multiperson field of theater and family.

Conclusions: The Ever-Expanding
Scope of Psychoanalysis

As I mentioned earlier, Freud gave up his dramatic interpersonal seduction theory in 1897. From this pivotal moment he took the less traveled road to his discovery of the Unconscious. In the case of Dora, Freud (1905a) eloquently described the complex situation Dora found herself in. He wrote that "we are obliged to pay attention in our case histories to the purely human and social circumstances of our patients. Above all our interest will be directed towards their family circumstances" (p. 18). He then plunged into an exploration of Dora's inner life which became the hallmark of psychoanalysis. The discovery of unconscious fantasies and conflicts flowed naturally from the psychoanalytic focus on the individual, and for nearly a century, "interaction" and "interpersonal" were viewed as but epiphenomena of unconscious fantasies and conflicts, not appropriate for analytic scrutiny. Yet the idea of acting out, enacting past conflicts in the present, has always been significant in psychoanalytic theory. In this essay on the influence of psychoanalytic theory and theater upon one another, I tried to demonstrate anew our appreciation that interpersonal and intrapsychic conflicts are but complementary sides of a coin. Intrapsychic conflicts, ever externalized, and intersubjectively linked to others' intrapsychic conflicts are what make the world, including the clinical arena, a stage for enactments. Our methods of observation, as modern physics teaches us, determine what we see: the particles of intrapsychic dynamics or the rippling waves of interaction.

I recently led an audience discussion of Michael Frayn's (1998) *Copenhagen*. In the play Werner Heisenberg, Niels Bohr, and his wife, Margarite, relive their lives before, during, and after their historic meeting in September 1941, about which uncertainty abounds. The audience members related their personal reactions. A lawyer saw the two rows of audience members at the back of the stage as a jury weighing the innocence or guilt of the participants. An analyst commented on the new role of "intersubjectivity" in psychoanalysis reflecting Heisenberg's uncertainty principle. A medical researcher saw a departmental meeting. One audience member after another saw different things in this play, and we experienced the uncertainties that the play dramatizes. Why did Heisenberg, the director of the German nuclear fission project, come to occupied Copenhagen to visit his former mentor and father figure and now enemy? Heisenberg and Bohr spin around and collide like electrons around Margarite Bohr, the mother nucleus. Were oedipal conflicts at play here? Did Heisenberg's miscalculation of the amount of uranium necessary to build the bomb represent an inhibition resulting from inner conflict? Did he want to deny Hitler the bomb? Historians differ in their views. Had Heisenberg been in analysis at the time, only his analyst might have known "the truth." Of course history is the main character in this play, as it so often is, in determining our lives. History, along with our genes, our unconscious conflicts, our families, and recently discovered social determinants out of our awareness (Bargh and Chartrand, 1999), influence our daily thoughts, feelings, and behavior—the dramas of our lives.

I conclude with Heisenberg's postmortem question of Bohr in Frayn's (1998) imaginative play. Why did he, Bohr, not assassinate him in Copenhagen in 1941, given the possibility that he might be building an atomic bomb for Germany? Bohr is nonplussed by the question and Heisenberg muses:

Most interesting. So interesting that it never even occurred to you. Complementarity, once again. I'm your enemy; I'm also your friend. I'm a danger to mankind; I'm also your guest. I'm a particle; I'm also a wave. We have one set of obligations to the world in general, and we have other sets, never to be reconciled, to our fellow-countrymen, to our neighbors, to our friends, to our family, to our children. We have to go through not two slits at the same time but twenty two. All we can do is to look afterwards, and see what happened [pp.79–80].

This serves as a reminder that in our field prediction eludes us, that we can not know precisely what happened. We can but look back, with uncertainty and humility, and continue to expand the scope of our understanding.

On the couch only one of many realities emerges. In the burgeoning neurosciences, in the ways individuals influence one another, as audiences perceive the arts, multiple realities compete. Freud's discoveries with their emphasis on drives and psychic forces emerged in the context of 19th-century science characterized by classical mechanics. Can psychoanalysis catch up with 20th-century physics? Can psychoanalysis integrate these multiple realities by further expanding its scope? Can we make the quantum leap from our "classical" model to include an ever-widening scope and again recapture a role on the stage of intellectual history?

References

Aaron, S. (1986), *Stage Fright.* Chicago: University of Chicago Press.

Appel, D. (2000), "Freud's Girls." Unpublished play—finalist for 2000 Eugene O'Neill National Playwrights Conference.

Arlow, J. (1981), Theories of pathogenesis. *Psychoanal. Quart.*, 50:488–514.

Artaud, A. (1970), *The Theatre and Its Double* London: Calder.

Auden, W. H. (1940), In memory of Sigmund Freud. In: *Another Time.* New York: Random House.

Balter, L. (1969), The mother as a source of power. *Psychoanal. Quart.,* 38:217–274.

Bargh, J. A. & Chartrand, T. L. (1999), The unbearable automaticity of being. *Amer. Psychologist,* 54:462–479.

Bennett, Susan (1990), *Theater Audiences: A Theory of Production and Reception.* New York: Routledge.

Bentley, E. (1969), Theatre and therapy. In: *Thinking About the Playwright: Comments from Four Decades.* Evanston, IL: Northwestern University Press, 1987.

Bergmann, M. S. (1973), Limitations of method in psychoanalytic biography: An historical inquiry *J. Amer. Psychoanal. Assn.*, 21:833–850.

——— (1992), *In the Shadow of Moloch: The Sacrifice of Children and Its Impact on Western Religions.* New York: Columbia University Press.

Binstock, W. A. (1973), Purgation through pity and terror. *Internat. J. Psycho-Anal.,* 54:499–504.

Blakemore, M. (2000), From physics to metaphysics and the bomb. *The New York Times, Arts and Leisure Section,* April 9.

Bosnak, R. (1996), *Tracks in the Wilderness of Dreaming: Exploring Interior Landscape Through Practical Dreamwork.* New York: Delacorte Press.

Brenman-Gibson, M. (1981), *Clifford Odets: American Playwright.* New York: Atheneum.

Brenner, C. (1987), Working through: 1914–1984. *Psychoanal. Quart.,* 56:88–108.

Breuer, J. & Freud, S. (1893–1895), Studies on hysteria. *Standard Edition,* 2:1–309. London: Hogarth Press, 1955.

Brook, P. (1968), *The Empty Space.* New York: Atheneum, 1983.

Calef, V. (1969), Lady Macbeth and infanticide. *J. Amer. Psychoanal. Assn.,* 17:528–547.

Edel, L. (1961), The biographer and psychoanalysis. *Internat. J. Psycho-Anal.,* 42: 458–466.

Edmunds, L. & Ingber, R. (1977), Psychological writings on the Oedipus legend: A bibliography. *Amer. Imago,* 34:374–386.

Esman, A. H. (1998), What is "applied" in "applied" psychoanalysis? *Internat. J. Psycho-Anal.,* 79:741–756.

Fenichel, O. (1946), On acting. *Psychoanal. Quart.,* 15:144–160.

Frayn, M. (1998), *Copenhagen.* London: Methuen.

Friedman, J. J. (1953), Psychology of the audience in relation to the architecture of the theater. *Psychoanal. Quart.,* 22:561–570.

———— (1953), Psychology of the audience in relation to the architecture of the theater. *Psychoanal. Quart.,* 22:561–570.

Freud, S. (1905a), Fragment of an analysis of a case of hysteria. *Standard Edition,* 7:7–122. London: Hogarth Press, 1953.

———— (1905b), Psychopathic characters on the stage. *Standard Edition,* 7:305–310. London: Hogarth Press, 1953.

———— (1912), Recommendations to physicians practising psycho-analysis. *Standard Edition,* 12:109–120. London: Hogarth Press, 1958.

———— (1913), *Totem and taboo. Standard Edition,* 13:1–162. London: Hogarth Press, 1955.

————(1914), On the history of the psycho-analytic movement. *Standard Edition,* 14:7–66. London: Hogarth Press, 1957.

———— (1919), Lines of advance in psycho-analytic therapy. *Standard Edition,* 17:157–168. London: Hogarth Press, 1955.

———— (1928), Dostoyevsky and parricide [1927]. *Standard Edition,* 21:177–196. London: Hogarth Press, 1961.

———— (1950), Extracts from the Fliess papers [and letters] (1892–1899). *Standard Edition,*1:177–280. London: Hogarth Press, 1966.

———— (1974), *The Contents of the Standard Edition, Volumes 1–23. Standard Edition,* 24, London: Hogarth Press, 1953–1964.

Gabbard, G. (1979a), The creative process of the actor. *Bull. Menn. Clin.,* 3:354–364.

———— (1979b), Stage fright. *Internat. J. Psycho-Anal.,* 60:383–392.

———— (1983), Further contributions to the understanding of stage fright: Narcissistic issues. *J. Amer. Psychoanal. Assn.,* 31:423–441.

Gabbard, K. & Gabbard, G. (1987), *Psychiatry and the Cinema.* Chicago: University of Chicago Press.

Goffman, E. (1959), *The Presentation of Self in Everyday Life.* New York: Doubleday Anchor.

Grand, H. G. (1973), The masochistic defence of the "double mask": Its relationship to imposture. *Internat. J. Psycho-Anal.*, 54:445–454.

Hasty, N. (2000), *The Director* (unpublished play produced at the ArcLight Theater, February).

Holland, N. (1966), *Psychoanalysis and Shakespeare.* New York: McGraw-Hill.

Holtzman, W. (1998), *Sabina.* Woodstock, IL: Dramatic Publishers.

Jiji, V. (1988), Reviewers' responses to early plays of Eugene O'Neill: A study of influence. *Amer. J. Theater History,* 29:1.

Johnson, A. & Szurek, S. A. (1952), The genesis of antisocial acting out in children and adults. *Psychoanal. Quart.,* 21:323–343.

Johnson, T. (1996), *Hysteria.* London: Methuen.

Kantrowitz, J. (1996), *The Patient's Impact on the Analyst.* Hillsdale, NJ: The Analytic Press.

Kaplan, D. (1968), Theater architecture and the primal cavity. In: *Clinical and Social Realities,* ed. L. Kaplan. Northvale, NJ: Aronson, 1995.

———— (1969), Stage fright. In: *Clinical and Social Realities,* ed. L. Kaplan. Northvale, NJ: Aronson, 1995.

Keill, N. (1982), *Psychoanalysis, Psychology and Literature: A Bibliography, 2nd ed.* Metuchen, NJ: Scarecrow Press.

Kligerman, C. (1962), A psychoanalytic study of Pirandello's "Six Characters in Search of an Author." *J. Amer. Psychoanal. Assn.,* 10:731–744.

Kohut, H. (1971), *The Analysis of the Self.* New York: International Universities Press.

Kris, E. (1952), Approaches to art. In: *Psychoanalytic Explorations in Art,* ed. E. Kris. New York: International Universities Press, pp. 15–63.

Lahr, J. (2000), Making it real: Mike Nichols' improvised life. *New Yorker,* February 21/ 28.

Lewontin, R. (2000), *The Triple Helix.* Cambridge, MA: Harvard University Press.

Lidz, T. (1975), *Hamlet's Enemy: Madness and Myth in "Hamlet."* New York: Basic Books.

Loewald, H. W. (1975), Psychoanalysis as an art and the fantasy character of the psychoanalytic situation. *J. Amer. Psychoanal. Assn.,* 23:277–299.

Main, T. F. (1966), Mutual projection in a marriage. *Comprehensive Psychiatry,* 7:432–439.

McDougall, J. (1985), *Theaters of the Mind: Illusion and Truth on the Psychoanalytic Stage.* New York: Brunner/Mazel.

Miller, A. (1949), *Death of a Salesman.* New York: Viking Press.

Modell, A. (1990), Play, illusion, and the setting of psychoanalysis. In: *Other Times, Other Realities: Toward a Theory of Psychoanalytic Treatment.* Cambridge: Harvard University Press.

Moreno, J. L. (1946), *Psychodrama.* New York: Beacon House.

Munro, L. (1952), Clinical notes on internalization and identification. *Internat. J. Psycho-Anal.,* 33:132–143.

Naiman, J. (1992), Freud's Jocasta and Sophocles' Jocasta: Clinical implications of the difference. *Internat. J. Psycho-Anal.,* 73:95–101.

Nuetzel, E. (1995), Unconscious phenomena in the process of theater: Preliminary hypotheses. *Psychoanal. Quart.,* 64:345–352.

Nuetzel, E. J. (1999a), Acting and enacting: A case study in the evolution of theatrical performance. *J. Applied Psychoanal. Studies,* 1:79–102.

———— (1999b), Psychoanalysis as a dramatic art. *The Annual of Psychoanalysis,* 26/27:295–313. Hillsdale, NJ: The Analytic Press.

O'Neill, E. (1974), *A Moon for the Misbegotten.* New York: Random House/Vintage.

Osborne, J. (1957), *The Entertainer.* New York: Criterion Books.

Pedder, J. R. (1977), The role of space and location in psychotherapy, play and theatre. *Internat. Rev. Psycho-Anal.,* 4:215–223.

———— (1979), Transitional space in psychotherapy and theater. *Brit. J. Med. Psychology,* 52:377–384.

———— (1992), Conductor or director? Transitional space in psychotherapy and in the theater. *Psychoanal. Rev.,* 79:261–270.

Pierloot, R. A. (1987), The analysand as a character in search of an author. *Internat. Rev. Psycho-Anal.,* 14:221–230.

Pirandello, L. (1925), Preface to "Six Characters in Search of an Author." In: *Naked Masks.* New York: E. P. Dutton, 1952.

Rank, O. (1932), *The Myth of the Birth of the Hero.* New York: Knopf.

Ritvo, L. (1970), The ideological wellsprings of psychoanalysis. *J. Amer. Psychoanal. Assn.,* 18:195–208.

Ross, J. M. (1982), Oedipus revisited: Laius and the Laius complex. In: *The Psychoanalytic Study of the Child,* 37:169–200. New Haven, CT: Yale University Press.

Rycroft, C. (1985), *Psychoanalysis and Beyond.* Chicago: University of Chicago Press.

Sander, F. M. (1974), Freud's "A successful treatment by hypnotism (1892–1893)": An uncommon therapy. *Fam. Proc.,* 13:461–468.

———— (1979), *Individual and Family Therapy: Toward an Integration.* New York: Aronson.

———— (1998), Psychoanalytic couple therapy. In: *Case Studies in Couple and Family Therapy,* ed. F. Dattilio. New York: Guilford Press.

Schafer, R. (1976), *A New Language for Psychoanalysis.* New Haven, CT: Yale University Press.

Scharff, J., ed. (1989), *The Foundations of Object Relations Family Therapy.* Northvale, NJ: Aronson.

Siever, W. D. (1955), *Freud on Broadway.* New York: Heritage House.

Simon, B. (1988), *Tragic Drama and the Family: Psychoanalytic Studies from Aeschykus to Beckett.* New Haven, CT: Yale University Press.

Slavney, P. R. (1990), *Perspectives on "Hysteria."* Baltimore, MD: Johns Hopkins University Press.

Solnit, A. (1987), A psychoanalytic view of play. *The Psychoanalytic Study of the Child,* 42:205–219. New Haven, CT: Yale University Press.

Sonnenberg, J. (1998), *Imaginary Landscapes.* Unpublished manuscript.

Spence, D. P. (1982), *Narrative Truth and Historical Truth.* New York: Norton.

Spitz, R. A. (1965), *The First Year of Life.* New York: International Universities Press.

Stanislavski, C. (1936), *An Actor Prepares.* New York: Theater Art Books, 1952.

Steiner, J. (1993), Two types of pathological organization in *Oedipus the King* and *Oedipus at Colonus.* In: *Psychic Retreats.* London: Routledge.

Stewart, H. (1961), Jocasta's crises. *Internat. J. Psycho-Anal.,* 42:424–430.

Stolorow, R. D., Brandchaft, B. & Atwood, G. E. (1987), *Psychoanalytic Therapy: An Intersubjective Approach.* Hillsdale, NJ: The Analytic Press.

Wangh, M. (1962), The evocation of a proxy. *The Psychoanalytic Study of the Child,* 17:451–469. New Haven, CT: Yale University Press.
——— (1976), Underlying motivations in Pirandello's "Six Characters in Search of an Author." *J. Amer. Psychoanal. Assn.,* 24:309–328.
Weissman, P. (1965), *Creativity and the Theater: A Psychoanalytic Study.* New York: Basic Books.
Willbern, D. (1978), William Shakespeare: A bibliography of psychoanalytic and psychological criticism. *Internat. Rev. Psycho-Anal.,* 5:361–372.
Winnicott, D. W. (1971), *Playing and Reality.* New York: Basic Books.
Wright, N. (1995), *Mrs. Klein: A Play.* London: Nick Hern Books.
Zinner, J. (1976), The implications of projective identification for marital interaction. In: *Foundations of Object Relations Family Therapy,* ed. J. S. Scharff. Northvale, NJ: Jason Aronson, 1989.

The Legacy of Freud in the Approach
to the Visual Arts

HARRY TROSMAN

For many of us, the visual arts have a strong emotional impact. Constantly we read about the high prices paid for a van Gogh or a Picasso, and although we may disparage such material emphasis, crass consumership becomes a further sign of the value which we attribute to the work. Because psychoanalysis is a body of knowledge that takes as its subject matter the central preoccupations of humankind, it is not surprising that some analysts find the study of art fascinating. Certainly during the past century, beginning with Freud's study of Leonardo da Vinci, psychoanalysts have not neglected the field of the plastic arts (Freud, 1910).

A variety of psychoanalytic approaches have proved helpful in understanding the impact of works of art, and I endeavor in this contribution to describe the main currents and to offer examples of each. First, there is the work itself. Although a work can be studied from the perspective of art history, stylistic and technical aspects, patronage, and other such perspectives, many works are of significance because of the psychological impact they produce in the viewer. One approach is to consider this issue in terms of audience response and to highlight the manner that makes a work evocative. The work resonates with certain aspects of the psychology of the viewer. Such depictions in narrative painting as the presence of similar unconscious wishes and conflict, modes of the resolution of conflict, varieties of defense, or mastery are meaningful to a viewer because they offer a visualization of similar internal tendencies expressed through an aesthetic context.

Freud was impressed with this quality of resonance when he pointed out that three of the great works of literature—Sophocles' *Oedipus Rex*, Shakespeare's *Hamlet*, and Dostoevsky's *The Brothers Karamazov*—have as a central motif, the similar theme of parricide. For Freud and for many psychoanalysts the centrality of the oedipal complex continues to have an emphatic and nodal position in emotional life and is a profound expression of a fundamental complexity in human relationships. Thus, a work that offers evidence for a psychological interpretation which combines sexual and aggressive components is likely to have a convincing explanatory role.

Analysts are interested in the mechanisms of mediation, that is, the manner by which psychological experience is expressed in the artistic product. In the analogous field of dreaming, the dream work mechanisms of condensation and displacement transmit latent thoughts into forms of plastic representation not unlike the visualizations we find in the plastic arts (Freud, 1900). In addition, Freud found jokes a fertile arena in which to explore the nature of mediation. He pointed out that joke work transforms emotional and ideational content in order to evoke an appropriate response in a listener (Freud, 1905). Manipulated by the joke work, the listener undergoes a buildup of tension that is liberated and discharged at the end. The form of the joke creates a listener who is primed. The listener is likely to build up a complicity, as well as a resistance of an inhibitory nature as the jokester carefully plans his tactical placements until, with the well-timed punch line, the inhibitory energy becomes no longer necessary. The release of laughter expresses the saved expenditure of energy. Freud (1900) wrote of the process of artistic transformation in terms of "cunning delays of ever-mounting excitement—a process that can be likened to the work of a psychoanalysis" (p. 262).

In addition to considering the evocative nature of the artistic work in terms of central psychological preoccupations and means by which the artist brings about the desirable effect, the psychoanalyst is interested in the mind of the creative artist. One of the results of Freud's biography of Leonardo da Vinci has been a continuing interest in the impact of intrapsychic conflicts of the artist on the work itself.

Through the years much has been made of Freud's errors in translation in the original Leonardo contribution, and much has been added in terms of Freud's defense (Wohl and Trosman, 1955; Eissler, 1961; Trosman, 1985; Collins, 1997). Collins's recent book is an excellent example of a careful assessment both of Freud's early volume and its pertinence to ongoing and further psychoanalytic studies. Psychoanalytic findings are incorporated seamlessly into outstanding biographies of literary artists (Edel, 1953–1972). Psychoanalysts continue to be interested in personalities in whom pathology is rampant and yet are capable of great creative achievement. Gedo (1983), in a study of Caravaggio, whom he described as a "paranoid monster," marvels, as we all do, that this man whose life seemed so filled with violence and malice yet was able to achieve works of such high magnitude.

In addition, psychoanalysts continue to be preoccupied with the origins and manifestations of the creative process itself. How is it possible for some individuals to create works of art that illuminate the human condition? What is the psychology of creativity? Does the creative process have to be guarded by the artist against the intrusion by the psychoanalyst, or can it be more openly investigated? A contemporary American artist, Jim Dine, has been open about the relationship between his work and his personal life culled from analytical experience. In contrast, while teaching a seminar on creativity at a local psychoanalytic institute, I asked one of our leading novelists to participate and discuss his own creativity. He demurred and asked wryly, "Does a fish talk about swimming?" Meaning what? I assume he meant that if a fish became excessively self-conscious, it would interfere with the automatic mechanism that was necessary for performance. A creative artist may fear an intrusive violation.

Considering the overall contribution of psychoanalysis to art, I am reminded of a comment by Susanne Langer, brought to my attention by Bradley Collins in his 1997 publication:

> The Freudian interpretation, no matter how far it be carried, never offers even the rudest criterion of *artistic* excellence. It may explain why a poem was written, why it was popular, what human features it hides under its fanciful imagery; what secret ideas a picture combines and why Leonardo's women smile mysteriously. *But it makes no distinction between good and bad art"* [192, n.1].

The gauntlet she throws down is worthy of careful consideration. To a large extent, she grants a good deal. To be able to explain why a poem was written, its popularity, what is hidden within in, and how these features combine is no small achievement.

I would like to set aside the issue of quality and look at some of the achievements Langer is willing to grant psychoanalysis in terms of its explanatory power. She credits psychoanalysis with the capacity to explain "what secret ideas a picture combines." In Freud's book on Leonardo da Vinci, he viewed Leonardo's *Madonna and Child with St. Anne* (Figure 1) as a work of art only Leonardo could have painted. The painting reflects Leonardo's early childhood in that he had two mothers. Because he was born out of wedlock, he condenses the mother with whom he had spent the first years of his life and the stepmother whom his father married and who subsequently raised him. For Freud, the painting is a psychological document; it creates a visual fusion of the forms of the two women to the extent that the viewer has difficulty distinguishing between the lower parts of the two bodies. In addition, the two women appear to be of similar ages in spite of the fact that St. Anne is the Virgin's mother. This too is compatible with what we know about Leonardo's childhood caretakers. Consistent with Freud's interest in biographical antecedents for works of art, he suggests that the serenity and peacefulness visible on the face of the Madonna is understandable as reactions against the envy and rage the biological mother concealed when she had to give up her infant to her lover's legitimate wife.

Figure 1. Leonardo da Vinci, *Madonna and Child with St. Anne*. Louvre, Paris.

In rebuttal Schapiro (1956) points out that Freud made too much out of the similarity in age between the two women, that a tradition of making St. Anne and the Madonna similar in age already existed in quattrocento Italian art. For the art historian, age and smile are not critical. However, the achievement of the painting is to be discerned in the interrelationship between the individual figures, the pyramidal structure of the composition, and the fact that—although each figure is permitted an individualized movement—together they create a coherent unity, an ensemble which, although pulling in several directions, has a focal center.

Such an achievement, which is a vital contribution of Leonardo to High Renaissance art, can be understood as a response to the confusion surrounding Leonardo's early life. The disharmony in early life is compensated for in the mastery achieved in the wished-for artistic unity. Freud accepted too readily the romantic theme, which he inherited from Dmitri Merezhkovsky's (1963) novel, *The Romance of Leonardo da Vinci,* of the unhappy mother longing for the child taken from her. Today we would tend to attach less importance to the artwork as a veridical biographical statement and much more to the work as the attempt to master traumatic experiences through the sublimations in fantasy which art enables.

A subsequent foray of Freud's into the analysis of an artwork led him to an analysis of Michelangelo's statue of Moses (Figure 2). Here Freud did not interest himself primarily in biographical material about the great sculptor. He did, however, in passing, comment on Michelangelo's *terribilità,* the emotion of rage being by no means an irrelevant issue in his analysis of the statue.

Freud's main concern, however, was with the work of art itself, not with the personality of the creator. His ingenious interpretation was to be differentiated from an analysis of the statute in terms of its formal attributes. In fact he disclaimed that he could respond to works of art in terms of formal beauty. He began his anonymous contribution by stating, "I have often observed that the subject-matter of works of art has a stronger attraction for me than their formal and technical qualities. . . . I am unable rightly to appreciate many of the methods used and the effects obtained in art" (Freud, 1914, p. 211). In spite of such a disclaimer, it is striking to note the care that Freud took in describing the statue, particularly to positions of the hands and fingers, the contrast between the two legs, the variations in the folds of drapery, and the specific angle with which the tablets are held under the right arm. He went so far as to conceive of the statue as depicting a state prior to the version Michelangelo gives us.

Freud imagined that Moses was caught in a pose that concealed an aborted movement, thus stripping the figure of its position as a corner of the large tomb for Julius II. Freud proposed that Moses was portrayed at a moment subsequent to his descent from Mount Sinai, where he had been given the Ten Commandments. To his deep chagrin, he sees the Israelites worshipping the Golden Calf.

Figure 2. Michaelangelo, *Moses*. S. Pietro in Vincoli, Rome.

His impulse is to rise in a rage and express his extreme wrath by condemning the people who had betrayed him. Momentarily, however, he becomes aware of the precious tablets in his right hand and sensitive to the potential loss, he controls his fury in order to preserve the tablets. Although his fury is intense, he exercises a masterful self-control. Frenzy must be controlled when a great cause is at stake.

There is little doubt that Freud's reading is a reflection of his own feelings when faced with the defection of Jung and Adler, adherents who broke away and betrayed his own great cause. It is clear that a reading of a work of art can be motivated by a tendency to see the work in terms of one's own inner preoccupations. Freud's awareness of this highly subjective reading may have been a factor in encouraging him to publish the work anonymously. Freud, however, builds a good case for his interpretation. He makes a contribution because of the care with which he formulates his argument. And, in fact, not only does Freud identify with the need of Moses to inhibit his potentially disequilibriating rage, but he also sees himself as the object of Moses' fury. He writes about his reaction subsequent to seeing the statue in San Pietro in Vincoli:

> Sometimes I have crept cautiously out of the half-gloom of the interior as though I myself belonged to the mob upon whom his [Moses'] eye is turned— the mob which can hold fast no conviction, which had neither faith nor patience, and which rejoices when it has regained its illusory idols [1914, p. 213].

He not only is the violent destroyer, but he is also a guilt-ridden idolator who deserves chastisement.

Thus we see that Freud's contributions to the study of the visual arts follow two major currents. The structure of the artist's personality, conflicts, early experience, and developmental history play a role in influencing a work of art. Freud's other major interest concerns the analysis of the work itself, subjecting the work to the kind of critical acumen which is characteristic of the psychoanalytical clinical situation. Here the analytic scholar interested in an individual work of art functions like the analyst behind the couch who examines carefully every communication and expressive nuance with the expectation that a detailed investigative approach will lead to understanding; a close analysis of the associations will provide material for interpretations. Although Freud neglected to pursue the technical means by which a work brings about its effect, it has been left to subsequent psychoanalytic studies to examine more closely these technical matters.

There is one arena in which the two strands of Freud's investigations come together in an integrated fashion. This is the area of self-portraiture; if biographical aspects concerning the artist's life and experience are combined with a detailed study of the artwork itself, fruitful results can accrue.

In this regard I examine two self-portraits by Rembrandt—one in the Frick Collection in New York (Figure 3) and the other at Kenwood House in London (Figure 4). We know that Rembrandt, for whatever reason, must have had a great interest in representing himself because he did so in at least 75 times in paintings, drawings, and etchings. Are we to assume that Rembrandt was engaged in

Figure 3. Rembrandt van Rijn, *Self-Portrait.* The Frick Collection, New York. Copyright The Frick Collection of New York.

a quasi-analytic task? Some have doubted that self-reflection was a motive. Wright has written "it may well be that many of [the] portraits were demonstrations of his abilities, displayed in order to impress the prospective patrons; a kind of showing-off which has nothing to do with self-analysis" (1982, p. 26). On the other hand, why should self-portrait be a better display of his talents than other

Figure 4. Rembrandt van Rijn, *Portrait of the Artist c1665.* Kenwood House, The Inveagh Bequest. English Heritage Photo Library, London.

representations, particularly because Rembrandt was no great beauty and his portraits certainly do not flatter him?

It is possible to trace an evolving pattern in Rembrandt's self-portraits. In some of his very early etchings, he appeared to be particularly interested in depicting grimaces and exaggerated facial expressions. He portrays himself in a variety of outlandish costumes, oriental garb, military gear, and wearing a beret with a gold chain around his neck as if he had been granted such an honor by an aristocratic patron (Chapman, 1990).

The Frick self-portrait is dated 1658, when he was 52. In this work, in contrast to others, the gaze is direct and piercing, immediately involving the viewer. His bearing is majestic and grand, and he holds his rod, a modified maulstick, as a king might hold a scepter. In fact, he appears to be inflating his role as an artist, emphasizing his importance and his status.

It was not until several years later, in the early or mid 1660s that he painted himself in the Kenwood self-portrait (Figure 4) for the first time as a painter. Here, there is no attempt at using external attributes to increase his status. He presents himself simply as an artist, a craftsman, dressed in work clothes, holding a palette and brushes. Many a critic and connoisseur has reacted to the Kenwood portrait as if it depicts a Rembrandt at the zenith of his abilities. Many have wondered at the two concentric circles in the background and their meaning. It has been suggested that they represent maps, which refer to universality. Or perhaps they are simply examples of the artist's skill in being able to draw a circle without using a compass. It is to the commendable credit of psychoanalytic adherents of Melanie Klein that no one has thus far suggested that the concentric circles represent enormous maternal breasts a background support away from which the artist turns.

Schama (1999) has read the Frick self-portrait as a *Jupiter*, and pointed out the similarity to Rembrandt's *Juno* of 1662–1665. Schama, too, views the majesterial pose as a reaction formation to the reality of Rembrandt's bankrupt state, castigated by the church for living with a common-law wife, and seeking an elevated status to protest his condemnation. Schama suggests that the Frick portrait depicts a sense of lordly amusement, a "Jovian impenitence" (p. 617) in the midst of the disasters of Rembrandt's life.

Berger (2000) reads the Frick self-portrait as that of a patriarch who, deeply indebted to Titian for his manner, yet, through the exaggeration of the grand pose, declares his vulnerability through a sense of specious superiority. A note of irony undercuts the Titianesque influence, and is a unique contribution by Rembrandt. Berger writes, "In this imaginary Italian journey, Rembrandt, as they say, is going Dutch" (p. 495). He is on his way to attaining full artistic autonomy.

Berger reads the slashes of paint which stand for the left hand in the Kenwood self-portrait as an indication that it is the paint itself that stands in place of a representation. The artist establishes his presence, not through the monumental and majestic pose of the Frick but in the assertion that it is through the manipulating of the tools of his trade that his identity is confirmed.

What is critical is that Rembrandt in the Kenwood self-portrait attains monumentality and dignity simply by presenting himself as a craftsman, a workman painter, rather than a sitter in the disguise of a king. Can we assume that such a shift results from a personality advance, a greater sense of maturity, a more secure identity formation? Reaction formation exaggerates grandiosity and posing. Such a defense becomes unnecessary in the face of self-acceptance.

It is possible that the repeated view of oneself in the mirror for some is accompanied by opportunities for narcissistic transformations. One can see oneself in terms of who one was, who one is, and who one would like to be. In this sense the Frick self-portrait depicts an idealized grandiosity; the Kenwood, a coming to grips with psychological reality. The Frick embraces the viewer; the Kenwood is even somewhat rebuffing so that one feels put off even by the blob of red paint on the tip of the nose visible in situ. We see a man moving toward independence and self-sufficiency.

It is in the category of the self-portrait that the artist and his biography are likely to bring forth speculation about the mind behind the work and the temporal circumstances which accompany the work in progress. In the case of Rembrandt, as in the case of van Gogh, there is much to interest the psychoanalytic investigator in how the artist himself is present in the work.

I propose at this point to examine several works of art which are other than self-portraits and which can be illuminated if a psychoanalytic perspective is taken into account. I believe that by doing so it is possible to add a deeper reading of the artworks and to identify the presence of psychological mechanisms that contribute to the aesthetic effect.

The first work that I will discuss is a painting by Giovanni Battista Piazzetta (1682–1754) entitled *Pastoral Scene* (Figure. 5). The painting is one of a series of pastoral idylls, painted by the eighteenth-century Venetian master which, although universally admired, has been considered enigmatic and puzzling. It has been stated that there are "few paintings of the Italian settecento that raise so insistently the question of the artist's intentions" (Maxon and Rishel, 1970, p. 88). Previous attempts at interpretation have been characterized by indefinite generalities or references to questionable social and historical conditions. The painting was described by Daniel Catton Rich (1937) at the time that it was acquired by the Art Institute in 1937 as a return to a pagan feeling characteristic of the poetic and semimythological compositions of the Renaissance, a blend of realism and fantasy. Sewter and White (1961) almost reversed this interpretation by seeing this painting within a religious context. They proposed that the painting presented a reference to Christ in the role of a peacemaker trying to calm and dissipate the doctrinal strife within the Christian Church, an attempt to check the sects of the Protestant heresy. On the other hand, Jones (1981) suggested that the

Figure 5. Piazzetta, *Pastoral Scene.* Courtesy of the Art Institute of Chicago.

woman in the painting is a prostitute who makes herself available for a sexual encounter. She suggests the boy is the infant Bacchus, who carries the grapes that thwart desire. What, in fact, do we actually see?

A young woman is seated beside a rock near a stream with her left arm extended on a rock. In front of her is a young boy with his right arm extended. The gesture is meant to restrain two dogs who are chasing a fleeing waterfowl that has been trapped by some reeds at the edge of a stream in the right lower corner of the scene. The two dogs are in the lower left-hand corner. In the right upper corner are two men, their heads close together, one of whom casts a sidelong glance at the woman. The woman is scantily clad, and part of her right breast is exposed. The boy is also partially nude, and his right chest and his genitalia are exposed. The woman gazes out at the viewer; her relationship to the two men is manifestly unclear.

Structurally, the top half of the picture is pictorially linked with the bottom half. The two men in the upper right are positioned like the two dogs at the lower left. Although the men are apparently huddled in conspiratorial inactivity, in contrast, the two dogs are actually pursuing the bird. The animals are carrying out the activity at which the human context only hints. Human action is inhibited, fixed, or confined to the area of thought. Insofar as there is a suggestion of aggressive sexuality in the human sphere, the aggression is displaced and projected into the animals that carry out the overt activity. Efforts at control are suggested by the young boy in his inhibitory gesture, and the general sense of ominousness or threat is mitigated by the sense that we are witnessing an idyllic pastoral scene rather than a heterosexual or homosexual attack.

In Piazzetta's *Pastoral Scene,* we may speak of a structural redistribution of libidinal and aggressive cathexes which permits an expression, as well as a concealment of the human motives. The vulnerability of the woman is represented by the entrapped bird, the latent thoughts of the huddling men are enacted in the image of the attacking dogs, the efforts at control by the restraining gesture of the young boy. The viewer is implicated by the direct gaze of the young woman, which directs one to her seductive pose. One may speak here of a displacement of sexual and aggressive interests from the human to the animal realm. The men, who remind one of predators present in paintings of Susanna and the Elders, are represented by the attacking dogs with whom they are spatially and pictorially identified. Thus an apparently idyllic scene contains elements that hint at conflicts of impulses in need of control.

Another work that allows us to apply a reading of unconscious content is a painting by the French academic painter, Jean-Léon Gérôme. In 1846, Gérôme painted *The Cock Fight* (Figure 6). On a canvas equally as large as the Piazzetta, Gérôme depicts a nude boy and girl watching a cock fight. The boy is doing more than watching, however. He pushes one fowl toward the other. The girl watches passively and shrinks away but appears enthralled. The commentator at

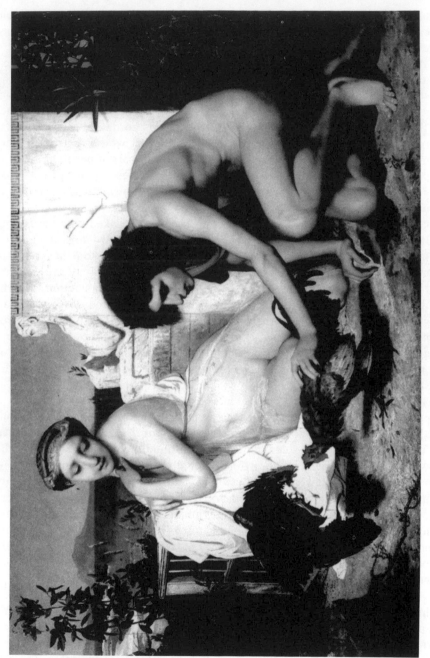

Figure 6. Gérôme, *The Cock Fight*. Musée d'Orsay, Paris.

the Gérôme exhibit, where the picture was displayed in the 1970s, states, "Underneath the action is a discourse on the vanity of temporal pursuits" (Ackerman, 1972, p. 30). Today we are more inclined to add a deeper meaning to the Victorian moralism.

The erotic tie in the relationship between the young man and woman, suggested by their nudity, is not represented by any overt interaction between them. Instead, the young man encourages a cock to attack another which withdraws from it much as the girl in the scene pulls back. The couple, however, do not fully repudiate the activity that they witness. In fact they seem deeply involved in it. The arm of the young man, in fact, is contiguous with the cock on the right; the elbow of the young woman forms an arrow that points at the head of the cock on the left. The entire scene is given an antique setting, which slyly legitimates and distances the impulse-driven content. The viewer is presented with animals engaged in a sadistic scene while the humans are relatively disengaged from one another and are innocent observers. There is a displacement of aspects of the self from the human to the animal realm and yet, at the same time, a participatory investment in the activities of the animals which suggests the identification with them. By instituting enticement and control on the animal realm, the humans reveal their inner preoccupations.

It is of interest to compare these two paintings with two others by Jan Vermeer in which the use of displacement is a means whereby an identification is permitted. In Vermeer's painting, *The Concert* (Figure 7), two women and a man are engaged in a musical performance. On the back wall behind the figures are two paintings. The one on the left is of an unidentified landscape. The one on the right is a well-known painting entitled *The Procuress* (Figure 8), by Van Baburen. In *The Procuress* there are also three figures, two women and a man, positioned very much like the figures innocently participating in the musical ensemble. In *The Procuress*, however, the man has his arm around the young woman, and offers her a coin, while the old woman indicates the financial nature of the transaction. Quite clearly, the sexualized component of the interaction among the players which is minimal in *The Concert* is stated overtly in the brothel scene on the back wall, and the figures are readily identifiable as similar to the ones playing. At the same time, the other painting of the innocuous landscape on the back wall introduces a note of stability and control in the face of too obvious a connection.

Last, in Vermeer's *A Lady Seated at a Virginal* (Figure 9), a woman is depicted playing a virginal. Although she is alone, she makes eye contact with the spectator. In the foreground of the painting is a viola da gamba, perched as if inviting the viewer to pick it up and join the lady in a duet. In this also seemingly innocuous scene, Vermeer again uses the painting, *The Procuress*, but here it is the viewer himself who is implicated in the inviting activity suggested by the welcoming look of the woman. Both she and the prostitute in the painting

Figure 7. Vermeer, *The Concert.* Isabella Stewart Gardner Museum, Boston.

are playing a musical instrument. Now it is the viewer's potential responsiveness that is hinted at by the painting on the wall.

   The psychological mechanisms of displacement, substitution, projection, and identification, which are discernable as technical devices in art, recall similar mechanisms in dreams. A similar theme is represented in a variety of instances, at some points more clearly than at others depending on the presence and success of disguise. In his famous Irma dream, which Freud (1900) analyzed in "The Interpretation of Dreams," it is Freud who merely looks into Irma's throat,

Figure 8. Van Baburen, *The Procuress*. M. Theresa B. Hopkins Fund. Courtesy, Museum of Fine Arts, Boston.

but it is the careless and negligent Otto who had given her a dirty injection. The displacement from the person of the dreamer (whatever malpractice was inflicted upon my previous patient wasn't my fault) permits a greater clarity to the expression of the potential underlying drive. In displacement we often assume that the direction in the investment of the representation is from an important idea to the less important one. In the examples from the paintings I have chosen to illustrate, particularly so in paintings within paintings, it is the seemingly less important work—such as the painting on the wall in the background—which gives us the clue as to the underlying meaning and also adds an extra fillip, the charge of concealed enjoyment. The apparently secondary scene is revelatory and indicative of the hidden interests of the more respectable foregrounded scene. This psychological mechanism, the establishment of similarity of theme among

Figure 9. Vermeer, *Lady at the Virginal.* National Gallery, London.

seemingly unrelated variations, accounts for a host of aesthetic responses and is linked to formal means such as counterpoint in music, subplots in drama, and the juxtaposing of apparently disparate characters in literature.

The legacy of Freud's interest in the visual arts has continued to be refined and elaborated by psychoanalysts who have followed him. As psychoanalysis itself has matured and expanded its clinical and theoretical base, the findings have been further applied to the visual arts, and thus have enriched our understanding of aesthetic response. Whether in the long run Langer's critique about the limitations regarding quality may ever be fully contradicted remains to be seen. At this time, we can say that similar mechanisms are discovered in paintings as diverse in quality as those by Rembrandt, Piazzetta, Gérôme, and Vermeer. Thus we have added to Freud's finding that art stirs us through subject matter by tapping significant emotional constellations, the awareness that art does so through recognizable psychological mechanisms.

References

Ackerman, G. M. (1972), *Jean-Léon Gérôme*. Dayton, OH: The Dayton Art Institute.

Berger, H. J. (2000), *Fictions of the Pose: Rembrandt against the Italian Renaissance*. Stanford, CA: Stanford University Press.

Chapman, H. P. (1990), *Rembrandt's Self-Portraits*. Princeton, NJ: Princeton University Press.

Collins, B. I. (1997), *Leonardo, Psychoanalysis and Art History*. Evanston, IL: Northwestern University Press.

Edel, L. (1953–1972), *Henry James, Vols. 1–5*. Philadelphia, PA: Lippincott.

Eissler, K. R. (1961), *Leonardo da Vinci: Psychoanalytic Notes on the Enigma*. New York: International Universities Press.

Freud, S. (1900), The interpretation of dreams. *Standard Edition*, 4 & 5. London: Hogarth Press, 1953.

——— (1905), Jokes and their relation to the unconscious. *Standard Edition*, 8. London: Hogarth Press, 1960.

——— (1910), Leonardo da Vinci and a memory of his childhood. *Standard Edition*, 11:63–137. London: Hogarth Press, 1955.

——— (1914), The Moses of Michelangelo. *Standard Edition*, 13:211–238. London: Hogarth Press, 1955.

Gedo, J. (1983), *Portraits of the Artist: Psychoanalysis of Creativity and Its Vicissitudes*. Hillsdale, NJ: The Analytic Press.

Jones, L. M. (1981), The paintings of Giovanni Battista Piazzetta. Unpublished doctoral. dissertation, University Microfilms International, Ann Arbor, MI.

Maxon, J. & Rishel, J. J., eds. (1970), *Painting in Italy in the Eighteenth Century: Rococo to Romanticism*. Chicago, IL: Art Institute of Chicago.

Merezhkovsky, D. S. (1963), *The Romance of Leonardo da Vinci*. New York: Washington Square Press.

Rich, D. C. (1937), A masterpiece by Piazzetta. *Bull. Art Institute of Chicago*, 11:98–100.

Schama, S. (1999), *Rembrandt's Eyes*. New York: Knopf.

Schapiro, M. (1956), Leonardo and Freud: An art-historical study. *J. History of Ideas*, 17:147–178.

Sewter, A. C. & White, M. (1961), Piazetta's *Pastorale*—an essay in interpretation. *Art Quart.*, 24:15–32.

Trosman, H. (1985), *Freud and the Imaginative World*. Hillsdale, NJ: The Analytic Press.

Wohl, R. R. & Trosman, H. (1955), A retrospective of Freud's Leonardo: An assessment of a psychoanalytic classic. *Psychiatry*, 18:27–39.

Wright, C. (1982), *Rembrandt: Self-Portraits*. New York: Viking Press.

Index

Aaron, S., 287–289, *295*
Abraham, H., 120n, *129*
Abraham, K., 113, *114*, 120, 238
Freud on, 42
Abraham and Isaac (Old Testament), 75
absurdity, 208–209
Ackerman, G. M., 315, *319*
Ackerman, N. W., 151, *158*
acting, psychology of, 287–288
actor and stage fright, the, 287–288
Adler, A.
Freud on, 42
affect, reversals of, 212–213
aggression, Freud on, 28–31
Aldington, H. D., 35, *46*
Alexander, F., 6, 37, 46
Allen, Woody, 242
altruism, 125, 127, 128
American psychoanalysis. *See also*
psychoanalysts, American
women; *specific topics*
stages in the development of, 161–162
analytic observational method,
development of, 106–108
Anna O. (Bertha Pappenheim), 17, 96
Ansbacher, H., 92, *102*
anxiety, 76–79
aphasias, 53
Appel, D., 291, *295*
Appignanesi, L., 161n, *175*
Arieti, S., 149, *158*
Aristotle, 74–75, 80
Arlow, J. A., 280, *295*
Artaud, A., 282, *295*

artistic creation, 172–173. *See also*
literary criticism
arts, visual
legacy of Freud in the approach to,
301–319
Aspern Papers, The (James), 224
assisted dying, 124
Atwood, G. E., 283, *299*
Auden, W. H., 3–4, 7, 291, *295*

Balint, E., 86, *102*
Balmary, M., 267, *275*
Balter, L., 284, *295*
Bargh, J. A., 294, *295*
Barthes, R., 218, *233*
"Bartleby the Scrivener," 206
Basinger, J., 243, *246*
Bauer, Ida. *See* Dora
Beck, E. M., 85, 95, *102*
Beit-Hallahmi, B., 274, *275*
Bellah, R. N., 272, *275*
Beloved (Morrison), 222–223
Benedek, T., 6, 46, 146, *158*
Benjamin, J., 219, *233*
Bennett, S., 289, *295*
Bentley, E., 285, 292, *295*
Berger, H. J., 310, *319*
Bergman, A., 70n, *82*
Bergmann, M. S., 280, 284, *295*
Bernstein, R., 270, *276*
Bertin, C., 87, *102*, 161n, *175*
Bible, 75
binary thought, 117, 118, 126, 127
Binstock, W. A., 281, *295*